D1527750

# Culture and Religion in International Relations

Series Editors:
*Josef Lapid and Friedrich Kratochwil*

## Published by Palgrave Macmillan:

*Dialogue among Civilizations: Some Exemplary Voices*
By Fred Dallmayr

*Religion in International Relations: The Return from Exile*
Edited by Fabio Petito and Pavlos Hatzopoulos

*Identity and Global Politics: Theoretical and Empirical Elaborations*
Edited by Patricia M. Goff and Kevin C. Dunn

*Reason, Culture, Religion: The Metaphysics of World Politics*
By Ralph Pettman

*Bringing Religion into International Relations*
By Jonathan Fox and Shmuel Sandler

*The Global Resurgence of Religion and the Transformation of International Relations:
The Struggle for the Soul of the Twenty-First Century*
By Scott M. Thomas

*Religion, Social Practice, and Contested Hegemonies: Reconstructing the Public Sphere
in Muslim Majority Societies*
Edited by Armando Salvatore and Mark LeVine

*Beyond Eurocentrism and Anarchy: Memories of International Order and Institutions*
By Siba N. Grovogui

*The Public Sphere: Liberal Modernity, Catholicism, Islam*
By Armando Salvatore

*Civilizational Identity: The Production and Reproduction of "Civilizations" in
International Relations*
By Martin Hall and Patrick Thaddeus Jackson (forthcoming)

*Global Islam: Between Fundamentalism and Cosmopolitanism*
By Jocelyne Cesari (forthcoming)

# The Public Sphere

# THE PUBLIC SPHERE

## LIBERAL MODERNITY, CATHOLICISM, ISLAM

Armando Salvatore

First published in 2007 by
PALGRAVE MACMILLAN™
175 Fifth Avenue, New York, N.Y. 10010 and
Houndmills, Basingstoke, Hampshire, England RG21 6XS
Companies and representatives throughout the world.

PALGRAVE MACMILLAN is the global academic imprint of the Palgrave Macmillan division of St. Martin's Press, LLC and of Palgrave Macmillan Ltd. Macmillan® is a registered trademark in the United States, United Kingdom and other countries. Palgrave is a registered trademark in the European Union and other countries.

ISBN-13: 978–1–4039–7473–0
ISBN-10: 1–4039–7473–X

Library of Congress Cataloging-in-Publication Data

Salvatore, Armando.
    The public sphere : liberal modernity, Catholicism, Islam / Armando Salvatore.
        p. cm.
    Includes bibliographical references and index.
    ISBN 1–4039–7473–X (alk. paper)
    1. Public interest. 2. Common good. 3. Islam and state. 4. Church and state. 5. Islam and justice. 6. Civilization, Western. 7. Civilization, Islamic. 8. Islamic sociology. I. Title.
JC 330.15.S24 2007
320.01'1—dc22                                                                 2006037218

A catalogue record for this book is available from the British Library.

Design by Newgen Imaging Systems (P) Ltd., Chennai, India.

First edition: July 2007
10 9 8 7 6 5 4 3 2 1

Printed in the United States of America.

*To the memory of my father, Antonio Salvatore (1925–2006)*

# CONTENTS

*Acknowledgments*                                                    ix

Introduction: The Genealogy of the Public Sphere                     1

1. Religion, Civilization, and the
   Redefinition of Tradition                                        33

2. Bridging Imagination, Practice, and Discourse                    69

3. The Public Reason of the Commoner                                99

4. The Collective Pursuit of Public Weal                           133

5. The Implosion of Traditions and the
   Redefinition of Common Sense                                    173

6. The Modern Public Sphere: Transforming Practical
   Reason into Prudential Communication                            215

Conclusion: After Genealogy—Toward a
Pluralist Theory of the Public Sphere                               243

*Notes*                                                            261

*References*                                                       267

*Index*                                                            283

# Acknowledgments

Work on this manuscript started in the year 2000 in the framework of a German Habilitation thesis in Sociology at Humboldt University in Berlin. In my earlier work, I had been confronted with the problem whether Western notions of the public sphere could "apply" to the Muslim majority word. I realized that the reasons why they could not are related to the contested nature of the notion of the public sphere within the West at large, and to the crucial—though often latent—role played by Islamic traditions in the long term shaping of the concept and its related practices.

I then embarked on a project linking a social and political theory problematic to a comparative historical sociology of discursive traditions in the West and in the Muslim world. I benefited from participating in a series of conferences held between 2000 and 2005 which articulated this nexus, first in Florence (European University Institute) and then in Essen (Institute for the Advanced Study in the Humanities). In this context, I owe thanks to Bo Stråth and Georg Stauth.

Yet the seeds for dealing with a genealogy of the public sphere also embracing Islamic traditions were implanted in earlier activities and cooperations. I benefited in particular from participating in a "Voegelinian" working group on religion and politics at the Free University in Berlin in the mid-1990s. I am thankful to Friedemann Büttner who invited me to the group. In those years in Berlin I also took advantage from attending seminars of the working group on Islam and modernity at Wissenschaftskolleg. I thank Aziz al-Azmeh, Georges Khalil, and Gudrun Krämer. Later I also benefited from intense discussions during the 2001–2002 Summer Institute, sponsored by Wissenschaftskolleg, Berlin and funded by the Alexander von Humboldt Foundation, Bonn, which I codirected with Dale F. Eickelman. I owe thanks to all fellows of the Summer Institute.

I am particularly happy to acknowledge the support of ISIM, Leiden, and in particular of M. Khalid Masud and Martin van Bruinessen, for granting me a visiting fellowship at a particular delicate juncture of the preparation of the manuscript, allowing me to produce a first draft. I am indebted to Dr. Masud for the many inspiring conversations related to social theory and the Islamic philosophy of law. Without these conversations, writing chapter 4—in many ways the hub of this work—would not have been possible.

I owe special thanks to the two main reviewers of the Habilitation thesis at the Department of Social Sciences of Humboldt University in Berlin, Klaus Eder and Johann P. Arnason, for their insightful comments. I also thank all other members of the commission, Hans-Peter Müller, Herfried Münkler, Claus Offe, and Peter Heine.

The help of all those distinguished colleagues who also read and commented upon the manuscript deserve a particular mention: they are Shmuel N. Eisenstadt, Mark LeVine, Cecelia Lynch, Setrag Manoukian, Frank Peter, Emilio Santoro, and M. Qasim Zaman.

The present work is a thoroughly revised and reduced version of the Habilitation thesis that I submitted to Humboldt University, Berlin in January 2005.

# INTRODUCTION: THE GENEALOGY OF THE PUBLIC SPHERE

## The Notion of the Public Sphere as the "Third Sphere" of Society

The notion of the public sphere has surged to worldwide significance during the 1990s, in the wake of the English translation of Habermas's German *Habilitation* thesis *The Structural Transformation of the Public Sphere* (1989 [1962]). This popularization of the concept of the public sphere on a global level and its understanding as the communicative engine of democratic politics (Calhoun 1992) coincided with the opening up of horizons of democratization in eastern Europe as well as — as it was hoped in the aftermath of the first Gulf War — in North Africa and the Middle East. Not surprisingly, the emerging discussion on the public sphere was tied to the revival of the companion notion of civil society (cf. Hall 1995). During the 1990s the public sphere was increasingly envisioned as the discursive infrastructure and the normative lubricant to a well-functioning civil society (cf. Cohen and Arato 1992; Fraser 1992, 1997). At the same time, parallel discussions interrogated anew the place of religious movements and discourses not only in the social processes of modernization but also in the public sphere (Asad 1993; Casanova 1994).

Increasing attention was devoted to developments in the Islamic world. The variety of cases illustrating the presence of religion in the public sphere could no longer be accounted for by a conventional search for gaps and deficits in the sociopolitical development of the Muslim majority world, in comparison with Western paths of secularization (Casanova 2001; Eickelman 2002; Asad 2003). At the same time when Habermas's theory of the public sphere along with its systematic ties to civil society were growing popular, they attracted criticism especially from scholars of the Middle East for not adequately reflecting the historic practices and institutions external to the European social worlds upon which the theory was built (cf. Asad 1993; Ayubi 1995; Salvatore 1997).

In this work I trace a genealogy and reconstruct a transculturally feasible notion of the public sphere and of the underlying concept of communicative action derived from the work of Habermas, and of some of his main critics and partners in the debates of the past fifteen years. I take seriously the seminal idea of a public sphere nourishing the social bond by fostering the rational and intentional dimensions of action, interaction, and communication. I investigate the long-term conceptual, practical, and institutional transformation and crystallization of ideas of publicness and of the underlying notion of the common good through an analysis focusing on three major breakthroughs in the social and intellectual history of the Euro-Mediterranean civilizational world beginning with the axial breakthrough of the first millennium BC. Axial transformation is explained here as the rise of a specific type of agency, interactivity, and reflexivity (Wittrock 2005) that is essential to the rise of public reasoning. The second major rupture that I examine is the renaissance of the axial framework of social interaction and communication that matured in the late Middle Ages and was anticipated by the emergence of Islam in the seventh century CE. Finally, I will focus on the early Enlightenment of the period 1650–1750 as a phase of intense restructuring of the axial postulates of social agency and rationality.

This path of investigation differs from Habermas's choice to sharply delimit the modern notion of the public sphere from what he lumped together as premodern concepts (Habermas 1989 [1962]: 1–14). He did not fail to notice that important roots of the modern public sphere are located in classic political theory and praxis. However, he did not specifically probe into the trajectory of emergence of the modern public sphere and significantly underplayed the role of religious traditions in its formation. This gap has been partly filled by other social theorists like Charles Taylor (1990, 1993), Craig Calhoun (1992), Adam Seligman (1997, 2000), and Shmuel Eisenstadt (2002). They have not only reaffirmed the public sphere as a European and Western formation, but have also suggested, from various angles, its comparability with long-term developments traceable in other cultures or civilizations. They have also pointed to transformations in the field of religion, mainly within Protestantism, Catholicism, and Judaism. One key idea in this undertaking has been to search for endeavors within different traditions to shape the idea of the centrality of ordinary life and the value of communication among commoners as the preconditions of the modern notion of the public sphere. My goal is to contribute to fill the gap in a more systematic way by devising a genealogical approach to the public sphere through the analysis of key transformations within Western traditions. The West is intended here as encompassing the entire Euro-Mediterranean civilizational area and its adjacent "Middle Eastern" fertile and desert regions. The Abrahamic traditions and the Hellenic political and cultural heritage equally share in this wider Western civilizational space.

The value of transparent communication and the practice of a communicative understanding among social actors from the microlevels of social life to the more organized collective arenas of deliberation reflect the political character of modern public spheres. A wider question concerns the extent to which the public sphere of modern societies is political, namely if there is a degree of autonomy of collective deliberation versus the power of bureaucratic steering and the rationality of capitalist markets in determining the political life of democratic polities. This is also the genuinely Habermasian question of whether there is a close-to-ground level of interaction and communication that holds society together and bestows a progressive scope onto the social and political process. This is less the question of distinguishing between a political and a nonpolitical—for example, literary—public sphere, than the issue of ascertaining the nature of the public sphere and of the modalities of communication it facilitates, with regard to the wider conception not only of society and the polity, but also, and especially, of the microfundament of the social bond where *ego* engages *alter*.

In other words: does the public sphere reflect or even constitute a political society? This work opens a different angle to the discussion by focusing on the genealogy of the social and symbolic-communicative microlink that allows for the emergence of macrostructures of deliberation making the public sphere an autonomous layer of society, a "third sphere," along with the economy and the political system (Somers 1998). According to the approach chosen in this work, the political determination of the public sphere depends on the various stages of its genealogy and cannot reflect an abstract typology.

In a study devoted to the genealogy of concept formation within Anglo-American sociopolitical theory with a liberal orientation, U.S. sociologist Margaret Somers has dissected the dense conceptual network combining notions of civil society, political culture, and the public sphere. Identifying in Talcott Parsons and Jürgen Habermas two different, but comparable masters of this compound theoretical approach that has gained a fresh popularity in social theory during the 1990s, she has exposed the distinctively "unpolitical" character of this type of conception. Somers has laid bare the predominance in this approach of a focus on factors and sites of social cohesion determined by the socioeconomic forces of a capitalist market economy. In particular, she has evidenced "a transmutation of personal and market privacy into the domain of 'public' issues regarding the management of the socioeconomic life" (Somers 1995: 126).

Through a sophisticated theoretical elaboration, these factors and sites of social integration are made to cohere into a "third sphere" situated between the economy and the bureaucratic state. Yet this sphere is conceived of as communicatively autonomous from the strictures of economic rationales and administrative steering. Nonetheless, its genetic links with modern commercial, industrial, and postindustrial society pose insurmountable limits to this autonomy. Its characterization as a "sphere" betrays the intrinsic normativity of the conception, bordering on wishful thinking and mystification (ibid.). Yet it is in this third sphere that cultural values, like those of commitment and tolerance, are allegedly formed. This sphere is therefore the seedbed of liberal civil society. In the characterization of the conceptual fabric centered on the public sphere, the genesis of its formation appears rooted in a predominantly Anglo-American stream of thought and vocabulary with important German and more generally continental variations and contributions drawing from a rich philosophical tradition. To sum up Somers's diagnosis, the public sphere as a third sphere of society promises a high degree of communicative integration of society that cannot however be convincingly grounded on a theoretical level, due to the liberal premises of the theoretical approach that do not clarify the degree of autonomy versus the determination of the sphere through economic factors.

Habermas's positioning toward this liberal trajectory is doubtless ambivalent. However, a genealogical link of Habermas to this tradition, in the sense elucidated by Somers, can hardly be denied. As often the case, such a connection is largely unintentional, though not casual. The core argument of his *Habilitation* thesis, written in the late 1950s, was reappropriated as part of the revival of interest and debate on civil society and the public sphere that climaxed during the 1990s, after the English translation of the work in 1989 (Habermas 1989 [1962]). As a matter of fact, Habermas's study was originally part of a distinctively German endeavor to cope with modern Germany's authoritarian and totalitarian trajectory. It was motivated by the urgency to explore the political causes that had till World War II set the country apart from the trajectories of Western liberal-democratic societies. Yet Habermas's work also represented a quite heterodox twist within the "critical theory" of the Frankfurt school (cf. Calhoun 1992: 4–6) that had proved inefficient in capturing with sufficient realism the main stakes of postwar political conjunctures. More specifically, Habermas's approach intended to prevent and cure the danger of a de-democratization allegedly inherent to the sociopolitical arrangements of postwar European welfare states and latent in the predicament of the *Bundesrepublik* of the economic wonder that quite abruptly superseded the catastrophe of Nazism and World War II.

Habermas's thesis was based on the view of a golden age of bourgeois civil society bringing into being a public sphere of citizens. This age flourished in parallel in Germany and in all other leading Western nations from the seventeenth to the early nineteenth century, and came to an abrupt end with the failure, all over Europe, of the revolutions of 1848. Without denying the singular tragedy of German authoritarianism and totalitarianism, Habermas intended to show that Germany participated in this golden age, not least through the work of Immanuel Kant. The decline of the public sphere in post–World War II welfare democracies was therefore a general problem of European and Western history and not a token of German exceptionalism. Not surprisingly the revival of the third sphere as the site of production of liberal-democratic values during the 1990s (first through the agitation of the banner of "civil society" in eastern Europe, then via an increasing attention to the communicative dimensions of the public sphere) recalled the importance of Habermas's earlier work.

Habermas eagerly elaborated upon those new developments. He stressed a line of continuity between this revival of the public sphere and the main theoretical idea on which he had worked since the 1970s, namely "communicative action." This was conceived of as a type of action rooted in the people's "lifeworld" that resisted colonization by the two-pronged system of economic and bureaucratic rationalization and therefore provided to the third sphere nothing less than its principle of agency and orderly interaction (Habermas 1990, 1992).

In a work basically contemporary to Habermas's *Habilitation*, the historian Reinhart Koselleck (1988 [1959]) adopted a different approach to the Enlightenment legacy. Instead of looking for a golden age of the public sphere, Koselleck attempted to show that the roots of all forms of modern totalitarianism in Europe had to be located in the absolutist conception of sovereign power that thinkers of the European Enlightenment had inherited from the absolutist monarchies and metamorphosed into a new idea of social autonomy and political agency. According to Koselleck, Enlightenment thinkers and their predecessors, like John Locke, charged with tensions the modern idea of politics by adding to the absolutist state's concentration of power the ambition to reconstruct society rationally—in spite of their lack of political realism.

The totalitarian catastrophes of the twentieth century were thus prepared by a singular blend of power absolutism and of a subject-centered liberal approach basing politics on a very abstract notion of the moral self. This conception laid the foundations of morality within an inner and even secret forum of conscience (cf. also Leites 1988). Koselleck's view had the merit to situate the rise of the bourgeois public sphere within a much more dialectical relationship between "publicness" (*Öffentlichkeit*) as a spatialized representation of public order, whose seeds were implanted (as also recognized by Habermas) by the modern European absolutist state, and the "inwardness" (*Innerlichkeit*) claimed by bourgeois ideology (be it liberal or radical) through metamorphosing selected Christian tenets concerning the moral responsibility of human beings into a new idea of social and political agency (see chapters 3, 5, and 6 of the present work).

Common to such attempts to redefine the public sphere is a need to rethink the conceptual network inherited from the Enlightenment tradition, be it in its liberal-Lockean or in its more radical-republican variants. More than a peculiar and distorted historical trajectory, German history often represents for German theorists a litmus test for this project of theoretical reconstruction. Since the 1990s the open character of this trajectory has been made more complex by the new chances and needs to reshape a European public sphere in order to find solutions to multiple dilemmas of integration in the old continent and to provide an adequate communicative arena to a constitutional process too tightly chained to institutional priorities and bureaucratic rigidities. This potential openness can be contrasted with the more self-enclosed character of the grand trajectory of Anglo-American sociopolitical theory, doubtless due to the smoother character of political development in noncontinental history. For these reasons the work of Habermas, though not the immediate object of the present study, represents the leading approach to the public sphere within the liberal tradition at large. It will be commented upon and constructively critiqued at several junctures of the argument deployed in the present study. Habermas's work is also particularly representative for its ubiquity within discussions on a European public sphere and for being closely conversant with the Anglo-American liberal tradition.

As diagnosed by Somers and further specified by another American social theorist, Jeff Weintraub (1997), Habermas's approach cannot be fully appreciated and critiqued if not placed within the conceptual coordinates of the liberal Anglo-American tradition. Weintraub shows that the Habermasian theoretical nodes that link German exceptionalism to the Anglo-American mainstream illustrate a larger problem in the conceptual framework delimiting the third sphere. He has denounced the pitfalls inherent in the liberal inclination to collapse civil society into political society, or vice versa, as a way to depoliticize the latter. This is a mistake that a leading thinker like Alexis de Tocqueville was attentive to avoid (Weintraub 1992), but that is common to both so-called liberals and so-called communitarians in their competition for capturing an integrated "third sphere" of society (civil-society-*cum*-public-sphere).

Weintraub has put in evidence the main shortcoming of the Anglo-American tradition and its conceptual fabric, namely the ambiguous passage from a postulate of structural determination of the third sphere to the view of a smooth "marriage of convenience" between the economic and the political spheres of modern society, as epitomized by capitalism and democracy. This approach tends to hypostasize the "third sphere" that holds them together. Weintraub has showed how the conceptual approach to the third sphere has disregarded factors of sociability that have constituted the lifeblood of public life not only in premodern Europe but also through various modern transformations, before being hijacked and largely suppressed by the modernization processes of the twentieth century. This dimension of public life has been stressed in various ways by different authors such as Philippe Ariès (1962 [1960]), Norbert Elias (1976 [1939]), and Richard Sennett (1978), who have explored the resilience of a public sociability paralleled by a domesticity not reducible to the parameters of a private sphere (Weintraub 1997: 16–25).

The concept of the public sphere has indeed a much more complex, plural, and conflicted genealogy than recognized from within the liberal tradition. In its kernel, the notion of the public sphere rests on the idea of acting, arguing, and deliberating in common in ways that are legitimated through a rational pursuit of collective interest, which also implies a fair degree of transparence of communication among the actors involved in the process. It is a complex concept that cuts across the formation of legal, civic, and religious traditions and the emergence and consolidation of modern notions of secular power. Its roots, etymologically and semantically, are in Roman legal parlance and "Greco-Roman" political theory (ibid.: 11). The Habermasian narration, instead, locates a mere "representative publicness" in the European premodern background against which the bourgeois public sphere took form, on the springboard of the commercial and civil society that arose in the seventeenth and eighteenth centuries (Habermas 1989 [1962]: 7).

In the Preface to the new German edition of his book, Habermas defended the specific character of the bourgeois public sphere as setting the "ideal type" for every public sphere based on a dialectics between "inwardness" and "publicness." He also criticized Richard Sennett's argument on the collapse of public culture (Sennett 1978) for ignoring the significance of this dialectics and for surreptitiously transporting key characters of the old representative publicness into the bourgeois, modern public sphere (Habermas 1990: 17). This criticism might be well grounded, but also reveals a scarce interest in attempting to reconstruct the long-term genesis of inwardness and publicness and the related combination of factors of continuity and discontinuity in the production of notions of acting, arguing, and deliberating in common. As a counterpoint to Habermas's closure to a long-term genealogy of publicness, Jan Assmann has convincingly argued that ancient Egypt produced a clear distinction between the "face" and the "heart" as metaphorical focal points of this dialectics of intersubjective engagement and communication (Assmann 2002 [2000]: 133).

Most criticisms of Habermas's theory of the public sphere (cf. Benhabib 1986, 1992; Fraser 1989, 1992, 1997; Boyte 1992; Calhoun 1992; Warner 1992, 2002; Negt and Kluge 1993 [1972]; Crossley and Roberts 2004) have evidenced one or a combination of the following limitations: (1) the lack of attention to class and gender based alternative publics or counterpublics, resulting in the singularization of a male bourgeois ideal type; (2) a minimization of national and historical differences among various instances of modern public spheres; (3) a lack of regard for the complex intertwining between local, national, and transnational public spheres; (4) the overly normative tenor of the characterization of the public sphere as singularly modern and Western. While benefiting from all these objections, my approach is less a critique of the Habermasian "model" than the reconstruction of a different, more complex genealogy within which Habermas's type represents an hegemonic yet specific development—through a series of historical and culturally specific ruptures—of a dialectics that has deeper roots. Here Assmann's Egypt plays the role of the historical and symbolic launching pad of this dialectics within the entire Euro-Mediterranean civilizational area (see chapter 1).

This work also intends to show that Habermas's model of the public sphere does not fully satisfy the criteria of rationality and universality that it requires in order to qualify as a Western, modern, rational prototype. It is a model based on a particular crystallization of the dialectics between inwardness and publicness, one to which German Protestant and post-Protestant culture decisively contributed (cf. Stauth 1993). The modern liberal dialectics of inwardness and publicness subverts and sometimes suppresses some fundamental characteristics of more ancient and often more complex trajectories of construction of public argument based on a comparable, yet different distinction, like in the example mentioned earlier from ancient Egypt.

My approach should facilitate clarifying key dimensions of the historic idea of publicness that are discarded or played down by Habermas and many of his critics. Some among these critics have attempted to render the original Habermasian model more open to issues of gender, class, and culture differences, while minimizing the normative tenor of the concept. While doing so they have not downplayed, but rather exalted Habermas's investment into a validation of the concept on a theoretical level as a quintessentially modern idea of social cohesion, as a third sphere. They have decried the deficits of the model and looked for its fulfillment: a truly modern—open, universal, democratic, nonbourgeois, not gender biased, and so on—public sphere.

Therefore in my analysis I need to draw from authors who have theorized on concepts and trajectories other than the public sphere, but which equally affect the problematic of acting, arguing, and deliberating in common. Among the key categories to which I will refer and that are essential to Habermasian theory are "practical rationality," "communication," and the "lifeworld." These rank quite prominently in this analysis. Among the other concepts that I elaborate upon though they are rejected, disguised, or invisibly metabolized within the Habermasian model, "authority," "faith/trust," and "imagination" occupy an important place: they are the key dimensions of human action that concur to establish the social and communicative bond in practice and so facilitate public reasoning. This perspective provides an alternative to the normative focus on inwardness as the inner forum of formation of the morality of the modern individual providing an ethical fundament to his public engagement. I focus on the microdimension of the *ego-alter* relationship as the cell of the constitution of the social bond, and on the dependence of this microdimension on patterns of communication and understanding.

I focus therefore on a sociologically relational microplatform of publicness and of its key conditions. I adopt the *ego-alter* relationship as the universalizable basis for any conceptualization of publicness, starting from how Abrahamic traditions seminally contributed to the shaping of this relationship. In this context I search for the seeds of Habermas's model of communicative action through a sequential contextualization of modes of communication as modalities of construction of the common, and in particular of the common good. I then relate Habermas's model to different stages of transformation of the social bond and of the symbolic-communicative link that supports it, reaching into the formation of modern European societies.

Therefore, several conceptual ingredients that I use in my genealogy are in common with Habermas's approach. Throughout this work I engage—critically but sympathetically—with his endeavor to provide to the public sphere a firm theoretical base through the concept of "communicative action." Whereas Habermas considers the potential universality of communicative action as inherent in its normative force, I adopt a genealogical approach that rejects the idea of justification that dominates moral philosophy and also affects Habermas's style of theorizing. My approach is based on a history oriented, civilizational contextualization of communication and of its normative conditions. This contextualization helps clarify how shifts in these normative conditions also change the repertoires of engagement between *ego* and *alter* and their attending power relations.

As a result, the present work responds to the necessity to redress Habermas's downplaying of the historical and transcivilizational complexity of the trajectories of action in common and collective reasoning that culminated in the construction of the "public sphere." He reduced this complexity in synthetic formulas within a dozen of pages at the beginning of his work (Habermas 1989 [1962]: 1–12). Habermas's swift references to classical antiquity, the Middle Ages, and early modernity, in order to summarize the "prehistory" of the modern liberal bourgeois public sphere, are basically correct and consistent. Yet, they are selectively combined to make the new type of public sphere stand out for its novelty, originality, and typological purity. At the same time, Habermas does not deny that the idea of the public sphere as a functional "sphere" is a key to the novelty of modern public argument that he highlights. The overtly functional character of his view of the public sphere reveals the ambivalence and fragility of the type of social integration explicitly or implicitly expected from the existence and working of this "third" sphere of society.

Moreover, the absence of any dealing with religious traditions in the rapid review done by Habermas is astonishing especially with regard to his reference to the late Middle Ages.[1] This absence appears even more surprising, and the loss of perspective in the trajectory of emergence of the modern public sphere even more serious, if we take into consideration those religious traditions that ingrained into the history and societies of the Muslim world—not to speak of the intersections and reciprocal impingement between Christian, Muslim, and Jewish traditions within the broader Euro-Mediterranean civilizational area (cf. Höfert and Salvatore 2000). Building on studies about Islamic public spheres or "public Islam" (cf. Salvatore 2001; Salvatore and Eickelman 2004; Salvatore and LeVine

2005), the present work contributes to the theory of the public sphere a shift of perspective intended to deprovincialize its genealogy. I perform this step through inserting an Islamic approach to the construction of the symbolic-communicative link into the genealogy of the European, Christian and post-Christian self-understanding that has shaped the bulk of the theoretical literature on the public sphere (chapter 4). The goal of this work is therefore neither a self-contained critique nor a self-enclosed genealogy of the public sphere. It explores the complexification and reconstruction of relevant historic streams leading to its theorization which have been marginalized within sociological theory.

The notion of practical reasoning (in Greek, *phronesis*) is here considered the stepping stone for assessing the genesis of public reasoning (see chapters 1 and 2) and its articulation in a variety of ways within different traditions (see chapters 3 and 4). *Phronesis* denotes a capacity of the agent that is partly discerning, partly communicative, and partly reflective of the consequences of action; it is therefore intrinsically interactive and deliberative, and potentially public. It indicates the agent's activity of finding means to ends, along with discerning the ends that a tradition defines and subjects to interpretation, more than dictating (see chapter 1). The present work sorts out the plural articulation of this notion of practical reasoning and analyzes its transformations, in order to facilitate understanding how different views of the public sphere and practices of public reasoning are configured. One background hypothesis is that we cannot make sense of the genesis of notions of publicness as based on reasoning for achieving public goods without taking seriously faith-based and other traditions that organically link concepts of practical reasoning to ideas of connective justice, and whose origin is situated before modernity and/or outside of the northwestern "core" of modern Europe.

The practical import of communication does not diminish, but strengthens the orientation to an understanding of *ego* with *alter*. The ethic of coping with otherness by entering into exchange and communication with the other is the key conceptual and practical stone for creating a sense of publicness. The modern liberal bourgeois development of a dialectics of inwardness and publicness as a steering mechanism for overcoming established authority, and building ties of trust and open and efficient communication is one specific, strongly streamlined solution to the problem of dealing with otherness and constructing the social bond. It is, however, not an exclusive approach, and not the end of history. If we turn this development into *the* standard of the public sphere, we just support a hegemonic, preemptive legitimization of a faculty of "public reason."

One should not neglect that such standardized ideas of public reason developed as part of a process of bureaucratic and economic rationalization, in Weberian terms, and are therefore in tension with the *telos*-oriented, though context-bound public reasoning promoted by other, prior or parallel, traditions. In the framework of traditions, reasoning is first practical and then public, and this double level immunizes both practitioners and observers against the danger of authoritarian definitions of an intrinsic finality of social and communicative action. An encompassing and fully autonomous public sphere as a third sphere is not envisaged.

The work suggests that traditional notions like the Roman *res publica* (later christianized into *respublica christiana*: see chapter 3), and the Muslim *maslaha 'amma* (an important concept that relates the pursuit and adjudication of specific goods to the definition of a more general good: see chapter 4)—both ideas that signify the "public good"—rely on the previously mentioned, Greek idea of *phronesis* and articulate *telos* (the goal or scope of action) in different and flexible ways. The liberal modern tradition (a tradition sui generis) that claims to be able to supersede all other traditions and domesticate *telos* and authority thus appears as the result of a metamorphosis of earlier such traditions. No doubt this specific, new tradition is often disruptive of the integrity of the older traditions. The extent to which these older traditions resist erasure of *telos* in constructing the social bond and authorizing communication—even in today's global society—can be interpreted not only as a symptom of the weakness of the universalistic ambitions of the idea of the public sphere as produced within the liberal tradition, but also of the necessity of a historically deeper genealogy of the public sphere.

## Axial Traditions and the Tradition of Modernity

This study intends to make intelligible the complex link between tradition and modernity in the emergence of the public sphere, a nexus that cannot be reduced to a radical opposition. To this end, it explores traditional notions of reasoning for the definition and achievement of the public good. These alternative genealogies are important because they do not only include the formation of oppositional movements (including several socioreligious movements inspired by religious traditions within Judaism, Christianity, and Islam), but are also essential to the relative stability of political, economic, and bureaucratic institutions of modern societies. The public goods of the modern states are, so to speak, partly parasitic on traditional patterns.

The discussion of the genesis and scope of practical reasoning leading to the public exercise of reason in spite of the existence of overarching systemic, functionalist constraints within modern societies is the principal question of the work not only of Habermas but also of Alasdair MacIntyre (cf. Kelly 1989–1990; Doody 1991). The main difference between these two thinkers is in how they conceptualize the universality of reason vis-à-vis the extent to which discursive traditions determine the potential and limits of universalizing projects. Habermas is firm in maintaining that modernity is bound to find reason in itself. Comparing Habermas's and MacIntyre's work, Michael Kelly has raised the question: "What else could 'itself' mean, however, if not that modernity is cast back upon itself qua tradition?" (Kelly 1989–1990: 71).

Habermas does not deny the tradition-bound character of communication, both factually and at the level of actors' competencies and motivations. He looks rather for universal features of communication that *justify* rational understanding on the basis of a strictly procedural rationality, and therefore irrespective of traditions (see chapter 2). The present work is not primarily interested in issues belonging to the realm of moral philosophy, like "justification." From a social-theoretical viewpoint, justification is only interesting as an intrinsic part of the processes through which discursive traditions seek their coherence and integrity. It should not however be surprising that justification plays such an important role within Habermas's approach: it is the symptom that his theory, which lays claim to evince the rationality of communication from modern imperatives, is part of a tradition, albeit sui generis.

My approach requires an investment in reconstructing a sociologically viable notion of tradition. This step was considered basically useless by Habermas, yet is necessary in order to genealogically situate the formation of modern discourse originating from its liberal trunk as a new type of tradition, and to reconstruct the emergence of the public sphere as a simultaneously descriptive, conceptual, and normative category playing a central role in this new tradition. MacIntyre has placed modern discourse in such a perspective and thus provides key elements for a theorization of tradition that are extremely useful from a social theory viewpoint. He suggests the following:

> It is central to the conception of . . . tradition that the past is never something merely to be discarded, but rather that the present is intelligible only as a commentary upon and response to the past in which the past, if necessary and if possible, is corrected and transcended, yet corrected and transcended in a way that leaves the present open to being in turn corrected and transcended by some yet

more adequate point of view . . . A tradition may cease to progress or to degenerate. But when a tradition is in good order, when progress *is* taking place, there is always a certain cumulative element to a tradition. Not everything in the present is equally liable to be overthrown in the future, and some elements of present theory or belief may be such that it is difficult to envisage their being abandoned without the tradition as a whole being discarded. (MacIntyre 1984 [1981]: 146–47)

As part of his conceptualization of tradition, MacIntyre provides a vivid insight into the modern notion of "morality" and into "moral philosophy" as the increasingly professionalized enterprise designed to provide rational criteria for determining what is moral, an enterprise that altered the rational modes of argument and judgment of tradition. Habermas's himself, namely his work, is part of this genealogy of morality, from which the social theory of the public sphere has not yet been emancipated (see chapter 6). It might appear paradoxical that the theoretical resources for emancipating the concept of the public sphere from moral and normative presuppositions come from a critical approach within moral philosophy like MacIntyre's. Yet it cannot be denied that the genesis of sociology itself in the nineteenth and in the early twentieth century is an integral part of the efforts to provide moral cohesion to modern societies (Gauchet 1997 [1985]). What we gain from MacIntyre's approach is a methodological notion that mediates between the theory of the public sphere and the need to calibrate genealogy as an analytical tool compatible with social theory, that is, as more than a deconstructivist weapon. "Tradition" provides such a notion. It is a concept based on a metaphor that stands for the tense search for, simultaneously, integrity and progress within patterns and procedures of reasoning applied to a vast array of practices.

I provide a social-theoretical definition of tradition in chapters 1 and 2. Suffice here to say that MacIntyre contends that the definition of patterns and procedures of practical reasoning and their yoking to concepts of justice are central to the deployment of tradition. It is so not surprising that traditions, if approached sociologically, are highly relevant for a genealogy of the public sphere, both on a methodological level and as units of analysis. Through an ongoing, also conflicted search, tradition grounds and justifies the microsocial bond, the patterns of relationship between *ego* and *alter*. In a discursive tradition, these patterns are hardly defined in the normative terms which, also according to Somers, prevail in the modern liberal Anglo-American parlance. More specifically, as I will try to show, the work of traditions does not yield the kind of dialectics between inwardness and publicness highlighted by Habermas and that is so central to his notion of the public sphere.

Even religiously connoted traditions, including Islam, have a potential to articulate the idea of a basic, factual autonomy of social processes (Houston 2004). The primary focus is on the elementary social bond between *ego* and *alter* and on the related "praxic" formations regulating understandings among agents. I will illustrate the role of the idea of God in this context within Abrahamic traditions (chapters 1 and 2). It is important not to short-circuit this focus into a view of these traditions as inherently prefiguring modern autonomy, intended as premised on a blend of technologies of the self and of domination: a theoretical move observable within the most recent strands of Axial Age theory (cf. Wittrock 2005). The strategy I follow consists in embedding the analysis of traditions within social theory and comparative historical sociology by retrieving traditions' own quasi-sociological understandings of the formation of the basic social bond and symbolic-communicative link. Throughout this work, the adjective "axial" is a qualification of "traditional."

Referring to the dialectics of inwardness and publicness as self-enclosed notions (best expressed in the German concepts of *Innerlichkeit* and *Öffentlichkeit* also used by Habermas) does not do justice to the complex development of the modern liberal, Anglo-American tradition, and even less to the more nuanced and conflicted European-continental variations of a tradition intimately related to Protestant and post-Protestant sociopolitical arenas within northwestern Europe, conventionally considered the cradles of modern Western notions of self, autonomy, and the modern social bond. Suffice here to say (just to anticipate some key elements of the genealogy reconstructed from chapters 3 to 6) that in Roman law, and even in its modern adaptation to Calvinist thought known as Roman-Dutch and Roman-Scottish law—other than in English common law—the notion of *publicus* integrated what we both understand as "public"—for example, by reference to a "good"—and what we understand as "common." This notion is moral and legal at the same time, precedes the differentiation of an autonomous field of operation of the moral self ("morality") and configures a practical-rational method to define and achieve certain collective goods, those falling within the range of the *res publica*. The development of modern liberal notions of the autonomy of the self and of the public sphere was complex and not as linear as the narratives of social theory often imply.

Comparable notions were developed, contested and transformed within other traditions, and here I mention the concept of *maslaha* or *maslaha 'amma* (literally: "general interest" or better "common good") within

Islamic jurisprudence (Zaman 2004; see chapter 4). The notion of common good as elaborated within Christian and Islamic theological and juridical traditions shows a considerable level of convergence, not only substantially, but also in terms of argumentative structures. This is particularly striking if one compares the work of the fourteenth-century Andalusi Islamic scholar al-Shatibi with the elaboration of the Spanish-Catholic scholars De Vitoria and Suarez, who lived in the sixteenth and seventeenth centuries (Masud 1995 [1977]: 59). To sum up, the dialectics of inwardness and publicness should be read and contextualized in its transcultural variability, yet by focusing on transmission, rupture, and reconstruction among and across different traditions.

Yet comparisons between traditions—and the analysis of their internal, plural, and inherently conflicted dynamics—should be conducted in a careful way. Philological and historical rigor should not be undermined, though the orientation of the present work to contribute to revision, reconstruction, and innovation within the public sphere theory compels me to adopt the scholarly standards of social science oriented theoretical work and not of classical humanities, in spite of my training in classical languages, including Arabic. This is a wider issue of theoretically oriented historical sociology. A systematic cooperation between historians, philologists, social scientists, and social theorists could dramatically improve this kind of undertaking. Examples of this cooperation have been numerous since the 1970s, also and especially within Axial Age theory. As a background to the present work, I have myself benefited from having shared in some such experiences of collaboration (cf. Arnason, Salvatore, and Stauth 2006). As far as the topic of this work is concerned, sustained interdisciplinary cooperation would need, however, to be pursued more systematically.

In order to build on my previous work (which also includes a thematic and methodological engagement with historically and philologically oriented Islamic Studies), and to overcome the danger of falling back into well-known Eurocentric traps, Muslim traditions, their formation, and transformations will be given significant weight in my analysis. I devote to these traditions chapter 4, and keep them as a permanent object of reference through the entire work, especially as far as the predominantly legal dimensions of practical reasoning (by reference to such concepts like *phronesis*, namely in the form of *iuris prudentia*, i.e., jurisprudence and its theory) are concerned. This option is also justified by the fact that the legal and jurisprudential dimensions of the construction of the categorical apparatus for the definition of public goods are particularly well developed and debated within Muslim traditions. Yet this perhaps sociologically counterintuitive choice of using Islam (the closest, yet antagonistic discursive tradition, if seen from a European Christian/post-Christian perspective) as a main reference point matches Habermas's wish that the validity of a theory of the public sphere be not dependent on the peculiarities of specific, post-Protestant and post-Enlightenment cultural traditions, like the political cultures that have nourished the Anglo-American conceptual network, or "Jefferson's fortunate heirs" (Habermas 1996 [1992]: 62–63).

Keeping a major focus on Islam facilitates gaining a different perspective. Islam is the last major instance of large-scale crystallization of a discursive tradition in the Euro-Mediterranean civilizational area related to the wider framework of "axial civilizations" (see chapter 1). Islam stands out for specific processes of translation of cultural patterns into institutional frameworks (Arnason 2006a; 2006b). Its authorities and practitioners have initiated and cultivated legal traditions, jurisprudential knowledge, and a distinctive philosophy of law. Particular attention was paid to the notion of practice and to its link to the organization not only of social relations but also of urban, public space. Islam could be characterized as a "Western" civilization in the wider axial framework, while comparative historical sociology is on its way to more radically deconstruct any "East-West" dichotomy (Arnason 2003a). Islam provides a particularly rich terrain for testing hypotheses on communicative action and the public sphere (Eisenstadt 2002; Masud 2005).

A recent collection of study on Islam and the public sphere has been explicitly situated within a comparative historical sociology linked to the axial framework of inquiry. Miriam Hoexter has so summarized the crucial link between divine norm (*shariʿa*) and the institution of charitable endowment (*waqf*) for the task of shaping Muslim public space and for orienting the pursuit of public goods, as well as for stimulating discussions about their determination:

> [I]f the protection against arbitrary acts by rulers was the main purpose of the chartered rights granted in Western civilization to various corporative organizations, the commitment of the Islamic ruler to uphold the *shariʿa* had a much broader significance. It implied an obligation on the part of the ruler to make sure that the public sphere in the territory under his control was construed in conformity with the basic moral norms and values of Islam. (Hoexter 2002: 125)

This picture suggests the existence of historical alternatives in the ways to frame the relation between practice, communication, and authority in shaping public space (see chapter 4 for a systematic treatment of Islam's contribution to the genealogy of the public sphere). It indicates that the concept of the public sphere should be assessed through the analysis of a variety of intersecting genealogies and traditions, wherein Islam as a complex "axial civilization" plays an important role.

Most studies that have dealt with the various facets of the "Islamic resurgence" that became visible in the mid-1970s (cf. Salvatore 1997) start with a caveat: that one should not consider sociopolitical movements inspired by Islam as articulations, under modern conditions, of a monolithic tradition trapped in its own repetitive discourse. Prior to Islam, however, it was Catholicism, in European post-Enlightenment social sciences, to be singled out for its doctrinal rigidity and organizational monolithism. Before Vatican Council II, the Catholic Church was stigmatized for preventing its members from entering modern social organization and embracing a view of society compatible with the realities of modern science, a modern economy, and the centrality of representative state institutions (Kallscheuer 1994: 44–73; Casanova 2001).

This negative consideration of Catholic tradition by post-Enlightenment social science was well grounded in the conflicts of the epoch but becomes a bias if extended backward to pre-Reformation dynamics. It is particularly problematic when it comes from an undifferentiated suspicion of a "medieval" closure of horizons behind any articulation of religious discourse that does not fit into the mainstream genealogy of liberal conceptions of science, democracy, and the public sphere. The present work avoids such bias toward religious traditions and locates their capacity to promote repertoires of intersubjective engagement and communicative understanding. It explores the genealogy of interventions undertaken from within the contests and struggles affecting the evolution of religious traditions. A crucial period for the reformulation of the conceptual apparatus of Latin Christianity was the thirteenth century, when an epoch of "Axial Renaissance" reached its intellectual climax and marked a turning point in the longer genealogy of the public sphere (chapters 3 and 4).

The Axial Renaissance provides a privileged terrain for comparing the transformation and internal variety of key religious traditions within the Euro-Mediterranean civilizational area. I investigate the role played by the new Christian monastic movements and by the Muslim Sufi mystical brotherhoods, along with their organizational differences, in shaping the great syntheses of the age via their interventions on the nexus between practical and public reasoning. I explore in particular the contributions of selected, towering Christian and Muslim scholars who authoritatively impacted on those synthetic formulas: the thirteenth-century theologian

Aquinas on the Latin Christian side (see chapter 3), and the fourteenth-century jurist al-Shatibi on the Sunni Islamic side (see chapter 4). This exploration is not finalized to a streamlined comparison between Christian and Islamic thought, but aims to instantiating key historical nexuses of practical and public reasoning providing a significant, albeit selective, historical contextualization to the theoretical discussion of chapters 1 and 2. This analysis of Latin Christendom and Arab Islamdom will also provide the essential background to the analysis of modern transformations and crystallizations of the public sphere developed in chapter 5 and 6. The modern public sphere will thus be examined in its complexity and ambivalence, as opening spaces of freedom but also as obstructing the further development of other traditions of intersubjective understanding, discourse, and social cooperation carrying different ideas for balancing practice and communication. Set against the background of the analysis of the achievements of the Axial Renaissance, these distinctively Western, predominantly Anglo-American developments variably tied to the Protestant Reformation will be reexamined not only with regard to their success in creating modern societies, but also as the manifestation of an implosion of earlier traditions and their cultural ecumene (cf. Wittrock 2005).

Both commonalities and differences between Christian and Islamic notions of practical and public reasoning will delimit the range of historically given crystallizations of the types of public spheres forged by subsequent transformations. My goal is not to deliver a typology of Christian versus Islamic forms or types of action that build the traditional backbone of Habermas's "communicative action" (see introduction, chapter 1, chapter 2, chapter 6, and conclusion). I aim rather to highlight different nodes in the construction of practical and public reasoning that emanate from the form of action premised on patterns of understanding and tension between *ego* and *alter*. In my analysis of different syntheses my primary concern is not to choose a Christian or an Islamic example as necessarily representative of a related "macrocivilizational" pattern.

A further major focus of the analysis is on the attempt to ground a new science of the constitution of the social bond, as related to authority, trust, and imagination, in the century (1650–1750) immediately preceding the zenith of the Enlightenment (see chapter 5). The specific attention that I will devote to the thought and method of the eighteenth-century thinker Giambattista Vico will also contribute to highlight the analogies and differences with a move performed by Habermas in the period between his *Habilitation* and his work on the theory of communicative action (Habermas 1978 [1963]). This was a crucial phase for shaping the later trajectory of Habermas's work, mainly remembered by observers for his debate with Gadamer, in which Habermas accused the Heidelberg philosopher of seeing "no antithesis between authority and reason" (Habermas 1986 [1970]: 315–16). It is the period when Habermas analyzed praxic notions like *phronesis* that could have led him in a different theoretical direction. Habermas appreciated Vico's employment of diagnostic analysis for the determination of the limits of a science of society dependent on modern scientific standards, a science that risked erasing the centrality of practice in repertoires of intersubjective understanding. But this appreciation evaporated in Habermas's later work on the theory of communicative action, for which such traditions of modern thought appeared to him still too much backward looking, and so unsuitable to a social theory adequate to the era of mature capitalism.[2]

Yet I would not be surprised if Habermas would think of his own theory of communicative action as the realization of Vico's stated program to build up a new theory of society that takes into account the modern techniques of power without falling prey to their functionalism. Without being a full-fledged social theorist in the contemporary sense, Vico came close to theorizing about society. Far from being the last of humanist thinkers (Apel 1978 [1963]), his approach moves into directions that seem to lead straight into the founding paradigms of modern European sociology (cf. Hösle 2001), even more than eighteenth-century Anglo-Scottish civil society theory did. He built up a sophisticated genealogical approach to praxic techniques of intersubjective understanding (Miner 2002). Unlike the Scottish Enlightenment and Adam Smith, to whose tradition Habermas has tried to reconnect in seeking to theorize about social integration via a third sphere, Vico consciously refrained from a mechanistic view of social integration and conceived instead of a permanently precarious social bond. This was seen as laboriously kept together through the discrete efforts of practical reasoning, against the backdrop of human efforts to draw social boundaries and the related drive to accumulate power and wealth. Here, like elsewhere, Habermas's scarce interest for religious traditions as platforms of reasoning connecting everyday practices to criteria of justice, and his wholesale depreciation of Vico's method as still trapped in an Aristotelian-Thomistic cage, might have played a role in pushing him to new shores of theorizing.

Yet the social thought of Vico presents the advantage of linking religious traditions to the emerging modern conditions of human society and in particular to the fragmentation of social authority effected by the concentration of political power in the hands of nation-states. Both phenomena were mediated by a new discourse of rights organically linking the individual and his liberties to the state and its guarantees. Vico's work reflects in a unique way the dilemmas and the attempted solutions produced in an era of intellectual upheaval inaugurated by Spinoza and named the "Radical Enlightenment" (roughly spanning the century 1650–1750), preceding the mature Enlightenment of the Encyclopedia and the *philosophes* (Israel 2001). These dilemmas, and the underlying arguments, reflect a remarkably open problematization of traditions' contributions to shaping the social bond and its patterns of understanding and communication. Through the analysis of these dilemmas we can better understand the extent to which modernity relied, elaborated upon, and metamorphosed—or rejected—specific concepts and arguments of traditions. During the Radical Enlightenment (which was to a large extent an "Axial Enlightenment," as I will suggest in chapter 5, for linking the radical questioning of traditions to a lucid consciousness of their axial origin), authority was dissected and trust recast, but the relations between "religion" and "politics," between religious authority and freedom, between faith and trust, were not yet rigidified and reified in the shape of differentiated social functions and fields. Moreover, the place of imagination in the construction of the social bond was given a privileged attention.

The feverish discussions and conceptual reconstructions of Vico's epoch of "crisis of the European mind" (Israel 2001: 14–22) are not just historical antecedents to the search for the light of reason culminating in the mature Enlightenment of the second half of the eighteenth century, but are critical passages in the long-term genealogy of the public sphere. They evidence still largely unsettled issues concerning potentials and limits of a universalizing construction of the social bond, based on a type of communicative action enlivening a third sphere of society (see chapters 5 and 6). These issues reverberate on today's agenda of social theory, crowded with such issues like the European sociocultural integration and the relationship between Europe and the Muslim world. They offer us precious conceptual clues that prevent a theoretical flattening of the analysis on the triumphant self-understanding of modernity inherited from the longer trajectory of rationalization of science and society of the nineteenth century, which was not by chance the century of the rise of sociology.

It is beyond doubt that the ruptures represented by the Enlightenment are essential to the genealogy of the public sphere. Yet these very discontinuities cannot be adequately evaluated without relying, methodologically and theoretically, on adequate conceptualizations of tradition. Alasdair MacIntyre shows us a promising track when he states:

> What the Enlightenment made us for the most part blind to and what we need now to recover is ... a conception of rational enquiry as embodied in a tradition, a conception according to which the standards of rational justification themselves emerge from and are part of a history in which they are vindicated by the way in which they transcend the limitations of and provide remedies for the defects of their predecessors within the history of that same tradition. Not all traditions, of course, have embodied rational enquiry as a constitutive part of themselves; and those thinkers of the Enlightenment who dismissed tradition because they took it to be the antithesis of rational enquiry where in some instances in the right. But in so doing they obscured from themselves and others the nature of some at least of the systems of thought which they so vehemently rejected. Nor was this entirely their fault. (MacIntyre 1988: 7)

The present work provides an investigation of the formation and transformations of major discursive traditions in the Euro-Mediterranean civilizational area. Latin Christianity and Sunni Islam are taken as the main focal points of the genealogy, as they are traditions that have not only shown both resilience and capacity to change, but also a high degree of discursive autonomy vis-à-vis the developments tied to the commercial, industrial, and political revolutions. At the beginning of the twenty-first century, these two religious traditions are well positioned on the communicative stages of global society and politics—and not as mere residues from a bygone epoch, or as relics of the Middle Ages. Defined through such traditions rooted in the axial breakthrough, public reasoning appears as antecedent to the public sphere, intended as the hub of a third sphere in the modern sense elucidated by Somers. Public reasoning is, nonetheless—as also shown by several modern and contemporary socioreligious movements (see Salvatore and LeVine 2005)—not essentially at odds with such a public sphere, but is on many levels its precondition.

## The Interlocking Genealogies of Traditions and Modernity

The modern crystallization of practices of public reasoning into the well-rounded idea of a public sphere has clouded long-term genealogies. The principles of the autonomy of reason and of the primacy of subjectivity inherited from the last phase of the Enlightenment have neutralized more complex trajectories. The newly emerging idea of the public sphere had to fit without traditional residues into a design of modern society built on new models of social solidarity and political participation. Alongside this centralistic and absolutistic quality of discourses variably affiliated with the Enlightenment, "alternative modernities" (cf. Eisenstadt, Schluchter and Wittrock 2000; Chambers and Kymlicka 2002) have developed from within various other traditions and their modes of social communication, motivation to action, and solidarity. These alternative traditions of modernity dislocate the dominant notion of the public sphere and provide fresh entry points into a transcultural reconstruction of the public sphere. Some of these alternative approaches have the potential to accelerate a transformation and cross-cultural validation of the notion of the public sphere itself and to facilitate new forms of pluralism within public arenas of engagement and communication.

This is why I argue in favor of a genealogical approach. The focal point of a genealogy is not a firm beginning, but tangible effects, which in this study are best reflected by a Habermasian dilemma: the necessity and simultaneous fragility of a public sphere as the main site of social integration within modern societies. The recourse to genealogy as a methodological tool should then be yoked to the theoretical centrality of "tradition" and made adequate to its final object, namely the "public sphere." The definition of the public sphere as a third sphere reveals instead a methodological and ideological bias in favor of the soft voluntarism underlying a constructivist approach, which is at odds with the idea of genealogy. I am not discarding constructivism per se. I rather attempt to put into perspective the transformations that generated a Habermasian type of voluntarism-*cum*-constructivism.

Both genealogy as a method and tradition as an object are helpful in this undertaking. Besides being an object of investigation, tradition also contributes to a methodological specification of the type of genealogical approach to pursue, thus making it an "axial genealogy." The notion of tradition is useful in neutralizing the excesses of two thus far opposed methods of social theory: the deconstructivist impetus of genealogy intended, in a Nietzschean-Foucauldian sense, as the unveiling of successive social and cultural formations brought about by wills to power; and the constructivist zeal of social theory facilitating a universalistic shortcut by identifying the "rational" with the "open" and potentially universal construction of communication and understanding, without however testing the closures that each and every moment of opening entails.

The construction of a self-enclosed public sphere is therefore excessively ambitious, if compared with the inevitable fragility of every new configuration of openness in the initiation of social action and communication. The goal of the present work is to situate the constructed public sphere against its complex and contradictory trajectory of emergence, without belittling the achievements of openness and agency reflected by it. The combined use of "genealogy" and "tradition" is congruent with the goal to make the theory of the public sphere less entrenched in a moral philosophy of the free and communicative agent. This approach will also provide a first step to unveil the anomalies of the notion of the public sphere vis-à-vis the antinomian metaphors of classical social theory, like movement versus institution, charisma/creativity/effervescence versus order/routinization, structure versus antistructure, and so on. The public sphere can never be reduced either to movement or institution, though it is inevitably, in some measure, parasitic on both. The elegant geometry of the third sphere, which promises to even out and neutralize the destructive creativity of movements and the uncreative disciplining of institutions, relies on a soft, voluntaristic, largely rationalizable construction work performed by free agents. My genealogy exposes the historical and cultural overdetermination of this geometry, without indulging in deconstructivist fury or seeking refuge into a soft constructivist voluntarism.

This is why I rely on a definition of tradition that innovates on how mainstream social theory has dealt with this concept so far. My approach is also intended to integrate the soft use of tradition made by Habermas's constructivist approach to the public sphere. This approach, while generically recognizing the role of "background" cultural orientation played by traditions, has not allowed for an accurate exploration of the methodological and thematic implications of a serious work on tradition. As noted earlier, a concept of tradition that builds, though not uncritically, on the work of MacIntyre, provides precious elements that feedback into the definition of the object of my research. This conceptualization of tradition also facilitates a refinement of approach, helping shape a genealogical method that is compatible with social theory and contributes to enrich it transculturally.

It should be clear now that with genealogy I intend here not a perspectivist reaction to the Enlightenment and its analytics of truth and falseness. While it is evident that the Enlightenment discourse of reason cannot be the exclusive source of conceptualizations, it also does not need to be radically combated or preemptively exorcized. Critique is here more specifically focused on how the Enlightenment's re-formation of universals has been conditioned by new metaphysics of the transcendental subject (in the Kantian sense), which yielded an imploded, more than an alternative form of divine transcendence (see chapter 6). The transcendental subject was also devised as a way out of an empiricism too narrow-mindedly modeled on the functional needs and emerging institutions of commercial and industrial society.

Genealogy is understood here first in its basic, metaphorical sense that in order to know somebody one has to know his ancestors, an idea that applies to human practices and institutions as well. This search cannot be implemented through an erudite passion for the etymologies of words and concepts. My focus is on how layers of concepts and series of arguments enrich and complicate the motivational prism of social and communicative agents in ways that the one-dimensional, mainly theatrical metaphors of the "social actor" carrying "interests," endowed with "skills," and playing the social "game," are not able to convey. Having a simple meaning and a prophylactic function, genealogy is not intended as a substitute for theoretical analysis. It rather integrates the genesis of modern social theory into the object of investigation.

Genealogical prophylaxis is also applied to a much too static view of religious traditions and to a strongly reified view of "religion" in sociological theory (see chapter 1). In the traumatic modern European experience of fragmentation of social authority that builds the counternarrative to the triumphs of industrial society, the welfare state, and representative-democratic institutions, religion was increasingly conceptualized as a transhistorical essence based on essentially private "belief." Within northwestern European modernity religion was therefore considered legitimate in the public sphere only if it helped overcoming discord and moralizing public life, optimally in one or the other form of "civil religion." The condition for operating in this socially functional manner is that religious authorities and institutions feed into the general framework of moral values of societies, increasingly organized under the aegis of modern nation-states. This normative understanding of religion is itself object of the genealogical exploration (cf. Asad 1993).

Genealogy here is not a perspectivist "unveiling" of the arbitrary character of points of origin, inevitably clouded in myth, but a more practical approach to continuities and discontinuities. This type of analysis focuses in particular on how ideas about the social bond among human beings, about the symbolic-communicative mediation of this link performed by the emerging idea of God in Abrahamic traditions, and about the resulting human "commonwealths," were finally metamorphosed in the context of emergence of a modern capitalist economy and even more of the modern state. This acknowledgement of continuities and discontinuities fits a type of genealogy that was practiced by Giambattista Vico. According to a contemporary interpreter of his genealogical method, Vico assumed that "a thing's present actuality is not fully intelligible until it is narrated as the end product of a sequence. Nature and process cannot be prised apart" (Miner 2002: 89). This approach facilitates a recognition of social contingence through continuities and discontinuities, while acknowledging the importance of identifying points of origin and rupture via an attentive analysis of the mythical and symbolic language through which they are formulated and narrated.

As a corrective to Habermas's basically negative appraisal of mythical knowledge as the antithesis of rational communication (Habermas 1984 [1981]; 1987 [1981]; cf. also Bertland 2000; Henry 2000), this genealogical approach to the symbolic-communicative dimension of the social bond builds on Vico's intuition that there could be no knowledge (not even legal knowledge, and therefore no civic institutions, no maintenance of the social bond, no human commonwealths) without mythical knowledge. This knowledge was produced as a reaction to the sacred fear inculcated in man by his exposure to powerful natural phenomena, epitomized by thunder. Vico also showed that this kind of nonrational knowledge is the foundation of authority *and so* of the social bond and of the possibility of communication and understanding among humans, and of their acting in common. In explaining the formation of repertoires of intersubjective engagement, understanding, and connectivity instituted by religious traditions, one cannot take for granted the erasure of authority as part of an evolutionary trajectory whereby tradition ends up bowing to Enlightenment reason. Vico explored how the evolution of practical and public reasoning out of their beginnings in *mythos* (myth, narration) can relocate and metamorphose authority while strengthening ties of communication and making them more transparent to participating agents. This occurs through the development among social agents of an increasingly strong sense of sharing goods, a process that culminated in the Latin invention of the idea of publicness. The process of sharing does not disguise material conditionings and their varied and fragmented forms of authority, including class stratification and conflict, as markers of ever more complex forms of society. Yet the rise of the *res publica* is a response to the clash among conflicting interests.

For Vico, the source of all authority is in the appropriation of space, resources, and modes of control of *ego* over *alter* and in drawing the boundaries that secure such appropriation. Yet mythological knowledge and symbolic communication are a sine qua non both for such processes of appropriation and acts of boundary drawing and for the challenge of authority through protest oriented movements. These movements defy the concentration of power and produce alternative frames of the symbolic orders and borders of society and its institutions. The private-public boundary and the institutions built thereupon are central to this Vichian genealogy of authority, action, and communication. For the Neapolitan thinker violence, which is inextricably material and symbolic, cannot be bracketed out from such a type of genealogy. The plebeians in Roman history are for him the prototype of such protest movements. They make use of organized—material and symbolic—violence to transgress the relations of power and authority. Unlike Habermas, for whom a "plebeian public sphere" can only approximate a bourgeois one, for Vico the historic rise of the notion of *res publica* and its institutionalization in Roman law are a direct consequence of the plebeian contestation of aristocratic authority (see chapter 5).

Habermas would probably object that the modern public sphere, built on its eighteenth-century bourgeois prototypes within English, French, and German societies, is a basically different site of social integration, for whose understanding the Vichian genealogy is of little use (see chapter 6). My approach overcomes such closure and traces genealogical links of continuity and discontinuity between various forms of public exchange, conflict and discourse. Vico did not conceal that at the root of the conflicted sociopolitical dynamics that led to the crystallization of *res publica* lay the two main types of patrimonial, authority-building, *ego-alter* relationships: between husband and wife and between the patrician patron and the plebeian client. It is well known that the Enlightenment did not abolish either marriage or property as the main foundations of authority, while commercial and industrial (or, simply, capitalist) society transformed and stabilized both institutions with the help of the new powers of the modern state. To analyze the modern bourgeois public sphere of Habermas outside of the web of institutional continuities is not a correct operation of social theory. Abrahamic traditions, on their part, gave a conditional blessing to the authority of both marriage and patronage by creating an external form of authority in the form of transcendence, namely the authority of God as superordinate father and patron. Genealogy helps identify continuities where the self-understanding of social sciences takes for granted the primacy of ruptures. But it also helps detect innovation where the impression of continuity and stagnation prevails.

Thus, my work hypothesis is that the Enlightenment discourse that provided the self-understanding to the modern public sphere was more the consequence of an implosion of traditions than of their collapse. In this sense, Enlightenment-based modernity is still hostage to the modalities through which religious traditions have instituted an external authority, a type of reasoning, and related techniques of intersubjective coordination functional to shaping the social bond. Unlike what is maintained by several strands of postmodern theory, the possible disillusionment with the capacity of Enlightenment discourse to produce and maintain a universalistic social science and social theory is not due to the fact that its discourse is too strong and absolutistic, but because it is—as adumbrated by sociological versions of Axial Age theory first pioneered, not by chance, by theorists of modernization—too weak an alternative to religious traditions and their authority.

Yet one has to give credit to Habermas for having produced the most powerful attempt to accomplish the social-theoretical potential of the philosophical discourse of modernity. The fact that this discourse is simultaneously hostage of the formulas of the axial breakthrough largely shaped by religious traditions on the one hand, and of capitalism and its related political formations on the other, is not Habermas's own fault. His grand merit is to have conceived of a reconstruction of social theory with the goal to create a common ground for social science and the humanities: this had been exactly, as Habermas acknowledged, Vico's program of the *New Science*, around a quarter of millennium before the Frankfurt social thinker launched his theory of communicative action.

While MacIntyre considers tradition and Nietzschean-Foucauldian genealogy alternative and competing methodologies (MacIntyre 1990), I opt for a genealogical approach of a Vichian kind, which relies on a notion of tradition. Genealogy and tradition are not necessarily, as in MacIntyre's definition, metatheoretical options, and as such radically alternative both to each other and to the mainstream approach that he identifies with the legacy of the Enlightenment and that reflects the concerns of modern and contemporary social theory. It is rather the theoretical legacy of the Enlightenment that needs to be complexified in such a way to create a stronger metatheoretical debate within social theory capable to integrate key elements of traditions into modern perspectives. It is less a way to theorize about "multiple modernities" than the recognition of the complexity of traditions' entangling within modernity.

Vico's approach to the mutual enmeshment between religious and civic institutions, to the genesis of public reasoning, and finally to "modernity," is a major source of methodological inspiration for the present work. Though subtly subversive, Vico's genealogical approach to modernity is a coherent alternative to the program of postmodern genealogy (Miner 2002). While anticipating Nietzsche's approach to language as a deconstruction of the development of moral concepts and social institutions (Rudnick Luft 1994, 2003), Vico's method has the merit of steadily highlighting the constructive character of ruptures and the *new*. The genesis of the new is framed by a socioanthropological understanding of the tense concomitance of contingency of action and directionality of history (Mazzotta 1999: 60). Vico's approach to society and history is thus a modern alternative to both Kant's transcendentalism and to Hegel's dialectics. Not by chance, it attracted the attention of Karl Marx (cf. Tagliacozzo 1983) and, more recently, of Edward Said (1975). Both, however, gave a reductionist reading (one too strictly aligned with their own political agendas) of Vico's research program in the *New Science*. The methodological bottom line of Vico's contribution to social theory consists in showing how political and religious concepts can only make sense as creations of specific social groups in history. The genealogy of public reasoning flows from this basic understanding.

Vico , especially in his dealing with religion, was indebted to one of his main targets in the intellectual debates of the epoch, the "laic saint" Spinoza, whose followers constituted a major force in the Republic of Letters—not only in Naples (cf. Stone 1997; Mazzotta 1999) but also in the whole of Europe—that emerged in the first half of the eighteenth century. A combined use of both Spinoza and Vico is particularly suitable to the alternative genealogy undertaken in the present work. They both worked at the definition of religion without, however, crystallizing it into a transhistorical essence, as subsequent Enlightenment thinkers did (Preus 1989: 89). Spinoza and Vico, whose lives spanned respectively the first and last phases of the century of the Radical Enlightenment (1650–1750)—that is also, as I attempt to show, an "Axial Enlightenment"—had to face the reality of a "disintegration of the Western body politic into a collection of mutually schismatic politico-religious bodies," namely the rising modern nation-states (Cooper 1998: 9).

However, unlike Spinoza, Vico did away radically with Cartesianism, perceived as an inert representational method of subjectification and objectification hostile to the task of capturing the intersubjectivity of the social bond that the Neapolitan thinker envisaged as the proper object of a new science of society. Tightly related to his reflections on myth, memory, and the genesis of law, Vico saw the origins of religion as grounded in fear, manifesting the anguish for an untamable world from which man feels separated and toward which he feels powerless

(Mazzotta 1999: 239). Vico argues that the rise of civic institutions followed up to the practices of divination that he considered "the source of intelligibility of the symbolic structures of the world" (ibid.: 240–41). These symbolic structures constitute the "common sense" that a certain kind of imaginative discourse, like the biblical "parable," tries to capture and to insert into the social process, via a critique of existing established institutions. Thanks to a combination of imagination and common sense, new public spaces and new institutions are created.

Vico's approach is made more sophisticated by his genealogical awareness that while man is the author of civic institutions, he can know them only from within. This is a caveat against all dealings with dichotomies like "religious" versus "secular," or "private" versus "public," in a geometric-Cartesian and scientist fashion. This insight is the springboard for reconstructing a viable notion of communication by relating it to the material human needs that constitute the social bond imaginatively and sustain it by establishing ties of authority and trust or distrust: a notion, therefore, other than pure *logos*, or discourse per se. The result are concepts of connective justice and equity based on the socioanthropological and historical observation that since man is able to communicate and adjudicate over *ego*'s and *alter*'s needs, justice cannot be an immediately causal determination of interest: "The utilitarian interest is the *occasion* of justice, not its *cause*" (ibid.: 111–12). Practical needs are shaped by practical reasoning, consisting in matching human necessities with the idea of equity. Repertoires of intersubjective engagement and understanding are the product of the largely communicative attempt to make needs convergence in this manner. This view contains the seeds for a work program of reconciliation of the notions of practice and communication which does not suppress but incorporate the modern idea of interest. This reconciliation is a necessary condition for reconstructing the theory of the public sphere in viable ways.

Vico's genealogy is thus "a counterexample to Foucault's claim that genealogy is necessarily impious" (Miner 2002: xv). It is based on the capacity "to find some truth in the perspective that is being undermined" (ibid.: 9). This is why this genealogy depends on a new conceptualization of tradition. As highlighted by Miner,

> Vico's genealogical approach seems to oscillate between two poles. On the one hand, it sets out to expose a phenomenon or discourse as something humanely constructed, as a *factum* that has no unique or special claim to truth. On the other hand, it seems eager to acknowledge that cultural formations, even those susceptible to being unmasked as

something other than what they pretend to be, manage to preserve a connection with truth insofar as they are participations in the divine *Logos*. Hence Vico holds a more positive view of the *factum*: "the true and the made are convertible" (*verum et factum convertuntur*). (ibid.: 26)

Traditions can only exist and thrive through this drive to connect facts to truths, *factum* to *verum*, *phronesis* to *telos*, by virtue of their claim to communicatively participate in a *logos* that transcends both *ego* and *alter* and allows for the construction of the common between them. This is what grounds a tradition and holds it together via a sustained search for coherence. This is also what makes the human communicative endeavors nonreducible to either power formations accessible through a deconstructivist Foucauldian genealogy or to a third sphere of social integration open to a constructivist Habermasian theory. In order to carry forward this program in ways that are adequate to respond to the challenges of modernity, Vico worked on situating the sociopolitical dimension of what we call "discourse," namely the only phenomenological concretization of *logos* — based on "rhetoric," intended as the classic art of persuasion — vis-à-vis the field of practice that Machiavelli had redefined as a political realm of strategy, expediency, and interest, within a first dramatic bid for divorcing "politics" from "religion" (and contributing to the reification of the latter). Vico reaffirms the centrality of rhetoric "since it combines the art of memory, invention, and judgment; it forges links between reason and will and can mold the passions; and as an art of persuasion it broadens the compass of the audience's imagination" (Mazzotta 1999: 70).

The present work might appear daring in its attempt to combine seeds from three fiercely competing schools that have fought for primacy within social theory in the last third of the twentieth century: theory (represented by Habermas), genealogy (condensed in the work of Foucault), and tradition (promoted by MacIntyre). I do refer to all three for the sake of clarifying the conceptual nodes related to a construct, the "public sphere," which most social science tends to take for granted, either glorifying it as the key to a scholarship committed to rationalization and democratization, or willfully ignoring it for disguising more relevant structural issues and cultural conflicts in society.

Provisionally, I would consider my methodological synthesis as drawing on the following assemblage of heuristic ideas. First, modernity provides the topical and theoretical dimension, since the "public sphere" is essentially given within modernity. However, theory is not self-sufficient, since — *pace* Habermas — modernity can discursively fold back on itself, but cannot produce, out of this self-understanding, a universally valid investigative method. Genealogy provides then the critical dimension of method that the "critical theory" of Horkheimer and Adorno (who provided an important theoretical background to Habermas and whose theory Habermas tried to supersede), ending up in postulating a "negative dialectics" of Enlightenment modernity, made purely diagnostic and antagonistic, and therefore analytically sterile. Second, it is through a "charitable," nondeconstructivist kind of genealogy that I suggest to discover the chain of continuities and discontinuities through which the search for coherence unfolds and to which modernity itself, though striving to overcome all traditions, is also subjected, thereby constituting itself as a tradition sui generis. Third, tradition provides a more tangible methodological dimension, and so the missing link for closing the circle with the topical dimension. Thus, the modern public sphere can be investigated through unraveling its self-enclosed constructedness via the recognition of its inevitable dependence on tradition, indeed on intersecting and sometimes conflicting traditions.

When I first formulated this research question, several years ago, in the framework of my *Habilitation* thesis at Humboldt University in Berlin, my knowledge of Vico was superficial. Deepening his study, I was delighted to discover in his work seeds of a methodological assemblage of components that later became separate in the three just mentioned approaches, and which for him were still represented by the classic triad of the topical, critical, and methodological dimensions of humanities. Though couched in a language, in categories, and in a style of writing that correspond to the baroque taste of the epoch and place (eighteenth-century Naples), such a synthesis was what Vico attempted to do, when he started, three centuries ago, to struggle for understanding the entanglements of inherited traditions and the emerging modernity, in order to explain how humans construct the common through discourse. I hope to contribute to carry forward a social-theoretical investigation within this Vichian tradition, one that sympathetically—though critically and genealogically—problematizes the universal scope of modern public discourse, while avoiding a rigid adherence to specific schools. Concerning the variety of social theory schools to which I refer in this work, with Vico I wish to say: *Nos vero, nullius sectae addicti* ("indeed, we do not belong to any sect").

# CHAPTER 1

# RELIGION, CIVILIZATION, AND THE REDEFINITION OF TRADITION

## The Microdimension of Tradition and Its Relation to Civilization

The notion of "tradition," as preliminarily illustrated in the introduction, is central to this work. In order to be defined in analytically acceptable ways, it first needs to be carefully disentangled from both "religion" and "civilization." Yet the concept of tradition also needs to reappropriate useful elements from both the sociology of civilization (or "comparative civilizational analysis") and the sociology of religion. My goal is to delineate a more general notion of tradition encompassing various levels of human action linking practice and reflection. This will include highlighting not only the religious dimensions of traditions but also their political, philosophical, legal, and "civic" components, which are in turn variously linked to what is often identified as the religious core of traditions.

Nobody would dispute the existence of a consolidated sociology of religion, whose beginnings basically coincide with the birth of sociology. A sociology of civilization articulated as a comparative analysis of civilizations has also gained a space in the social sciences. It combines the theory of axial civilizations with the civilizing process intended in an Eliasian sense (see Arnason 2001, 2003b; Mazlish 2001; Szakolczai 2001a). Yet there is no comparable "sociology of tradition" (see however Shils 1981). There are sufficient reasons for the absence of such a special sociology. Yet there are even stronger reasons not to leave the concept of tradition underdetermined. One of the leading social theorists of the last quarter of the twentieth century, Shmuel N. Eisenstadt, shifted his focus from "tradition" to "civilization" in his sustained endeavor to turn modernization theory into a theoretical program on "multiple modernities" (Eisenstadt and Graubard 1973; Eisenstadt 1982, 1985, 1998, 2000a, 2000b, 2001, 2003; see also Stauth 1998). I do not intend to develop a sociology of tradition that is distinct from the sociology of modernity or from social theory at large. However, I consider it important to recuperate a sociological notion of tradition that is useful to redefine and reconnect the notions of practice and communication within sociology at large.

This operation should facilitate capturing the genesis of repertoires of intersubjective understanding and connectivity which, rooted in the formation and transformations of traditions, led to the emergence of the concept of the public sphere as a quintessentially modern idea of social and communicative integration. It is with regard to this plastic notion of tradition, which I will specify in this chapter, that "religion" (and, secondarily, "civilization") might acquire the sociological sharpness that is needed for the present inquiry.

We can observe a peculiar fate of the concept of tradition within social theory and social science at large. It is the destiny of being an almost ubiquitous, yet residual category impregnated with a distinctively antisociological flavor. One does not need archaeological skills to unearth and display this derogatory idea of tradition, whose essential layer is often identified with "religion." For example, in a volume significantly titled *Detraditionalization: Critical Reflections on Authority and Identity at a Time of Uncertainty* (Heelas, Lash, and Morris 1996), that included contributions by leading social theorists like Bauman, Beck, Lash, Luhmann, Luckmann, and Sennett, "tradition," though central (in a negativized form) in the title, is taken for granted in most chapters. It is underdefined, or appears in reduced and conventional definitions, mostly invoking the authority of Shils (1981) and Giddens (1994). A constant feature of such reductionist sociological definitions of tradition is a focus on dimensions that configure the latter as a "predicative" aid to explain why religiously grounded societies—those still under the grip of "religious authority"—produce nonmodern or at best semimodern social worlds. Certain types of social conduct, belief, or mode of representation are predicated as "traditional" mainly for being associated with (unreformed) "religion."

For example, Anthony Giddens writes that "tradition ... is an orientation to the past, such that the past ... is made to have a heavy influence over the present" (ibid.: 62). Other authors, along similar lines, have contended that "tradition is what societies have before they are touched by the great transformation of capitalism, and what seems to characterize traditional societies most is that they are under the sway of religion" (van der Veer and Lehmann 1999: 6). More generally, people considered as rooted in a "traditional world" are thought to be living "out of time" and "out of history": in this way, tradition is identified with a notion of temporality that is simply inadequate to modern life. In this standardized view of tradition, it is also implied that the whole cluster of "social and institutional deficits" that afflict traditional social life are rooted in, or strictly associated with, a more deeply ideational or "cultural" retard.

To this consideration of tradition by, so to speak, sociological default, we should add other notions that attempt to turn the a-functionality or antifunctionality of tradition toward modernity into a potential, positive functionality. This alternative approach locates tradition into the matrix of "local cultures" or "communities" which cannot be disregarded in view of a society's entry into modernity. They should be taken into account or adequately "used"—so the argument goes—in order to avoid alienation, deacculturation, and their related backlashes at individual and collective levels. Traditional cultures are thus considered potential assets for enriching the motivational prisms of local actors and supporting those modernizing agents who intervene from outside to promote "indigenous" concerns on the way to social progress.

For instance, Robert Putnam (1993) praised the "civic traditions" of Tuscany, in Italy, as a generative source of social capital, in explicit contrast to the alleged absence of such traditions in southern Italy. The default negative view of traditions is turned here into a distinction between "good" and "bad" traditions. While there are innumerable empirical confutations of this approach, with regard to the Putnamian argument, as in the case of southern Italy (see Piattoni 1998), the theoretical point on which this discrimination rests has been challenged by a more sophisticated view of the complex relation between traditions and the rationalizing expectations of modern institutions, according to which traditions might ingrain into modern patterns of social differentiation while being however parasitic on them. The expected effects in terms of modernization are thus blocked or procrastinated (cf. Luhmann 1995).

While this is not the place to deepen discussion of the more sophisticated views of tradition that can emerge even from within modernization theory, it is sufficient to say that, sociologically, tradition is conceived either as an impediment to modernization or as a resource to it. Either way, traditions are conceptualized teleologically, that is, from the viewpoint of a path to (however conceived) "modernity." The resulting tendency to a reductionist view of tradition depends then on a still strong compulsion to essentialize modernity.

The minimal condition for bending this notion of tradition to analytical use and theoretical conceptualization is to ask the question: can an approach be chosen that conceives of traditions in positively sociological terms, while avoiding to reduce them to either cultural residues of the social worlds where modernization has not allegedly worked out well enough, or to local resources for modernization strategies? In spite of the inadequate elaboration on tradition in sociological theory, there have been other endeavors in the social sciences and the humanities which could be taken into account. These discussions deal with concepts that have a family resemblance with inherited sociological notions of tradition, though tradition in these instances is rarely invoked in an explicit way (not surprisingly, due to its predominantly negative connotation).

I refer here to those pieces of theory that are sometimes, but not always, lumped together under the label of "communitarianism," in some cases also linked to "pragmatism," which are best represented in twentieth-century U.S. social thought and that envision tradition in the form of "shared values," "cultural heritage," the "habits of the heart," or even as the roots of the type of civility that can produce a vital political culture. Edward Shils (1981) has been championing the creation of a link between this approach and the explicit use of the notion of tradition. Some among such approaches do make explicit reference to tradition and appear situated midway between the invocation of a religiously impregnated tradition, and the more contemporary, "progressive" views of "tradition as resource" (cf. Dewey 1927; Walzer 1968). Common to these views of tradition is that they point out action-orienting standards, deliberately and consciously shared and actively reshaped, and not passively inherited by social actors. These standards or values can therefore build the backbone of a vibrant civic spirit and public culture. Certain types of "religion"—often identified as "civil religion"—are explicitly construed as playing such role (Bellah 1970; 1992 [1975]).[1]

With few exceptions (see chapter 2), these discussions tend to conflate "tradition" and "religion" and do not produce a notion of tradition solidly tied to practice and communication. Following MacIntyre, who has dedicated the best part of his work to this issue, the notion of tradition that we need to reconstruct has, first of all, nothing to do with the ideological discourse of conservative political theorists, who contrast tradition with reason and the stability of tradition with conflict (MacIntyre 1984 [1981]: 218–20). On the contrary, tradition is positively related both to reason and conflict and is therefore, in many respects, the exact opposite of that conservative concept. More than being an eminent part of the motivational prism of the social agent—as in the approach to "tradition as resource"—tradition is, according to MacIntyre, essential to the grounding and understanding of repertoires of intersubjective engagement and connectivity, and therefore of both practice and communication. This approach no doubt privileges the intersubjective dimension of action and communication, but also entails a view of the rationality of the agent. This rationality, nonetheless, cannot be understood through a vocabulary borrowed either from economics or from law as specialized fields with distinctive modern rationalities. So far, MacIntyre's position seems to endorse Habermas's reliance—made clear in his contention with Gadamer during the late 1960s (Habermas 1977 [1970])—on tradition as a condition for building repertoires of intersubjective understanding between *ego* and *alter*. However, unlike Habermas, who considers reliance on tradition as a trivial platform of departure that does not necessitate further theoretical elaboration, MacIntyre deepens the point and stresses the agent's embeddedness in life narratives connecting him/her to a series of significant others. This connectivity is a condition for social agency, and, as we will see, for "communicative action" itself.

MacIntyre sees in life narratives not simply a quest for "identity," but a projection toward a *telos*, that is, the purposive construction of agency directed toward the pursuit of a hierarchy of goods that is necessarily transindividual and transgenerational. This *telos* is, however, not an abstract good or value—like justice per se—but essential to the faculty of discursive reasoning that facilitates the practical individuation and pursuit of more tangible social goods, for example, the building of structures of care based on solidarity that either dispense of, or are a condition for more functional patterns of insurance and assistance (cf. MacIntyre 1998 [1997]). Therefore, the scheme envisaged is not purely cognitive, in that it is apprehended through the acquisition of dispositions or *habitus*. MacIntyre brings here to the fore the same notion that once dominated the Habermas-Gadamer debate (cf. McGee 1998), namely practical reason or rationality, in the form of the Greek idea of *phronesis*.

*Phronesis* (a key notion that I have preliminary defined in the introduction) is, in this perspective, a simultaneously communicative and practical "metadisposition." It helps the agent finding means to the ends, along with discerning the ends that a tradition points out to. In other words, it is a notion essential to the sociological idea of communicatively mediated agency. The social-scientific determination of *phronesis* in Habermas's debate with Gadamer remained poor. Habermas was eager to collapse *phronesis* into a kind of prudential-practical knowledge of the "ancients" (Habermas 1978 [1963]: 48–87), so denying to it any explanatory power toward techniques of intersubjective understanding and connectivity to be found in modern society. Most probably, while he was engaged in the dispute with Gadamer, he was laying down the rails for the social-theoretical concept of communicative action that—he expected—would have made obsolete traditional notions like *phronesis*.

MacIntyre has preferred to work to give to *phronesis* a social-theoretical shape cutting through conventional definitions of tradition and modernity. *Phronesis* indicates a processual, both practical and interpretative engagement of the agent with the *telos* that is therefore, by definition, never really achieved.[2] Given a set of motivational inputs determined by social and psychological factors, *phronesis* is the work of the agent to rationally select, order, and relate these inputs to some notions of the goods that are appraised within the discursive tradition to which the agent belongs, as, for example, mother, lawyer, believer or unbeliever, citizen, or son. In this sense *phronesis* is not the token of a prudential calculus determined by pure expediency or the mark of excellence of a virtuous *phronimos*, which Gadamer intended as the agent of *phronesis* who creates the social bond hermeneutically, by interpreting the world, and not via social techniques, through acting in the world (McGee 1998: 20–24).

MacIntyre addresses *phronesis* with a sharper sociological sensibility for the need to address repertoires of intersubjective understanding and connectivity. He renounces the view of the *phronimos* as the ideal-typical agent, and situates the work on *phronesis* in the complex sphere of practice, communication, and connectivity which he calls tradition. According to this approach, notions of social goods are constructed within the structured social fields where agents, via their different or multiple social roles, pursue those goods. Yet these notions also depend on adequate mechanisms of transmission and renewal through generations. A tradition so defined, consisting of a synchronic and a diachronic dimension, ingrains into social fields but is not reducible to their functioning.

So far, a tradition is still close to Habermas's understanding of a lifeworld-based structure connecting agents, furthering their mutual recognition, and facilitating their sharing of motivations to action. Habermas also accepted that the authorizing power of a so conceived tradition is a fair model for investigating patterns of understanding in more general terms (Habermas 1977 [1970]). This acceptance inoculated Habermas's approach against the risk of a pragmatist reduction of agency to a purely "situational" (or "playful" and "theatrical") pattern of interaction. Therefore, we have here a thin, yet meaningful, least common denominator between MacIntyre's and Habermas's approaches that can be used to work out a predominantly microsociological definition of tradition, laying a stress on the communicative competencies that agents acquire by their exposure to a tradition.

Though tradition by necessity embraces a micro and a macrodimension, sticking to this bottom-line definition is essential to avoid falling back onto the kind of mainstream notions of tradition which are often negatively charged, conceptually underdefined, and are therefore, by default, generically macrosociological. This is not to deny (see chapters 3 and 4) the importance of capturing this macrosociological dimension in the definition and analysis of traditions. A refined macrosociological and "civilizational" match to the microsociological definition adopted here can be found in Arnason's interpretation of Marshall G. S. Hodgson's understanding of tradition. Not developed by chance in the context of his encompassing study of Islam (Hodgson 1974) and in a critical attitude toward the prevalent, trivialized notions of tradition, in particularly those in use within the modernization theory circles of the University of Chicago, Hodgson stressed creative action and cumulative interaction as essential traits of traditions. In this sense, civilizations by necessity rely on traditions and are defined by them (Arnason 2006a: 24–28).

Yet the work to remove the elitist *and* normative flavor that accrues to defining agency in "telic-phronetic" terms, as it appears in the Gadamerian discourse on the *phronimos*, who is almost a hero of action guided by right judgment, is still to be completed. My strategy consists in keeping a social-theoretical orientation, without however falling prey to the conceptual indeterminacy of some key sociological concepts. In order to do so, I draw benefit from the social-theoretical insights of MacIntyre, while avoiding the pitfalls of a bare (since traditionless) theory of action and communication. The permanent center of gravity of my analysis is given by the microlevel of conceptualization of repertoires of intersubjective understanding and connectivity premised on the dilemmas and ambivalence of the *ego-alter* relationship.

The debates where pragmatist thinkers have engaged, alternately, with the work of Jürgen Habermas and Pierre Bourdieu on, respectively, "communicative action" and the "logic of practice" (see chapter 2) will help me find a common terrain between the vocabulary of action—which has an inherent voluntaristic ring and normative tenor—and the vocabulary of practice—usually intended as habitual and dispositional, and therefore often trapped in a deceivingly "factual" circularity. MacIntyre's approach is helpful to overcome the gap between practice and communicative action affecting several such social theory debates. On a theoretical level, my approach is indebted not only to MacIntyre and Vico (see Introduction), but also to other contemporary authors, most of them idiosyncratically situated vis-à-vis the main currents of social science and social theory, first and foremost Bakhtin (1993), Wittgenstein (1974 [1953]), and Krippke (1982). In particular, my work on a sociological notion of tradition matches well the idea of a nonprivate language (cf. Krippke 1982), for reasons that will be further explained in chapter 2. Through the combined discussion of the work of Habermas and Bourdieu in chapter 2, I will attempt to show how tradition as the "track" linking agents to their praxis of pursuit of social goods entails a concept of "with-ness" or intersubjectivity that agents acquire via discerning and reasoning, and therefore though communication. Yet I avoid dealing with the theoretical issue of the intentionality of action, in which MacIntyre and others also participated, following Winch's elaboration on Wittgenstein (Winch 1958). The present work remains primarily concerned with the communicative dimension of the social bond and the related repertoires of intersubjective engagement and understanding.

To use Martin Buber's vocabulary, I am assuming the axial primacy of the I-Thou over the I-it relationship (cf. Buber 1983 [1936; 1958], 1992). This is also why the present work particularly focuses on the religious dimensions of traditions, since they put a special emphasis on the I-Thou type of relationship and on the symbolic-communicative mediation needed in maintaining the relationship. At first sight it might seem that, compared to Habermas's theory of communicative action, Buber's approach privileges the sacred or the search for ultimate values, yet its proper focus, in sociological terms (and he was also a professional sociologist), was on intersubjective communication and understanding (Eisenstadt 1992). Unlike the original formulations of the *ego-alter* connectivity by Buber which were still imbued with an enthusiasm lingering on oracular opacity—though they were probably in consonance with the spirit of Buber's overall oeuvre on the social and cultural foundations of religious traditions—I am not assuming a primal phenomenological or lifeworldly reality of the I-Thou to the detriment of the I-it relationship. Yet I share Buber's view of the reach of the I-Thou dimension beneath the reality of historical discourse, and its role in constituting sociality through meaningful practices based on *ego*'s engagement with *alter*.

I adhere here to the hypothesis that this primacy was enforced by the axial breakthrough (see introduction and further in this chapter). It is the overlaying of the I-it practical relationship through the I-Thou connectivity, indissolubly conjoining practical advantages and meaningfulness, that facilitates a phronetic "upgrading" of practical rationality and its subsequent feeding into public reasoning for the definition and implementation of the "common good." This is a peculiar type of good mediated by the work of those traditions variously associated with the axial breakthrough, and in particular of their "Western" variants. Crucial to these traditions are distinctive relationships between practical reasoning and justice, which are connected by their simultaneous dependence on conceptions of human and social goods and their hierarchy (MacIntyre 1988: 23). The crucial step in the analysis consists in moving from the level of practical rationality to the communicative potential to generate public reasoning, based on notions of justice. While it is possible to conceive of an agent who does not envision a public realm or a public good, since "publicness" is a derivative notion produced within specific traditions (see chapters 3, 4, and 5), an apprehension of what is practice, intended as a connective engagement with the other, belongs to the definition of the agent itself. Publicness then requires a further narrative and discursive determination—which I identify with the axial breakthrough—indicating both the instrument to collectively pursue the higher goods (a specific kind of reasoning, "public reasoning") and the rules and spaces governing this distinctive pursuit (what in due course of time will be defined as the "public realm" or the "public sphere").

Therefore a type of reasoning that allows for the identification of distinctive goods to pursue and means to attain them is here at stake, more than a sociologically pre-given category of social goods or "interests" defined as public. I draw from the general definition of tradition here adopted in order to pursue an analysis of the emergence of the public sphere from the axial breakthrough to modernity, by extrapolating from the genealogy of specific traditions (see chapters 3 and 4) key sociological motives that directly affect the construction of repertoires of intersubjective engagement and connectivity and are relevant for contemporary public sphere theory (see chapter 2).[3]

One can pursue such debates on connectivity and practice backward into key theoretical contentions from the age of triumphant modernity, the nineteenth century. It did not escape the attention of MacIntyre that in his early critique of the notion of civil society and in his focus on practice, in particular in the *Theses on Feuerbach*, Karl Marx neglected that practice, since it cannot just rest on the interest of atomized individuals, has to be informed by some embedded theory, *telos*, or higher goal or good: a good that is never achieved and often only vaguely defined, yet activates the phronetic and interactive capacity of the individual (cf. MacIntyre 1994). In the more sophisticated vocabulary of the contemporary theory of practice this capacity is referred to as the "teleoaffective structure" of practice (Schatzki 2001: 50). Marx came close to admitting this property of practice when he referred to it as an "objective activity," an expression first used by Hegel and Fichte. However, the politicization of his theory in particular after 1848 led him toward a completely different critique of the notion of civil society, one based on "structures" and not on relations.

According to "the road not taken" by Marx (MacIntyre 1994), *telos*, and the individuals' ability to conceive of "goods," is of essential importance, even if this *telos* is never really "shared" but individually interpreted in different or even in conflicting ways. In other words, the notion of *telos* is important to explain practice even if one admits that individual actors are positioned differentially within social relations, not in the least because of power imbalances and unequal distribution of resources for action. In a similar vein, the abandonment in modern social theory of the notion of "goods" is a serious problem, which derives from the attempt to create a more objectivist language that overcomes or preempts ideological quarrels. As evidenced by Laurent Thévenot by reference to contemporary debates on "the practice turn in the social sciences":

> With its inaugural rupture from political and moral philosophy, sociology distanced itself from ideas of good . . . they replaced them with concepts—like "norms" or "values"—which are supposed to be neutral and descriptive. This has led to the strange situation in which most sociologists, while deeply concerned with political and moral issues (sometimes overtly, sometimes not), generally offer accounts of the social world which poorly acknowledge actors' preoccupation with the good. (Thévenot 2001: 59)

Habermas's own strategy to remedy such deficits was first built on a familiarity with several nodes which he found in the theoretical work of Vico, Marx, and Hanna Arendt, on the one hand, and with the pragmatist tradition, on the other. Yet Habermas also insisted on a relentless pursuit of the type of objectivist program of a social science that he considered adequate to the era of modern science, since emancipated from philosophical discourse. This approach has contributed to create additional shortcuts to the more genuinely North American pieces of liberal theory. Marxian and post-Marxian dilemmas (see introduction), especially since Habermas's growth in popularity in the United States during the 1990s, after the "end of communism," have been more circumvented than solved.

Crucial to Habermas's combined dealing with practice and communication, and to the development of the concept of "communicative action," is the idea of *Lebenswelt* (lifeworld). This concept, while rooted in philosophical terminology—notably in the field of phenomenology—cannot be easily explained in sociological terms, as Habermas admits (Habermas 1987 [1981]: 119–20). However, the notion of lifeworld presents a potential to open up sociological analysis to a social dynamics of situated and evolving traditions, or, as Habermas sometimes prefers to formulate, in a Hegelian vocabulary, "customs" (*Sitten*). The lifeworld is presented as a locus of "communicative action" facilitating mutual understanding between social agents, based on a relatively open negotiation of the definition of the interactive situation (Habermas 1984 [1981]).

The lifeworld is for Habermas a primary prism of socialization, social integration and "cultural reproduction" which is separate from the social "system" proper, the modern machinery of society that functions via capitalist enterprise and the steering power of modern bureaucracies (Habermas 1987 [1981]: 113–97). The lifeworld is then the social locus where practical rationalities develop and ground a sense of justice, a concern for the common good, and the communicative capacity of a public discourse to determine and claim this type of good. In the final analysis, the lifeworld is the generative source of a "discourse ethics" whose final function is to provide a bottom-up legitimacy to the institutionalization of law (Habermas 1996 [1992]). For Habermas the good side of tradition—that is seldom named as such after his debate with Gadamer, but often clearly implied—is this raw practical and communicative material cohering in the lifeworld, prior to its rationalization into discourse ethics and the law. This raw material is given a first discursive form by communicative action, that is, by speech finalized to intersubjective understanding.

Communicative action ensures this mutual understanding and the concomitant definition and authorization of modes of action and interaction by incorporating a "telic" movement toward a communicative consensus among actors. The *telos* is consensus itself, to be reached through the interpretation of the situation and the appreciation of shared goods autonomously performed by the agents. The potentially dark side of this process is the imposition of customary ("traditional") norms not based on a scrutiny of reason, on *Aufklärung* (Enlightenment). This possible mismatch can be due to the incapacity of tradition unredeemed by reason—that is, of a nonrationalized lifeworld—to legitimate and universalize norms through transparent and power free procedures of deliberation, which is exactly what laws and constitutions guarantee.

Habermas therefore denies to tradition any autonomous rationality able to bring about such a procedural consensus. However, the potential of rationalization is seen as inherent in the lifeworld, to which he attributes a fair degree of autonomy from the forces that rationalize in a purely functionalist way the social system, that is, the forces of modern capitalism and of modern state bureaucracy. What is interesting is that Habermas does not reiterate the usual sociological dichotomization between "tradition" and "modernity," but sees a tension and a dualism within the lifeworld itself, depending on whether its rationalizing potential is activated or not.

Habermas's lifeworld provides a microsociological platform for grounding the public sphere on a power-free fundament, as according to him power is located in the system vectors (or "media") of money and administrative steering. I retain this idea of a communicative autonomy and the accompanying effect of "taming sheer power" as essential to repertoires of intersubjective understanding and connectivity culminating in the public sphere. However, I intend to show that a power-taming communicative force is not equal to a power-free fundament and does not entail an authority-free social basis. On the contrary, the basic way of taming power through traditions is via allowing for a transmission, and whenever necessary for a contestation, of patterns of authority in any given social formation. This process depends on the mechanism through which traditions try to immunize their practitioners from viewing power as an end in itself of social action. This mechanism is obviously no magic formula, but has to perform well, for the tradition to thrive or at least to survive. The price a tradition has to pay for an enduring failure in this immunization effort is a state of disturbance, a deep crisis or even an outright collapse and dissolution.

Comparable mechanisms of immunization produced by liberal modernity to offset or attenuate a one-sided compliance with a will to power are—when available—of a different nature (see chapters 5 and 6). They are grounded in a private sphere carefully delimited from the public sphere, much more than in the exercise of public reason via practical rationality. Indeed, the issue of taming power is shifted to, and encapsulated within a newly defined sphere, the private sphere, and subcontracted to the "autonomous subject."

Habermas's choice to erect the lifeworld to the most basic fundament of social integration, via its polarization with the functionally integrative force of the social system, depends on strong presuppositions. These consist in regarding the lifeworld as the social and communicative space where actors reach mutual understandings by selectively drawing on traditions, through the help of the rationalizing potential of communicative action (for a similar interpretation, see Casanova 2001). In this guise, Habermas seems to provide a sophisticated variant of the earlier mentioned approach to "tradition as a resource" that the actors employ for interpreting a social situation and gaining orientation in the world, or even as a resource for institutional solutions to wider social problems. Traditions appear then as the source of multiple resources for building, rebuilding and maintaining social relations, structures of cooperation and welfare, as well as networks of mutual support. However, this approach would not suffice to regard tradition-based lifeworlds as sources of social integration. This effect could only be warranted by adopting a macrosociological, Durkheimian notion of society based on organic solidarity.

Habermas clearly works in this direction in his theory of communicative action (Habermas 1987 [1981]: 43–111) but in so doing activates a short-circuit between the microlevel of understanding between *ego* and *alter* (a microsociological a priori) and the macrolevel of "society" (a macrosociological a priori). This is apparent in the growing ambivalence, through the works that followed Habermas's *Habilitation*, of his coping with the Durkheimian-functionalist matrix of mainstream sociology. This challenge induced him to circumscribe, on the one hand, the areas of social action governed by a functionalist logic, and to strengthen, on the other, the focus on the principle of "social integration," by looking for a kind of alternative, namely communicative functionality. Long before Habermas the question of social integration, which is constitutive of modern sociology, had generated a reifying redefinition of the notions of "religion" and "society" as well as of their mutual relationship in the trajectory of emergence and development of sociology (Salvatore 1997: 23–40). The idea itself of a society bound by organic solidarity was seen as the upgrading of the integrative potential inherent in "religion."

## "Religion" and Axial Transformations

The Marxian intervention that followed Feuerbach's radical deconstruction of religion de facto severed the link of religion from practice and made it the kernel of the ideology of tradition. Religion was described as a crucial instrument of domination and as the principal manifestation of human alienation, to be transcended through the dialectics of historical materialism. It was nonetheless through Durkheim's successful shaping of a sociological canon that religion was repackaged and essentialized. Preceded by increasingly interconnected theological and anthropological innovations, culminating in the work of the theologically motivated anthropologist William Robertson Smith (Asad 2003: 32–33), Durkheimian sociology reinterpreted religion as an almost pristine force of social cohesion through which the subject appropriates and internalizes the power located in the collective world of social relations. Durkheim considered ritual as the symbolic-communicative bridge between subject and object, as the warrant of the objectivity of the social bond, which confers normative force to social obligations via an organic solidarity dispensing of a discursively formulated consensus. Religion thus becomes a strategic moment in the process of production of cohesion within modern society, continually resourcing its underlying civic morals (cf. Robertson 1970; B. Turner 1991, 1992; Kippenberg 1996).

Through an evolutionist approach to religion as the organic force of social solidarity and cohesion, Durkheim severed the nexus between religious practice and the ideational dimension of the higher goods in God and His attributes. He neglected how dogma and practice are shaped and transmitted; in other words, he deprived religion of any constitutive tie to tradition intended in a MacIntyrean sense (cf. also Tarot 1993). Following Durkheim's footsteps, the sociology of religion has too often assumed the identity of an underdefined tradition with a quite overdefined religion. Religion as the modernizable key to social integration remains archaic and "traditional," when it is not upgraded along this evolutionary line. Weber positioned his sociology of religion differently within his wider social theory. He provided valuable elements for defining tradition while avoiding any essentializing overdefinition of religion.

But before turning to Weber, it is appropriate to pause at the attempts done to recondense the Durkheimian-functionalist heritage into a renewed emphasis—especially among various U.S. theorists of "shared values" and "civility"—on religion as a major cohesive force of society, a crucial provider of "social integration." "Civil religion" emerged in the last third of the twentieth century as a notion denoting a cultural force capable of reconciling tradition and modernity (Bellah and Hammond 1980; for the application of this paradigm to Islam cf. Hefner 2000). A leading sociologist who has carefully unearthed the implications of a sociological approach to religion before attempting any shortcut to "civil religion," while dwelling on the phenomenological view of the lifeworld, is Peter Berger. In what has become a classic of the sociology of religion (Berger 1967), he asserted that "religion is the human enterprise by which a sacred cosmos is established" (ibid.: 25), which "is confronted by man as an immensely powerful reality other than himself . . . Yet this reality . . . locates his life in a ultimately meaningful order" (ibid.: 26). The origins of the idea of a comprehensive law or *nomos*—affecting Abrahamic religions, in their complex relationship with the Greek philosophical heritage—lie in this confrontation. According to Berger, the concept of the *nomos* became a source for legitimizing various social arrangements and institutions. Thus, it functioned as the root of normativity within social relations. Religion is here first made functional to a stabilization of the relationship between the subject and the world as experienced by the former, thus rooting the subject in the lifeworld. In a further twist, however, religion is seen as alienating the subject from the sources of his/her power, perceived by the human actor as located outside of himself/herself.

In spite of his invocation of Weber for linking religion to a process of rationalization through which man redresses this experience of alienation, Berger's main reference remains, not surprisingly, Durkheim. Berger does not reject Durkheim's functionalism, but remolds it through relocating the macronormative function of religion into the *nomos* as subjective meaning, now reinterpreted in a mildly functional way. This relocation is facilitated by deepening the implications of social differentiation. Berger no longer holds on to the phenomenological assumption of the lone subject facing the world, but focuses on the tasks of a subject who copes with sector specific, "subsystemic," differentiated rationalities. The subject is not a social being separated and potentially alienated from objective reality, but is called to reconstruct the microorder of life across bits of fragmented experience, by giving a meaning to it.

In this way, Berger—immediately followed by Luckmann (1967)—constructs an anachronism by providing a transhistorical definition of religion largely stemming from the remolding of religion's meaning and function which was crystallizing in the 1950s and early 1960 in the United States and, to a lesser extent, in Germany, during a period of breathtaking modernization and intense "cultural change" increasingly conducted under the banner of individualization. The result was a reduction of religion to a subjective search for meaning with normative power. Other leading social theorists like Robert N. Bellah and Clifford Geertz further elaborated on this approach, though from different angles. Most notably, Geertz saw instances of a religion conceived as a cultural system subject to change at work in various manifestations of Islam in such distant places—not only geographically, but culturally—like Morocco and Indonesia. As a "cultural system," religion is shaped in different ways if we move from one cultural world to another, but its basic function is invariant (Geertz 1973: 87–125). This type of definition of religion can be defined as a softly functional search for "meaning."

According to this approach, the specialization of religion as a source of holistic meaning and as a *nomos*-provider is applicable to the most modern among Western societies, starting with those with a strong Protestant background, and ending with the new postcolonial nations, where a cultural function of religion as a provider of collective identity acquires strong public connotations. Both types of cultural functionalization reflect and, so to speak, upgrade the pristine function of religion. Berger himself decried this kind of functionalization, which was put in evidence in an even stronger fashion by his colleague Thomas Luckmann, who completed the job by reducing religion to the notion of individual "religiosity." This concept reflects the centrality of the search for the "ultimate" significance of life, so that even movements of sexual liberation might be regarded as manifestations of such individualized, internalized, largely privatized, and often invisible religion (Luckmann 1967: 69–114). However, by stressing the continuity of the religious-nomic function against any cultural dilution of religion, Berger encouraged an even sharper short-circuit in the definition of religion as a transhistorical essence. He sealed "religion" in an updated Durkheimian-functionalist fashion matching distinctive, post–World War II processes of individualization.

Talal Asad, an anthropologist, stands out as the most uncompromising critic and genealogist of this view of religion. He has exposed this monolithic, largely internalized, and well delineated notion of religion as being radically severed from the social connectivity of practice and power. Thus "religion" appears as a modern Western norm engendered by a post-Reformation anthropology peculiar to the West, or parts thereof (Asad 1993: 28; cf. also Tooker 1992). Asad denies the possibility of defining religion in universal terms, "not only because its constituent elements and relationships are historically specific, but because that definition is itself the historical product of discursive processes" (Asad 1993: 29). Concerning in particular the notion of symbol as used to define the essence of religion like in the work of Geertz, Asad denounced its use for designating a sheer carrier of meaning. He underscored how a symbol has the more complex function of bringing together and establishing relationships between objects or events which are impregnated with relations of power (ibid.: 31). The crucial focus of analysis should lie therefore on how symbols are enacted through practices, as it occurs within the domain of elaboration of a given tradition. The next step in Asad's critique is, not surprisingly, a radical objection to erecting religion to a "system" on its own:

> Religious symbols . . . cannot be understood independently of their historical relations with non religious symbols or of their articulations in and of social life, in which work and power are always crucial . . . From this it does not follow that the meanings of religious practices and utterances are to be sought in social phenomena, but only that their possibility and their authoritative status are to be explained as products of historically distinctive disciplines and forces. (ibid.: 53–54)

This critique implies that we cannot compare "religions" as systemic units, but should rather study the wider traditions within which religious concepts inform complex conceptual schemes, woven into discourses that are tied to and authorize specific practices and life forms (ibid.: 17).

There is evidently a risk of oscillating between a transhistorical, but in fact post-Protestant definition of religion as a "sphere," "field," or even a "system" (centered on inwardness, meaning-giving, and, in a modern context, privateness), which is pivotal to a large and influential part of the sociology of religion, on the one hand, and an extremely diffused semidefinition (or indirect definition) of religion, that often becomes diluted into another concept, "civilization." This indeterminacy often undermines an integrated analysis and reiterates the old dilemma of how to match "Jerusalem and Athens," that is, the religion of the Jews and the civilization of the Greeks (see chapter 2). In order to avoid this oscillation and indeterminacy, I begin here to develop an analytical framework that tries to relate different traditions of practical reasoning inherited from the crucial time that spans the late Middle Ages and immediately precedes the conventional beginning of modernity, to the earlier, epochal breakthroughs that have propelled the key civilizational formations of the Euro-Mediterranean area and their interlocking components. In the rest of this chapter, I start to assess the contribution of Axial Age theory to the elaboration of this analytical framework. In chapter 2, I relate this discussion of the "axial" dimensions of traditions to how repertoires of intersubjective understanding, the most genuine legacy of the axial breakthrough, can be better understood through the concept of *phronesis*/practice, which is central to the working of traditions.

First, we should give credit to Max Weber, in many ways an early inspirer of the axial framework, for his avoidance of a transhistorical definition of religion. He was not interested in drawing general anthropological conclusions from the observation of man's experience of a cosmic gap, but rather focused on reconstructing how different theodicies and soteriologies (the paths of justification of God before the evidence of earthly evil, and therefore paths of individual salvation) contributed to ground specific forms of life conduct via their elaboration by specific social and cultural "carriers." This approach yielded a focus on the emergence of patterns of rationalization of daily affairs especially among cultural-intellectual elites (cf. Sadri 1992). As such, religion is not simply faith enhanced to objective belief, secret to the sacred identity of community, or collective ritual formulated as doctrine. Therefore, religion cannot be defined in an objectifying and functionalist way. It is rather a crucial engine of the production of "values" and standards of conduct that promote cultured behavior—not merely intellectual modes—via the cultivation and inculcation of dispositions beyond the restricted circles of the elites themselves. Weber endeavored to give a systematic, sociological shape to the Nietzschean approach to civilizations—and in particular to Western Christian civilization—through a genealogy of subjugation, transfiguration, and implementation of an increasingly organized (and internalized) will to power manifest in "world religions" (cf. Szakolczai 1998; cf. also Abaza and Stauth 1988).

Yet a notion present in Weber's work came closer to a cultural objectification and functionalization of religion. It is the notion of *Kulturreligion*. Focusing on this concept can be impairing, since it trivializes—as done by several generations and schools of modernization theorists throughout the twentieth century—Weber's main argument on the inherent complexity of the relationship between religion and society. It is true that Weber, unlike Durkheim, tried hard not to define too bluntly either. Yet the notion of *Kulturreligion* is strictly dependent on a view of religion as the primary engine of the rationalization of life conduct. Therefore it prefigures the last twist of rationalization of a tradition that is a prelude to its dissolution qua tradition. This is epitomized by the Protestant and occidental case, through which the "value" rationality of the *Kulturreligion* becomes intrinsically ambivalent. Value thus operates as the permanent source of instrumental rationality clothed in the ethic of modern professionalism and bureaucratic steering.

The half-objectified notion of *Kulturreligion* should be read in terms of the models of life conduct that the cultured elites promoted and inculcated in the practitioners of the traditions. It is noteworthy that one of the most acute interpreters of Weber, Wilhelm Hennis, even if aiming to get rid of all trivializations of Weber's sociological theory—among which he included the paradigm of disenchantment as the foil of the last occidental twist of rationalization—could only reinforce the impression that Weber's core problematic (and therefore also the hub of his sociology of religion) was "life conduct" (Hennis 1987). In the rest of the analysis in this chapter and in the following chapters, I try to show the extent to which this notion of life conduct, though more credible than any transhistorical concept of religion and of any concomitant idea of disenchantment, is still entrenched in the self-understanding of a post-Reformation, Western social world. Nonetheless, life conduct can provide a challenging entry point into a work of reconstruction and incorporation of the notion of tradition within social theory, and of the definition of the "religious" dimensions of traditions.

The best way to dereify the conceptual clusters used by Weber with reference to religion and to circumvent the danger of a functionalization and trivialization of Weber's theory (and, as far as the notion of religion is concerned, its "Durkheimianization": cf. Szakolczai 1998), is by linking his general sociology and his sociology of religion to the "Axial Age" framework of a comparative historical sociology, which was initiated by such scholars—variously linked to Max Weber and Weberian circles in Heidelberg—like Karl Jaspers (1953 [1949]) and Alfred Weber, with Eric Voegelin taking a parallel road partly enriching, partly subverting the framework and its basically Weberian inspiration. This framework is useful to dynamize the concept of religion underlying Weber's approach, and simultaneously to better relate the notions of religion and civilization to a notion of tradition.

Johann P. Arnason has observed that Max Weber's sociology of religion and in particular some passages from an article on Hinduism and Buddhism published in 1916 in the *Archiv für Sozialwissenschaft und Sozialpolitik* prefigure the core hypothesis of Axial Age theory (Arnason 2005: 22). This theory is based on a comprehensive hypothesis concerning the nature of the radical transformations that made possible a momentous breakthrough in the complexification of community life and the differentiation of social fields out of archaic communities regulated by cyclical and mythical views of the cosmological order. The axial approach facilitates examining on a comparative basis the essentially simultaneous discovery of "transcendence" across various civilizations. This construction builds the symbolic engine and the discursive kernel in the redefinition of patterns of imagination and authority called to give shape to the increasing complexity of social relations. Like the present work, Axial Age theory is concerned with the development of repertoires of intersubjective understanding that match increasingly complex forms of definition and governance of self and community, and therefore prefigure the kernel of patterns and institutions of public reasoning.

At its root, Axial Age theory is a research program for locating and explaining, in historical-comparative, sociological terms, the type of breakthrough that allowed, through the shaping of notions of transcendence, for the emergence of a type of human reflexivity conventionally identified as the passage from the narrativity of *mythos* to the rationality of *logos* (Jaspers 1953 [1949]). As maintained by Björn Wittrock, transcendence is not to be interpreted in strictly theological terms, but as the emergence of a form of reflexivity that transcends those activities tied to the daily necessities of human beings, as also reflected by mythologies of cosmological shape. The main novelty of the axial breakthrough resides accordingly in "the capacity of human beings to reflect upon and to give expression to an image of the world as having the potential of being different from what it was perceived to be here and now" (Wittrock 2005: 62).

Axial Age theory provides therefore a heuristic device and a theoretical tool not limited to understanding the self-propelling dynamics of social differentiation and complexification. It facilitates an explanation of the relocation and transformation of selfhood and community and of their reciprocal constitutive relations. Even if intended in more strictly religious terms transcendence can, nonetheless, hardly be explained away from the axial framework. The crucial axial discovery lies in a tension between the mundane world of material needs and power drives, and another world, mostly indicated—notably in the Western-Abrahamic version of axial civilizations on which I focus here—as the "thereafter." This space is regarded as the generative source of repertoires of intersubjective understanding and related patterns of authority basically alternative to those—identified with structures of domination and economic processes—located in the mundane sphere. Transcendence is the main expression of this tension. The emergence of this tension and its institutionalization in form of theological, juridical, and philosophical discourses authorized a basic differentiation in the leadership of human communities. It is the differentiation between priests, scribes, and scholars, on the one hand, and the ruling class, on the other. This differentiation also legitimizes the institution of a moral authority of the former over the latter.

As suggested by Arnason, "the axial transformation broadens the *cognitive horizon* and therefore the *strategic scope* of power centers and elites, but the growing quantity and diversity of cognitive resources is at the same time an *obstacle to the monopolization of power*" (Arnason 2005: 47). On the other hand, one should mind the caveat that this sociopolitical dimension of the axial breakthrough cannot be rigidly equated with the demise of a certain type of cosmology (the narrative cosmology of the *mythos*) and its replacement with an outright new cosmology, assuming theological, juridical, and philosophical traits (a cosmology of the *logos*). Yet the most crucial character of axial transcendence stands out most vividly if we renounce inserting it into a cosmological typology and consider it the engine of a specific type of discourse pointing out the unsustainable character of this-worldly order and the need to transcend it—in one way or another, through taming or denying the mundane, sociopolitical order, in any case by making the power holders accountable to a transcendent power or divinity, which takes over the traits of unitary and supreme majesty not only over the cosmos, but over human society, and especially over the individual soul, whose discovery (or invention) can be considered a genuine product of axial transformations.

## Transcendence, Prophecy, and Philosophy

While Axial Age theory conventionally locates the apex of the process of rupture in the time around the middle of the first millennium BCE, Eric Voegelin's analysis of Hebrew prophecy and Greek philosophy lays the focus on a longer and more suffered trajectory of transformation. The Biblical narrative and the role of the prophets assume a certain primacy in this approach, usually located at the margin of the Axial Age framework. The Greek philosophical venture, in spite of its unique character, is then read in terms of its capacity to complete and compete with the institution of transcendence by the Hebrew prophecy.

Voegelin discloses a chain of subsequent, momentous shifts in the prophetic discourse that targets the sociopolitical order. At the crucial stage entered by prophecy around the beginning of the era when the axial breakthrough is conventionally placed, he evidenced the progressing "metastatic" character of waves of instructing-exhortative discourse based on a densely creative, exponential reassembling of symbols of mundane and transcendent order and majesty. The axial division of functions between rulers and clerics appears as the result of a tumultuous process, not of a linear and neat differentiation. The metastatic character of the prophetic discourse that triggers out the division lies in its continual reformulation facilitated by the prophets' efforts to stubbornly push forward the boundary between those orders, up to a breaking point: the critical threshold when Hebrew prophecy, though still rooted in the vocabulary of the Ten Commandments, was no longer concerned with the restoration of the Covenant with Yahweh that Moses had promulgated in the name of the "chosen people."

A notion of "salvation" emerges in the process and crystallizes through the metastatic power of prophetic imaginative discourse

(Voegelin 1956: 428–513). In this manner, successive prophetic voices metamorphosed the meaning of Exodus, the Covenant, and the attainment of the "promised land." The climax of the axial breakthrough was reached when the prophets Jeremiah and Isaiah showed that "there are problems of order beyond the existence of a concrete society and its institutions," but also—and this is a crucial corollary to the axial postulate of transcendence—that there is no one-for-all covenantal solution to the problem of order (ibid.: 491). The unattainability of a solution is one with its transcendence, and can only be tackled via an ongoing discourse, in which we can see the onset of a discursive tradition (see chapter 3). It is this start of the "Exodus of Israel from itself" that condenses the kernel of the axial breakthrough carried by prophetic discourse: the understanding that transcendence has less to do with specific doctrines of the thereafter and salvation, than with the articulation of a discourse facing "the experience of the gulf between true order and the order realized concretely by any society" (Voegelin 1956: 491).

The consequence is that "the *terminus ad quem* of the movement is *not* [my emphasis] a concrete society with a recognizable order" (ibid.). Transcendence is here a token of a never accomplished, unattainable, yet necessarily and perpetually reformulated *telos*. Transcendence is a potential to transcend social and even cultural boundaries, and integrate new groups and social arrangements (and institutions) into the salvational path (cf. Schwartz 1975). Here lies the main sociological thrust of Axial Age theory. Transcendence is the key to the institution of the social bond and to the construction of the common on a new basis, compared with "pre-axial" formulas of ritual reconstruction of the cosmos that encapsulate the form of the community and the place of individuals therein (cf. Assmann 2002 [2000]).

The axial transcendence of social boundaries certainly depends on the theological notion of transcendence, which facilitates the translation of prophetic discourse into repertoires of intersubjective understanding and connectivity below the level of political domination, and largely independently from it. The inclusion of the fellow human being into a given community of salvation is an expansion of the *ego-alter* dyadic relationship originally buffered by cosmological myth and ritual, from the undifferentiated collectivity of Mauss's *mana*, the force that humans see as intrinsic to things (Tarot 1993: 565–67), into the *ego-alter-Alter*/God triadic relationship supported by transcendence.

In adherence to the categories of Mauss's sociology, the axial pattern of I-Thou connectivity mediated by a transcendent God replaces primordial forms of the contract as a gift. It is a rupture of archaic sociality that marks, after the fragmentation of social relations into dyads, its reconstruction through the triad of *ego-alter-Alter*/God. God is the transcendent *Alter*. The breakthrough disengages agents from a dependence on the mediating capacity of objects as gifts. It thus transposes the "it" of things into the "It" of divine transcendence. Godly *Alter* is then both He and It; it is personal-impersonal, and as such surges to the role of ultimate instance of mediation in social relationships and, therefore, authority.

"Transcendence" as the tension between mundane and transcendent spheres should be then explained through the dilemma and prism of the triad. Far from being an anthropological given, the dyad is stabilized, through the axial breakthrough, into a triangling with a third element. The making of a triad is cemented by a common faith in a God combining the attributes of wrath and mercy (cf. also K. Burke 1961). Transcendence thus conceived is at the root of a major shift in the relationship between self and other. This is also the formula for making practice no longer encapsulated in the logic of daily necessities contained within ritual reconstructions of the cosmos. Transcendence is the key to ground more inclusive and transformative repertoires of intersubjective understanding through a common orientation to a mildly reflexive *telos* pivoting on the concept of divine justice.

However, this potential is not based on a movement of the mind. It can only unfold through the ongoing sociopolitical and theological dialectics between orthodoxies and heterodoxies. It is cyclically the task and turn of heterodox doctrines to cross new boundaries in opposition to orthodox elites more interested to enforce the boundaries (Voegelin 1994). Heterodox movements periodically critique institutional crystallizations of repertoires of intersubjective engagement, of *ego-alter* relationships (between man and woman, the rich and the poor, the old and the young), when they are divorced from daily needs and practice. More than merely protesting, these movements start to legitimize different, alternative practices into a new *doxa*. This dialectics between established institutions and oppositional movements is embedded in a new—albeit partial—consciousness of the immaterial techniques of power that regulate and discipline the self, the other, and their fragile nexus. The main such technique is the discursive exhortation to perform good and combat evil.

Axial transformations are sociologically relevant as the momentums of constitution of the reflexive social bond. This reflection is strongly rooted in a communicative idea of practice and in particular in the "call." First emerging in its prophetic form, it is nonetheless, as I indicate later, equally present in the Greek axial framework. Axial transcendence and the call that grounds discursive traditions matter sociologically as a kind of social-communicative a priori not subject to explanation through "sub-sociological"—be they anthropological, philological, or theological—methods.

The analytical potential of Axial Age theory is augmented if we admit that there is no single, consolidated such theory or crystallized variants thereof, but an ongoing debate on the heuristic—more than factual—usefulness of such an approach for a sociological, comparative-historical analysis, and theoretical systematization. This view privileges a microsociological focus on communicative repertoires of engagement between *ego* and *alter*. One receives from the Axial Age approach key inputs for reconstructing the intersubjective character of the social bond and the underlying idea of "connective justice" (Assmann 2002 [2000]). This view is matched, at a macrosociological level, by a focus on the relation of tension between sociopolitical and religious institutions, on the one hand, and oppositional socioreligious movements, on the other.

Axial transformations can be then understood as a particularly radical metamorphosis of the distinction—that is typical of pre-axial religions and concomitant social worlds—between sacred and profane, or between pure and impure realms, a binary code that still belongs to the basics of the anthropology of religion. Jan Assmann (2002 [2000]; 2005) sees this breakthrough exemplified by the paradigm of the "Mosaic distinction" between true and false (cf. also K. Burke 1961), which lays the basis for the subsequent complexification of prophetic exhortations to perform good and prohibit evil. In the narrative of Moses and the Exodus "Egypt appears as the symbol not so much of 'false religion' (paganism and idolatry), but, above all, of 'false politics', as the 'house of serfdom'" (Assmann 2005: 149). On the other hand, the Covenant with God on the Sinai is represented as a liberation from such serfdom, namely from human, not divine rulership. The result is that "monotheism appears both as a political movement of liberation from pharaonic oppression and as the foundation of an alternative way of life, where humans are no longer subject to human rule but freely consent to enter into an alliance with God and adopt the stipulations of divine law" (ibid.). Assmann concludes that the axial breakthrough is basically a revolution in the model of authority, which is solemnly declared independent from political domination. This is the permanent, though changing source of visions of connective justice among human beings. The notion of "salvation," accordingly, is not a purely "religious" concept, but is a vector of the crystallization of a radical, metastatic alteration of authority.

Salvation is an intermediate outcome of the transformation or break-through, not its engine.

Assmann condenses the axial breakthrough into a "semantic relocation" of the discourse on piety and authority. The discourse is so redirected toward a contestation of authority, without however suppressing it, but rather shifting its source from the King-God (Pharaoh) to the God of the Old Testament. This is a decisive step that opens up the cataracts of a continual and cumulative ("metastatic") discursive deepening—or rather spiraling (see chapter 5)—of the processes of legitimization of authority inherent in axial transformations. These processes produce new techniques for ordering social relations facilitated by the opening of a spectrum of different interpretations of the relation between the cosmological and the social orders. The main sociological operator of this continual dynamics of potential transformation is the rise of virtuosi of authoritative discourses, coupled with the increasing differentiation of their institutions from the apparatus of domination, with a scope and function quite clearly distinct from domination: the administration of paths to truth and "salvation" which are equally incumbent on all members of community, including the rulers.

The rooting of these paths to truth in "scripture," that is, within Abrahamic traditions, in texts recording God's revelation via prophetic voices, is not a necessary condition for the axial breakthrough but one of its possible forms of crystallization or traditionalization. The virtuosi are a particular category within the wider class that Craig Calhoun has called "authorized arbiters of correctness" (Calhoun 1993: 79). By time, the formulations of theodicies and soteriologies impacting on life conduct and on available repertoires of intersubjective understanding intersected the ethical philosophies that were initially based on a search for truth not based on any revelation, as it happened in particular during the Axial Renaissance of the late Middle Ages (chapters 3 and 4). One can conceive of the rise of a largely autonomous and institutionalized class of clerics as the basic functional differentiation anticipating the much further range of differentiations making out the complexity of modern societies. However, this is a differentiation that one cannot explain in a functionalist way but needs a thematization of discursive traditions.

The activity of defining and administering paths to truth and salvation within specific traditions was not politically neutral. It was often used by clerics in different historical contexts, in an ongoing process of conflict, mediation, and compromise between several social factions and the rulers (Eisenstadt 1982; see also, for a more eclectic view,

Gellner 1991 and, more specifically on Islam, which inspired his general theory, Gellner 1981). Yet, this activity was never a political tool like any other, since the class of the scholars/clerics was never a social group like any other, as if defined by a specific class "interest."[4]

In order to avoid the pitfalls resulting from merely looking at the political institutionalization of discursive traditions upheld by the scholarly class within Western axial civilizations, we should not forget that the main solution to the tension of transcendence was conceived as engaging *ego*'s relationship to *alter*, supported by the work of—and upon—individual souls mediated by specialized clerics. The collective dimension of the search for truth was no immediate consequence of axial transformations. It resulted from the large-scale institutionalization and integration of worship, of the emerging idea of a justice-based law, and of related ethical systems, via the ongoing discourse of instruction and exhortation administered by the clerics and performed by the practitioners. This is why the discourse itself—and in particular its theological orientation—cannot be analyzed in isolation from the repertoires of intersubjective understanding and connectivity with which it was associated.

From the viewpoint of the guardians of the discursive traditions originating from the axial transformations the mundane political order is therefore mainly a "second level order." The interpretation of the relationship between this order and the "first level order" defined by transcendence is subject to considerable variation, not only among, but also within traditions. The main dimension of contestability of order concerns exactly the relationship between its two levels. However, a common axial feature of the link between both orders is given by the concept of accountability of the ruler to God or, more specifically, to God's law. Referring to Egypt and the Exodus (more than to Mesopotamia) as the embodiment of the pre-axial order and of the axial exit from it via the "Mosaic distinction," Shmuel N. Eisenstadt has written that "the King-God, the embodiment of the cosmic and earthly order alike, disappeared, and a secular ruler, in principle accountable to some higher order, appeared" (Eisenstadt 1986: 8). The transcendent order, which is the order of the soul walking on the path to salvation, is constructed as autonomous and delimits the scope of the second level, mundane order. This is what legitimated the post-Exodus Hebrew prophets to make the kings and the people accountable for their misdeeds.

Prophetic warnings, excoriating, and exhortations, directed at both rulers and simple practitioners, were couched in a poetic-imaginative language. The patterns of relationship between the two orders, nonetheless, became more precise in the postprophetic era that is specific to each religious tradition: for example, with Christianity, it was inaugurated by the coming of the Messiah, while with Islam, were messianism is put at the margins or outside orthodoxy, this era started with the Qur'anic revelation, which was given to Muhammad, proclaimed as the seal of all prophets (see chapter 4). Yet both in Christianity and Islam during the postprophetic era the role of thematizing and reclaiming the implications of the imperatives of the salvational path for the sociopolitical order was most typically performed by heterodox movements that contested the orthodox interpretations of the relationship between the two orders. Usually these movements claim to restore prophetic charisma, and are sometimes reabsorbed within institutional orthodoxy as "reform" movements, before the major rupture, within Latin Christendom, of the Protestant Reformation (see chapters 3 and 5).

The cluster of concepts of "transcendence-order-salvation" which resulted from axial transformations was rooted in an enhanced consciousness of death. This consciousness transcended the prior dealing with mortality within pre-axial cosmogonies and cosmologies based on collective adaptations to a cyclical rhythm perceived as natural and conveniently sacralized. These arrangements did not require a highly systematic concept of a differentiated transcendent order, but an incorporation of deities as forces within the cosmos. The idea of a "pagan world" caught up in myth and ritual and that existed before the axial transformations that ushered in the era of transcendence and discursive reflexivity is therefore not analytically neutral. It is itself a product of axial transformations, finalized to build the image of a counterorder, a world of chaos and ignorance, preceding the opening of a path to truth and salvation. For instance, this counterworld was depicted in Islam as a *jahiliyya*, the realm of human pride untamed by the knowledge of the true and only God. As the latest manifestation of the axial breakthrough, it is not surprising that Islam provides the most coherently dichotomist conceptualization of the axial order and of the pre-axial counterorder of heathens.

The idea of the axial breakthrough itself is by necessity a duplication of the discourse of the carriers of axial civilizations. Axial Age theory overdetermines the breakthrough and runs the risk "to deny the historically previous civilizations in a way that cannot be made compatible with available historical research itself" (Wittrock 2005: 67). This distorted perspective also includes an anachronistic accentuation of "reflexivity" as a distinctive axial achievement. Commenting on the problem of the interpretative presuppositions of this strand of theory,

Arnason has stated that "it seems legitimate to assume that our attempts to understand the Axial Age will reflect a *Vorverständnis* derived from Western sources—more specifically, from the changing combinations of Greek and Jewish sources that have been central to Western traditions" (Arnason 2005: 27).

This is also why it might be more convenient to ground the analysis of the traditions originating from axial transformations on the exploration of a theoretically defined microlevel of understanding and connectivity among human agents, rather than on macrocivilizational narratives. To the extent that the stakes of the *ego-alter* relationship transcend daily necessities—and fear and faith are projected onto a transcendent other—repertoires of intersubjective engagement and understanding gain new degrees of sophistication. With Martin Buber, we would say that in the process the practical I-it relationship is increasingly absorbed within the dominant I-Thou relationship (Buber 1983 [1936; 1958], 1992).

The exit from the circularity of life and death in natural cycles and the resulting dread of individual damnation mark the simultaneous birth of the intrinsically intersubjective concept of the responsible soul-self and of sophisticated dramas of salvation. These require a much more elaborate, both narrative and exhortative structure of discourse than it was the case with prior ritual formulas. To formulate the shift or breakthrough in sociological terms, this new discourse is condensable in a view of human agency as guided by a *telos* transcending particular situations and interactions. It is a *telos* directing practice toward a set of hierarchically ordered goals and goods, the highest ones being nonmaterial goods, and in particular goods of salvation, but also including the implementation of justice, which is inevitably rooted, in spite of its lofty status, in the daily connectivity of the *ego-alter* relationship. *Telos* provides orientation to this relationship.

We see here how much we risk overstating reflexivity as part of the breakthrough and as the marker of an entirely new civilization, culminating with the achievements of Western modernity, to the detriment of a focus on the emerging intentionality of action, or, in bare sociological terms, agency, as intrinsically tied to new communicative mechanisms. It is less subjective reflexivity than a reflexive, conscious, and purposive attitude in the pursuit of the higher goods that forms the core of the shift. As much as this idea of *telos* defines an ideal horizon of human interaction unmatched by real practice, real practice is only possible as a good or bad approximation, or as a negation of that ideal. *Telos*'s function is never to be realized completely, transcendence never to be attained in full. They are the necessary engines of the counterfactual dimension of human action, including what Habermas defines as "communicative action" (see chapter 2).

Abrahamic monotheism as a formula for axial transformations solved some key problems of the reconstruction of order through the creation of a permanent field of tensions, between the first and the second level of order, between orthodoxy and heterodoxies, and between centers and peripheries, involved in the administration of the orders and in the definition of the underlying salvational paths. The key solution consisted in the constitution of the *ego-alter-Alter*/God triad. This idea of order could not be purely ideational and discursive but had (as I show in chapter 2 in more detail) to take root in the ongoing process of shaping the *ego-alter* relationship via repertoires of intersubjective engagement and connectivity.

A major crux in the social worlds where these traditions play a role concerns the creation of a field of authority for administering the truth, a step which opens the lid to the dialectics between orthodoxies and heterodoxies. Weber's formula of the "value rationality" of traditions only works halfway in capturing these traits and modalities. One could say that tradition as defined for the purpose of the present work consists in the crafting of discursive and initially only mildly institutionalized mechanisms for a disciplining of people's life conduct through the shaping of repertoires of intersubjective engagement, understanding, and connectivity. Therefore, such traditions have to build and intervene upon forms of practical rationality. These waves of intervention are mainly manifested through the cyclical rise and waning of prophetic voices. Warning about the consequences of wrong behavior is a way to elicit and transform patterns of everyday practical reason, to stress the importance of a regulated interaction, and to orient it to patterns of order that transcend a rationality of daily necessities.

It is in particular the format of prophetic discourse that constitutes a corrective exit from everydayness. As stressed by Voegelin (1997a: 69–85), the "parabolic" nature of prophetic discourse requires to build a symbolically dense and highly creative nexus between injustice as inherent in ordinary interactions among people and a sense of disintegration of the cosmological order. This disintegration was originally the consequence of the fall of the integrative force of the ancient empires of the Nilotic and Mesopotamian areas, and occurs therefore in periods and situations of enhanced "liminality" (Eisenstadt 1985; Szakolczai 2003). The prototypical example of this liminal situation is in the prophet speaking out that the order collapses—and the order disintegrates indeed from inside: like in the case of the Assyrian empire, the first "world empire" based on conquest, around 600 BCE, right at the beginning of the crucial period of the axial breakthrough (Szakolczai 2001a, 2003).

This approach also helps avoiding the anachronism of dealing with "religion" as a given sphere, field, or (sub)system within society. With it, we do not need to presuppose the existence of specifically "religious" forms of social action facing those based on a "civic" understanding of social and political life, paradigmatically enshrined in Greek democracy, philosophy, and its "Western" heritage. A "civic" model of organization of human life underlies the more sophisticated axial model (see chapter 5; cf. Eisenstadt and Giesen 1995). The Greek way to the common good (Kirner 2001) can therefore be reabsorbed within the approach to axial civilizations, while maintaining and highlighting its original contribution, as confirmed by its influence on Jewish and even more on Christian and Islamic traditions and on their underlying conceptions of human action and interaction, a process of influence that culminated in the Axial Renaissance of the late Middle Ages (see chapters 3 and 4).

It has been observed that "the image of the *polis* as a community of citizens could be interpreted as a transcendental model in permanent tension with the mundane orders of really existing *poleis*" (Arnason 2005: 39). Yet the emergence of this framework of transcendence was a gradual and not a painless accomplishment of the challenge of the existing *poleis*, also and especially of Athens, through distinctive developments of Greek philosophy that created and instituted refined visions of transcendence (cf. Humphreys 1975; Humphreys 1986; Elkana 1986; Raaflaub 2005). The political-discursive praxis of the Athenian *polis* was highly unstable in the era of the sophists. The leadership of Pericles, right after the middle of the first millennium BCE—when the apex of the axial breakthrough is conventionally located—revealed ever deeper contradictions. At that time, coinciding with the zenith of Athens's political power and civilizational achievements, the practice of public life in the Athenian *polis* had entered a cycle of deterioration because of the difficulty to find a consensus on the intrinsic value to attribute to the deliberative procedures of democracy.

In his pursuit of power externally and internally, public discourse, which in the *polis* coincided with political discourse without residues and was mediated by the technique of rhetoric, was deployed by Pericles through excluding from rational debate "that shared background of beliefs about the desirable and undesirable which provide for democratic Athenians the first and ultimate premises of their arguments" (MacIntyre 1988: 56). The tension between shared background values and rational debate and procedure will also affect modern notions of public reason and the public sphere (see chapter 6). Indeed the Periclean case prefigures modern dilemmas: due to the erosion or loss of the reference to shared values, the technical primacy of procedures had to be compensated by the imaginative construction of a collective identity ("We, the Athenians") that finally pervaded, visually and ritually, the public space, much to the detriment of discourse. Paradoxically, the primacy of rhetoric and deliberative procedures diminished the centrality of rational argument by opening up public space to the iconicity of sheer identity. As highlighted by MacIntyre,

> the Periclean vision was itself inseparable from the rhetoric by means of which it was expressed, a work of an imagination which took form in the building and sculptures of the Parthenon as well as in words. Images are more fundamental to the Periclean standpoint than either concepts or arguments. (ibid.: 57)

The restoration of the primacy of argument and public reasoning could not consist in restoring a pre-Periclean status quo, when argument was still amalgamated with the mytologemes of the Greek heroic age. It required the creation of a new level of reasoning that transformed—to use Vico's vocabulary—what were still largely imaginative universals into intelligible universals (ibid.), with all the risks entailed by the passage. The transition was accomplished during the classic phase of Athenian philosophy, which symptomatically coincides with a postclassic era in Athenian democratic life. This was a momentous turning point that had an enduring impact on all subsequent reconceptualizations of discourse and reasoning in the Euro-Mediterranean civilizational area, through the influence that Platonic and Aristotelian philosophies had on both Christianity and Islam. Through a basically uninterrupted commentary on Aristotle's ethics, this breakthrough has exercised a determinant influence not just on the "West," but on the development of the theoretical and dogmatic fundaments of the late-medieval crystallizations of all Abrahamic religions, those formed during the "Axial Renaissance" (see chapters 3 and 4).

As observed by MacIntyre, the passage from Pericles's public rhetoric to Plato's foundation of value in transcendence could be interpreted as the sole theoretical way to overcome the Periclean primacy of goods of effectiveness and power. The solution lay in a more solid speculative underpinning of "goods of excellence" or "values," those deeply rooted in the (pre-axial) "heroic age." The basic critique leveled by Plato at

Athenian democracy pointed out its incapacity to promote an enduring primacy of those goods of excellence attainable through the dispositions that preclassic discourse had already defined as "virtue" (*areté*). Plato's *Republic* was a refutation of the assumption that the highly ambivalent political discourse and public deliberation within Athenian democracy would be conducive to the higher goods of the polity. The cultivation of virtues was mainly valued to the extent it contributed to particular interests, to goods of effectiveness, and therefore to pinpoint power relationships and win games of power (MacIntyre 1988: 63–64). As opposed to this limit Plato provided "a well-articulated theory as to what human excellence in fact consists in and why it is rational in the light of that theory always to subordinate the goods of effectiveness to those of excellence" (ibid.: 68). This is in a nutshell the Greek version of the axial breakthrough.

Plato's point was that "without *areté* you cannot be either theoretically or practically rational and that without rationality you cannot have *areté*" (ibid.: 69). The vocabulary of the virtues centered on the axis between *phronesis* and *telos* is the most genuine Greek philosophical contribution to axial transformations. Plato reacted to Thucydides's appraisal of Pericles's *polis*, which was a kind of deconstructionist critique that exposed how justice by necessity depends on the will of the most powerful, and that the discourse of justice follows such determinations of power. Thucydides depicted a sociopolitical discourse functioning as a sheer technique of power, inexorably overpowering and instrumentalizing *areté* in all kinds of interpersonal and public relationships. Against Thucydides, Plato maintained that there are no games of power, and no corresponding pursuits of goods of effectiveness which are self-sustaining and long lasting: a lack or deficit of excellence, and especially of the virtue of justice, ultimately puts in jeopardy the pursuit of those goods.

This approach entails a radically different view of the technique of rhetoric. While the Periclean rhetoric was sustained by a view of skills allowing for a strictly instrumental means-end operationalization, which usually ends up with a nonargumentative manipulation of citizens' will, Plato (or, to be more precise, the Platonic Socrates) asserted that "no one is master of a *techné* who does not understand how and in what way the end which that specific *techné* serves is a good, and that understanding requires a knowledge of goods and good in general" (ibid.: 70). The work on a notion of justice external to the dynamics of pursuit of goods of effectiveness, but also independent from the imposition of any collective identity, is a crucial passage in the transformation.

However, it is important to locate this transformation in a wider perspective, which—using again a Vichian vocabulary—relates to the momentous transition from the (pre-axial) "heroic age" to the (axial) human age of "civic commonwealths." The goal is to acquire a better perspective for tackling the more basic issue of the reconstruction of the social bond through practical repertoires of intersubjective understanding and connectivity, which underlie the attainment of notions of context-independent justice (see chapter 2). Symbolic evocations of order have to be solidly based on this microlevel of sociality. It is important to focus on the crystallization of conceptions of "virtues" as neither tokens of heroic honor nor mere Periclean "skills" or technical competencies, but as tensional dispositions facilitating intersubjective connectivity and communication. This crystallization was the result of a longer process much more than of a sudden breakthrough.

In the "heroic age," *dikaiòs* ("just") designated the man who respects and does not violate the order of the universe. However, a subtle but momentous discursive shift occurs by the end of the fifth century BCE. One starts to question if it is "just" to do what the established order requires. It became possible to disagree even radically on what is to be just, if it is not simply to act in accordance with the established order. This transformation is no less than—and indeed probably the best example of—the axial breakthrough laying the basis for reflective judgment and opening up a space for discursive contention on what the *telos* consists of, the hierarchy of goods or values it covers, and how they should be defined and pursued. One of the main concerns of Socrates was that the ordinary usage of current concepts, or a passive reliance on received knowledge, would no longer yield a self-sustaining moral vision and therefore would result in the collapse of the pursuit of goods of excellence, and consequently in the disintegration of the entire order of the *polis* (MacIntyre 1988: 134). A reflexivity based on transcendence was not a philosophical option among other, but the only way to restore the order, indeed to create a new one.

True, the all-encompassing view of the *agòn* as competition (in fact, almost an ubiquitous institution, in all Greece and not only in Athens) embracing all sorts of contest within political, dramatic, and philosophical arenas, and linking them all in an organic way, was the suitable scenario for Socrates's attempted educational reform through rational-exhortative speech. Yet it was not a guarantee of the survival of the setting itself. The discourse of positing and inculcating axial values was agonic and dialogic at the same time. Athens had a quite integrated public space epitomized by the *agorà* (market place and "public square"), which was the product of a deep metamorphosis of the kinship ties and obligations of the Homeric age. It was, nonetheless, not self-sufficient for guaranteeing an enduring and effective public reasoning (ibid.: 138). The concept of *telos* was essential to this educational reform project launched by the philosophical triad of Socrates, Plato, and Aristotle. Concomitantly, the notion of the virtues was detached by them from ascriptive social roles and inscribed into a vision of good life with a potentially universal extension. Here *telos* calls for an inscription of virtues as repertoires of intersubjective understanding and connectivity into some view of transcendence.

Transcendence then surfaces in the fourth century BCE and takes root during the Hellenistic era. We cannot think of Greek politics without Aristotle, who built transcendence into his system, along with the discourse of virtues. Most notably, he achieves what Plato did not, namely to yoke practical rationality to public reasoning according to modalities that will successfully—albeit variably and selectively—penetrate subsequent axial transformations within the Abrahamic tree, like in the rise and crystallization of Christianity and Islam and during the Axial Renaissance of the late Middle Ages. If there is an axial "anomaly" in the Greek case, it is not ideational, or due to a lack of transcendence, but rather institutional. This institutional peculiarity consists in the communitarian self-enclosure of the Greek *poleis*, reveals limits in the universalization of concepts of man, and leaves the impression of a primacy of the "civil" versus the "religious" dimension in Greek axiality. Alternatively, one could maintain that the Greek case proved weak in configuring a civilizational pattern, in creating norms of order clearly external to the given community (Arnason 2005: 46–48). Or, as noticed by MacIntyre, the problem consisted in the fact that "both poets and philosophers for the most part do not distinguish in their accounts of these relationships what is universal and human from what is local and Athenian. The claim is often explicit; Athens is praised because she *par excellence* exhibits human life as it ought to be . . ." (MacIntyre 1984 [1981]: 133).

Therefore, more than being the seedbed of "Western civilization," the Greek model generated a rich and complex heritage that was to be raided by successive and different discursive traditions, notably Christianity and Islam. The Greek axial counterpart to the "Mosaic distinction" is in the discovery of an exclusive truth set apart against falseness (Assmann 2005). The strength of this model is in the thorough conceptual elaboration of the implications of this discovery as concerns the phronetic rationality of human action. The Greek invention of politics emerged as an overarching practice that cannot survive on the sole basis of techniques of persuasion (rhetoric), but needs exactly a wider notion of *telos*/transcendence to underpin the social bond beyond a historically and sociologically restricted, albeit at times successful, communitarian project. This invention can be summarized as follows:

> The only form of community which could provide itself with such a standard would be one whose members structured their common life in terms of a form of activity whose specific goal was to integrate within itself, so far as possible, all those other forms of activity practiced by its members and so to create and sustain as its specific goal that form of life within which to the greatest possible degree the goods of each practice could be enjoyed as well as those goods which are the external rewards of excellence. The name given by Greeks to this form of activity was "politics." (MacIntyre 1988: 33–34)

This is why the trajectory of reflection initiated by Socrates, Plato, and Aristotle did institute a relationship between a first (transcendent) and a second (mundane, sociopolitical) level of order comparable with other axial civilizations of the Euro-Mediterranean area. Apart from the issue of the "Greek anomaly" and its final "normalization," all three main Abrahamic traditions thrived within a field of tension between scriptural narratives and Greek philosophemes.

# CHAPTER 2

# BRIDGING IMAGINATION, PRACTICE, AND DISCOURSE

### Tradition, Practice, and "Communicative Action"

In this chapter I develop a more sustained argumentation for explaining the impact of discursive traditions originating from the axial breakthrough on the formation of key concepts and practices of "communicative action." This discussion is essential for providing theoretical depth to the genealogy of the public sphere that is the object of all subsequent chapters. Beneath the level of validation and canonization of discursive traditions belonging to the "high politics" of the clerics, there are close-to-ground, communicative tools which actors adopt for seeking practical coherence and a collective coordination of their actions.

A seminal idea, presented in chapter 1 and worth developing further, is the view of Abrahamic traditions as a prophetic discourse evolving out of mythical and poetical forms of imagination—and therefore as the historical and institutional source of the fundamental social bond between *ego* and *alter* and as the platform for its stabilization and upgrading into a triangle with God. This idea, originally elaborated by Islamic philosophers and later refined by Spinoza, was made more precise by Vico's elaboration on the morphological affinities between Greek-Homeric and Hebrew-Mosaic narratives (Preus 1989: 72–73; see also chapters 3, 4, and 5). Spinoza's prophets and Vico's poets have in common the capacity to speak imaginatively and in parabolic form in order to communicate virtue and piety *inter rudes*, among the common folk (ibid.: 80–81).

While authors from within the theoretical circles working on the idea of axial transformations have often dealt with "civilization" and "tradition" as partly interchangeable notions, or at least as concepts with largely overlapping meanings, the ensuing discussion provides a sustained elaboration on tradition as a concept linking practice to discourse thanks to the cognitive mediation of imagination. At stake is a discourse, like the prophetic one, painfully emerging out of a mythical stage, but never completely abandoning myth even after the crystallization of the idea of *logos*. The same, *mutatis mutandis*, also applies to philosophical traditions, particularly those influenced by Platonism.

The work of relating everyday life and practice to the new ordainments of transcendence was part of the process of making prophetic discourse applicable to the governance of the self-in-community or to the maintenance of the social bond between *ego* and *alter* through specific forms of "communicative action." Prophetic discourse fulfilled this task through bridging the gulf between the first and second level orders of reality illustrated in chapter 1. It created new forms of authority, finally ushering in new repertoires of intersubjective understanding and connectivity—only partly new, if compared to the pre-axial age, as far as the necessary imaginative dimension of action is concerned (see chapter 5).

Tradition fulfils in this case the task of keeping together discourse and practice over time, retains a root in the creative sources of mythical imagination, and allows for balancing stability and change, as well as the ideational-discursive, the institutional, and the practical layers of the intervention on social worlds by axial virtuosi of the word. The main operational formula of a tradition is therefore their practitioners' "search for coherence" between all these levels and layers, in spite of a fairly good degree of consciousness—among the "guardians" of traditions—of the existence and persistence of tensions.

The sociologists who took over the Axial Age theoretical framework have focused on axial transformations as a sort of precondition to the subsequent breakthrough of modernity. I am more specifically interested in the dynamics of tradition as a way to grasp better the complexity and fragility of the modern breakthrough and of the emergence of a quintessentially modern public sphere, reposing on the Enlightenment ambition to supersede all traditions, and on the attending concept of autonomous agency. I pursue this analysis of the ambivalence of the public sphere not on the wing of a deconstructivist zeal, but with the goal of discovering the tensions in the relationship between practice and public reasoning as inherited and transformed in modern settings. MacIntyre is helpful, in this instance, in that he stresses the contingent positivity of the starting points and breakthroughs within traditions. However, one has to be aware of the difference between the contingency of breakthroughs and the practical and communicative working of traditions in "routine" times. I also concentrate on the latter, delimiting a field of change no less remarkable than those momentums labeled as ruptures.

Once established, traditions work through an internal program authorizing specific procedures of debate and contention, and delegitimizing other procedures. In this way traditions immunize themselves against a lethal level of exposure to the contingency of communication. At the same time, traditions need and effect change. MacIntyre's approach is here sociologically more plausible than Axial Age theory, while it helps in raising the interesting hypothesis that transcendence and contingency pervade the motivational and reflective prism of the agent simultaneously. The Axial Age approach has not yet completely shrugged off a Hegelian teleology of history that goes back to Jaspers and predictably lays stress on a revolution in the constitution of the self as a key variable. This is basically a postulate of self-understanding and identity carried by a grand philosophy of history, which is quite difficult to fold into a full-fledged sociological work hypothesis. Focusing instead on the workings of tradition beyond the revolutionary breakthroughs, MacIntyre has stressed that

> in systematizing and ordering the truths [the traditions] take themselves to have discovered, the adherents of a tradition may well assign a primary place in the structures of their theorizing to certain truths and treat them as first metaphysical or practical principles. But such principles will have had to vindicate themselves in the historical process of dialectical justification. (MacIntyre 1988: 360)

Yet commenting on MacIntyre's view of tradition's orientation to change and merging this notion with Wittgenstein's concept of form of life, John Shotter has suggested to conceptualize the creativity of microruptures within traditions as essential to their vitality:

> If a community is to sustain living traditions within its forms of life, its forms of life must afford opportunities not only for what one might call second-order discussions or arguments, that is, arguments about what should be argued about, and why, but also opportunities for the occurrence of unique, essentially poetic, events that lead us to acknowledge within them aspects of our circumstances that up till now have passed by us unnoticed. (Shotter 1996: 16)[1]

On a second step, we need to place transcendence and the contingency of creativity not in a framework exalting the subject or, alternatively, his "lifeworld," but in a setting of social relationships evidencing the primacy of intersubjective connectivity. Subject-constitution is an unassailable motive within the post-Hegelian self-understandings of the "West." Phenomenology has perfected both the ideas of the subject and the lifeworld and has transmitted them to some of the theoretically most ambitious branches of post–World War II sociology of religion, like in the work of Berger and Luckmann (see chapter 1). This approach is sill part of a Cartesian genealogy, which sets subjects over against an objective or phenomenological reality. This reality, "although it yielded to our manipulations as third-person outsiders, . . . did not respond to us as first or second-person interactants" (Shotter 1996: 5). Therefore, the phenomenological approach risks to subvert the microsociological operation underlying the axial breakthrough; it subsumes the I-Thou (and even the I-Thou-God) relationship under the I-it relationship. In axial terms, instead, the "it," the phenomenological medium of communication and understanding, can only result from the I-Thou-God triad and its enduring tensions. The "it," indeed, becomes the "It," the communicative force of cohesion of the triad, the *logos*.

Taking inspiration from the work of MacIntyre and Asad, I further develop here a notion of "discursive tradition" that ties, in a Wittgensteinian fashion,[2] life form and language game, and thereby circumvents the pitfalls of phenomenologically impregnated visions of the "lifeworld," as well as postphenomenological versions of pragmatism that resist incorporating a notion of tradition. This conceptual discussion should also help grasping the dynamics of change triggered out by and within discursive traditions. These are transformations that a privileged macrosociological focus on the civilizational dimension is not adequate to account for. On the other hand, Habermas's theory of communicative action and the underlying notion of lifeworld, which he inherits from phenomenologically oriented social scientists but redefines according to his "formal-pragmatic" approach, should be rediscussed as providing, at the same time, a fragile solution to the earlier mentioned aporias, and tracks for ways out of the theoretical impasse—and possibly ways into the theorization of discursive traditions as essential to the genealogy of the public sphere.

The concerns of Habermas's theory of communicative action and the goal of the present work overlap to a large extent (see introduction); so is also some of the conceptual apparatus adopted. As observed by Hans Joas, Habermas sees "lifeworld as represented by a culturally transmitted and linguistically organized stock of interpretive patterns" (Joas 1991 [1986]: 114). The notion of communicative action constructed by Habermas is assigned two main tasks: to capture the self-regulating character of social interaction and to construct a category of action that is communicative to the extent it is noninstrumental (ibid.: 101). Yet Habermas warned against the danger that "language and cultural tradition take on a certain transcendental status in relation to everything that can become an element of a situation." Habermas's first—though vague—way out of this uneasiness is to admit that "language and culture are constitutive of the lifeworld itself" (Habermas 1987 [1981]: 124–25).

Set against this background, we can better understand Habermas's definition of the lifeworld with regard to his notion of language, and the residual importance he attributes to tradition via language:

> From a perspective turned toward the situation, the lifeworld appears as a reservoir of taken-for-granteds, of unshaken convictions that participants in communication draw upon in cooperative processes of interaction. Single elements, specific taken-for-granteds, are, however, mobilized in the form of consensual yet problematicizable knowledge only when they become relevant to a situation. (ibid.: 124)[3]

What is remarkable is that in defending his theory of communicative action against various critiques, including Joas's, Habermas took on board the notion of "cultural tradition," defined in basically negative terms, as in most sociological references to tradition (see introduction and chapter 1). It is also interesting that he focuses on the issue of language, probably assuming that tradition is by default part of language. He believes that traditions persist in language only in a symbolic form.

While Habermas admits that a distinction between the linguistic structure or "organism" of language and the living practice of speech is now a recognized acquisition of language theories, he sees an insufficient stress in most contemporary theories on the dimension of "intersubjectivity," that is of the mutual understanding facilitated by conversation (Habermas 1991 [1986]: 215). Pursuing a radical inoculation of his theory of communicative action against any philosophy of the subject, Habermas interestingly stresses the importance of

> the relation of an ego to an alter ego, *of simultaneous and equal origin.* Between the two, the space opens up for an intersubjectively shared life world . . . A communication-theoretical concept of society hinges on this social space for a lifeworld inhabited in common that emerges in the course of dialogue. (ibid.: 218)

Habermas concludes that the Humboldtian idea of the rational potential of speech is reflected in "the *telos* inherent in the very process of reaching understanding though language" (ibid.: 219). Admitting this *telos* would preempt—so the sense of Habermas's argument—the basic objection to procedural-communicative rationality, formulated by Charles Taylor and others, according to which rationality cannot be divorced from "substantive" views of the good life. The alley into such procedural-communicative rationality conceived by Habermas as a kind of—quite paradoxical, and indeed, as we will see, untenable—nontelic *telos* is the process of rationalization of the lifeworld, consisting in "the constant revision of fluidized traditions: traditions which have become reflexive" (ibid.: 224).

Habermas does not engage in defining tradition in an accurate way with regard to his theory of communicative action, so one is left to recall the semidefinitions that were part of his earlier debates with Gadamer (see introduction and chapter 1). Further and more importantly, it is not clear what the normative, linguistic, and communicative threshold of a "fluidization" of traditions should be, for them to be enabled to provide suitable "raw material" to the rationalization of the lifeworld. The consequence of a lack of definition of tradition and of the normative assumptions about the conditions for their fluidization is that Habermas strongly implies that tradition is by definition nonreflexive and not subject to an inherent process of revision. The present work argues that a consistent, nonreticent, nonresidualist definition of tradition stresses reflexivity, change, and constant revision as indispensable markers of tradition.

Yet the most striking and dubious assumption is—as evidenced by Habermas's rebuttal of the substantivist objections to his proceduralist view of reason—that he considers traditions like a "cultural mass" without form. In what follows, I try to show that quite the opposite is the case, namely that traditions are mainly forms for shaping, collating, and governing modes of speech, dialogue, and reasoning into synoptic ensembles which are in a permanent state of unbalance. This permanent movement is due to the ever new demands posed to discursive traditions and arising from concrete situations faced by their practitioners, so that the same or similar traditions can carry highly varying or even diverging cultural contents within shifting contexts. However, this does not mean that only context and situation matter. It is quite the opposite: in order to understand a situation, one has first to know the repertoires of engagement enabled by the form of traditions, that is, the forms of life and language games invested into the situation by the agents. This issue calls into question the link between communication and practice.

As previously seen (see introduction and chapter 1) the earlier strategy followed by Habermas consisted in invoking a notion of practice partly inspired by the Greek philosophy of praxis and partly by modern thinkers hostile to a mechanistic view of society, first and foremost Vico (see chapter 5). At that stage, Habermas was working on a phronetic notion of action. This means that at the start of the long trajectory that would finally lead him to the theory of communicative action he was well aware of the complexity and richness of the concept of practice, whose wider implications his foremost concern with communication finally prevented to integrate in his theory.

Joas comments that "it could indeed be the case that there are more reasons for rejecting the limitation of the practical to the technical than can be derived from the concepts of communication and interaction" ( Joas 1991 [1986]: 99), so manifesting his skepticism about Habermas's "discovery" of communicative action as *the* essentially dialogic, rational, noninstrumental, and nonfunctional form of action. In this context Joas mentions some of such "more reasons" by invoking Durkheim's, Parsons's, and Gehlen's anti-utilitarian views of ritual, intended as a norm-constituting type of action, almost the kernel of a counterprogram to the instrumentalist restriction of the concept of action. Thus Joas puts in evidence how Habermas's argument on communicative action is indebted to a broader sociological tradition of search for such noninstrumental basis for action (ibid.: 100).

Yet, while Habermas recognized this debt, it cannot be denied that he attempted a more drastic breakthrough. In order to pinpoint the irreducibility and self-resourcefulness of human communication, Habermas singles out "communicative action" both from "instrumental action" and from "teleological action." While "teleological action" is not a sociologically acceptable way to describe the nonfunctional yet nonirrational kernel of action, we have also to come around Habermas's uncertain postulation of a *telos* of understanding residing in the exchange itself and backed up by a procedural rationality that has to be at least partly external to the exchange, notably for being posited and administered by external agencies, by post-axial arbiters of the correctness of rational procedures. In other words, we have to solve the dilemma of a nontelic *telos* and attain a sociologically clearer consideration of *telos*. This can be done via a theoretical approach to tradition that can still benefit from coping with Habermas's work.

What is needed is to recall the reflections on the *telos* of practice conducted in chapter 1 and relate them to the way Habermas conceives of the *telos* of communicative action, in order to treasure upon the strength of this Habermasian view (not least vis-à-vis pragmatism) and amending its weaknesses (also evidenced by parts of Joas's objections inspired by pragmatism). One key statement by Habermas is that "the medium of the language and the *telos* of reaching understanding intrinsic to it reciprocally constitute one another. The relation between these is not one of means and ends" (Habermas 1991 [1986]: 241). This statement reveals an effort to look for the integrative factor of interaction that cannot be accounted for by the pragmatist one-dimensional notion of the "situation" and by the concomitant claim that "actors find their ends in the situation."

In particular, one needs to admit that it is not sufficient to postulate a spontaneous dilution of *telos* into "intersubjective understanding" by invoking a virtue inherent in human communication, namely the capacity to develop "communicative action." Moreover, we have to recognize that the medium and language of a conversation, however embedded in a situation that is always and by definition unique, has both a history and a set of parameters through which its rules are authorized, maintained, criticized, changed, and redressed. The urgency of redeploying Habermas's idea of communicative action out of its paradoxical and circular definition is further highlighted by the fact that the gap between situation and medium was bridged by Habermas through the sociologically obscure remark that "the very medium of mutual understanding abides in a peculiar *half-transcendence* [author's emphasis]" (Habermas 1987 [1981]: 125). Through this statement, Habermas probably tried to translate into a halfway sociologically understandable language Karl Otto Apel's elaboration on the theoretical notion of an *apriori* of communication (Apel 1972, 1988). Evidently, Habermas's attempt to make obsolete *telos* and *phronesis* in order to account for techniques of intersubjective understanding and connectivity was still fraught with conceptual aporias.

In order to conceive of action as bent on understanding, communication, and connectivity I propose to refer explicitly to traditional notions and to analyze them genealogically, instead of making reluctant, out-of-context half-references to their ghosts. What makes out an action is the capacity to yoke *phronesis* to *telos* in ways that are specific to the situation yet are also set against an ensemble, a chain, and a narrative of resembling situations. The ensuing communicative dimension of action incorporates a *telos* that is apprehended rationally from within a certain tradition of inquiry and good life. The limit of Habermas's approach lies in his insistence that tradition only provides the cultural raw material but lacks per se a rational form of inquiry and understanding. For fear of compromising the originality and modernity of communicative action, he prefers to resort to unclear references to the nontelic *telos* of communication and to the "half-transcendence" of its medium.

As a corrective to this view, I propose that a full-fledged *telos* does not configure a "substantive" anchoring of specific conceptions and hierarchies of the goods pursued but is the given, yet contestable and revisable form of argumentation and reasoning. This function is clarified by *telos*'s relationship to *phronesis*. The *telos* would have no existence in social practice without providing direction to *phronesis* intended as the "capacity to judge and to do the right thing in the right place at the right time in the right way." For sure "the exercise of such judgement is not a routinizable application of rules" (MacIntyre 1984 [1981]: 150).

In its formal dimension, the relation of this type of reasoning to the Habermasian notions of "procedure" and "procedural rationality" has still to be ascertained. Yet to deny to discursive traditions a capacity to give form, also procedurally, to specific situations would perpetuate a grave misunderstanding based on a too rigid dichotomization between "modern" and "traditional," "formal" and "substantive" types of rationality. The main issue at stake is rather which kind of procedure, which kind of rationality, and which kind of modernity can be configured by which kind of tradition. Habermas's quite abrupt abandonment of praxic concepts like *phronesis* and *poiesis* after the launch of his theory of communicative action did not facilitate his task of capturing the complexities of the synchronic (situation-related) and diachronic (tradition-based) dimensions of communicative action.

Taken into account the shortcomings of Habermas's operation, it is not surprising that the idea of *phronesis* has continued to appeal to social theorists (cf. Bourdieu and Wacquant 1992: 128; Flyvbjerg 2001). Symptomatically, however, it has been mostly considered as divorced from *telos*, without which, however, *phronesis* looses its power of activating the agent. How *phronesis* was divorced from *telos* and in which historical and conceptual setting, is the object of chapter 6. It was the severance of this link that made possible to social theorists like Parsons to postulate the existence of "telic systems" of social action without attributing *phronesis* to its actors, a step that was rightly criticized by Habermas (1987 [1981]: 250–56). Habermas indicted this view for configuring "a region that *indirectly* influences communicative action via the symbolic reproduction of the lifeworld" (ibid.: 256), in what appears as the final metaphysical twist of Durkheimian-functionalist macrosociology. Habermas was not willing, however, to completely reject such an indirect link between symbols and communication. The consequence is that his theory of communicative action is kept hostage of the same kind of macro-micro short-circuit that he decries in Parsons, where the social integration of the social system is presupposed in the individual capacity to act. Habermas's theory is at pain to redress the short-circuit into a theoretically persuasive micro-macro link showing that communicative action is a major source of social integration.

In the present work I have opted for defining as "communicative action" a type of action that is not instrumental, but praxis-oriented and incorporated in a tradition. In this way I do not refute but critically reconstruct Habermas's own notion, through its embedding in a sociological concept of tradition. This type of action, rooted in practice as learned (not just individually, but through transmission and revisions across generations), evidences the way in which means are related to ends in response to the continual need for praxic creativity and adaptations to ever new situations. A so redefined and situated communicative action is one with the interactive and situation-bound reconstruction of the rule that also includes a dimension of reflexivity as to the justification of the rule. Unlike Parsons's notion of "telic systems," there is, sociologically speaking, no "ultimate concern" (in the late Protestant language of Paul Tillich from which Habermas also distances himself) to be postulated. For this type of action to take place, the only condition is that the agent is guided by a capacity to order goods to be attained via the relentless and creative repetition of practice. The definition and the hierarchy of the goods are adjudicated upon dialogically and agonically, diachronically and synchronically, within a given tradition of apprehension and pursuit of the goods and (increasingly in modern contexts) through its exposure to the challenge of rival traditions.

This view also allows to define "instrumental action" as a type of action that is built on a different apprehension of the goods, usually one dictated by some notion of interest, and privileging goods of effectiveness over goods of excellence (see chapter 1). Reasoning is applied not to the dialogical and/or agonic ordering of the goods, but to the calculation of the best means to achieve any ends contingently dictated by interest. As I show in chapter 6, this kind of instrumental action was reformulated in the course of the eighteenth-century metamorphosis of *phronesis/prudentia* into the Anglo-Scottish "prudence," which denotes exactly this kind of prudential-calculative rationality. Accepting such a basic distinction between these two types of rationality of action is crucial, because it subverts any basic partition of the motivation of social action into, for example, a "religious" versus a "secular" type of mindset or motivational prism. For both telic-phronetic and prudential-calculative action can be vindicated by various kinds of religious, nonreligious, and antireligious discourses or "substantive" ethics. It is the emergence and largely the success of prudential-calculative reason that makes tradition—any tradition—a potential enemy, or at least an obstacle, to modern liberal views of the rationality of the socioeconomic actor.

To complete this strand of argument, "communicative action" should be redefined by making explicit the role of *phronesis* and *telos* in it. Practice is not excluded from, but essential to a redefined notion of communicative action. From now on I will refer to practice in a sense very close to the meaning elucidated by MacIntyre, as including an essential communicative dimension:

> I shall be using the word "practice" in a specially defined way which does not completely agree with ordinary use . . . any coherent and complex form of socially established cooperative human activity through which goods internal to that form of activity are realized in the course of trying to achieve those standards of excellence which are appropriate to, and partially definitive of, that form of activity, with the result that human powers to achieve excellence, and human conceptions of the ends and goods involved, are systematically extended. (MacIntyre 1984 [1981]: 187)

The significance of MacIntyre's definition of practice has been acknowledged by leading theorists of practice like Barry Barns (2001) and Theodor Schatzki (2001). They have observed that MacIntyre's notion of practice is more specific than most of those in use in the social sciences and in social theory debates. It is part of a tradition of critique of post-Kantian concepts of practice, communication, and agency with wide currency in the social sciences. MacIntyre, nonetheless, has worked on making his concept of practice ever more generalizable in social-theoretical terms. He maintains that it is symptomatic that in the ancient and medieval worlds the grounding and development of households, towns, and wider communities was considered a practice in the sense elucidated by him, so as to include arts, sciences, family life, games, and politics in the classic sense (MacIntyre 1984 [1981]: 187–88). This is why in developing and keeping standards of excellence in the pursuit of goods, one has to accept the authority of standards of excellence which help measuring the degree of aptness versus inadequacy of one's own performance of a given practice (ibid.: 190). Therefore, while it is true that the aims and goods of practices are subject to contention and change, in a given moment they are influenced by the authority of the most gifted practitioners.

MacIntyre also warns against a too optimistic view of practice as self-sustaining and as fully external to games of power. Practices need institutions, which are at least as concerned with acquiring and providing goods of effectiveness as they are to facilitate the pursuit of the goods of excellence internal to the practices they facilitate. Yet the two institutional concerns are often in tension. Therefore "the cooperative care for common goods of the practice is always vulnerable to the competitiveness of the institution" (ibid.: 194). The fact that practices are exposed to an institutional overpowering does not mean that they are encapsulated within fields essentially governed by power and interest. Some dispositions catalogued as higher virtues by discursive traditions (like justice, courage, and truthfulness) are key to safeguarding practices against the logic of power incorporated in institutions (MacIntyre 1984 [1981]: 194), like a hospital, a school, a university, a law court, a charitable foundation, or a cultural foundation. MacIntyre does not hesitate to include the family among the set of such constructed, and therefore vulnerable institutions, although it was certainly one of the first institutions to be sanctified by several religious traditions (especially those belonging to the Abrahamic tree). This institution is viable only as long as it can guarantee a balance between enabling practices and avoid an institutional overfunctionalization, which is, however, exactly what occurred to it within modernity through its relocation at the core of the "private sphere" (see chapter 6).

The notion of "virtues" and even the more neutral notion of "dispositions" should not be considered theoretical concepts, but key ideas that build the motivating prism of the agents who respond to a given tradition. As concepts, they are tautological, as also evidenced by Wittgenstein (Bouveresse 1999: 61), yet they reveal tautologies which are essential to the discursive dimension and effectiveness of a tradition. At the same time, virtues are not an exclusive token of religious traditions. The crudest utilitarian approaches like Benjamin Franklin's also produce their catalogues of virtues (MacIntyre 1984 [1981]: 198). On the other hand, a notion of justice as the highest virtue does not require by necessity a cosmology of transcendence.

## Tradition as Life Form and Discourse

The diachronic and intergenerational dimension of the transmission of practices and the corresponding shifts and transformations of authority are of crucial importance. Apart from the contingent situation to which a particular model of good life is applied through practice, the underlying dispositions are inculcated and transmitted over time through a variety of expectations, legacies, and commitments (MacIntyre 1984 [1981]: 220). We can speak of "macrotraditions," which are often identified with "religious-civilizational" attachments and senses of belonging, even when their practitioners no longer profess their faith in a traditional way. It is necessary to bear in mind, however, that such macrotraditions should not be intended as cultural monoliths, and therefore as the substantive cultural matrixes of neatly differentiated civilizations. They provide broad frameworks of narrative identification and instruction and are therefore like arenas for intersecting language games. Practice, on the other hand, is more directly determined by the "microtraditions" providing instructions as to how to live a good life with regard to a particular role, or indeed a multiplicity of roles (how to be a good physician, a good mother, a good student, and so on, but also how to be a good Muslim physician, a good Catholic mother, a good atheist student, and so on).

Where can we locate a strong link between micro and macrotraditions, or between living traditions and life forms, on the one hand, and wider arenas of language games, on the other? This link can be seen in the use of discourse and its modes of argument and reasoning in order to transcend, via creativity and criticism, the limitations of the interpretations and definitions of the goods and the solutions to problems thus far delivered within a given tradition. Solutions are envisioned by referring means to ends or goods. Therefore, an institution like a university, or a farm, which is the product and the carrier of a tradition defining and supporting practices, has to deploy a continuous argument specifying the manner and the extent to which the university, or the farm, as an institution, is supportive of the notion of the good of higher education or of good farming. To be in good order and thrive, a tradition cannot escape conflict but has to accept and process it conveniently as essential to its survival. As formulated by MacIntyre,

> Traditions, when vital, embody continuities of conflict. Indeed, when a tradition becomes Burkean, it is always dying or dead . . . A living tradition then is an historically extended, socially embodied argument, and an argument precisely in part about the goods which constitute that tradition. (MacIntyre 1984 [1981]: 222)

John Shotter has suggested that by "dead" tradition one should intend

one sustained by a form of life in which the final form of everything is already supposedly known, and thus, all difficulties are problems that, with enough effort and insight, can be routinely solved. In such a "dead" form of life, there can be no more surprises, no more utterly unique, unrepeatable, first time events. (Shotter 1996: 15)

It is evident that traditions thrive or die out through the work and interventions of subsequent generations. MacIntyre points out, however, that there is at least one area of human activity that is essential to keep macrotraditions and their institutional configurations in good order, at any given time. This is given by the shape of law, which cannot be considered as a mere social "field" or "subsystem" among others.[4] Or, to express the same point from the other end of the argument, if one can, in a given social setting, theorize of law as nonreducible to the functional operations of a social field or subsystem, then we have a thriving tradition at work within law. Law, or the regulative dimension of traditions, cuts through several other dimensions and fields of practice. Sunni Islam provides a case that helps understanding more deeply the link between macrotraditions and law. Even more importantly, the case of the *shari'a* tradition (chapter 4) along with its comparison with the Roman law tradition as reconstructed by Vico (chapter 5) can help highlighting the extent to which law is immediately linked to the phronetic dimension of practice. Chapter 6 will then offer insights into the effects of a full functionalization, positivization and de-traditionalization of law in modern settings.

Though not the primary object of this work, law is a privileged arena of human discourse and social practice for testing the match or mismatch between microtraditions, anchored within practices that can never be fully formalized and functionalized, and macrotraditions that are more prone to institutionalization and formalization. The training of the good judge and the instruction of the commoner into being a good member of the social body ideally coincide, since no law is specific enough to be applied immediately and without reasoning. However, the reality gap between the law (any kind of, including divine law, as the Decalogue that Moses received on Mount Sinai, according to the biblical narration) and its application is exactly what opens the cataract of prophetic discourse, admonishing commoners and practitioners for their infringing, circumventing or minimizing the sense of the law.

Through this kind of discourse *phronesis* is extended to the commoners, even if it was originally an heroic aristocratic virtue denoting the capacity to take pride in claiming one's due (MacIntyre 1984 [1981]: 154). From being one major virtue among others, through axial transformations (see chapter 1) *phronesis* becomes a potentially universal metadisposition, required for any apprehension of the goods and related practices, and therefore as the condition itself of agency, intentionality and reflexivity. However, the types of intentionality and reflexivity required to the agent are determined by the shape and the evolution of a given tradition that grounds phronetic agency. The form that discourse attributes to the individual-agential "will" or equivalents thereof can not only vary from one axial tradition to the other, but is subject to contestation within each tradition (see examples for chapters 3 and 4).

The extent to which I have laid stress on the notion of "discursive tradition" (including its kernel of "living tradition") versus life conduct, lifeworld, life form, or *habitus* (not to speak of the too generic notion of "culture") is due to the necessity to highlight the importance of discourse in mediating between practice and institution. This move highlights the dimension of governance and stratification that creates and reproduces authority and places it in the hands of "guardians" of the tradition. Such a process makes authority contestable through shifting sociopolitical configurations and generational change. A view of tradition of some theoretical complexity allows for a particularly balanced view of the production, maintenance, and transformation of repertoires of intersubjective understanding and connectivity at the delicate juncture between practice and institution, with a focus on their reciprocal implications of mutuality and tension.

A much needed specification of this approach to traditions is provided by Talal Asad (1986, 1993, 1999, 2003). While maintaining a distance from a Weberian approach, Asad has attempted to define the workings of a discursive tradition on an anthropological and microinstitutional level. He has provided an analytical angle that can complement and correct the mainly macroinstitutional orientation of Axial Age theory, and facilitate a focus on the microdimension of repertoires of intersubjective connectivity much more than Habermas's approach, more oriented to the search for communicative mechanisms of social integration, is able to do. Asad maintains that a discursive tradition cannot be understood through its collective and civilizational rooting (in institutions or movements variably challenging those institutions), but should be analyzed first through the communicative-performative mechanism linking *ego* (the faithful in Abrahamic traditions) to *alter* (who is no longer simply another human being, but a potential recruit to the community of truth).

The engine of this call through which *ego* addresses *alter* consists in the former's attempt to win over the latter to the true faith and to the obligations inherent in it. The maintenance of tradition depends on this exhortative, microdimension of discourse. This is an important qualification of MacIntyre's insight into the reasoning dimension of discursive traditions which, even if it allows for disagreement and conflict, risks to echo the limitations of Habermas's "power-free, seminar room model" of the public sphere, or the dichotomization of communicative action and "power." For the moment, let us just retain the Wittgensteinian lesson that language is inherently instructive and educational, as much as it is responsive and reactive. In other words, a "call." Discursive traditions are then densely complex instances of language in use.

Particularly within Christianity and Islam the calls to act virtuously and piously are formative to the faith and its transmission. In Islam the call is subsumed under the canonical formula (itself an obligation incumbent on the faithful) of "commanding good and prohibiting evil" (further to this point, see chapter 4). This formula—unsurprisingly—has been historically subject to a broad range of interpretations. While obviously the obligations—and prohibitions—are defined through processes of crystallization of their catalogues in parallel to doctrines, the differences concerning the interpretations of the formula concern the means and media themselves of the exhortation (commanding and prohibiting), which can range from gentle reminders to forceful inculcation (cf. Cook 2000), in analogy with Augustine's prescriptions for the education into the Christian virtues.

Whatever the interpretation, the Islamic injunction epitomizes the exhortative form that is central to this type of discursive tradition. Clearly, the salvational path can neither consist solely in the participation in extraordinary, community-making, collective rituals, and in the attending of, more routine-like, rites of purification, nor in a solitary caring for one's own soul. It is neither a matter of building up a "collective identity" (the Durkheimian way), nor simply a "constitution of the subject" (the Foucauldian, but also the phenomenological way). Caring for the virtuous life conduct of other members of the community, and winning over an external or internal other as a potential brother or sister in faith, are probably the most striking similarities—in spite of all momentous differences—between Christianity and Islam. Against Habermas's insistence in viewing traditional reason as "substantive," the exhortative call is a form that can be grounded on a wide and potentially unlimited range of contestable, binary oppositions between the "good" to be commanded and the "evil" to be prohibited. It is inevitable that, however high the formalization and proceduralization of the mutual understanding among participants in a discourse as envisaged by Habermas's communicative action, participants base their discourse on some binary view of what is good or just, and its negation.

Even if in most cases discursive traditions converge on the assertion that the final adherence to a salvational call should be the product of a conscious act of assent on the part of the faithful, this dimension of tradition entails that teaching should be complemented by warning. This is a process of persuasion whose complexity cannot be reduced to an extremely formalized procedural rationality of sort, since it appeals to symbols and sentiments resonating with the mind of the practitioner. It therefore includes the inculcation of fear and entails a reasoned and organized application of authority. Augustine summarized this essential aspect of the discursive tradition as *disciplina* (Asad 1993: 34): "Particular discourses and practices were to be systematically excluded, forbidden, denounced—made as much as possible unthinkable; others were to be included, allowed, praised, and drawn into the narrative of sacred truth" (ibid.: 35). It is important to bear in mind that the nonreducibility of traditional religious discourse to a simple pattern of procedural rationality finalized to mutual understanding among participants in a discourse should not induce us to see in a discursive tradition the realm of blind fear and of unchecked, arbitrary authority—nor the domain of a substantive reason devoid of any procedural underpinnings.

Asad has analyzed the complexification and sophistication of discipline through the patterns of medieval monasticism (see chapter 3). Discourses authorize certain practices and prohibit other, including an ever increasing spectrum of topics and genres, as well as a wide assortment of modalities of inculcation. These range from a selective rejection or adaptation of "pagan" practices, the authentication of specific miracles and relics and the condemnation of other practices as spurious and unauthentic, to the writing of saints' hagiographies; from the standardization of penitential practices, to the authorization of certain religious movements in the form of rule-based orders and the concomitant stigmatization, repression and suppression of other movements identified as heretical. Remarkable, however, is that "the medieval Church did not attempt to establish absolute uniformity of practice; on the contrary, its authoritative discourse was always concerned to specify differences, gradations, exceptions" (Asad 1993: 37–38).

The maintenance of a tradition requires forms of admonition and formulas of conversion, and therefore the structuring of a discourse that is able to transcend the pure transmissibility of knowledge that occurs via the authentication, falsification, and canonization of scriptural sources. This task cannot be the exclusive prerogative of a specialized personnel, the class of scholars and clerics administering ritual and discursive procedures and their complex application. One needs instances of control, mediation, and communication that warrant an adequate degree of practical appropriation (or circumvention) of commandments and prohibitions by the practitioners themselves, the "commoners." The members of the specific community defined by a tradition (which is a "community of salvation" in the case of Abrahamic traditions) are called to act upon the tradition from within their everyday life. In order to be a real insider, it is not sufficient to adequately know the discursive rules for engaging *alter* (this is what neophytes do best), but one also needs to master on a practical level the case-by-case modularity of application of the rule itself. This does not constitute a "substantial," but a complexly formal type of rationality.

Anthony Giddens, who shared a negative conceptualization of tradition as a backward-looking culture with most social theorists, was nonetheless able to observe that "the 'integrity' of tradition derives not from the simple fact of persistence over time but from the continuous 'work' of interpretation that is carried out to identify the strands which bind present to past" (Giddens 1994: 64). The discourse of tradition forms the self-in-community through a permanent recourse to a transindividual and transgenerational *telos* activated through the exhortative matrix of the discourse directed at *alter*. This mediatized vector can be administered but not monopolized by religious personnel.

The basic procedures for constructing the *telos* and inserting it into a certain model of social action and interaction deserve a specific attention, in order not to fall back into a Habermasian typology of motivations pointing out—and usually stigmatizing—a "teleological" orientation of action as opposed to a "communicative" one. *Telos*-oriented praxis is facilitated by an orientation to the other that results from a specific ordering of the social and transcendent goods, within which usually justice as the correct interpretation of the binary tension between good and evil, between right and wrong, ranks prominently. Justice, before incorporating a "substantive" version of the sense of right and wrong, provides a formal coherence between the discourse emanating from the lineages of prophetic charisma and the virtuous practice of the members of community. At the bottom, however, this praxis requires the gestural dimension of instructive talk in calling out the responsive reactions of *alter* (Shotter 1996: 10). Even Luhmann, whose social theory is the farthest from any substantialist temptation, admits that communication by necessity incorporates this dimension of "call" (Luhmann 1998: 60).

This type of praxis supported by an allocutional competence that is itself a key practice, is a sort of self-resourcing program for a tradition in permanent search for coherence. Nonetheless, it cannot absorb the much more complex and multilogical character of the action of any practitioner of a given tradition, which has to combine, in creative and often improvised manners, several language games, repertoires of engagement, and registers of judgment. To recapitulate, spelling out such a notion of tradition is not intended to oppose a "substantive" to a "formal" ethic (Schnädelbach 1986). Tradition specifies a basically different and in many ways more sophisticated *form* of discourse than a "discourse ethics," in the sense elucidated by Apel and Habermas, and consisting in "the exchange of arguments and counterarguments as the most suitable procedure for resolving moral-practical questions" (Habermas 1992: 447). On the level of form, while life forms and their associated language games are by definition embedded in situations, living traditions do not provide an extremely formalized metalanguage inaccessible to the commoner, but an articulate narrative allowing to bundle life forms and language games together via largely coherent series of phronetic judgments. This type of judgment is supported by a capacity of arguing that transcends the specific goods to be sought in a specific situation and embraces the more general—and in this sense formal and even procedural—definition of those goods (see the example in chapters 3 and 4).

This form is supported by a basic understanding between *ego* and *alter*, which is something different from a sheer procedure relying on a "critical mass" of underlying "cultural resources." It is a technique for reassembling and giving coherence to goods/values and for creating synoptic ensembles among them. On a matter of content, the variety of forms of argument and reasoning, including those that have been hegemonic in specific religious, civic, and legal traditions, should be acknowledged and analyzed case by case. In this sense, "culture" does not underlie the form of tradition but is rather its contingent and unstable product. Habermas is ready to concede on the cultural variability of moral contents while he sticks to a uniform formula of "procedural rationality" that does not give sufficient weight to hegemonic configurations and shifts of authority in the making of traditions (cf. Salvatore and Amir-Moazami 2002; Salvatore and LeVine 2005). These are either excluded, or marginalized and taken for granted within Habermas's discursive approach to ethics (see chapter 6 and conclusion).

A discursive tradition is therefore a form of discourse oriented neither to a pure hermeneutic understanding nor to the sheer success of cooperative or collective action, to the attainment of goods of effectiveness. Tradition is based on a discursive form shaped by the "call" and finalized to the fulfillment of good life. Good life is often, but not always and necessarily, embedded in a soteriological form of life, mediated by a notion of supreme, divine justice projected onto the Day of Judgment.

88 off *The Public Sphere*

## Tradition and *Habitus*

We should now deepen the analysis of the nexus between the sociological usefulness of a notion of tradition and the concept of practice. Pierre Bourdieu's work on a theory of practice (1977 [1972]; 1990 [1980]) and his use of the concept of *habitus* are of foremost importance. For Bourdieu practices are self-organizing bundles of human activity crystallizing in *habitus*, intended as the common understanding of practice linking individual skills with the collective alignment of action within a certain group or with regard to a particular field of human activity. Yet one is left with wondering what cements these bundles of human activity, and which is the warrant of the ensuing "logic of practice." Craig Calhoun has convincingly shown that a coherent notion of tradition is exactly what is missing in Bourdieu's theory of practice (Calhoun 1993). This deficit reveals the difficulty to have a theory of practice without a concept of tradition linking practice with communication.

As Calhoun reminds us, tradition in its wider, diachronic dimension transcending situated practice was derided by Bourdieu as pertinent to the realm of social philosophers. Against such a prejudiced sociological closure to the notion of tradition, Calhoun suggests that tradition might help to relate the concept of practice to the idea of regulation, or of coordination of action, a nexus that remains obscure in Bourdieuian *habitus*, which in this sense is no less tautological than the notion of disposition or even virtue (ibid.; Bouveresse 1999). A discussion of the notion of tradition through Calhoun's reflection on the deficits of Bourdieu's theory of practice could help narrowing—though not entirely filling—the gap between practice and communication, by recognizing that a discursive engagement between *ego* and *alter* is essential to practice (cf. Thévenot 2001).

Moreover, a critical discussion of Bourdieu's self-enclosed and largely circular notion of *habitus*, which the French sociologist defined most synthetically as an "open system of dispositions" (Bourdieu and Wacquant 1992: 133) upholding practice, can be useful to give sharper contours to the mechanisms of coordination of action that are latent in the definition of tradition. Calhoun believes that a notion of tradition can be valorized by relating it to its primary meaning as transmission of knowledge (Calhoun 1993). What is transmitted is no plain information or rigid modules of instruction but rather the know-how of practical rationality, which Bourdieu himself on some occasions identified as *phronesis*. Herewith the notion of *habitus* can be used for clarifying the sociological implications of the concept of tradition, provided we understand the latter through the prism of a discourse (that is, as a discursive tradition) called to bridge practice and communication.

Let's then discuss the potential and limits of *habitus*. The pragmatist philosopher Joseph Margolis made the interesting observation that

> if we ask *what* the *habitus is*, what the telling features of its functioning structures are, what we get from Bourdieu is a kind of holist characterization that never comes to terms with its operative substructures. For, consider that the spontaneous play of ordinary life is *not* like an actor's performance: the actor's skilled "inductions" (in Bourdieu's image) are triggered *by a finished and familiar script*; whereas (to continue the image) the ordinary human agent (in "acting his part") creates a fresh script nearly always and continually. (Margolis 1999: 69)

Margolis questions whether it is sufficient to identify *habitus* with the "feel for the game" nourished by the "logic of practice" emphasized by Bourdieu. He contends that it does not help much to explain the logic of practice if we shift focus, with Bourdieu, from "rules" to "strategies" (ibid.: 70). The first problem lies then in the Bourdieuian presumption that there is a system by necessity referred to (or "recalled" by) any disposition or any specific act resulting from a certain disposition. This is no doubt a genuinely pragmatist objection, based on the fear to evoke a "totality" beyond the "situation." Yet the second weakness pointed out by Margolis, interestingly enough, moves in the opposite direction, since it concerns Bourdieu's easy assumption of a "fluency" of acts and underlying dispositions without indicating anything holding them together.

A first remedy is found by referring to Wittgenstein's notion of form of life, which warrants "the improvisational continuity of an open-ended practice in which neither 'rules' nor 'strategies' could yield sufficient closure" (ibid.: 71). As we have seen earlier in this chapter, this is a useful way to spell out the notion of tradition on a microsociological level. At this point Margolis makes the contentious statement that "there *is* no principled distinction between the 'folk' competence of basic predicative discourse and its professionalization: there is only a difference between the various societies whose *Lebensformen* are invoked" (ibid.: 75). Here we find another important feature of the notion of tradition as specified earlier in this chapter: the fact that a tradition's coherence and integrity depends not only on its transmission over time and generations, but also on the capacity of its guardians or arbiters to keep a permanent, two-ways flow between the "commoners" and "professionals" or virtuosi of the practices enacted by tradition. The way Margolis helps us specify the similarity between the notion of tradition and the idea of life form (that we saw present but underdeveloped in MacIntyre's argument on tradition) should not prevent us from retaining a distinction between practice and institution. They are necessarily—albeit tensely—linked in and through tradition in a way that does not neatly reflect the dichotomy between ordinary competencies and expert knowledge.

The sociologically interesting aspect of tradition is given by the extent to which tradition does not only connect *ego* and *alter* but also provides coordination to social activity, a function that is too obscurely present in *habitus'* circular reference to the "logic of practice." Calhoun sees this property of coordination as emanating from traditions' capacity to change and adjust to various aspects of social reality, in order to ensure the success of the "practical projects" that the tradition inscribes in the *habitus* of its practitioners (Calhoun 1993: 78). We see here that the notion of tradition modifies, completes, and absorbs the concept of *habitus*. The link between the problem of coordinating action and the motivational prism of the agent should be warranted by what Asad sees as the engine of tradition's capacity to adapt and change, namely its ongoing "search for coherence." This cannot be provided only by reference to internal debates about the nature of the goods to pursue and their ordering, but vitally depends on the need to make the pursuit viable in each agent's social "environment" (cf. Thévenot 2001), in various "fields" of social action.

In this sense, coherence is not what characterizes a particular type of discourse and action (that would be defined as "teleological" according to Habermas's typology), but is the necessary, though often latent and elusive reference of individual action to a wider collective framework of justification that is transported by the ongoing discourse of tradition. However, we only stop halfway on the route to clearing up the notion of tradition's search for coherence if we do not tackle the relation between the creative and the imitative dimensions of action, and between the imaginative and the rational aspects of the discursive tradition.

As maintained by Spinoza, prophetic imagination and discourse were based on the capacity to upgrade *imaginatio* ("imagination") and *experientia vaga* ("vague experience") into an ability to build universals that are morphologically homologues with those of "common sense." This is a tricky notion to be revisited (see chapter 5), since it is within modernity that it was reestablished and gained currency. Vico gave much importance to the concept, but suffice to say that he saw common sense as merging the cognitive and the practical dimensions of action, the know-that and the know-how. Rooted in mythical imagination, common sense allows to "think particulars in universal form" (Preus 1989: 83–85). Therefore a further element pinpointing the search for coherence of traditions—alongside the internal debates and contentions through argument, the adaptation of the arguments to social reality, and of registers of justification to the "environment"—is in the daily work of human actors to base the abstraction and universalization of discursive formulas of exhortation on the imaginative inputs of common sense. For Vico, the paradigmatic example of the human fear of thunder as the origin of both religion and civilization serves exactly this need: to show the mechanism of crystallization of shared representations of divinities, followed by the summoning of practically relevant meaning via divination, which he considered the first institution of human society:

> As everyone runs to shelter from the thunder, all in a state of fear, they all do in fact come to act in the same way in the same circumstances. What the "inner mechanisms" are that bring this about, is not of Vico's concern here. His concern is with the "outer," practical, social conditions conducive to such a possibility. And here, it is the fear induced activity shared in common which provides the first fixed reference point which people can "find again" within themselves and know that for all practical purposes, the others around them "feel the same." (Shotter 1996: 6)

Every tradition bases the search for coherence on a refinement and a rhetorically conscious steering of this basic mechanism. Therefore, it is possible to say that the prophetic exhortative discourse is a medium capable of enhancing certain features of the properties of language consisting in gathering dialogically those experiences and images that are first formed and receive crystallization through poetic imagination (cf. also K. Burke 1961). The prophetic discourse strives toward matching the symbolism of the commoners—that is an inextricable part of ordinary practice—with the universalizing virtues, values, and goods rhetorically constructed through the axial breakthrough by its agents. This rupture was nourished by the realization that pre-axial cosmotheistic languages and institutions of divination do not preserve the community from disintegration. However, this work is mostly destined to reproduce a mismatch between imagination and discourse due to the "metastatic" quality of prophetic speech (see chapter 1), so that the tension—and the corresponding search for coherence—is perpetuated.

This view of prophetic discourse facing ordinary practice and its underlying symbolic-communicative web is a good antidote against any subjectivist shortcut that sees a pattern of human agency confined to the "inner space" of the "mind," a view that has deeply penetrated social science, and not least the sociology of religion (see chapter 1), thus accommodating or even nurturing methodological individualism in various shapes. As maintained by Charles Taylor, "what this kind of consciousness leaves out are: the body and the other. Both have to be brought back in if we are to grasp the kind of background understanding which Wittgenstein seems to be adverting to" (Taylor 1999: 33).

This insight shows the need to review the notion of coordination of social action, for which the "sharpened sense of the game" purported by the notion of *habitus* is not enough, especially since it is confined to a model-like, one-dimensional, routinized aspect of social life. Most important, as further observed by Charles Taylor, "integration into a common rhythm . . . can also come into being outside the situation of face-to-face encounter. In a different form it can also constitute . . . a political or religious movement whose members may be widely scattered but are animated by a sense of common purpose" (ibid.: 36). Prophetic discourse can then be regarded as the matrix of successive waves of socioreligious movements that do not simply provide a collective identity, but also the necessary coordination among its members in the task to match the "common sense" of ordinary practices with the values, virtues, and goods promoted by a discursive tradition.

What, however, Taylor seems to share with Habermas—all their differences notwithstanding—is a shortcut from the I to the We facilitated by viewing communicative action as leading straight up to collective movements[5] and a heavy investment into a thick view of language as the basically autonomous—and, as Habermas remarked, "half-transcendent"—medium of mutual understanding connecting to social practice and opening up to a public sphere (ibid.: 37). This option results in making an immanent *logos* out of language. More plausible is, instead, Taylor's reflection on the degree of uncertainty surrounding all of what is involved in apprehending and implementing a rule (in a Wittgensteinian sense), a situation that requires finely tuned judgments.

Taylor sees in this predicament the roots of *phronesis*. "There is, as it were, a crucial 'phronetic gap' between the formula and its enactment, and this too is neglected by explanations which give primacy to the rule-as-represented" (ibid.: 41). Therefore, a major limitation of the notion of *habitus* as embodied understanding and transposable disposition is a lacking of, or only a superficial attention to, *phronesis* as a complex and never stable achievement, one necessarily produced, administered, and adapted by traditions. Bourdieu admits that the institution is, along with *habitus*, a mode of objectification of past history, and that norms are incorporated in institutions more than rules *tout court* (ibid.: 43). However, Bourdieu failed to see the complexity of the relationship between *phronesis* and institution, exactly because he regarded *phronesis* as nothing more than the expression of an *orthe doxa*, a correct rule. He stopped halfway in grasping the telic-phronetic character of action when he affirmed that "the agent does what he or she 'has to do' without posing it explicitly as a goal, below the level of calculation and even consciousness, beneath discourse and representation" (Bourdieu and Wacquant 1992: 128).

Set against this discussion about how to pinpoint a sociological notion of tradition, the most important achievement of the axial breakthrough might be reconceived less as the invention of transcendence—as a shift in subjective and semantic sensibility—than as the creation of integrated— albeit tense—practical, discursive, and institutional mechanisms to ensure coordination of action and coherence between discourse and practice. The deployment of *ratio*, that is, of argument in Aristotelian or other forms—and the development of "fundaments" for philosophical, theological, and jurisprudential discourse—is therefore the highest achievement of the axial breakthrough. It is the link between the search for coherence inherent in practice and the need for a discursive and institutional coordination that cannot be warranted by practice on its own, within the circular logic of *habitus* (cf. Margolis 1999: 74), but requires a sustainable concept of tradition.

Bourdieu tried to overcome this deficit of the theory of *habitus* by invoking the notion of "codification of culture in complex societies" (Calhoun 1993: 79), so losing sight of the fact that there are other social worlds located between the two extremes, on which he worked, of tribal Kabylia and republican French society. But he also reproduced a too dichotomic view of the opposition between the logics of "official cultures" and the forms of practical knowledge, and, in parallel, reduced theoretical knowledge to a specific social field, with its own *habitus*, interests, and so on. It is true that in his more nuanced dealing with the religious field (Bourdieu 1971) he acknowledged different stages and levels of codification, but he related them too rigidly—coherently with his more general theory of fields, *habitus*, and interest—to the search for dominance by the religious personnel over their field.

Traditions are not restricted to the canonization of dogmas and rituals, to the institutions sanctioning the domination of written and codified forms, and therefore to the textual "inscription" of cosmologies dictating interpretative rules. Not only oral and more fluid forms were never completely suppressed, but in the rearrangement of continuity and discontinuity of communicative forms, pre-axial potentialities never disappeared within axial civilizations. They were partly incorporated, partly suppressed, and largely lived on as a permanent challenge internal to axial civilizations, as a token of the perpetual instability of traditional formulas of regulation and coordination of practice.

On the other hand, more than through the suppression of pre-axial forms of knowledge and practice, orthodoxies emerged via the establishment of a hierarchy between different such forms. The establishment of orthodoxies should be seen as the product of a laborious and complex balancing between such different layers, as a passage from attitudes of indifference vis-à-vis pre-axial cultures, toward an activist discursive and institutional hierarchization and selective suppression vis-à-vis these cultures (Calhoun 1993: 80). This kind of approach was favored by the inter-civilizational exchange and competition that characterized all major waves of axial transformations. What is specifically "axial" in the process is the structuring of a specialized metalanguage for hierarchizing and balancing different forms, an achievement that set the stage for an ongoing contestation over the correct interpretations. The open contestation is then only possible through the use of the same metalanguage. Thus, the development of traditions became tied to building up the encyclopedia for providing the required metalanguages.

Sharing a *telos* is therefore not a formula for communitarian homogeneity, but the engine of the search for coherence within the conflicted reproduction of the encyclopedia, in the ongoing redefinition of worldly and transcendent goods and their ordering (cf. MacIntyre 1988: 349–69). Conflict is largely managed, and even generated, from within the search for coherence.

> A tradition is an argument extended through time in which certain fundamental agreements are defined and redefined in terms of two kinds of conflict: those with critics and enemies external to the tradition who reject all or at least key parts of those fundamental agreements, and those internal, interpretative debates through which the meaning and rationale of the fundamental agreements come to be expressed and by whose progress a tradition is constituted. (ibid.: 12)

The building of the dispositions of the subject which occurs via exhortation, instruction, and education, corresponds to specific interpretations of the ordering of goods that can be only attained through intersubjective engagement and understanding. Personal and collective identities are therefore important, but only as secondary crystallizations within processes of constructions of modes of engagement shaping *ego*, *alter*, and the mediating symbolic structures ordering the goods of excellence to achieve. The ensuing concept of the person, which is central to all traditions of the Euro-Mediterranean civilizational area including Islam (cf. Mauss 1985 [1938]; Waardenburg 1989; Nashi 2004), can only be understood with regard to a *telos* that is concretely related to those repertoires facilitating a pursuit of hierarchically ordered goods through practice. The *telos* warrants the coherence of the tradition's discourse through generational changes and the transformation of sociopolitical circumstances. It is the sharing of a *telos* that opens up spaces for both dialogic engagements and interpretative contentions. The search for coherence is a much more complex and dynamic force than the integrity imperatives—or even holistic drives— adumbrated in Giddens's definition of tradition quoted earlier. Traditions thrive, collapse, or implode on the basis of their capacity or incapacity of warranting the sharing and contestation of *telos* through argument, contention, and conflict.

Via theological, philosophical, and legal discourses, by techniques of narration and abstractions, universalizing values are sifted out of the imaginative universals carried over poetically by common sense (see chapter 5). Traditions' arbiters have to maintain a balance between the contingency faced by common sense driven everyday practice and the universality of the instructing, directive, and exhortative discourse they produce. Habermas recurrently denounces what he sees as the inexorable limits of this balancing act of traditions for hiding arbitrary authority behind any reason claimed by the traditions themselves. Therefore he wants to extract a normative universality from beneath the crust of singular traditions and to show that it is this operationalizable universality that provides intersubjective understanding, not the contingent and arbitrary manifestation of imaginative universals in the form of tradition.

The recipe he recommends in order to "solve" and "fluidize" traditions and retrieve the operational universality inherent in lifeworlds consists in constructing a procedural rationality, optimally incorporated in "discourse ethics." He does not take seriously enough the risk that by solving traditions into discourse ethics, the lifeworlds themselves might dissolve. At the very least, since the operational universality can only be supported—communicatively even before than ethically—by some linguistic-traditional form, the retrieving of operational universality, if it has to be successful over time, can only be the product of artificial indoctrination or of a massive cumulative process of internalization of norms of the kind described by Elias (1976 [1939]) as a civilizing process reshaping the personality and agency of the social actor.[6]

To conclude, let us revisit one of Habermas's main point of theoretical crystallization:

> The medium of the language and the *telos* of reaching understanding intrinsic to it reciprocally constitute one another. The relation between these is not one of means and ends. As a consequence, "aims" which an actor pursues in language and can only realize together with Alter cannot be described as if they resembled conditions which we can bring about by intervening casually in the world. (Habermas 1991 [1986]: 241)

Pragmatism's reply, following John Dewey, would be that while social action cannot be conceived as the pursuit of ends established a priori, and that therefore ends are "found in the world," in concrete practical situations, a moment of conscious intentionality can only be admitted "when the imprecise directedness with which customary actions are performed proves insufficient to overcome the resistance encountered in a particular situation" ( Joas 1991 [1986]: 101–2). This claim is acceptable in order to recognize the directedness of action, which is imprecise exactly because it is—inevitably, since one does not need any theoretical insight in order to act—embedded in a particular situation. However, what is perplexing is the frequent pragmatist obscuration of the theoretical relevance of the nexus between action and the reflexive consciousness (mediated by arguments and reasoning) that by necessity not only follows, but precedes action. For the "follow-up" reflection can only take place by retrieving stored knowledge and applying it, phronetically, to a future given situation.

In sum, pragmatism's critique of both Habermas and Bourdieu proves useful for elaborating on a sociological notion of tradition which escapes the dilemmas encountered by the theory of communicative action in accounting for the rise, transformation, and variability of techniques of intersubjective understanding, connectivity, and coordination. In fact, Habermas's response stimulated by Joas's critique is quite acceptable— if we discount the illustrated reservations toward the notion of "lifeworld," mentioned earlier, and those toward "consensus." This issue will be tackled again in chapter 6. And, to further dynamize the picture, in search of a sustainable notion of tradition, the following statement is also of some interest:

> A directional dynamics is built into the communicatively structured lifeworld in the form of a polarity between a state of pre-established pre-understanding and a consensus to be achieved: in the course of time, the reproductive achievements switch from one pole to the other (Habermas 1991 [1986]: 224) . . . The *manner* in which the transition is effected is regulated by the logic of argumentation; *whether* and *when* we are supposed to accomplish it depends on the faculty of judgment inherent in communicative action itself. (ibid.: 226)

While this conclusion is largely acceptable, to force discursive traditions into notions of either self-realization or collective identity (variably a concern of both Taylor and Habermas) would be misleading. The basis of such traditions is the problematic character of the *ego-alter* relationship in the construction of social and communicative spaces, and it would be an anachronism to project back into this relationship a dimension of "collective identity," modeled on citizenship within the nation-state as a pattern of collective or "republican" upgrading of the interactions taking place within "civil society" (see chapter 6). The *ego-alter* relationship is regulated by discursive traditions through a triangling toward a God of justice effected via prophetic discourse. For example, within Islamic traditions, the living, vital core is represented less by scripture (the Qur'an) and more by what the prophet Muhammad did and said to other Muslims on specific occasions (see chapter 4). We have here the construction of a model of social relationship and trust between *ego* and *alter* that is mediated by the common faith and fellowship in God (the triad *ego-alter*-God), but also, and more immediately, by the exemplary life conduct of a prophet. It is the transcendent otherhood that helps the human self connect to his terrestrial otherhood through a common fellowship in God mediated by authoritative examples and related narratives. We see that within Abrahamic, faith-based traditions the Aristotelian ethics "is complicated and added to, but not essentially altered" (MacIntyre 1984 [1981]: 53).

Therefore, as the operational engine of discursive traditions, the search for coherence should not be equated to a homogeneity of discourses and their contents among the practitioners of the tradition, or even to conformism of rules of conduct. It is allowed within discursive traditions that different speakers and interpreters ensure coherence in widely divergent ways. However, whenever contradictions are spotted in the operations of the discourse, these will have to be amended and coherence restored. This imperative places a bonus on those arguments that are capable of restoring the coherence: if necessary, through a reform or even through major ruptures within the continuity of a tradition. Therefore a knowledge of the methods of arguing and reasoning is demanded from the practitioners of discursive traditions, as much if not more than the dealing with the scriptural sources.

In the process of inscription of telic-phronetic reason into practice and discourse, the hegemonic power of the arbiters of correctness and warrantors of coherence should not be overestimated. Calhoun offers us a synthetic statement that escapes the pitfalls of the views of Bourdieu, Habermas, Taylor, and the pragmatists:

> Most tradition is not passed down in situations—for example, ritual performances or schools—in which the passing down is itself the main manifest project. On the contrary, most passing on and subsequent affirmations of culture take place in the course of interested actions in which people pursue a variety of ends, both conscious and unconscious. (Calhoun 1993: 78)

The specific type of reason inherent in the job of warranting coherence does not prevent the multilogical character of social practice of members of the community. Specific forms of reason and corresponding discourses require, to be practiced, repertoires of intersubjective understanding among the practitioners. Linguistic competencies are necessary but not sufficient since a tradition cannot be reduced to a hermeneutically articulated language. Moreover, it is important to lay stress on the existence of a plurality of conceptions of *phronesis* even within the same tradition (MacIntyre 1984 [1981]: 180–81). As *telos* is not singular, so is, even less, *phronesis*.

# CHAPTER 3

# THE PUBLIC REASON OF THE COMMONER

## From *Res Publica* to *Respublica Christiana*: An Axial Renaissance?

One of the main nodes of Axial Age theory concerns its dealing with the aftermath of the "primary" axial breakthrough around the middle of the first millennium BCE. This is no minor issue, since it affects the historical development, institutionalization, and transformation of axial civilizations. It is the stage of their inscription into conceptions of history and models of society or "commonwealth." It is also the process of "canonization" and "traditionalization," of institutionalizing repertoires of intersubjective understanding and connectivity, forms of reasoning and inquiries into the goods, and, not least, the patterns of reflexivity supporting the process.

Momentous new foundations like the rise of Christianity and the emergence of Islam can then be considered as resystematizations of axial elements across civilizational boundaries, facilitating the creation of more solid orthodoxies based on more compact, often more radical visions (cf. Arnason 2005). One could see this development as a plot where, after the initial breakthroughs and the grounding of institutions administered by clerics deputed to "speak the truth," it is precisely the failure to speak a definitive truth, its continual procrastination, which prepares the ground for the appearance of a new type of prophetic figures, "final prophets." The plot deploys as the final unfolding of the discursive metastasis highlighted by Voegelin (see chapter 1), which finds a new healing or at least more stable institutional cures on new foundations. The new prophetic voices and their disciples, who became the founders of new religious traditions—like Jesus, Mani, and Muhammad—made use of a discursive approach that linked the parabolic form of prophecy to more continuous and effective mechanisms of inculcation and dissemination of the message (cf. W. C. Smith

1962). These transformations made preaching particularly important as a discursive genre.

This perfecting of the effectiveness of the exhortative instruments of the discursive tradition went along with major reformulations of the attending forms of reasoning and of justifying the supreme good. Within this discourse, a more mundane notion of the "common good" gradually emerged, occupying a central stage within the hierarchy of goods of excellence. At the same time, a clearer view of the faithful as the "commoner" took shape. By the seventh century CE, Christianity found a valid emulator and a powerful challenger in Islam (see chapter 4). The centrality of preaching is a strong element of commonality between Christianity and Islam in spite of all institutional and dogmatic differences, which also reside in the different status of "scripture" as *logos* and truth speech, within the discursive economy of the tradition.

This chapter and the next do not aim to engage in a conventional comparison of Christianity (in particular, the Catholic tradition) and Islam (in particular, the Sunni tradition) as religious-civilizational monoliths. My approach consists in examining, within an integrated genealogical perspective, key instances of largely successful, discursively based, strongly proselytizing, and universalistically oriented religious traditions. The method consists in looking at some crucial developments in the formulation of the sophisticated repertoires of intersubjective engagement, understanding, and connectivity deployed within these two traditions. I trace a trajectory through which the empowerment of the "commoners"—or the making itself of the subjective and agential category of the commoner—facilitated revisions and transformations of the discursive traditions via a crystallization of notions of common good and public reasoning. These concepts will later provide the state-of-the-art theoretical repertoire to those modern thinkers who will reconstruct comparable notions across the traumatic transformations of modernity (see chapters 5 and 6).

Latin Christendom's trajectory is examined in particular with a view to the empowering of the commoner as the agent of public reason. Sunni Islam's developments are later explored by looking at the largely horizontal, softly hierarchical, and institutionally scalable modalities of tradition-making supported by a method for ascertaining and adjudicating the good in a given social situation, so as to yoke practical rationality to public reasoning. This is not a comparison, in that I highlight two different dimensions of the construction of public reason within discursive traditions.

One main character of Christianity and Islam and of specific movements and groupings within them is an orientation to proselytizing that goes beyond the community paradigms of the first axial breakthrough, associated with the Jewish and the Greek models. For Christianity and Islam it is not sufficient to accomplish canonically prescribed duties or to actively participate in collective life and ritual in order to attain salvation. It is imperative to win over other fellows to the faith and to a virtuous life conduct, and to convert them to the "straight path" (a key Qur'anic expression) if they are still mired in "pagan" superstitions, that is, if they are not yet committed to a type of social bond based on a fellowship in faith and on the idea of a God-willed connective justice. This proselytizing élan is based on the double postulate of equal dignity and accountability of all individual souls before God and relies on the formation of a vanguard of virtue within the community of believers.

Though the latter is a sectarian leitmotiv often associated with heterodox movements, Catholicism and Sunni Islam were equally able to fold it into orthodoxy. Of course, the principle of equal dignity does not translate into equal status, for differences determined by gender, tribal affiliation, kinship, patronage, and not least slavery and other forms of serfdom endured, albeit modified and usually tempered by the common faith and a sense of shared humanity. The combinations of the legal dimension of such relationships with the idea of brotherhood between *ego* and *alter* created configurations of social relationships whose degree of complexity—sometimes reflected by the difficulties in studying them through the scriptural, exegetic, and apologetic sources—usually exceeds those found in pre- or proto-axial contexts.

I focus on the "transpersonal" operational dimension of tradition-making, consisting in installing and maintaining a relationship between *ego* and *alter* governed by the "connective justice" warranted by a third instance, represented by God and, usually, his challenger, Satan (see chapters 1 and 2). The action performed in order to win over somebody to the true faith is an act of exhortation. This act is not part of an interpersonal type of relationship based on ties of family or clan; it cannot also be reduced to the sole working of the personal charisma of a particular religious personality over a discrete—however large—number of others. This type of action can only exist thanks to a third element that is found in the symbolic-communicative mediation of transcendence, carried by the legitimate heirs of prophetic lineages. Furthermore, the authority of, and faith in God, the angels, and the prophets—the kernel of dogmas both in Christianity and Islam—has to be supported by commentaries to the "scriptures" which ground this authority and so become crucial to tradition-making, or traditionalization. This key activity of the axial arbiters of correctness and, among them, more particularly of the virtuosi of the word, splits in genres ranging from the strictly theological to the more specifically juridical fields. These genres reflect the authority of the clerics in ways that have been clearly recognized by Axial Age theory (see chapter 1).

The institutionalization of tradition proceeds in parallel to the redefinition of the tension between rulers and administrators of salvation. This long process of conflicted institutionalization depended on existing power structures within the Roman Empire, whose heritage was of crucial importance for the various trajectories of traditionalization of Christianity, both in the West and in the East. As stressed by Johann P. Arnason (2003a: 32–33), drawing from recent research on the transformation of the Roman world one can maintain that the empire did not collapse, but was divided up into a Roman Catholic, a Greek Orthodox, and an Arab Islamic legacy (cf. Fowden 1993), whereas for the schismatic Shi'a component of Islam the heritage of the other "world's eye," the Persian Empire (ibid.: 12–36) was of utmost importance. The sociopolitical predicament and the cultural mosaic of the Roman Empire had a formative influence on the new faith represented by Christianity, when both the empire and the religion were at a critical stage of expansion, first on a collision course, then in institutional symbiosis.

In its early repositioning and systematization work, Christianity presents itself not only as the true interpretation of the revelation on the Mount Sinai, but also as the best philosophical school of the empire. In this operation, early Christian leaders spoke the language of mainstream philosophy and Greco-Roman cultures, while defining the limits of those same cultures, which Christianity was making obsolete through its higher capacity to provide orientation in daily life to an expanding range of social groups, including slaves. In discursive terms, the key feature of Christianity was the capacity to transcend a confinement to a particular "community" or cultural language and to shape life forms and discursive formulas for a call to conversion to a new life suitable to a translation into several languages (cf. Stroumsa 2005).

The Greek-Athenian experience had made clear, both in philosophical terms and through the vicissitudes of its political life—dramatically centered on the quasi-martyrdom of Socrates—the nature of the problem of order and transcendence (see chapter 1). The way out of the Greek dilemmas and the overcoming of the limited translatability of the Aristotelian solutions was facilitated by a radical reorientation of the Abrahamic heritage which capitalized on the arguments produced in the earlier pursuit of those limited solutions. The way was open for a reformulation of the Aristotelian heritage. As suggested by MacIntyre:

> Insofar as ... argumentative conflicts concern the nature of justice, that of practical reasoning, and their mutual relationship, the relevant histories cannot be made intelligible without a recognition of the degree to which they are an extension and a continuation of a history of conflict found in the Athenian social and cultural order during the fifth and fourth centuries B.C. ... even the understanding of divine law has in certain important episodes been partially but crucially determined by modes of argument and interpretation stemming from Athenian debates. (MacIntyre 1988: 13)

These debates set the terms for subsequent contentions within traditions and between antagonistic traditions, which are relevant even today. What emerges out of these developments is that the Aristotelian solutions transported into these contentions a conundrum of potentials and limits for reformulating repertoires of intersubjective engagement, understanding, and connectivity articulating formulas linking the *ego*'s agency and reflexivity to the welfare of a wider community.

Aristotelian public reasoning was limited to the *polis* with its restrictive and exclusive criteria of citizenship. Conscious of these limits, Socrates was the first to suggest that the pursuit of the higher goods required a universalizing notion of humanity or human community (*koinonìa*), and the concomitant guarantee by some divine form of law and justice. Similarly, but more effective in political terms, the crossing of the boundaries of a given political community was part of the history of the crisis and redefinition of public reason within the Roman Republic, and during the transition to empire.

While the Stoics had led the way to the first clear formulation of a membership within humanity to be conceived in universal terms, Cicero began to disassociate *res publica* from the political community and gestured toward a larger common and public good whose borders were no longer "political" in the Greek sense. This type of supreme good, though not erasing the juridically manageable terms of public good intended as "utility"—which in fact inspired the edicts of the imperial age—was increasingly formulated via a transcendent notion of justice encompassing a larger and potentially universal human community. It is in this context that Cicero developed the idea of *caritas* to make viable the still too abstract view of justice of the Stoics. *Caritas* so became a crucial virtue for acquiring membership in the human community. It is important to bear in mind that this notion was developed from within the Roman juridico-political-philosophical discourse prior to the emergence of Christianity. The care of the individual *ego* outside of a sustained engagement with *alter* appears now insufficient for perfecting the soul. Pursuing *caritas* gradually appears as the only alley to shape and govern the transpersonal social bond and the related repertoires of intersubjective understanding and connectivity (MacIntyre 1988: 148).

In this type of discourse the identity of the self-in-community is still enveloped in a system of coordinated expectations and regulated reciprocities, even if the strictly legal regulations are no longer considered self-legitimizing. The conception is still basically juridical. Its main product, the *ius gentium*, is still a specific development of the Roman law tradition. The real breakthrough across the borders of a republic and the overcoming of a public reason still conceived in juridical-political terms could not come either from Aristotelian philosophy or from Roman law. What was required was a relocation of the Abrahamic model of the axial breakthrough and more specifically a reshaping of the matrix of divine law that according to Biblical narratives God had given to Moses on Mount Sinai (ibid.: 149).

The model of the Decalogue (the Ten Commandments) enjoins certain types of action and forbids others irrespective of circumstance. "To live according to them will be to act for one's own good at all times" (ibid.: 150). The Deuteronomic narrative was universalized into the Christian *ecclesia* ("church") through Paul, who in his letter to the Romans asserted that all human beings know God and his law. This key statement posited a natural basis for divine law and the adherence of the Ten Commandments to this natural law (ibid.: 152; see also Agamben 2000).

It was finally Augustine who merged the discourse of Cicero and Paul and transcended the mundane *polis/civitas terrena* into the institution of a *civitas Dei*, "that divinely ordained form of community into which every human being is summoned to find his or her due place and within which every human being may finally receive, not his or her desert, but something far better" (MacIntyre 1988: 153). Discussing Cicero's *De Re publica*, Augustine fully agreed that a commonwealth should be based on the citizens' agreement on a standard of justice, but he clearly stated that there had never been such a justice in pagan Rome where individual pride prevailed in motivating people to action. Therefore, he concluded, there never was a true republic. The bases were laid to see the only true commonwealth in an ideal of *respublica christiana*. This ideal body was nonpolitical, in the Greco-Roman sense, yet strongly political in a potentially new, more sophisticated and flexible sense, which was still largely to be elucidated.

The subsequent Christian dealing with the legal and political institutions of Roman origin was guided by the assumption that those same institutions were not purely civic in nature, but reflected the function and, to that extent, the embryonic "truth" of the *falsi Dei*, the false gods of the pagans, as the symbols of the sanctity of social relations. These gods—which were first those of the patrician *gentes* and then the gods of the democratic republic—were later swept off by a monotheistic and, above all, transcendent God. This was the "leap of faith" that allowed for the rise of the idea of a republic of mankind.

In this way Christianity in general—and Latin European Christianity in particular, under the influence of Augustine—altered an assumption widely shared in basically the entire Euro-Mediterranean civilizational area till Late Antiquity, and also reflected by Roman civilization: namely that religion was inherently related to the well-being of the political community. The resulting deep ambivalence toward human society and political government that Latin Christendom will share with Sunni Islamdom, in spite of all differences, has to be considered as a further twist of an axial potentiality of complexification of the relationship between religion and politics which the lineage of Biblical prophets had not been able to solidly inscribe into Jewish traditions. In analogy with how Sunni Islam (after the golden era of the prophet Muhammad and his companions and in spite of the astonishing military conquests) developed a notion of autonomy of Islamic traditions from the whims of even those rulers whose Islamic credentials were not in question (see chapter 4), Western Christianity never confused the Christianized Roman Empire with the ideal of the City of God (cf. Stroumsa 2005). The same will apply, with some restrictions, to the medieval Sacred Roman Empire.

The impact of Augustinian theory on the reconstruction of public reason within the medieval *respublica christiana* was ambivalent yet seminal. From that perspective, medieval political theory cannot be considered as inherently problematic—since peculiarly "medieval," and therefore "transitional"—as if we anachronistically adopt post-Enlightenment normative notions of the separation between "politics" and "religion." These standards derive from the theoretical acceptance of the monopolistic claims to force by the modern nation-state and the concomitant submission of Churches to a state-regulated religious field. Therefore they are not suitable to assess genealogically how medieval Christianity developed a distinctive model of "community-creating power" based on a tense combination between the notion of *res publica* and the Christian tenet that salvation is not to be located in the political community (Szakolczai 2001a: 357).

Pope Gelasius I (492–96) formulated a system of checks and balances between spiritual and temporal powers gravitating around the idea that any office or power, including secular government, was a service to the *telos* of Christianity. The main unintended consequence of Gelasius's theory became evident in the sharp institutional dualism which crystallized between the pope and the emperor as authorities competing on the same, double terrain, determined by the authority that performs the highest service for the distinct but twin goals. However, this competition was incongruent with the recognized gap between the mainly temporal legitimacy of the emperor and the predominantly spiritual legitimacy of the pope. This gulf prefigured severe limits to all subsequent attempts to institutionalize the conception of *respublica christiana*, and also ignited the contention over how to conceive and implement such an institutionalization.

While the institutional contradictions eroded, in the long run, the viability of the specific Gelasian formula, the proper terrain of implementation of the *respublica christiana* was, nevertheless, not primarily located on the institutional terrain. We have here to do with a salvational project inspiring modes of individual and community life for the Christians, a project initially not affected by the ambition to build a compact theocratic edifice. Yet with Pope Gregory VII (1025–1085) the Church pushed for a compact institutional solution to the dualism of powers. It is important to analyze this case in order to understand better the potentials and the limitations of the vision of the *respublica christiana*. After the launching of the project by Gregory VII, the balancing of institutional power and of the practiced virtues in the *respublica christiana* was at the center of a continual conflict between shifting orthodoxies and ever new, potentially heterodox socioreligious movements.

At the center of Gregory's visions there was the *ecclesia* as teacher of the virtues, whose implementation was to be facilitated by unequivocal institutional arrangements upholding the institutional primacy of the pope (Voegelin 1997b: 87–91). It is symptomatic, however, that even Gregory's view of the pope as God's viceroy of a *civitas* encompassing the entire universe was the result of a movement of renewal from within the Church (also called the "papal revolution") which was tensely but positively linked to the pressure exercised from below by popular movements. The project of Church renewal reasserted the autonomy of distinctively ecclesiastical organizational forms against the erosion of celibacy, the spread of simony, and the chase for mundane goods and privileges. In other words, the more institutional part of the larger movement of renewal was also set against a conception of power and greed unbridled by the papal authority, which was considered ultimately grounded on God's sovereignty.

## Yoking Practical Rationality to Justice

Justice (*iustitia*) is central in this scheme, as manifesting the equality of all human beings within a universal, divinely ordained community. Gregory's view entailed a passage to a full-fledged *societas christiana*, a more structured and secular notion than the ideal of the *respublica christiana* imbued with the transcendence of the *civitas Dei*. In Gregory's vision, proclaiming divine justice was not enough, if not translated into a notion of law (*ius*) inherited from the Roman legal tradition. This idea of law consisted in sanctionable rules for the regulation of the conduct of the members of the human society under God's sovereignty. The Gregorian project triggered a codification process of the law, whose institutional underpinning was the view of the pope as the guardian of the mundane order of justice, whose authority was seen as encompassing the control of secular rulers and even the right to depose them.

This project was not the mere result of theocratic ambitions, but the cusp of a larger movement of construction of a new synthesis between the universality of the law and the pragmatics of everyday existence under the umbrella of a *respublica christiana*. The revival of Roman law centered in Bologna during the twelfth and thirteenth centuries "was the most important single event in the process in which the new forces, individual and collective, generated an order of inner-worldly action as well as a method of inner-worldly legal reasoning" (Voegelin 1997b: 160).

In order to understand the synergy between the religious and legal revivals of the High Middle Ages we need to look back at some key stages of the crisis and transformation of the Roman law tradition since Late Antiquity. The medieval revival of Roman law in Western Europe was from its inception in a relation of tension with the Ciceronian conception of Roman law as a "higher" law. This classic notion was based on an idea that proved to be untenable after the collapse of the Western Roman Empire, namely on the claim that the *lex* of Rome coincided with the cosmic *nomos-logos* propagated by the Stoics. On the other hand, the Ciceronian conception had impoverished the power of the Stoic *nomos-logos*, because the assumption that the spiritual order was embodied in the intramundane order of the *res publica* suppressed the tension between this order and the hereafter and diluted the very impetus of the axial breakthrough (ibid.: 163).

Therefore, even in the sixth century CE, the Western monastic rule of Benedict of Norcia (ca. 480–547) continued to be viewed as the superior recollection of the Christian way of life (ibid.: 164) and as the source of inspiration for the new proliferation of religious orders through the passage to the late Middle Ages; the reconstruction of Roman law facilitated by new commentaries provided the tools for institutionalizing the link between practical rationality, ideas of the common good, and the emerging practice of public reasoning within the rising secular worlds of urban economies. Indeed the religious revival that picked up during the eleventh century and culminated in the thirteenth century was largely produced within those secular worlds directly interconnected to the reconstruction of Roman law. The combined religious and secular movements marked the constitution of a new type of commoner.

As mentioned previously, there was a remarkable response to this grass roots movement through the high politics of the Church. The *Deliberatio Papae*, a document issued by Pope Innocent III (c. 1161–1216) in the year 1200, tuned down the quasi-theocratic ambitions of Gregory VII, but at the same time systematized and rationalized digests and codes via procedural rules and casuistic argumentation and refutation. This document marks not only an important moment in the ongoing power game between pope and emperor but also testifies how the innerworldly logic of action had legitimately penetrated the discourse of the highest spiritual authority. Most importantly, the text reflects a primacy of procedure in a way that silences any recourse to charismatic inspiration. It confers a sense of procedural certainty to actions previously experienced as transcendentally determined. In other words, it reflects "a new mode of 'covering' the contingencies of action" (ibid.: 174–75).

It is important to appreciate the full extent to which this outcome was heir to the myth of Roman law as an absolute order to which the historical laws of the *civitates* were expected to conform, for being a common law for all men. This myth was—in spite of the Augustinian dichotomist view of the *civitas Dei* and the *civitas terrena*—kept alive in practice by the Church, not least because, as an institution, the Church perpetuated its existence under Roman law (ibid.: 167). Moreover, it was the Church's merit to use the evocative power of Roman law to bridge the gap between *res publica* and *imperium* on a theoretical and symbolic level.

This ideational performance attained in the High Middle Ages contrasted with the level of existing political regimes within the older Roman politics, discontinued by the rupture determined by the traumatic transition from republic to empire. The former encouraged the citizen's participation; the latter contained this participation while guaranteeing and even reinforcing the prevalence of public interest. "Public utility" (*utilitas publica*) had been often invoked in imperial edictal legislation, yet in a vertical decisionist way that had eroded the participatory promise of the notion of *res publica*. While the tension between the republican-participatory and the authoritarian-centralized components continued to animate the historical redeployment of the notion of publicness well into the modern era (cf. Weintraub 1997: 11–14; see also chapters 5 and 6), this tension was preempted in the High Middle Ages by the crystallization of a balanced tension between the *respublica christiana* as an ideal of common good finalized to salvation, and the *sacrum imperium* as a political-theological formula at the service of the *respublica christiana*.

What is particularly interesting here are not the innumerable shifts in institutional conceptions, disputes, and arrangements between the papacy, the emperor, the autonomous cities, and the early developments of what will become nation-states—along with the final demise of the theological and ideological core of the imperial idea. The main focus of interest concerns how the framework of *respublica christiana* oriented momentous systematizations of the link between the practical rationality of intersubjective repertoires of understanding and connectivity, the motivational prism for new models of agency in the secular worlds of the rising urban economies, and the consolidation of the idea of public reason as mediated by notions of justice incarnated in a reconstructed axial idea of transcendence. It is important to grasp the fundamental tensions of this political theology as a further development of the essential axial tensions and promises, without indulging in measuring the degree of success or failure of the one or the other contingent institutional arrangement, which is far beyond the scope of this analysis.

The achievements of Latin Christendom as a discursive tradition in this delicate task resulted from reappropriating *caritas* as a tool for taming the new tensions emerging within the secular worlds. A new discursive synthesis was elaborated which was enshrined in the work of Aquinas. *Caritas* provided the missing, crucial link between the repertoires of practical reason, on the one hand, and a justice-oriented public reason, which was directly related to the emergence of a new type of commoner in urban economies, on the other. The resulting theology presupposed a reconstructed anthropology, which in turn allowed for new forms of reconstructive politics—mainly micropolitics—based on more solid universalistic visions than allowed by prior axial transformations. The ideational root of this reconstruction was in the Augustinian tension between the *civitas terrena*, founded on misdirected human will motivated by pride, and the *civitas Dei* opened up by Christ through the gift of grace that directs human will toward the higher goods (MacIntyre 1988: 155). In the context of the Axial Renaissance of the High Middle Ages, the Augustinian idea becomes nonetheless a key stone in a much more complex mosaic. A sophisticated political theology incorporated a new conception of human agency based on a radical reshuffling of the axial tension between mundane and cosmological orders.[1] Augustine's simultaneous affirmation of divine grace as essential to the directing of the will toward the supreme good, and of the free character of the will's assenting to grace, was preserved as a starting point (ibid.: 157). In that early conception, however, practical, phronetic reason was bereft of *telos* and therefore powerless in determining right action. Reason lacked the key to produce right willing. The notion of the agent and the concomitant ideas of connectivity and communication were still defective. The crucial elaboration on axial formulas of correct action by the thinkers of the Axial Renaissance occurred through a direct intervention on the political theology and on the underlying anthropology, and found a key manifestation at the level of discourse. The voluntary character of agency needed to be married with a communicatively effective but also politically acceptable idea of speaking the truth.

Recognizing and speaking the truth had been one of the main formulas of the axial breakthrough. In the macroinstitutional arena of the Greek public square, the *agorà*, which had been exposed to an art of persuasion centered on the primacy of the pursuit of goods of effectiveness (see chapter 1), *parrhesia*, the virtue of truth-telling, had been reduced to saying whatever one wanted to, so configuring a principled openness of speech and critique. However, philosophical reflection had redeveloped *parrhesia* into an essential tool for the Socratic and Platonic attempts to resurrect the proper functioning of the *polis* in the crisis that began during Athens's apogee of power, in the Periclean age (see chapter 1). The virtue of *parrhesia* thus signified speaking truth to power, so becoming a key public virtue. In a further specification, it provided in the New Testament a formula of fidelity to prophetic discourse. Through this development, it acquired the status of a key tool of intersubjective understanding and connectivity, epitomizing the type of speech for teaching the virtues and exemplary life conduct (Szakolczai 2001a, 2003; see also Raaflaub 2005).

Reasserted in the patristic literature, the virtue of speaking the truth acquires an even clearer discursive connotation, though one distinct from, and antithetical to, the sophistic quest for goods of effectiveness. This trajectory helps us understand more deeply the discursive power incorporated in the processes of axial traditionalization. Under the aegis of Augustine's epistemology, speaking the truth becomes the hub of an ever more sophisticated set of practices and disciplines: from prayer, to reading scriptures, through the crucial genre of preaching, this program became central and was further articulated in the medieval monastic disciplines (Asad 1993: 155). *Parrhesia* was metamorphosed into preaching and confessing techniques, conforming to a vision of "the perfection of discourse as investigative and educative power" (ibid.: 121). The notion of a truth to be searched for, pursued, and almost extracted from the sinning, initiated a restructuring of the *ego-alter* relationship in the formation of increasingly complex communities. This process not only thrived inside of the monasteries, but also penetrated into civic life, which in the twelfth and thirteenth centuries was characterized by an accelerating social differentiation. In the process, the classic intersubjective genre of *parrhesia* was increasingly subsumed under *caritas*.

Axial Age theory has framed this process of redefining and institutionalizing *caritas* in the Christian discursive tradition as part of an epochal momentum of cultural crystallization in the history of humankind, characterized by major synthetic efforts. Björn Wittrock has recently proposed the term "ecumenic renaissance" to define this period of intellectual and institutional crystallizations across the Afro-Eurasian civilizations which occurred around and especially after the turn of the first millennium CE, roughly from the middle of the ninth century to the middle of the thirteenth century (Wittrock 2001). Johann P. Arnason has suggested classifying this era of transformations as the last axial breakthrough preparing the advent of modernity (Arnason 2005: 39). I have opted for the term "Axial Renaissance" to refer to this period, and especially to its last part, to which I give ample consideration in the rest of this chapter and in the following one. In chapter 4, I also suggest that the rise itself of Islam could be considered an early manifestation of the Axial Renaissance more than a late manifestation of the axial breakthrough.

While these transformations, like the original axial breakthrough, also encompassed civilizational regions other than the Euro-Mediterranean area, like China and India, in Europe they coincided with the advancing vernacularization of language and identity. They also resulted in the crystallization of what Marshall G. S. Hodgson (1974) called "Islamdom," a term indicating the formation of an ecumene comparable in form with Latin Christendom. Through subsequent waves not only of military conquest but also of religious conversion (that were in most cases temporally disassociated), Islamdom became a simultaneously Euro-Mediterranean and Asian ecumene, building a strong presence in Central Asia, China, and especially in India. However, its Abrahamic root and its selective and largely creative appropriation of the Greek philosophical heritage facilitated keeping major centers of intellectual elaboration, throughout the Axial Renaissance, on the Euro-Mediterranean side. One major element of commonality that developed between Latin Christendom and the still largely Arab-centered Islamdom during the Axial Renaissance was the challenge of mystically oriented movements drawing on the imagination and needs of the commoners (see chapter 4).

These movements were partly fought as heretic, but for the most part were successfully integrated into the orthodox mainstreams and have thus affected the institutional outlook of both Catholic and Sunni orthodoxies till our days. In Europe the rise of heterodox movements and the simultaneous emergence of nonoppositional, yet radical, new mendicant orders manifested the pressures, on ecclesiastical institutions, of the practical necessities and desires of renewal which spread among popular classes and the rising urban middle classes. A similar role was played within Islam by the emergence of Sufism and the struggles surrounding its co-optation into the crystallizing forms of orthodoxy (see chapter 4).[2]

The institutional implications of the Axial Renaissance in Europe can be summarized in the following way: by the time of Gregory VII, the institutionally fragile ideal of the *respublica christiana* had not been successfully articulated into a functioning and consensual mechanism. Now the main issue for the Church was, increasingly, to make sure that divine law was taken seriously, practiced, and lived out in the emerging secular societies outside the monastery walls. The discursive tradition of Latin Christendom had to fit into the increasingly differentiated social realities of towns' economies. The following question had to be rediscussed from its ground: what kind of education could promote a type of human agent able to translate monastic virtues into a secular social bond? As indicated by MacIntyre, these are

> the problems of a society in which the central and equitable administration of justice, universities, and other means of sustaining learning and culture and the kind of civility which peculiarly belongs to urban life are still in the process of being created ... somewhere between the particularistic claims of the intense local rural community which threatens to absorb everything into custom and local power and the universal claims of the Church. (MacIntyre 1984 [1981]: 170–71)

The ingredients for such new institutional formulas were already available: monastic discipline, a revived Roman law, a refurbished papal leadership, a notion of fiduciary relationships inscribed in the feudal world, and the new élan—not only commercial but also "spiritual"—of urban life entwined with the teaching circles formed in the universities. The main glue, however, was still missing. The classic *polis* was clearly not a viable model of sociopolitical integration of increasingly differentiated socioeconomic worlds, for the host of reasons examined earlier this chapter. More in general, the issue was not one of pure institutional engineering. The social bond between *ego* and *alter* had to be radically reconstructed, on the basis of the available inputs, for meeting the new challenges.

Knowing how to die a martyr was no longer a central need, while a capacity to relate to the ever more complex forms of daily life was what the Christian was expected to learn. The first sketch of the equation for solving the problem configured the practice of the four cardinal (and in this sense secular) virtues of justice, prudence, temperance, and courage as fitting into the theological virtues of faith, hope, and especially the pivotal *caritas*. While this integrated classification of the virtues was first established around 1300, the various terms of the equation were laid down much earlier. The key to solve the equation was to focus on the definition of the act of the will, of intentionality, as the kernel of agency. It increasingly appeared that "the true arena of morality is that of the will and of the will alone" (MacIntyre 1984 [1981]: 168).

This definition of the will as part of a wider arena of morality centered on the pursuit of the common good within a Christianized *res publica* could not be retrieved from any prior axial inheritance. Insufficient were the immediate antecedents to the Axial Renaissance, in particular from the "ecumenic age" of Late Antiquity with the texts from the New Testament and, further down the lines of tradition, Stoicism. The way out of the dilemma whose two corns were the Aristotelian virtues based on an exclusivist partnership in sharing a *telos* between virtuous men of a circumscribed community, and the inclusive universalism of Stoicism that neglected any concrete form of partnership, was found in a new emphasis on a type of practice that the Old and the New Testament had consecrated as more than virtuous. This practice was essential to the construction of the social bond itself and was therefore considered sacred: the practice of forgiving debts, intended in a general, not merely (though certainly also) material or financial sense.

Forgiveness requires a complexification of justice, and it is in the folds of this complexity that an agential surplus was enacted during the Axial Renaissance. While justice, pronounced from God on his throne, is administered by an authority representing the entire community, forgiveness requires the proactive agency and will of the offending party.

It bestows a strongly "transpersonal" dimension on the social bond. It represents a sort of synthesis between an impersonal justice and personal *pietas*. The corresponding virtue of forgiveness was subsumed under *caritas*—not a novelty itself, as we saw. Yet its specification, like in Aquinas's *Summa Theologiae*, reached unprecedented levels of sophistication in capturing the differentiation of the social worlds.

There is another dimension of the new synthesis achieved during the Axial Renaissance, which impresses on it a further degree of refinement toward both the Stoic view and the Biblical formulas. During the Axial Renaissance, Aristotle's *telos* was increasingly reconceived in a historical mode that incorporated the subsequent waves of Biblical narratives as sequential shells of a salvational history. The medieval visions situated the pursuit of the goods not just in sociologically identifiable contexts, but in specific institutional spaces and constraints that were themselves embedded in historical spaces. Medieval thinkers developed a strong conception of human life as inevitably historical, to the point that the reformulation itself of the virtues could not be understood other than as an essential equipment to survive evil and perform good in the drama of history (MacIntyre 1984 [1981]: 175–76).

Notwithstanding the nearly totalizing systems developed by thinkers like Aquinas and Dante Alighieri, an important, indeed creative feature of the reconstruction work of the age was the impossibility to fully close the circle of systematization of the religious and political orders, since the possibility to retrieve a full-fledged Stoic conception of a compact order based on an impersonal rationality was no longer feasible. Yet we should not interpret this lack of closure as a deficit. It could be assessed in the opposite way: in the late-medieval outlook on the fragility of the equipment of human agency and intentionality in performing good we can see an immunization, with some sociological insight, against any naive, mono-dimensional view of human agency like the one that will triumph in the subsequent, modern era in parts of northwestern Europe and some of its settlement colonies overseas (see chapter 6).

During the Axial Renaissance agency and intentionality were scripts of a narrative that rationalized and expanded the biblical terms of the I-Thou relationship (see chapter 1). The shortcut of theorizing about an unchanging human nature modeled on one particular representation of the social bond, as it will emerge, within modernity, with Grotius, Pufendorf, and Selden, was carefully avoided (see chapter 5). Therefore, the best spirits of the age provided—in literary, theological, and juridical terms, as well as in other genres of the emerging vernacular literatures—visions of the social bond incorporating a capacity to regulate the *ego-alter* relationship. These visions were rich with socioanthropological insights into the limits and potentials of elevating practical to public reasoning, local to universal issues. This capacity was matched by a notion of the law inherited from the Roman tradition and therefore largely immune from the totalistic and communitarian presumptions of the model of the *polis* (MacIntyre 1984 [1981]: 176–78).

Thomas Aquinas (1225–1274) lucidly situated his contribution to the Christian discursive tradition and his energetic theoretical underpinning of its hegemonic ambitions in a sphere of competition and contention with other traditions. In that sense, it was not a mere self-celebration of Latin Christendom's imperialistic ambitions, at the stage when the conflict with Islamdom—which after the fading crusader spirit that looked East, concentrated in the progressing *reconquista* in Spain westwards—was being ever more consciously framed in terms of intellectual battles. These struggles were conducted with theoretically comparable discursive and conceptual weapons, due to the fact that both Christian and Islamic traditions were nurtured by Abrahamic narratives and Greek philosophical legacies, though the syntheses achieved and in particular the methods of coping with those narratives and legacies were quite different (cf. Brague 2002 [1992]).

As summarized by Voegelin, Thomas maintained in his *Summa Contra Gentiles* (Aquinas 1975 [1259–1265]) written for the Dominican mission in Spain, that "with the Jews we can argue on the basis of the Old Testament, with the heretics on the basis of the New Testament, but with the Muslims we have to argue by appeal to the authority of the intellect" (Voegelin 1997b: 211). This intellect was conceived according to axial parameters and was nurtured by a complex anthropology viewed as the condition for a theological reconstruction. The bottom line of any intra-axial contention was therefore to be found on a terrain of definition of the best type of human action that can help reconstructing and attaining the highest goods and justify a strong nexus between individual agency and collective action.

Aquinas's anthropology operates with an the idea of the free—and mature—Christian subject, a complex creature quite neatly distinct from the simpler Aristotelian *zoòn politikòn* grown free and able to inhabit a natural community nourishing his (more than her) virtues. Unlike the Aristotelian approach, where the concept of individual freedom is one with the virtues, freedom is connected by Thomas to the idea of *multitudo*. Therefore, partnership is the result of free and creative cooperation. In order to allow for that, it has to be a partnership sustained by sharing in the love of God and the directionality of a human life of mutual help geared toward the attainment of eternal beatitude. Love of God is the warrant of the human bond of affection (ibid.: 219). Having reconstructed the *homo Christianus* in this way, Aquinas claims that he is indeed an *animal politicum*, but with the important qualification that the socioanthropological roots of politics are defined in new ways. As illustrated by Voegelin, the degree of innovation of Aquinas's view cannot be overestimated:

> Under the hands of Thomas the term *political* begins to assume its modern meaning; the Gelasian dichotomy of spiritual and temporal powers began to be replaced by the modern dichotomy between religion and politics. With Thomas, the political sphere, in the modern sense, was still completely oriented towards the spiritual, but the beginning of the momentous evolution that led, through the Lockean privatization of religion and the assignment of a public monopoly to politics, to the totalitarian integration of an intramundane spirituality into the public sphere of politics can be discerned. (ibid.: 220)

The paramount twist within Aquinas's anthropology occurs through its turning Aristotle's political friendship into a triangular partnership of faith between *ego* and *alter* mediated by their voluntary and trustful faith in God and facilitated by the apprehension of the highest good (*summum bonum*). This partnership can only arise through voluntary action, carried by a human will formed by love and intellectually reposing in the apprehension of the supreme good that is beatitude (Hollweck and Sandoz 1997: 36). In the *Summa Theologiae* (Aquinas 1981 [1265–1273]), after the specification of the end of human life, Aquinas devotes his main analytic effort to discerning the means by which to attain beatitude. It is sociologically interesting that Aquinas sees the "internal" principles of human action in "powers and habits," which he therefore neither denies nor confines to the diabolic passion of self-love (*amor sui*). On the other hand, the "external principle" giving directionality to man's action is and remains God, who instructs man via the law, in order to direct his actions toward beatitude (Voegelin 1997b: 223). As observed by Voegelin, here "law is defined as an ordinance of reason (*ratio*), for the common good, made by him who has the care for the community, and promulgated in it" (ibid.: 224).

Yet even the stress on beatitude as the supreme good is finalized to what Voegelin termed a "totalitarian integration into intramundane spirituality," so typical of the thirteenth century's climax of the Axial Renaissance within Latin Christendom. Aquinas framed the intentional dimension of action as expressing the agent's determination to do what is good for himself in the present, *hic et nunc*, as a means to the end that man adopts through a deliberation guided by the intellect (MacIntyre 1988: 189). He took the action that manifests this *electio* (a notion coming close to "choice," if not interpreted anachronistically, as in the modern liberal tradition) of the good as a genuine act of the will, which he calls *intentio*. This will is set against mere desire, and this is what grounds human action.

This concept revised Aristotle's weakly sociological view according to which action follows automatically from the agent's moral character. Neither *akrasìa* (a lack of force of the will), nor Aristotle's denunciation of scarce education as conducive to defective reason can explain, according to Aquinas, a defaulting action in the pursuit of the goods. He constructed the responsibility of the human agent as starting from a relatively early age through his/her incorporation in a tight web of ongoing interactions nurtured by communication, trust, and legitimate authority. This view encompassed a stronger universal model of the agent, in opposition both to the elitist and communitarian Aristotelian view (ibid.: 191) and to the Augustinian fragmented soul that can only be rescued by God's grace. While the path to the anthropology of liberal modernity will be paved by a revival of the Augustinian view as opposed to the Aristotelian one — starting with some thinkers and movements contemporary to Aquinas, including Aquinas's friend and colleague, the Franciscan theologian Bonaventura of Bagnoregio (cf. Milbank 1990: 14–17; Santoro 2003 [1999]: 83–86) — Aquinas had the courage and capacity to reject both views simultaneously, before recuperating crucial parts of them in order to forge a new synthesis adequate to the demands of his age.

An articulate anthropological vision underlies Aquinas's theory of the common good. The basic elements of the common good are self-preservation, the preservation of the species through procreation and education, the preservation of the rational nature of man warranted by his desire for the knowledge of God, and the inclination toward civilized life. Human participation in this common good does not depend on individual illumination, but on the singular will (*voluntas*) of the "Christian human being" (*homo christiano*) joining his/her brothers and sisters in a path of cooperation geared toward a legally ordered community (Voegelin 1997b: 226). The nexus between Aquinas's anthropology and theology resides in a philosophy of law that theorizes of a "perfect community" through a highly elastic formula possessing unpredictable potentialities. The law is conceived as necessarily opposite to human hardship and in harmony with local traditions. These traditions enable human actors to give due consideration to circumstances of time and place, are characterized by certainty, stimulate the assent of participants, and therefore are most suitable to serve the common good and the public weal (ibid.: 228). Another interesting aspect is that Aquinas holds that unjust laws, contrasting with natural and divine law, do not require obedience. More than that, they simply do not have the force of law, so they do not even deserve this name. This obviously applies a fortiori to tyranny as an organized regime of injustice.

What Thomas called the "new law" (*lex nova*) of Christianity was first the form of voluntary action which he described as written by grace into the heart of the faithful; only on a second step, this law was a written, positive law (ibid.: 230). In this sense, it was neither a reflection of the feudal system at its apex of perfection, nor intrinsically incompatible with the socioeconomic formations of mercantile capitalism which at Thomas's time were beginning to take form.[3] Voegelin is quite straightforward in saying that "the dissolution of the *polis* forms the background of Stoicism just as the dissolution of the *sacrum imperium* forms the background of Thomas's transcendental ontology" (ibid.: 227). Aquinas's views had therefore a potential for impacting those modern reconstructions of the social bond that will not entirely bow to the political realism represented by the power of the emerging states. We can find important traces of his view of individual freedom, power, and self-preservation, as well as of the conception of human beings as multitude, even in a radical thinker like Spinoza (see chapter 5).[4]

Going beyond the perspective of Voegelin, MacIntyre sees in the work of Aquinas not just a distinctive systematization of a specific tradition or an original synthesis of basic elements of two traditions, the Aristotelian and the Augustinian, which in the consciousness of thirteenth-century European thinkers were considered in tension, if not overtly antagonistic (MacIntyre 1988: 166). MacIntyre also sees in Aquinas's work no less than the best exemplification of the complex social workings of a tradition, namely of what it, as a discursive tradition, necessarily contributes to the building of the social fabric. Referring to a passage of the *Summa Theologiae*, MacIntyre says that the key to understand how Aquinas's theory exemplifies what traditions contribute to the social bond is the fact that he describes the partnership in faith among *ego* and *alter* as a relationship of inquiry, before it is seen as a relationship of authority and brotherhood. Aquinas sees partnership in faith as a practice that incorporates an ongoing work of definition of the goods and their hierarchy. This description clearly shows that the *telos*, within a discursive tradition, is never given a priori, except in cases of an authoritarian degeneration of traditions, which usually threaten their very existence. *Telos* depends on a sustained cultivation and transmission of knowledge (ibid.: 179–80).

We see in Thomas's legal philosophy a much higher sociological determination of the ideal of the *res publica*, than in its antecedents within the Roman law tradition and in the earlier medieval elaborations. With him the divorce of this concept from the Gelasian political theology of the *sacrum imperium* is accomplished. There is still, however, a sociological underdetermination of the resulting *societas christiana*. Symptomatically, this sociological underdetermination goes along with an anthropological overdetermination. This stricture prefigures the sociological underdetermination of several political visions of Western Enlightenment (see chapter 6). It consists in the view of a *societas* as extended to all mankind, resting on one main mechanism that does not focus on the subjects to include in this social form, but on those to exclude, namely those moved by a "bad will" (*mala voluntas*) that enfeebles reason through a lack of humility (a typically monastic virtue that acquires here a much more secular justification), generates sin, and leads to the self-exclusion of the sinner.

This simplistic construction of "society" is facilitated by an overdetermination of the traits of the human being's capacity to rule oneself, in that this potential to self-rule, or autonomy, is turned into a duty. This anthropological overdetermination leads to a deficient sociological grasp of the contingency of social factors influencing this human capacity. While Aquinas provides a quite balanced picture of the interplay of intentionality and contingency in social action and interaction, his theory reflects an inflated view of intentionality. We will see that within the Islamic philosophy of law a more balanced solution will be provided, by using categories that are largely comparable to those employed by Aquinas (see chapter 4).

It is important to observe that in Aquinas's case, Aristotelianism was not just a philosophical system to be reevaluated since central to the nonscriptural legacy of Euro-Mediterranean axial traditions, and to be accommodated with the Abrahamic-scriptural traditions influenced, in Latin Christendom, by the Augustinian construction of the will. Aristotelianism also represented a challenge coming from some of the most vibrant schools of the Islamic tradition (*falsafa*: see chapter 4) which had hitherto been much ahead of Latin Christendom in the adaptation and elaboration of the Greek philosophical heritage. Thomas's solution of imbuing Augustine's theory of the will with the Aristotelian view of *phronesis* produced an elegant sociopolitical theory based on the powerful anthropology of the free and cooperative social agent. The situation faced and the solutions devised by him are therefore an important historical precedent to the type of dilemmas that religious traditions of Abrahamic roots encounter today while confronting a competing and potentially hostile tradition. The strategy adopted by Aquinas, consisting in rejecting the Aristotelian and Augustinian legacies as packages and in recuperating and reshaping concepts and motives that are central to them, is noteworthy, since it was a genuinely theoretical undertaking based on respecifying the notion of goods and their hierarchy, the *ego-alter* interaction, the process of common deliberation, and the purposive character of action. It was, in other words, much more than an exegetical exercise. This is why MacIntyre takes it as the best case of an attempt at grounding a new tradition—here the tradition of Latin Christendom radiating from Europe.

Aquinas's main intervention on Aristotelianism—or rather on the part of that system that was relevant to his work program—aimed to redress a defective construction of *telos* within human agency. The lacking definition of the voluntary character of action and the ethnocentric and restrictive construction of political community—and of the corresponding goods—around the *polis* in Aristotle's theory were the reasons for this deficit. In Thomas's approach, the apprehension of the ultimate good is not enough. The notion of *telos* needed to be profoundly reconstructed, in order not to become circular and normative. Practical life is for Aquinas an ongoing inquiry, sustained by practical rationality, into how our present pursuit of goods can or cannot lead us to the ultimate good. Self-education and self-awareness give us, so to speak, a sense of direction, via the acquisition of the set of virtues that will sustain our ongoing practical inquiry into the goods and the best ways to pursue them (MacIntyre 1988: 192–94).

However, as social beings humans enter into relationships via their own pursuits of the goods, and so the individual paths to the supreme good can only be part of a collective endeavor that becomes manifest as public reason. The open character of the collective determination of public reason according to Aquinas is evident. Obeying divine commandments is a necessary, but not sufficient condition to pursue the path of individual salvation and of collective construction of the *societas christiana*. Aquinas is explicit in saying that universal rules can only be a first guide for the difficult phronetic task of defining and ranking goods and especially of choosing appropriate means to those ends. Practical rationality governed by a prudential attitude is the real key to the conception of the free and cooperative agents who are capable to deliberate in common.

Without *prudentia* (the Latin equivalent of *phronesis*), both judgment and action are directionless. *Prudentia* becomes here *the* crucial virtue, on a par with *caritas*, as the human activity of matching, so to speak from the bottom up, on the basis of real practical needs, the ordering of creatures to their *telos*, which is properly reflected in the idea of providence.⁵ While the bottom line of *prudentia* consists in the attainment of household-related goods, its higher forms require a sustained public reasoning about the type and hierarchy of the shared goods of the sociopolitical community (MacIntyre 1988: 196–97). There is no public reasoning without practical rationality based on *phronesis/prudentia*, which ends up towering among the four cardinal virtues and building an essential synergic link with the foremost of the theological virtues, namely *caritas*. *Prudentia* without *caritas* is a sociologically blind type of reasoning, blind to the needs and dignity of *alter*. Even justice, consisting in rationally directing oneself toward right conduct, is subordinated to prudence and to its privileged axis to *caritas*.

Yet public reasoning requires both prudence and justice. *Iustitia* retains its importance, because *caritas* without *iustitia* would be deprived of the latter's directionality in regulating *ego*'s relations to *alter* and can degenerate in a sentimentalist élan. There is one dimension of justice that immediately affects the exercise of public reasoning: "justice prohibits open, angry speech which reviles another, and quiet, insidious speech which spreads calumny or detraction" (ibid.: 200).

Thomas also confirms the importance of the classic virtue of *parrhesia* (truth-telling) versus lying, yet this virtue will not enter the catalogue of the seven golden virtues. This has to do with the primacy of *phronesis*/prudence that might advise not to tell all one knows. The arguments Aquinas examines, and rejects, about whether and under which circumstances lying might be permissible, clearly show that truth-telling is not a means to a specific end, to some self-enclosed good of excellence like building a truthful and rightful self (a crucial Stoic virtue), but is a relational disposition and so an integral part of the project of living a good and truthful life individually and collectively. Therefore it is essential to public reasoning as a way to attain this form of life. Truth-telling as a standard for public reasoning keeps its importance, but is yoked to prudence and thus rendered more interactional and communicative, and less subject-centered.

A pure and unbridled truth-telling—one that does not care about the reactions of the audience—appears as a token of excellence that can only be demanded to truly prophetic speech. Aquinas, and the Dominicans in general, were teachers of teachers and advisors of advisors, influential within universities and courts. This teaching and advising activity targeting the learned and the powerful might have also entailed the requirement not to lie. Indeed the arguments Thomas rejected about the permissibility of lying were those current at his time and due to gain further popularity in the centuries to come in grounding various forms of political "realism." This realism was based on the necessity to pursue those goods of effectiveness without which the pursuit of goods of excellence in the *societas christiana* would recede into a purely otherworldly ideal, thereby reproducing a sharp dichotomy between *civitas Dei* and *civitas terrena*.

The sociological strength of Aquinas's balanced position on the importance of transparence in publicly relevant communication, which contrasts with an overemphasis on *parrhesia* as a technology of subjectivity, is evident on a number of points. First, it grounds public reason solidly on the practical construction of the social bond, and not on a self-centered truth-seeking activity whose power implications when translated into public speech are always uncertain, since the truth-speaker might construct on its basis a personal charisma to the detriment of the charisma of the community of truth. Not to speak of the danger that truth-speaking might be rhetorically staged, but not truthful at all, and that it might not change the subject and its relationship to *alter*: this is an axial issue as old as the denunciation of the "false prophets" and the "tricksters." Second, the view of conflicting rationalities and truth-claims leading to error, like those found in Greek tragedy, and which *parrhesia* was originally called to supersede, is expunged at its root by Thomas's vision that the issue of agreement versus disagreement of values is considered important not in itself, but primarily insofar as it impacts practical life.[6]

## From the Monastery to the *Civitas*

Thomas's synthesis, far from blindly legitimizing the existent institutional structures and doctrinal catalogues, emphasized faith and freedom of the will to an extent that reflected the motivational prism of the emerging actors of the socioreligious movements of the age: the "commoners." This consideration should help putting his work in its proper sociopolitical context, as being part of a larger movement of mendicant orders rapidly turning, during the thirteenth century, into an intellectual vanguard militating for a practical rooting and an institutional reconstruction of the *societas christiana*. At the same time, Aquinas's work was also intended to cope with the challenge of a more radical spiritualism, propagated by Francis of Assisi earlier in the century. Aquinas's emphasis on *caritas* as the pillar of his entire anthropology and as the queen of all virtues, on a par with prudence, was at the root of the spiritual ferment from which his own order, the Dominicans, had sprouted. They then engaged in a brotherly competition with the more radical Franciscans, as exemplified by the partnership not only in faith and friendship, but also in knowledge, between Aquinas and the fellow Franciscan Bonaventura of Bagnoregio. Nonetheless, the competition was fierce. The Franciscans configured a type of socioreligious movement that, unlike the Dominicans, rejected intellectualism and insisted on the power of *caritas* and grace in a fashion that the Thomistic synthesis was only partly capable to capture and systematize. The deeper radical character of the Franciscans lies primarily in a much stronger evocation of the community of the politically free, which led them—who, in spite of the original anti-intellectualism, were due to prove no less successful than the Dominicans to take root in European universities—to develop an even stronger capacity to permeate social life and work as intermediaries in civic contentions (Voegelin 1997b: 231; Santoro 2003 [1999]: 71–88).

Apart from the innovative character of their discourse, new monastic orders had started to play a central role in movements of revitalization and reformation of the Christian, theological-political ideas of order since the beginning of the climax of the Axial Renaissance. Earlier in this chapter we have seen how this reform impetus came to fruition during and after the unsettling of the fragile institutional balance of the *respublica christiana* effected by various macroinstitutional failures in the redefinition of the authority of the pope and the emperor, as well as of the pastoral role of bishops and priests. This is also why one cannot understand the impact of Aquinas's theory without looking at the monastic revolution as a whole. On the other hand, the Dominican and Franciscan vanguards and new intellectual elites that were formed during the thirteenth century represented the culmination of a longer "movement of the commoner" whose beginnings stretch back across the millennium turn into the first attempts to reconstruct a new order after the instability of Late Antiquity (see chapter 4).

Among earlier waves of monastic reforms, the Cistercian approach had played a particularly important role, led by the personality of Bernard of Clairvaux (1090–1153). The core organizational novelty brought forward by his reform was a strong emphasis on spiritual fatherhood and sonship in the relationship between monks, in the form of an institutional tightening of the intersubjective approach laid down in the Christian notion of *disciplina*, based on specific patterns of authority, trust, and communication between the abbot and the monk (Voegelin 1997b: 70–71). The subsequent rise of the mendicant orders shifted the focus of renewal outside the monastery walls. The new orders launched a program for capturing and domesticating the popular drives to heterodoxy and incorporating them into innovative life forms compatible with the monastic tradition and doctrinal orthodoxy. In this way, the new orders became the true social vanguards of the renewal and reform not only of the Church, but of society at large. Their tasks ranged from redesigning the imitation of Christ through a life of poverty, to healing the sick, but also to performing a capillary work of preaching and conversion. The powered discursive arsenal resulting from the resystematization of the Christian virtues makes no sense without the deployment of a type of mobility directly functional to the refinement of the power of speech (Friedrich Silber 1995: 140).

This latter function required a swift progress in the organization of adequate education. As a result, the newly grounded universities became centers of excellence for a sustained theological and philosophical activity, which finally culminated in the work of the Dominican monk Thomas Aquinas, just examined, and of his master Albertus Magnus, but also of their Franciscan contenders Bonaventura of Bagnoregio and William of Ockham (for their challenge of the emerging Thomistic order see Santoro 2003 [1999]: 83–89).

It is important to see that in spite of the importance of the wider framework of turbulence in the institutional architecture of the *sacrum imperium* in the struggle between pope and emperor about their respective prerogatives and powers, the new monastic orders did not significantly intervene on the level of conception of the *respublica christiana*. That struggle was basically a dispute over jurisdictions, an arena of political-institutional confrontation where traditional arsenals of arguments were continually redeployed (Voegelin 1997b: 89). The focus of the movement and the reconceptualization endeavors of the new mendicant orders lay, not surprisingly, elsewhere. Their efforts focused on the institutional innovation represented by the constitution of the *universitas* as a body increasingly independent both from *imperium* and *sacerdotium*. However, their terrain of action and innovation was still oriented to a renewal of the ties of authority and trust as laid down by the *Regula* of Benedict of Norcia in the sixth century CE. A strong continuity in the capacity of transformation of monasticism as a long-term "movement" is undeniable (cf. Bergmann 1985), and we cannot reduce Dominicans and Franciscans to a half-secularized elite personnel of the new universities and the new secular worlds. The *Regula* was a simple but articulate blueprint grounding a school of prayer and work at the service of God. Not surprisingly, it was especially through monks inspired by Augustine that the theory of human will had been developed, before the intervention of Aquinas. It would be impossible to introduce the achievements of Francis of Assisi without linking them to the inherited theory and practice of the monastic tradition. Crucial to the formation of the will of the monk was the virtue of humility, which opposes the worst of all sins, pride. In the *Regula*, the progress through several steps in the ladder of humility is crucial. Moreover, in the virtue of humility, the monkish disciplines of the self depend strictly on the relationship to *alter*, and therefore are part and parcel of larger and more structured repertoires of intersubjective understanding and connectivity. The Benedictine rule makes explicit and details how the triadic relationship between *ego*, *alter*, and God operates in the Christian tradition grounded on monastic virtues (Asad 1993: 135–47).

Success in implementing the monastic discipline is measured through relations with others. While Foucault, when he tackled the issue, seemed to concentrate his attention entirely on the "microcosm of solitude" of the monk, the famous "steps of humility" of the Benedictine rule were in reality enmeshed in human relationships and intended as not simply a disciplinary regime, but as a path to the attainment to the higher goods. In the dominant form of medieval monasticism (coenobitic, that is, "communitarian," as opposed to eremitic, or "solitary"), the technology of the self, which lies at the heart of the combat of chastity, is itself dependent on the institutional resources of organized community life. The body, which Foucault identified as the arena for that continuous labor of inspecting and testing, was experienced as integral to the monastic body as a whole. In this area there was no single point of surveillance from which the self examined itself, but an entire network of functions through which watching, testing, learning, and teaching took place. Thus, the monastic body observed and tested itself, and its members learned, painfully, the obedience that formed the disciplined will of each as the will not of the self but of the Lord (ibid.: 112–14). It emerges from the practice of the *Regula* that mutual observation was essential for the working of this network of relations. Moreover, for its very centrality and complexity, this mutuality of observing and monitoring could not be captured by explicit precepts, but had to emerge through the practice-based refinement of this concerted movement (ibid.: 161).

There are several layers of meaning beneath the *disciplina* of the Benedictine rule. From its Latin application to the domains of domestic life, politics, and especially war, the Biblical *disciplina* matches, on a first level, the Greek *paideia*, intended as the building and cultivation of the virtues. The twist of meaning that *paideia* acquires in the Biblical narrative denotes the divine source of education, directed to an entire people and implemented through surrender to God's law, implemented in particular via the exhortations of the prophets. In the monastic elaboration on this concept and narrative, its military connotation was recuperated in the notion of the Christian's combat against the devil. What was clearly different from its classic meaning was the neutralization of the strategic dimension of discipline, since too strictly tied to the pursuit of goods of effectiveness. More generally, in medieval Christianity, including the non-monastic realm of the bishop's authority over the laity, *disciplina* ended up covering the entire apparatus of injunctions and instructions, the whole disciplining network deemed essential to govern the faithful by directing their will to the will of God (ibid.: 135–36).

Texts like the *Regula*, but also other instruments (including breviaries), illustrate the exhortative dimension that the theory of monastic life drew from the patristic contributions and consigned to the larger discursive tradition for further uses, potentially not restricted to the monastery. These programmatic texts combined a synergic variety of discursive forms: recommendation, injunction, authorization, justification. However, an essential role in mediating between program and performance was played by the practices through which the texts were simultaneously inter-preted and applied to the regulation and disciplining of the monastic community. A particularly strong focus was laid on instruction. Talal Asad has forcefully argued that the centrality of mediating practices precludes a view of the relationship between program and performance as either a strategic game or a theatrical play. In this form of speech there is no autonomous notion of a relation of the discourse to an audience or to a clientele, but rather an intrinsic relation among the performers themselves as an overlapping multitude of, simultaneously, *ego*s and *alter*s (ibid.: 140).

The virtue of *caritas* is central to this program and is by necessity based on the raw material of human love that most of the monastic recruits of the epoch of the Axial Renaissance—unlike those of the earlier centuries since Benedict—had experienced in their previous mundane life. *Caritas* is love for God manifested through love for the creatures, after *libido* (intended as "unlawful desire," that is desire for the wrong objects, including glory) has been subdued and eliminated (ibid.: 141–42). The rise of *caritas* to a pivotal virtue is therefore part of the process through which Christian monastic life "colonized" the increasingly complex social and urban worlds outside of the monasteriy walls, and developed a quite accurate sociopsychological knowledge of the potentials and limits of secular life.

The process through which the disciplines of monastic life were adapted to organize the life of a vast array of social classes, notably in the resurgent urban centers, can be first detected in the trajectory of the penitential manuals, specifying sins and corresponding penance.

They helped to propagate the practice of penance among the mobile population of the towns considered most exposed to heresy. This secular use of penance spread out long before it was declared compulsory by the Lateran Council of 1215 (ibid.: 115). The new mendicant movements, in particular the Franciscans and the Dominicans, were instrumental to the extension of the Church's discipline to the urban classes via preaching, arguing, and disputing for the orthodox faith, aided by the study and teaching of law, theology, and logic, in the rising universities (ibid.: 117). The types of social roles among townsmen and their families were carefully sorted out by the monks, in order to prepare preachers and confessors to meet different cases. Types of sinful thought, speech, and action were given a differential treatment according to the occupation and skills of the portion of urban population targeted (ibid.: 120).

Francis of Assisi (1182–1226) started his activities at the beginning of the thirteenth century as one among large crowds of lay individuals inspired by the hermitic-penitential tradition (Merlo 1997: 5). These lay people turned their attention to the poor and derelict by considering themselves poor and derelict, and therefore as the poor's peer. As maintained by Voegelin, "the Christ of Saint Francis is an innerworldly Christ of the poor; he is no longer the head of the whole *corpus mysticum* of mankind" (Voegelin 1997b: 142). Based on a fresh and radical reading of the New Testament, this approach operated a shift from the idea of *caritas* as doing good thus far understood and practiced in the Church. It added to it a genuinely dialogic layer that the mendicants saw as the essence of the New Testament: a solidarity-oriented "conversation among the poor" (*conversatio inter pauperes*; Merlo 1997: 6). This is the sharing of the Christian ideal among pure Christians, who are poor and therefore divested from any other identity, yet coming from and going back into the social worlds of the commoners.

The subject and target of the conversation is the lay poor. The new discourse stems from a *caritas* purified of any power imbalance between the giver and the receiver. *Caritas* was thus conceived as an ideal type of exchange attending to the elementary construction of the social bond between *ego* and *alter*, as the bottom-like technology of intersubjective understanding, engagement, and connectivity, to be practiced before and outside any systematic architecture of community-building: like through assisting the lepers, repairing modest churches laying in ruin, and so on. It is doing good for doing good, for connecting to *alter*, not for a systematic scope, which always entails, or produces, strong and unbalanced power relationships. The trouble for Francis arose with the sweeping success of his activities, with the formation of ever bigger groups following his call. This raised the question of how to position the movement vis-à-vis consolidated institutional patterns within the Church in general and with regard to the traditional monastic practices in particular (ibid.: 7).

Voegelin stated that "the action of Saint Francis . . . emanates from a self-assertive, unbending, dominating will, creating a style of existence for the simple layman, the *idiota* without feudal or ecclesiastical rank" (Voegelin 1997b: 135). The radical character of his message resulted in nothing less than an onslaught on all key social institutions of family, property, inheritance, governmental authority, and the fabric of intellectual discourse, including—or even especially—theology. Only the Church *as* grounded by Jesus Christ was spared. The attack was cast in the discursive form of personal preaching, but also of the "open letters" disseminating the message to the commoner, like in Francis's epistle *To All Christians* of 1215. This approach revealed the new pathos of the townsman gaining the confidence to speak to the Christian public like a pope or an emperor.

This was the culmination of a process through which during the Axial Renaissance the self-styled urban commoner was becoming a self-conscious and autonomous force within European Christianity: a socioreligious actor initiating movements disassociated, at least at the beginning, from how social power and temporal authority had been thus far integrated into the grid of the Christian charismata. Francis was the leader of a wider movement whereby the *idiotae*, the commoners, started to build an autonomous community, however obeying to the Church, or rather a sort of new, parallel *ecclesia*, its new-old kernel (ibid.: 137–40).

This approach made the movement attractive well beyond the circles of urban commoners and appealed to the new intellectual stratum of university students and masters. Yet this radically anti-institutional discourse exalting the bare and power-free nature of the social bond was already history by the time a frustrated Francis wrote his Testament. It was finally sublimated in Francis's canonization in 1228, after which churches and monasteries mushroomed under his name, and a specifically Franciscan pastoral activity based on preaching and confession took root. This activity was fully legitimated by the Church, although it was in evident competition with the latter's official institutions, including all other established monastic orders. The establishment of Franciscan jurists and theologians in the universities also occurred with stunning rapidity.

Yet the radical character of the discourse could not be absorbed completely and influenced the course of resystematizations and contentions in the Church, in the universities, and in society at large. The rise and spread of the Franciscan discourse was well timed to offer students and masters a new model for linking the production of knowledge with religiously legitimated forms of life (Merlo 1997: 18). In this process, the Franciscans found models and competitors in the parallel trajectory of the Dominicans who had been eagerly recruiting monks from among personnel and pupils of European universities. In other words, this is not simply a story of monks turned professors, but also of students turned monks, albeit of a new type.

The success of both orders was finally recognized by the Council of Lyon of 1274, which proclaimed their "evident usefulness" (*evidens utilitas*) for the power and goals of the Church (ibid.: 30). That was also the year when Aquinas died and that so marked the beginning of the end of the propulsive force of the new monastic socioreligious movements of the Axial Renaissance, and the zenith of the Church's capacity of institutional absorption of the reform impulses emanating from those movements. This phase was to be followed, in the fourteenth and fifteenth centuries, by an increasing repression and authoritarian centralization, beginning in particular with Bonifacius VIII, during which the Church was entangled in ever more complicated power games largely detached from the thematic contentions of the Axial Renaissance and increasingly distant from the idea of *respublica christiana*. The Church's counterpart was ever less an imperial authority at its sunset, and ever more the emerging national states. Toward them the Church, if intended as the pivotal institution of the *respublica christiana*, found itself increasingly on the loosing side, and saw its authority vanishing, while it consolidated the mundane power of the "pope-king" as rooted in an expanding territorial state existing alongside more powerful ones.

However, underneath the erosion of the high politics of the Church, the Franciscan friars worked particularly well in order to reshape the notion and practices of civic cooperation and public life through their engagement in towns and cities, in which they were incorporated from the inception of their movement. They did not have to get out of the monastery walls since they had understood themselves from the beginning as the purest commoners and townspeople. Therefore, even during and after the process of institutionalization of their order, they eagerly invested their newly acquired powers into the job of addressing wide sectors of the urban populations, up to local elites (Rigon 1997: 260). They put aside the radical dimension of the original message and invested Franciscan authority in routine-like tasks of reproduction of social bonds. They became fiduciary persons in giving witness and executing testaments, guaranteeing all sorts of agreements, and providing counsel to individuals and organized groups. In exceptional cases, when a city's factionalism heightened their authority as arbiters, some monks were even conferred direct ruling responsibilities (ibid.: 262).

Their most original and socially creative role lay in their promotion and sponsoring of autonomous associations that merged monastic and civic ideals, like a vast array of lay brotherhoods and congregations, up to "peace and faith" militias. There the friars tutored lay citizens (especially those from the merchant and artisan classes) into practicing Christian virtues, while preparing them to take up tasks and offices in public life (ibid.: 266). They were also able to infiltrate patronage networks, without disrupting them, but by building up a parallel hierarchy in their midst, based on religious-*cum*-civic virtue and corresponding authority as an alternative to patron-client relations (ibid.: 269). In the final analysis, they were able to create a tight link between the Christian practice of doing good upheld by the discursive tradition, and more purely social types of civic habitus related to socioeconomic life and to its modes of entrepreneurship, class solidarity, and patronage.

As their institutional roles ingrained deeper into civic life, the Franciscans capitalized on the widely appreciated added value of "poverty" (*pauperitas*) to be invested into *civitas*. The former provided the bottom line to the much needed position of neutrality in city factionalism. They incarnated a civic spirit severed from any particularistic interest. Franciscan friars did not simply penetrate the mechanisms of civic life by infusing them with *caritas*, but played a leading role in constructing and managing public utilities in ways that could not grow out of civic dynamics themselves. They showed that the revived Roman law was necessary but not sufficient for setting up city statutes and governing city life. Interestingly enough, a key field of their activity in reshaping the social bond was their assisting and influencing testamentary practices. Thus they linked a typically private law instrument for the preservation and transmission of family assets to the Christian practice of doing good through *caritas* (ibid.: 270–71). This kind of legal practices showed the extent to which the domain of private law was technically, but not ideally autonomous from the pursuit of the public good. This practice marked a continuity with the Roman law tradition, and was due to be contradicted by later developments whereby the private and the public will delimit rigidly separate "spheres" (see chapter 6).

In all these cases the role of the Franciscans in the city as religious brokers upheld the "common utility" (*utilitas communis*) in quite explicit and immediate ways. In their quality of often welcome outsiders, because free from particularistic, material interests, they were able to reflect on the social conflicts they were confronted with, and to communicate to society the results of their reflection. They could finally translate these reflections into noncoercive suggestions of solutions to specific collective problems. They were a living example of how a reflective process of stepping back from particularistic interests constitutes a sine qua non of public life (ibid.: 275–79).

Genealogically, they laid the grounding stone for the discourse of the free and cooperative agent capable to engage *alter* in a power-free arena of communication and public deliberation. This was a development facilitated by their liminal position toward social structures and civic institutions. Any theoretical reconstruction of the public sphere based on purely structural factors of interaction between the "third sphere" and the spheres of politics and the economy appears from this historical angle quite improbable (cf. introduction, chapter 6, and conclusion).

# CHAPTER 4

# THE COLLECTIVE PURSUIT OF PUBLIC WEAL

## Tradition-Making in Islam and the Role of Jurisprudence

There are several reasons why focusing now on Islam can substantially enrich the post-axial genealogy of intersubjective repertoires of understanding, connectivity, and communication within discursive traditions. This concerns in particular the nexus between practical and public reasoning in the construction and maintenance of the social bond. Islam is the last in the family of Abrahamic, prophetic religions. Its scriptural basis and the ensuing traditions reflect the awareness by the prophet Muhammad and his successors among the leaders of the Islamic community that they were grounding—via revelation, its recording, canonization, and authoritative interpretation—a religious civilization repristinating and remolding key elements of the previous "religions of the book," that is, Judaism and Christianity.

The Greek philosophical heritage had a substantial influence on some key aspects of Muslim traditions. Several scholars (Goldziher 1889–1890; Nallino 1942; D'Emilia 1953; Schacht 1957; Crone 1987; Hallaq 1989) have also taken into consideration the impact of some aspects of Roman law on Islamic jurisprudence. As a result, it is fair to say that Islam has attempted to bring to perfection a crucial feature of axial civilizations in the reconstruction of the social bond, notably the construction of an uncontaminated triad between *ego*, *alter*, and God (Salvatore 1997: 5–22). As aptly formulated by Shmuel N. Eisenstadt,

the emphasis on the construction of a political-religious collectivity was connected in Islam with the development of a principled ideological negation of any primordial element or component within this sacred political-religious identity. Indeed, of all the Axial Age civilizations in general, and the monotheistic ones in particular, Islam was, on the ideological level, the most extreme in its denial of the legitimacy of such primordial dimensions in the structure of the Islamic community . . . In this it stood in opposition to Judaism, with which it shared such characteristics as an emphasis on the direct, unmediated access of all members of the community to the sacred. (Eisenstadt 2002: 148–49)

The rise of Islam is therefore the last and most consciously managed manifestation of the axial civilizational breakthrough within the Euro-Mediterranean area. For being so, it is also the beginning, or an early signal, of the Axial Renaissance (see chapter 3). The Qur'an gives prominence to the earlier chains of prophets, from Noah through Abraham and Moses to Jesus, and lays a strong emphasis on the opposition they met in their call to submission to God's will, which is condensed in the meaning of the Arabic word *islam*. In this sense, Muhammad's message was neither new nor intended to be new, but was conceived as a restoration, completion, and renaissance of the true Abrahamic faith through a final and unequivocal revelation of God's word and will to humankind. However, not only the content of the Qur'anic message but also the communicative infrastructure itself of prophetic discourse and its means of inculcation were made particularly effective by Muhammad and the chains of Islamic scholars who came after him. God's message, revealed through the earlier prophets, had been received and incorporated in Judaism and Christianity in imperfect ways—as claimed by Muhammad—due to human pride and egoism and religious sectarianism.

Islam, the new-old call to submission to God, was to overcome sectarianism and embrace mankind in a truly universal *umma*, a community of all believers, superseding all sectarian *and* tribal affiliations. It was the sweeping success, after initial resistance, of Muhammad's career, between Mecca and Medina, in the specifically Semitic tradition of the "armed prophets," that made the turn from parabolic exhortation to an activist reconstruction of the social bond a crucial part of his preaching and leadership during the last part of his own life. While it is an exaggeration to state that Muhammad was a conscious empire builder (Fowden 1993: 138–52), his practice and judgment as the last prophet and as the first leader of the new *umma* in shaping and regulating human relationships acquired paradigmatic value beyond the Qur'an itself. This scripture, centered on the call to conversion and on the retelling and reshaping of several Biblical and other mythical narratives, only dealt—unlike the encompassing Deuteronomic Torah—with a limited number of issues immediately related to the ordinance of social life.

The Qur'an reflected the new irruption of God's word into human history through his messenger, as the carrier of a divine command that awakes in the human souls the discernment between good and evil that God the creator has infused into their hearts, but that, without the call to conversion and to the "straight path" in a life of devotion and righteousness, lies dormant and impotent, exposed to the insistent devil's whispers. Far from being an exhaustive catalogue of discrete exhortations and specific commands, "the Qur'an emerges as a document that from the first to the last seeks to emphasize all those moral tensions that are necessary for creative human action" (Rahman 1979 [1966]: 35). God's command (*amr*) is ceaseless, and in order to implement it man is called to collaborate with God on a permanent basis and with sincere commitment: this is the core meaning of faith. Islam is therefore the tie of faith/trust that makes human will and command adequate to God's will and command. Through obeying God and his law, man is entitled to act as his vicegerent on earth (*khilafa Allah*).

A sociological profile of the nexus between salvation and human action is evident in the Qur'an. Islam's primary document is a teaching chiefly concerned with producing the right attitude for human action. It considers *correct* action to be *'ibada* or "the service due to God." The Qur'an, therefore, emphasizes tensions and psychological factors that generate the correct moral frame for action and interaction. A very crucial warning in the core Islamic scripture is against positing human agency as proudly self-sufficient, while on the other hand the Qur'an also scorns passivity and hopelessness. A key exhortation to man is to be on one's own guard via fear of God (*taqwa*), while the faithful is also reassured about God's mercy toward his creatures, in the assumption that man has been created good in essence (ibid.: 241).

Before delving on the analysis of some crucial nodes concerning how the new prophetic discourse translates into specific practices, institutions, and forms of reasoning, that is, into a tradition, it is worth having a look at the nexus of Islam with Late Antiquity. It has been stated that the early political success of Islam "consummated rather than contradicted the themes of late Roman history" (Fowden 1993: 157), thus influencing decisively the medieval and modern developments of European Christendom (ibid.: 10; cf. also Crone and Hinds 1986). Yet the most important issue of continuity concerns the shape of the self-in-community, and therefore the form of collectivity or commonwealth. This form can be hardly reduced to the question of the degree of success of an imperial process. Peter Brown has suggested that Islam relates to the nonprophetic predecessor cultures in the Euro-Mediterranean civilizational area in a more organic way than the conflicted and fragmented revolutionary irruption, and subsequent accommodation, of Christianity into the world of Late Antiquity (Brown 1984; see also Rosenthal 1965).

Starting from the life of the prophet Muhammad, Islam's construction of the model of exemplary conduct was certainly in tension with the civilizing exemplars of the Byzantine and Persian imperial cultures, but it was also morally distant from the pure saint of Christian asceticism. The pattern of intersubjective repertoires that Islam set out to reconstruct was closer to that of the late-antique philosopher, the "saint of the *paideia*," (discipline, education) for which the disciplines of life were not to be projected toward a *civitas Dei*, but to be put to work quite immediately into the social networks linking leaders and commoners within the community (Brown 1984: 32). The path to internalizing the dictates of divine law, the *shari'a*, was mediated by an identification with the life of the prophet Muhammad, whose model combined an impressive range of signs of excellence within various spheres of human action. Here piety as *taqwa* stood central but was not singled out as a stand-alone virtue, and indicated rather the pinnacle of exemplary conduct (cf. Chittick 1992: 9–12).

Within medieval Christian models of authority, trust, and communication the implementation of divine will and law rested primarily on those who had turned *disciplina* into practices of self-monitoring and rituals of renunciation (see chapter 3). With the new monastic movements and the civic resurgence of the Axial Renaissance the problem of extending moral authority to the increasingly complex social worlds was solved through the transposition, adaptation, and application of ascetic paradigms of discipline and piety to the expanding laity. A celibate clergy, who even in the case of the Franciscan ideal of the commoners or *idiotae* (originally belonging to the laity) incarnated a monastic paradigm of excellence, attempted to impose a control on the "lower" life of the *saeculum* (Brown 1984: 33–34).

In contrast to this model, and similarly to the late-antique philosopher, the Muslim *'alim* (scholar) does not inhabit a singled out space like the monastery, but lives into the social bond without prior institutional mediations. Therefore he carries from the beginning the burden of constructing and preserving a tradition of knowledge and excellence providing the necessary moral authority to the shaping of the social bond and to its governance, based on axial criteria of understanding and connectivity among human actors. For the Muslim scholar "appeal to tradition appears to be a case of *reculer pour mieux sauter* in the present" (ibid.: 35–36). In order to fully appreciate the process of tradition-making in Islam, Peter Brown advised to avoid an obsessive focus on the most visible streams of the tradition, and to look instead at "the barely perceptible network of capillaries by which this tradition was both handed on and perceived anew in every generation" (ibid.: 36).

This is why the Islamic case offers us a privileged terrain for the analysis of traditionalization and canonization of prophetic discourse, and of its combination with other sources and forms of post-axial and post-prophetic conceptions of legal and political order. The synthetic fixation of the basic profile of the tradition was accomplished at an extraordinary pace, within one century after the death of Muhammad. It was based on an original combination between the precepts of the Qur'an and the elaboration on the practice of the pristine Muslim community, on the one hand, and the post-Hellenistic legal and political traditions as found particularly in Syria, to which the center of the Muslim Caliphate shifted in the century between 650 and 750, on the other (cf. Crone and Hinds 1986).

The two main notions that capture the concept of tradition and its underlying problematic within Islam are *sunna* and *hadith*. *Hadith* is "a short report of what an authoritative figure of the past said or did in connection with a certain problem, each report being prefaced by a chain of transmitters guaranteeing its authenticity" (Crone 1987: 23). *Hadith* denotes therefore tradition in a very specific sense, as a contestable work of authentication. The *sunna* is instead the report, or a set of reports considered authentic, in the moment they acquire a regulating force. Yet there is a further and probably more important level of differentiation residing at the core of tradition-making. It is not by chance that the *sunna* of the prophet Muhammad has for the Muslim a higher practical importance than revelation itself for its capacity of providing orientation to everyday life: it brackets out the "wondrous" character of revelation and—supported by the Qur'an itself that praises the exemplary conduct of Muhammad—becomes living practice or "living tradition" (Hodgson 1974: 64; Rahman 1979 [1966]: 45).

According to the view of some scholars within Islamic studies, the collection and authentication of *hadith* reflected the legal controversies taking place two centuries after Muhammad (Crone 1987: 3). Centered on the traditions directly linked to the deeds and sayings of Muhammad as the last prophet, *hadith*s were feverishly collected all over the Islamic world in a sort of collective run for knowledge (ibid.: 25; cf. also Juynboll 1983, 1987, 1996). The consolidation of *hadith* collections took place in the third Islamic (AH, "after *hijra*") century (corresponding to the ninth century CE). *Hadith* presupposes a commitment to a search for truth, but is in the final analysis built on expert disputes on authenticity, which went so far as to encompass the truthfulness of the transmitters of a given *hadith*. The fixation of *hadith* is therefore a canonization process, whereas the ongoing importance of the *sunna* as the actual incorporation of God's command through human command (mediated by prophetic practice and reflection on practice) is the sociologically more diffuse but also more interesting dimension of traditionalization in the sense of tradition-making. It evidences its bottom-up, nonspecialist dimension.

Starting from the late nineteenth century, scholars of Islam like Ignaz Goldziher (1889–1890) characterized the *sunna* as a living tradition. Their analysis is of sociological interest not only for elucidating the process of traditionalization and canonization within Islam, but also for characterizing the process as a most promising case for studying tradition-making in general. The *sunna* appears as actual social practice filtered out through the selectivity of memory and spontaneous reflection. It is the product of individual and collective reasoning on actual problems based on the authoritative examples of the last prophet and of the other fore-bears who lived in the era of Qur'anic revelation. On the other hand, the canonization of *hadith* that started in the middle of the second century AH proceeded in a chronologically inverted manner; it reconstructed traditions backwards, first by referring the authoritative sayings and deeds to the prophet's successors, then to his companions, last to Muhammad himself (Rahman 1979 [1966]: 46–47).

One *hadith* has it that the prophet once said: "Whatever of good speech there be, you can take it to have been said by me." The result is to effectively consecrate as normative the practice of the pristine community, and to minimize any later contention as to whether any tradition was confirmed by prophetic charisma. This closure of the circle between prophetic discourse and actual practice becomes determinant in completing the definition of Islam itself: meaning submission to God's will and law in the first instance, the actual way to implement this submission is through the emulation of what the prophet said or did (Makdisi 1983: 73). And there is no avenue to relate to the prophet's sayings and deeds other than the *hadith* (Rahman 1979 [1966]: 66).

It should also be considered that, while the Qur'an itself consecrates the prophet's *sunna* as authoritative—and Muhammad did adjudicate and pronounce authoritatively on a number of problems or disputes during his life—it is also clear that most social transactions in the pristine Muslim community were settled without the intervention of the prophet or his close companions (ibid.: 51). We see a specific strength of Islam in how prophetic discourse acquires paradigmatic value through its application to social practice, so closing the normative gaps of earlier Abrahamic manifestations of prophetic voices that had "metastatically" anticipated a just world of reconciliation with God (see chapter 1). These pre-Islamic voices within the chain of Semitic prophets had to relocate the tension of the origin and justification of commanding and doing good ever and again, through a direct management of the gap between this world and the thereafter. A final closure of the gap was only possible through theological speculations and eschatological narratives. In contrast to this path, in the Islamic mainstream the discourse will be mainly kept at the service of the paradigms of moral-practical guidance and legal adjudication.

In his endeavor to make sociologically transparent the process of tradition-making in Islam, Fazlur Rahman has convincingly objected to the view of a separation or enduring tension between *hadith* and *sunna* entertained by European Orientalists.[1] He has argued that if on the one hand it is true that the *sunna* can be considered a living tradition, whereby tradition is mainly nonverbal, silent, and produced *in actu*, on the other hand in spite of being "living" and therefore nonexpert based, tradition cannot renounce discourse. "Men do not merely act and follow (and innovate) but also talk and report. There was, therefore, at least an informal verbal tradition" (ibid.: 55). This informal tradition became a deliberate activity among the younger generation of the prophet's companions. As a consequence, the extension of the authoritative character of prophetic discourse to prophet-centered practice did empower the prophet's companions as authoritative though "lay" spokesmen for the Islamic community. This primacy of the lay in tradition-making was largely new to Abrahamic traditions, and was therefore an early sign of an Axial Renaissance laying an emphasis on the commoner's agency. In earlier instances of Abrahamic-prophetic discourse, this kind of lay empowerment was accepted only by way of acquisition of prophetic or saintly charisma. Therefore, Islam is original in allowing—at its inception—for a tradition-making dependent neither on the transmission of charisma nor on a strictly specialized knowledge.

In spite of the quite swift crystallization of groups and schools of experts, the orthodox mainstream of Islam consistently prevented the formation of a class of consecrated specialists or priests. In principle, whoever acquires knowledge, *'ilm*, is entitled to speak as an *'alim* (plural *'ulama'*), that is as a scholar, or better as a participant in the collective run for knowledge. There is no charismatic, and not even a ritual consecration of a distinct class of scholars. Specialization primarily depends on a dynamics of school-building. Sociologically speaking, this feature contributes to making Islam a unique object for the study of tradition-making and of its impact on models of practical, legal, and public reasoning.

The process of tradition-making was not centralized. Disagreement emerged and crystallized, affecting not only the identification of substantial rulings of authorized tradition, but also the issue itself of what tradition is and how, with which method, it must be reconstructed. Curiously enough, what emerged as "orthodox," Sunni Islam was characterized by a principled acceptance of this type of disagreement and by the concomitant rejection of any other charismatic source of authority in adjudicating the "dogma" (in fact, the *sunna*).[2] The orthodox Islamic community, that is, Sunni Islam, emerged as a basically lay ecumene of managed disagreement in public reasoning. Yet the inherent risk of fragmentation created a counterimpulse to search for nonscriptural ordering principles, which were found, as we will see, in the principle of *ijma'* (consensus) and in the notion of *maslaha* (covering a semantic terrain close to common good, public weal, and *res publica*).

Essential to both the principle of consensus and to the search for implementing the common good was the method of *ijtihad*. This was intended as an original "endeavor" in jurisprudential reasoning necessary to supplement the insufficiency of the other main sources of the law. However, *ijtihad* was gradually hijacked by a more basic and less creative method of analogical reasoning (*qiyas*) which in particular the Shafi'i school of law succeeded in sanctioning as a canonical method on a par with *ijma'*—yet with a factually much larger influence in orienting jurisprudential activities. *Qiyas* was a quite strict method of deduction of rulings by analogy from other rulings anchored in the text (Qur'an or certified *hadith*). Therefore it imposed strict limits on *ijtihad*, which required a more inductive, less text oriented, and therefore more creative kind of reasoning (Rahman 1979 [1966]: 71–77).

*Ijtihad* was originally developed between the second/eight (AH/CE) and the third/ninth centuries independently from *qiyas*. It reflected the systemic character of the type of original jurisprudential thinking intent on balancing method, adaptation to circumstances, and creativity. *Ijma'*, on the other hand, was understood as an ongoing process of reciprocal accommodation among the positions represented by the various scholars and schools, and therefore as a device of complexity-reduction in the fixation of the normativity of tradition at any given moment. Neither *ijtihad* nor *ijma'* were ever fully institutionalized. The former depended on the commitment of the individual scholar in pushing forward jurisprudential reasoning beyond its textual limits, whenever no solutions were available on the basis of the analysis of the main sources. *Ijma'* was a pragmatic approximation of the ideal, never accomplished situation where all the actors who possess knowledge agree, by necessity, on the right interpretation. As a whole, *ijtihad* and *ijma'* were designed to guarantee a suitable blend of creativity in thinking and arguing and of a commitment to common standards of reasoning (ibid.: 74–75).

Muslim jurists remained private individuals grouping first in informal schools or currents (*madhhab*s), competing with each other in terms of correctness of interpretation of the law and of corresponding moral and intellectual influence (ibid.: 261). Though never forming a corporation of jurists—since such a notion of corporate personality was never developed (Schacht 1950 [1935])—they did constitute a body of professional jurists institutionalizing their competencies and teaching skills through the instrument of the pious foundation (*waqf*). In analogy with the tradition of Roman law, they based their factual corporate identity and function within society on developing and upholding clear jurisprudential standards. The emergence and consolidation of four schools within the Sunni "orthodox" mainstream (the Shafi'i, the Maliki, the Hanafi, and the Hanbali schools, all named after their founders) out of several hundreds restricted this potential of creativity. The ensuing myth of a "closure of the gates of *ijtihad*" emerged by the tenth century CE.

Yet more than a closure, the process imposed a reformulation of the conditions for exercising *ijtihad* in such a restrictive way as to make this method unfeasible for normally talented practitioners. The curbing of *ijtihad* did not reduce disagreement nor did it redeem the scholars from the necessity of an ongoing invocation of a largely fictive consensus. The lack itself of a Church presiding over dogma made the voicing of disagreement through scholars a physiological mechanism for the administration of the tradition. This meant that a scholar who did not agree with another scholar's position on a given matter had in principle not simply the right, but the obligation to manifest his disagreement.

It cannot, however, be neglected that *ijma'* (the principle of "consensus"), facing now a truncated *ijtihad*, ended up being even more emptied and, as such, absolutized as a sheer principle (cf. Hallaq 1986). The resulting doctrine of the infallibility of *ijma'* severely restricted its original sense of consecrating the authority of the living tradition through ongoing, pragmatic accommodation. This authoritarian dogmatization of consensus was no replacement for the required procedure for reaching a consensus, since it did not foresee *concilia* like those that in the Catholic Church preside over the fixation and revision of dogma. The infallibility of *ijma'*, along with its authoritarian potential, remained largely fictitious and scarcely effective. It simulated the existence of an impossible consensus, while spaces of autonomy were preserved as essential to Sunni jurisprudence.

We can now start to appreciate the degree of complexity, fragility, and sophistication of tradition-making in Sunni Islam, which makes it a unique case for conceptual and theoretical reflection. The grand scheme of classification of action within Islamic legal-moral traditions—under the five categories of *wajib* ("mandatory"), *mandub* ("recommended"), *mubah* ("permissible" or "indifferent"), *makruh* ("reprehensible"), and *haram* ("illicit," "forbidden")—offers an articulate grid of categories to all practitioners, including the commoners. It encourages a diffuse effort at categorizing types of action and determining the degree of creative interpretation permitted versus undue innovations (or "heterodox" practices).

The consequence is an ongoing, demanding activity consisting in reconceptualizing the spaces of freedom and the responsibility of the agent within given contexts of action, and the concomitant necessity to persuade a Muslim audience that any such solution is plausible (Asad 1993: 211–12). Being based on a grid and not on a strictly binary code of good and bad, the human actions that are covered by the three central categories are subject to a general rule of "resoluteness and relaxation." This rule exalts the nexus between the agent's phronetic judgment in the application of a given rule in a specific situation and the corresponding modulation of his will. What is demanded is not the articulation of a subjective *voluntas*, but a channeling of the agent's "intention" (*niyya*) into a specific interaction. This operation does not require a substantiation of the human will as it happens when the *telos* of action consists in the avoidance of sin. Thus Sunni Islam escapes the risk of a hyperinflation of subjectivity, which characterizes the Augustinian, and, to a minor extent, the Thomistic elaboration on the notion of intention (see chapter 3).

The agent's playing into a given situation or interaction is to be guided by a reflective understanding of the situation. While the Qur'an aims at creating a good and just society by shaping righteous human beings who voluntarily submit to a God enjoining good and prohibiting evil, the emphasis is on faith guiding action via a permanent adjustment guided by reflection (Rahman 1979 [1966]: 85). While *'ilm* was intended as knowledge in the sense of learning, the activity of *fiqh* denoted the capacity to understand a situation on the basis of *'ilm*. *Fiqh* denotes first of all a phronetic interpretative activity, and only through the consolidation of the legal schools does it end up coinciding with (juris)prudential work, which is the way *fiqh* is usually translated (ibid.: 101, Crone 1987: 103). However, *fiqh* still retains a shade of the meaning of phronetic judgment that cannot be completely normalized into a body of knowledge, that is into *'ilm*, even if intended as knowledge with a primarily jurisprudential value (Rahman 1979 [1966]: 103).

We see here how the conceptual and practical toolkit of Islamic tradition was first assembled without the decisive intervention of the notion of *shari'a*, an idea signifying the Islamic normativity emanating from divine will. *Shari'a* is a theological concept hardly central in the Qur'an and *hadith* and therefore basically external to the first decisive wave of traditionalization. Its core meaning is "the divinely ordained pattern of human conduct" (ibid.: 68). The subsequent rise of the importance of this notion and its taking the central stage within the Islamic tradition reflects a growing influence of theological *and* philosophical reflection within this tradition. Both speculative theology and philosophy flourished in the formative stages of Islamic tradition and beyond them, and related in complex ways to each other, to various currents within jurisprudence, as well as, most importantly, to Sufism (*tasawwuf*). Sufism was the name given to the emerging, organized forms of mystical practices. This mystical path within Sunni Islam presented a particularly insidious challenge to jurisprudence since it appealed simultaneously to scholars and commoners. Sufism invoked both the Qur'an and the *sunna* in its program to sustain the centrality of a personal commitment to faith—often helped through mystical practices of renunciation—against the formalized character of the emerging body of *fiqh* literature.

The elaboration on the notion of *shari'a*, at first a concept not essential to the repertoire of the legists, was a prerogative of the theologians, who were often engaged in tense contentions with the custodians of the law. *Shari'a* developed in parallel with speculation on *din*, which unlike *shari'a* features quite central in the Qur'an. *Din* is the term usually translated as "religion," and indicates the partnership itself between man and God. It is a term covering neatly the triadic relationship between *ego*, *alter*, and *Alter*/God which is at the basis of axial intersubjective repertoires discussed in chapter 1. *Din* embraces several layers of meaning, one of which denotes the way to be followed for human beings to reach God (a meaning close to *shari'a*), while another layer attends to the idea of judgment, as in the Qur'anic notion of *yaum al-din*, the Day of Judgment. This further significance is reflected in the mirroring relationship between God's judgment and human judgment, as in the Arab proverb "as you judge, so you will be judged" (cf. Salvatore 1997: 17). The new community of the faithful, the *umma*, was seen as constructed on the basis of equal dignity among human beings, in their double identity as subjects and objects of *din*. In contradistinction to this meaning of *din*, *shari'a* was framed—starting from its rare use in the Qur'an—as more immediately related to—or emanating from—God as commander.

Theologians tended therefore to see *din* and *shari'a* as two sides of the same coin, the former identifying the intimate link between creator and creature, the latter the path of rules and disciplines, concerning both the man-God relationship and the *ego-alter* intercourse, which has to be followed in order to preserve and nourish the link. The theological synthesis of the leading theologian and Sufi Abu Hamid al-Ghazali (1058–1111) showed that *shari'a* without *din* is an empty shell (Rahman 1979 [1966]: 106). By that time, which was the beginning of the climax of resystematizations of the Axial Renaissance (see chapter 3)—also through the stimulus represented by the increasing success of Sufism that posed a challenge to the legists—the synthetic achievement of al-Ghazali enriched the process of *ijma'* (consensus). As we have seen, *ijma'* was permanently at risk of becoming an empty formula preventing innovation in the tradition. By that time, various currents within theology and mysticism had successfully started to penetrate the arena of consensus-building, thus far hegemonized by the canonical law schools.

In order to better understand the role of *shari'a* within Sunni traditions we need to take a step back. Before al-Ghazali authoritatively intervened in defining the nexus between *din* and *shari'a*, during the last period of the formative phase of canonization of the Sunni way, in the third/ninth century AH/CE, theologians and legists had fought a major battle that enduringly impacted the modalities of the consensus. We saw the ambivalent influence that Stoicism had on early Christianity (see chapter 3). That leading school within Late Antiquity, in conjunction with an Aristotelian arsenal of metaphysical concepts, also influenced the theological reflections of a school of Muslim scholars, called Mu'tazila, which enjoyed a hegemonic position during the third century AH. Whereas these thinkers subsumed the idea of God under the notion of cosmic justice, the Sunni legal schools did the opposite, so reaffirming the centrality of the Qur'an and of revelation. In one of the major direct clashes for the prevalence of one of the two main components of Axial discourse—prophetic speech versus philosophical-theological speculation—the legal schools resisted the claims of speculative theology on the ground that it threatened to disrupt the delicate work of traditionalization thus far performed, and to upset the resulting, unstable balance between Qur'an, *hadith*, *sunna*, *ijma'*, *ijtihad*, and so on.

In the perception of some leading legists, speculation risked to erase the piety enjoined by the God of the living tradition, who is the compassionate commander of good deeds, among other numerous attributes.

The Mu'tazila thinkers aimed to obliterate all such attributes, since they considered them as diminishing the notion of God as a pure essence of justice, as an Aristotelian prime mover. This clash was the only moment in Islamic history where one major party in a dispute tried to eradicate disagreement and win a contest through the use of inflexible judicial means against not just the one or the other thinker suspected of heterodoxy, but against a whole class of scholars, here the legists and traditionists. The Mu'tazila succeeded in inciting the caliph al-Ma'mun to institute the *mihna*, a sort of inquisition, through which numerous scholars were interrogated and punished because of their doctrines, and among them the founder of the most radically antitheological and antiphilosophical among the four canonical Sunni schools, Amad Ibn Hanbal (780–855), a personality surrounded by an aura of piety and a fame of endurance. The population of Baghdad supported the persecuted scholars against the caliph and the Mu'tazila. This was a decisive battle to affirm the principle of centrality of the Sunni mechanism of tradition-building against any temptation to establish a centralistic orthodoxy based on the fixation of dogma (Hurvitz 2002: 17–18).

Not unlike the Christian elaboration on Greek philosophy, Islamic philosophy (called *falsafa*), which flourished right after the epoch of canonization and through the age of the Axial Renaissance (between the tenth and the twelfth centuries CE) established a dual relation of absorption and rejection between Islamic high culture and the Greek philosophical heritage. At the same time, Islamic philosophers seriously coped with the main theoretical thrust of the reflections and contentions of the legists, the theologians, and the mystics: in other words, they took Islam seriously, although the strains they had to sustain in their reflections were particularly severe (Marmura 1983). Yet unlike thinkers like Aquinas in Latin Christendom, the practitioners of *falsafa* identified themselves as philosophers, and by this very identification they took one step out of the consensus. It is not surprising that, in spite of its importance and active contribution to the process of reshaping the consensus, philosophy and its modes of reasoning did not end up featuring centrally in the Sunni synthesis, in contrast with Christian Europe, where not only Aquinas, but also some of his adversaries, did not conceal the extent to which their own discourse was indebted to the legacy of the Greek metaphysical corpus, while remaining within the orthodox consensus as theologians and legists.

A nonspeculative, largely antimetaphysical philosophy of law will lay the basis for the reconstruction of public reasoning in Islam well into the modern era. It would be however a gross mistake to think of speculative philosophy as being excluded from any stake in the intricate politics of the Islamic consensus. Islamic philosophy contributed key elements to a theory of prophetic discourse that not only affected, albeit indirectly, the most penetrating reflection of the Islamic philosophy of law, but also contributed invaluable seeds to much later discussions on religion and scripture within European modernity.[3] The leading Islamic philosopher, Ibn Sina (980–1037), known in Europe as Avicenna, formulated the pathbreaking hypothesis that prophetic discourse received its strength and persuasiveness from being imbued with mythical imagery.

This discourse was best shaped to match the imagination of the commoners and induce them to perform good. This does not mean—so his argument—that prophetic discourse is untrue. The use of imaginative symbols is here considered necessary for effectively communicating the truth of religion. Inspired by his predecessor al-Farabi, Ibn Sina was the prime formulator of a theory of religion as an equivalent of philosophy of and for the masses which would find eager new interpreters in leading modern European thinkers such as Spinoza, Vico, and even Gramsci. According to this theory the prophets translated the philosophical maxim "if you pursue moral good, your mind shall attain the real spiritual freedom which is bliss" into the command "if you are virtuous and perform these *specific acts*, you shall enter Paradise and will be saved from the flames of Hell" (Rahman 1979 [1966]: 119–20; Marmura 1983).

Ibn Sina's theory and Islamic philosophy in general had a strongly intellectualist bent and elitist overtones. It was mainly for this reason, more than for any allegedly heretical character toward Sunni dogma, that its approach raised the suspicion of the orthodox legists. Yet Islamic philosophy provided the most ingenious systematization of the relationship between revelation-based and speculation-driven strands of axial thought (see chapter 2). Its later influence on the modern European coping with prophetic discourse as "religion" shows how this theory was a unique contribution to the long term, post-axial debate on the fundaments and modalities of public speech, and on its effect on the commoners. The contribution of philosophy to the redefinition of public reasoning within Islamic jurisprudential traditions will also leave enduring traces, however, indirectly. Many among the scholars who coped with the rational methods of *falsafa*—like Fakhr-al-Din al-Razi (d. 1209)—or argued against them—like al-Ghazali—or took a prudent distance from them—like Abu Ishaq al-Shatibi (d. 1388)—contributed to introduce philosophical rigor into theology, Sufism, and, finally, as we will see, into the theory of jurisprudence and law.

Another major turning point in Islamic history that affected the framing of *shari'a* within Sunni traditions occurred around the end of the seventh century AH, between the thirteenth and the fourteenth centuries CE, after traumatic events such as the Mongol invasion and the demise of the Caliphate in Baghdad. The Islamic notions of order had to be rescued from the effects of a crumbling political authority and from the impasse of a speculative rationality incapable of pinpointing the transcendent order without destroying it. It is in this phase that Sufism became ubiquitous in the Muslim world thanks to a fresh wave of diffusion and institutionalization of mystical paths as practiced in the confraternities (*turuq*). Partly through an effort to come to terms with this rise of Sufism, Ibn Taymiya (1263–1328) represents the point of view of the *'ulama'*, the leading formulators of the transcendent order, and their relationship to a political order that was at its deepest point of crisis since after the rise of Islam. Ibn Taymiya's strategy was to reaffirm a synthetic view of *shari'a*'s centrality in Islam, encompassing the inner truth of the Sufis (*haqiqa*), the rational approach of the philosophers and theologians (*'aql*), and obviously the law (*shari'a*) (Rahman 1979 [1966]: 111).

*Shari'a* was redefined by Ibn Taymiya as the source of Islamic normativity originating in divine will, as the essential condition for the law, and therefore as much more than its mere outward dimension, which was how some Sufis saw it. In order to endorse this conception of *shari'a*, Ibn Taymiya had to specify it as purposively affirming the wisdom and command of God, against all theological speculations that considered the purposive character of God's will as diminishing his omnipotence. Since *shari'a* ordains human behavior, Ibn Taymiya's reaffirmed through it the telic and intentional character of human action (ibid.: 113–14). Here *shari'a* coincides with the good commanded by God and implemented by man. This formulation of *shari'a* opened the way to a new reconstruction of its foundations and objectives to be pursued through a renewed philosophy of Islamic jurisprudence.

## The Challenge of Pietistic Movements

While *shari'a* was relocated from the edge to the center of Sunni tradition, the rise of Sufism represented the most serious challenge to the hegemony of the legists. The competition between Sufism and jurisprudence not only contributed to redefine the place of *shari'a*, it also affected the ongoing tension between intellectual speculation, on the one hand, and practical, juridical, and public reasoning, on the other. Unlike the philosophers, the Sufis did not raise the banner of rational speculation. They reinterpreted the tension between the spiritual and the practical levels of the Islamic tradition. The advantage of the Sufi "pietistic" approach, compared to that of the theologians and the philosophers, consisted in the fact that Sufism anchored its spiritual claims within ritualized collective practices and repertoires of intersubjective engagement and connectivity, so avoiding a dogmatist impasse and an elitist bias. In what follows I attempt to show that the precarious balance that resulted from the Sufi challenge favored the crystallization of "scalable" models of governance of the social bond between *ego* and *alter* mediated by faith.

The roots of Sufism are as old as the endeavor of putting Muhammad's message into practice by his companions and the new Muslim community. From a first nucleus of Medinese piety and asceticism inspired by the Qur'anic notion of faithful trust in God (*tawakkul*) and of love for God, the Sufi path took its first contours during the first two centuries of Islam. This initial growth was sustained by the widespread sentiment that the process of canonization led by the legists did not exhaust the truth of Islam, and that therefore a parallel tradition of piety immune from formalistic fixings was required (Rahman 1979 [1966]: 130). This approach was favored by the fact that the absence of priesthood in Sunni Islam facilitated equating the sincere faithful, the practitioner, and the commoner. It was however not before the eleventh and the twelfth centuries that Sufism was included into the mainstream consensus and took up a clear organizational form (Hoexter and Levtzion 2002: 12).

The path of Sufism was highly innovative in that it formulated a solution to the problem of the relationship between rational speculation, on the one hand, and prophetic discourse along with its impact on the categories of practitioners, on the other. This inherently tense relationship seemed to have reached a grave stalemate with the work of Ibn Rushd (d. 1198), known in Europe as Averroes. His rationalist philosophy became the object of vehement attacks by the *fuqaha'* (singular *faqih*, practitioner of *fiqh*, "jurist") in spite of the fact that he was also an active jurist. Sufism exploited this tension to its advantage in order to prove its commitment to orthodoxy by focusing on the exemplary value of the *sunna* of Muhammad. This was regarded as a path that the single believer had to appropriate in a disciplined training under the guide of a master, in order to gain access to the essential truth, the *haqiqa*. This inner truth could only be achieved through establishing a close relationship to the human being who is particularly close to God, the prophet Muhammad, and to the other "friends of God," the new Sufi saints.

The *shari'a* was not rejected by the Sufis. It was considered as the necessary, outer shell of truth. The Sufi path contributed to reconstruct the fragile consensus in a manner that neither abstract rational speculation nor the plain administration of the law could achieve on their own. In spite of the fact that Sufi masters mostly belonged to the ranks of the *'ulama'*, they saw their primary task not in administering the *shari'a*, but in experiencing and communicating the tensions of the cosmological order in a primary form, and in distilling a practice of piety out of the experience. In the course of time, organized, collective mystical practices emerged. The *shari'a* was regarded by Sufis as a norm governing the *ego-alter*-God relationship in routine-like, daily situations. It was felt that a deepening of piety needed a commitment both to the inner truth of the *haqiqa* and to the regulating framework of *shari'a*. The investment into this blend of practices and commitments represented an important step in the construction of an ethic of personal responsibility that contributed to later, modern reconstructions of the public sphere (cf. Eickelman and Salvatore 2002).

Sufism took upon itself the task of shaping that form of faithful trust among brothers in faith that the *fuqaha'* discourse was not able to capture on its own. This is why several interpreters, including the authoritative Muslim reformer Fazlur Rahman, tend to see the relationship between Sufism and jurisprudence more as a division of labor than as a conflict between sharply competing approaches to Islam. Noteworthy is the fact that the crystallizing orthodox formulas of Sunni Islam as described earlier prevented Sufism from establishing a form of monasticism, which was not unknown to the spiritual ferments in Arabia immediately antecedent to Muhammad's preaching. Similarly, however, to the new monastic movements of the Axial Renaissance in Christian Europe, the consolidation of Sufism took from the beginning the form of a socioreligious movement of the commoners laying a claim to grasp the essence of the truth. This similarity stands out in spite of all deep differences with the European experience for what concerns the institutional environment and the organizational forms of the movement and its understandings of the basic disciplines involved.

The most interesting aspect of the wave of institutionalization of Sufism during the Axial Renaissance is that while the new monastic orders in Europe colonized and shaped the renaissance of civic life, the Sufi movements entered a much more symbiotic relationship with urban associations, providing them a permanent source of ties of trust underpinned by the authority of the shaykhs (masters) of the brotherhoods. There were some associations whose organizational lines partly overlapped with the brotherhoods: the craftsmen guilds (cf. Gerber 1994: 113–26), some military or paramilitary organizations, like, among the Ottomans, the Turkish Janissaries, including autonomous units of frontiers warriors, as well as the urban *futuwwa*, a sort of youth gangs whose action was inspired by a chivalry code aimed to the protection of shared values and honor (Rahimi 2006: 62–63).

Sufi leaders played a role of conciliation and arbitration in civic disputes, up to the point that their houses were considered sanctuaries, in the double sense of revered places and extraterritorial sites for peace and arbitration gatherings, and therefore a safe haven from factional violence (Levtzion 2002: 110). Sufi orders reached out to a variety of constituencies, like traders, townspeople and peasants. Sufi leaders used not only scholastic Arabic but also the vernacular languages of the region. Ruling authorities were often deeply suspicious of the Sufi orders because of their autonomy and capacity for independent action, linking the local arenas with much wider spheres of influence. For the same reasons, some rulers sought links and advice from Sufi shaykhs.

In analogy with the new monastic movements described in chapter 3, the Sufi orders, without coinciding with civic associations, provided to them moral leadership, a discourse of justice, and a permanent channel of communication that facilitated connections between commoners and authorities (ibid.: 117). The monastic movements in Europe were able to take over the fabric of local sainthood and so to mediate between popular sentiments and the Church's fear that popular pressure could unsettle the centralized procedures of saints' canonization. In this way, the monastic movements contributed to make local saints the symbols of civic allegiances. The Sufi brotherhoods practiced a more radical path: they instituted on their own a notion of saintliness that was in principle extraneous to Sunni doctrine. This was and still is a contentious issue. The Sunni incorporation of prophetic charisma into a highly fragmented notion of authority does not recognize, in principle, authoritative sources external to the Qur'an and the *sunna*. Therefore, the making of saintliness through movements and groups other than the schools of law and which laid a claim to the preservation and transmission of Qur'anic piety was perceived as a challenge to the authority of the jurisprudents.

It was al-Ghazali who, at the very moment he was engaging in an onslaught on philosophy, made an important step in incorporating Sufism into the Sunni consensus, without extinguishing the tension among them. The authority of the Sufi masters—often elected to living saints—was able to shape the will of adepts much more than what the legists, from the vintage point of a balanced view of *shari'a*-based piety, would have liked to see. Apart from theoretical systematization and dispute, the main reason for the rise of the authority of Sufi leaders as not only spiritual masters but also as managers of social trust, is that the waves of conversion to Islam, which in most cases did not immediately follow the military conquests, were often the work of Sufi missionaries and networks. It is noteworthy, however, that the more orthodox forms of Sufism, rejecting the nonorthodox rituals practiced by less orthodox Sufis, like tombs worship, singing and dancing, and body piercing, were close, at their root, to the sentiments of the most radical among the Sunni schools, Hanbalism, for their shared anti-intellectualistic emphasis on the purity of faith based on its genuine Qur'anic expressions uncontaminated by formalisms.[4]

In organizational terms, the Sufi movements, especially through the incorporation of their more orthodox practices into the Sunni consensus during the age of the Axial Renaissance, impacted on the sociopolitical configuration of forces in both urban and rural contexts. The making of saintliness became strictly associated with autonomous civic powers, mostly linked to professional organizations, similarly to Europe. The main difference from Europe, apart from the weaker religious legitimacy of political power in increasingly fragmented and enfeebled Muslim potentates after the eleventh century, and toward which the Sufi organizations acted as sites for autonomous social organization and as a permanent source of popular unrest, was that the organizational unit of Sufism, the *tariqa*, was kept much more fluid than the monastic form of organization prevalent in Europe. The *tariqa* did not necessarily coincide with a brotherhood, nor with a lay confraternity like those promoted by the new monastic movements in Europe (see chapter 3). A *tariqa*, which literally means a "way," was basically a network of variably organized levels of master-disciple relations, kept together by strong congregational moments epitomized by the collective séances of the adepts.

We can therefore locate in the urban centers a variable geography of legal schools (several hundreds in the early centuries, then consolidating into a dozen, and with four emerging as "canonical schools": Makdisi 1983: 79), guilds, and brotherhoods, alongside ethnic communities. This organizational map found a transversal institutional glue in the mechanisms through which public services were funded: not by municipalities, but by pious endowments, originating from the institution of *waqf* (cf. Mardin 1995: 286–87). In this institutional environment, the *'ulama'*, many of which were tied to Sufi brotherhoods as much as they were to the formal educational curricula, took over the role of community leaders. The category of the *'ulama'* (or "men of knowledge") becomes therefore broader than the category of the legists/jurisprudents (the *fuqaha'*, or specialists of *fiqh*).

Sociologically speaking, the *'ulama'* encompass those cultural elites who, basing their credentials on some "orthodox" form of knowledge and leadership, were best positioned to shape a viable social environment nourishing public space. The diversity of opinions among them on various issues of both practical and conceptual interest and the ensuing disagreements encouraged them to seek the support of the restricted public of their peers (*al-khassa*), for the more theoretical questions, and of the common public (*al-'amma*), on the questions of public interest (Rahman 1979 [1966]: 261–62). Their wider ethic of public service consisted in providing moral guidance on life conduct and social intercourse, from a broadly social, to a specifically religious or legal level. Their multiple functions — as teachers, jurisprudents, notaries, judges, guardians of orphans, preachers, and, not least, Sufi masters — brought them into daily contact with all segments of the populations. As de facto representatives and interpreters of a variety of interests, they shaped and channeled public opinion. The autonomous organizations to which they provided leadership and ranks, but which were kept short of an entirely formal organization, were the Sufi brotherhoods and the colleges of learning (Hoexter and Levtzion 2002: 11). In both sets of organizations, the ties between master and disciples and the related networks prevailed over formal organization.

There emerged a clear division of responsibilities between rulers (including caliphs in the old Umayyad and Abbasid empires, and in the modern Ottoman Empire) and *'ulama'*. Even more than the caliphs, other sultanic authorities[5] generally refrained from interfering with disputes among *'ulama'*, although the *madrasa*s, that is the *waqf*-based colleges of learning, often kept close ties to the rulers. This configuration appears like the inside-out version of the situation in Christian Europe, where the universities were autonomously constituted as corporations of teachers and/or students, while the religious personnel, largely drawn from the mendicant orders, was tied to the Church.

Both in the realm of socioeconomic activities and in the world of learning, the discourse of the *'ulama'* was ubiquitous, yet highly articulated internally due to the plurality of schools and orders. As summarized by Sharif Mardin, "this lifeworld of Islam had a dynamic of its own, recursive in its reference to a golden age of Islam but progressive in the sense of gradually mobilizing an increasing number of Muslims for the elaboration of an Islamic ideal" (Mardin 1995: 289). More than a prevalence of informal ties in the relationships among scholars and between scholars, commoners, and rulers, we see here an organizational approach of a more "scalable" kind than in their European counterparts, in terms of degree, and reversibility, of formalization. This is well illustrated by the institution that best reflects the inclusion of the commoners in the practices and discourses of doing good: the institution that incorporates the public weal also via the physical shaping of public space, the *waqf*.

While *shari'a*-based jurisprudence provided the normative ideal to Muslim society, and Sufi orders supplied it with moral leadership, the *waqf* represented the structural and even fiscal infrastructure that secured the public weal, especially in the two fields that we today define as "educational" and "charitable." Though being a full-fledged type of institution unlike the legists' schools and the Sufi orders, the *waqf* retains and optimizes the scalability of formalization and flexibility in the use of resources for the pursuit of its institutional ends, although it could not provide secure guarantees of protection from abuses and diversions of resources from their institutional objectives. Yet the light and flexible level of formalization was guaranteed by a de facto civil law of *waqf*.[6]

The *waqf*, an endowment made by any faithful able to afford it—though mainly by the rulers and the political, bureaucratic, and economic elites—was the largest source of funding for public services. It is not surprising that among such services the rulers were particularly eager to institute and fund the colleges, in order to employ *'ulama'* and attract their benevolence. The establishment of charitable endowments benefited the elite in that it fostered bonds of loyalty with the lower classes via the mediation of the authority and trust generated by the *'ulama'*. It so compensated the inherently fragile legitimacy of the leadership of those in a privileged position within society. The centrality of the *waqf* increased, instead of declining, in the Ottoman Empire, which was by far the clearest case in Islamic history of a political-administrative, territorial state entailing an organization and hierarchization of public functions. In an Ottoman context, the *waqf* did not change its function due to the stronger centralization and legitimacy of political power, but became particularly complex and ubiquitous. It embraced numerous villages and several revenue-consuming institutions, including Friday mosques, *madrasa*s, poor kitchens, and so on. It is significant that even when rulers had a higher inherent legitimacy—as in the case of the Ottoman ruler, who after the conquest of Constantinople/Istanbul resurrected the ancient institution of the caliphate—they often preferred to provide basic services in the form of personal bestowal rather than through a faceless bureaucracy (Gerber 2002: 75). In an optimal situation, one could observe the existence of a large network of *waqf*s providing a variety of public services, a largely autonomous network run by the public itself through the *'ulama'*, whereby the rulers' intervention was reduced to a minimum (Gerber 2002: 77; for the relation of *waqf* to Ottoman law, see Gerber 1994: 101–9).

The term *waqf* is an abbreviation of *sadaqa mawqufa* that means something close to "perpetual charity," a permanent source of doing good for the sake of God, as specified in all *waqf* manuals. A valid purpose for the endower/founder to initiate a *waqf* was a *qurba*, which means any motive liable to bring him/her closer to God. The charitable scope was defined in this way, but the endower had a wide decisional freedom as to the beneficiary, which could range from family members to freed slaves and poor belonging to particular ethnic groups or urban neighborhoods, or to the poor in general—but also to a specific law school or Sufi brotherhood, to the building of basic infrastructures like water supply or bridges, and obviously to the construction and maintenance of mosques and annexed colleges (Hoexter 2002: 122, 128). A close equivalent of an idea of *caritas* was incorporated in the principle of *qurba*. Yet in the case of *waqf* this idea defined a continuum between private and public concern, both considered essential constituents of the welfare of the community of believers. This practical version of *caritas* is less a subjective virtue, and more a legally defined modality of interaction where God mediates the link between *ego* and *alter* as the celestial Other in whose name—or better, for the sake of whose closeness—the charitable act is performed, finally to the benefit of the terrestrial other.

Yet it is less the concept than the management of *waqf* conglomerations that best reflects Islamic notions of duties, rights, and responsibilities underlying collective welfare. First, the institutionally unmarked character of the *umma*, the community of believers, made *waqf* a terrain of competition for leadership measured by a capacity to care for the common good. The rulers were considered responsible for the public order, but were not per se, as rulers, deputed to care for the public weal. They were expected to create the practical conditions for its pursuit. Therefore, it is not surprising that while the rulers guaranteed public order qua rulers, they competed on the provision for the public weal as endowers, that is as community leaders among others (ibid.: 123). And it is remarkable that the *'ulama'* retained a central role not only in the formulation of the common good, but also in its daily and concrete management via their staffing of *waqf* institutions. These required a considerable administrative and especially legal competence in accommodating the composite and mobile interests that the *waqf* was called to satisfy.

It is fair to say that the rational, organizational, and jurisprudential tools for managing accommodation and change within the sphere of interests covered by *waqf* were in the hands of the *'ulama'* (ibid.: 127). A sociologically focused definition of the *'ulama'* would be as those community leaders who shape public space by employing their public and legal reasoning in running *waqf*. This function legitimized and facilitated their role as intermediaries between rulers and commoners even more than their possession of knowledge per se, or more than their role as scholars, teachers, and preachers. The fact that complaints were often filed for improper management of *waqf* in the Ottoman Empire, in the frequent court cases involving the *waqf* administration, shows that each and every citizen had the right to file a lawsuit in the name of a public interest. Local communities saw themselves as the first instance of monitoring on the proper use of *waqf*, that is on its use for the benefit of the various sectors of the population to which *waqf* services were directed (Gerber 2002: 76). The imperatives of *caritas* were best served by a continuous renegotiation and interpretation of all legitimate interests at stake, and therefore an "ongoing discourse" on the common good and the associated methods of public reasoning emerged, formulated and mediated by the *'ulama'*. This approach produced a rich jurisprudential knowledge, but also one that eschewed rigid codification. I now turn to the theoretical fundaments of this ongoing, practical and juridical discourse on the common good.

## The Triumph of *Phronesis* and the Sunset of the Axial Renaissance

Jurisprudence and the theory of its "fundaments," *usul al-fiqh*, required a method of reasoning different from that of theology and philosophy. A focus on the simultaneously intentional and interactional dimension of human actions was required, in order for man to be held not just morally but also legally responsible for his acts. It has been stated that the main issue of the philosophy of law was that "since obedience to Divine Command . . . depends on human volition, the Command must be shown to be motivated by the consideration of human interest" (Masud 1995 [1977]: 119). It is therefore unsurprising that especially from the eleventh century onward various thinkers concentrated their reflections on the idea of *maslaha* (common good/public weal) as the universal general principle permeating all commands with legal value (ibid.: 122). *Maslaha* provided the conceptual proof stone for underpinning theoretically informed but practice-oriented views of the common good which were suitable to become platforms for concrete articulations of the pursuit of public weal.

The notion of *maslaha* is based on the root *s-l-h* that denotes being and becoming good, in a sense that conveys the full scale of positive values from uncorrupted to right, honest, virtuous, and further up to just and righteous (ibid.: 135). In time, *maslaha* and the related notion of *istislah*—stemming from the same root, and indicating the method of reasoning for seeking *maslaha*—became the principal key words in the discussion. The emerging method of reasoning associated with this wider theoretical reflection stood out against other approaches that sought an exclusive basis on scriptural sources. In the method of the Maliki school, one of the four canonical Sunni legal schools, the one that most consistently upheld the centrality of *maslaha*, this approach was also employed to discard the earlier mentioned limitations of the notion of *ijma'*, or consensus.

The approach to *maslaha* still stands out as the most flexible and rational method of Islamic legal reasoning to date. It appears, symptomatically, not only less text bound and more context friendly than other methods, but also based on a view of the common good emancipated from the fictitious, fragile, and largely arbitrary view of consensus that prevails at any given time. This methodology was from its inception quite suitable to shift the boundaries of any existing consensus, via the modes of public reasoning concretely applied to any given situation (ibid.: 137).

Using in particular the method of induction and generalization shaped by the Hanafi school, and merging it with the Maliki notion of the common good as intrinsic to *shari'a*, the Andalusi jurist Abu Ishaq al-Shatibi asserted that the principle underlying all *shari'a* rulings is and cannot be other than *maslaha*. It is the intent of God the Lawgiver as incarnate in the objectives of the law (*maqasid al-shari'a*) that makes *maslaha* central to legislation. In other words—so al-Shatibi's claim—legal reasoning cannot focus on a single doctrine or case while looking at the legal sources, but has to relate to the *telos* of the law. The theological premise of this reasoning was quite simple: "the premise is that God instituted the . . . laws . . . for the . . . good of the people, both immediate and future" (ibid.: 118–19). According to this approach, reliance on *qiyas* (analogical reasoning) was not acceptable, because it limited legal reasoning to deducting rulings from a particular text, thereby inhibiting any inductive reasoning based on aggregate textual evidence and not on a single text (ibid.: 128).

Furthermore, *istislah* as the method of inductive search for *maslaha* differed from the *istihsan* preferred by the Hanafi school. The latter promoted the discretion of the individual jurist in searching for the most useful solution to a given case (and has been therefore compared to the notion of "equity" in common law) whenever the reasoning by analogy (*qiyas*) yields a solution harmful to such utility. *Istislah* instead originated from an integrated method for identifying and promoting the public weal and has therefore been compared with the Roman law principle of *utilitas publica* ("public utility"). In spite of its simple theological premise, *istislah* is a sophisticated method of reasoning resting on the theoretical notion of *maslaha*, while *istihsan* consists in deploying an equitable approach to specific cases. In this sense, *istislah* departs form a merely utilitarian logic. Based on *maslaha* and on the related method of *istislah*, a ruling should not be simply useful in itself, that is by reference to a notion of utility seen as inherent in a given empirical situation and in a specific legal case, but by reference to a wider concept of common good, equivalent to *res publica*. This goal is attained by applying existing rules with the backup of a wider collective interest that corresponds to the basic finality of the law itself (ibid.: 129–31).

*Maslaha* differs from utility in that, theologically, it is not limited to this world but links the good in this world to the hereafter, and sociologically, does not limit the common good to material utility, and especially not to the sum of the utility of various agents (ibid.: 132). Moreover *maslaha* does not show the limitations of the *utilitas publica* of Roman law (Crone 1987: 11). In the Roman imperial epoch the faculty to reinterpret a law in the name of the public weal degenerated into the prerogative of edictal legislation to undermine the traditional law and legitimize ad hoc rulings (ibid.: 104–5). The legalistic notion of *utilitas publica* hijacked the wider normative concept of *res publica*, while *maslaha*, though suitable to a juridical operationalization in form of *istislah*, remained closer to an interpretation of *res publica* in principle uncontaminated by any compromise with contingent exigencies of the ruler. Following *maslaha* inoculates the law against any abuse for an expediency dictated by considerations external to the legitimate interests at stake in a given situation.

There is, moreover, a sense of *caritas* incorporated in *maslaha*, which crosscuts the service function of the *waqf* institution, as the pivotal establishment for seeking and implementing *maslaha*. However, this cannot be equated with the incorporation of *caritas* implemented within Latin Christendom, via the elaboration on the notion of a *respublica christiana* reconstructed in chapter 3. The latter was the product of the combination of at least two different traditions, the Christian tradition of *caritas* and the legal tradition of Roman law. *Maslaha*, while incorporating several layers of traditional legacies ranging from Greek philosophy, through the influence of Judaism and Christianity, to Roman law itself, was developed in a more linear and sustained fashion from within the ongoing—though precarious—search for an Islamic consensus.

At the same time, the notion of *maslaha* can be articulated in a plural way, in the form of the *masalih* (plural of *maslaha*), which are the goods to be sought in different situations and legal cases. *Maslaha* could be elaborated upon simultaneously in theological-theoretical and legal-practical terms, while *utilitas publica* remained a strictly jurisprudential notion and *res publica* became a too strongly theoretical concept increasingly divorced—during the Axial Renaissance of Latin Christendom—from the legal field. *Maslaha*, however, is never identical with a particularistic good even when it is identified with a discrete good. Various species of *maslaha* refer to *maslaha* as a genus. It is noteworthy that in a *fatwa* (legal opinion) on a *waqf* controversy issued by al-Shatibi, the principle of *maslaha* was applied in order to safeguard the nature of *waqf* as a type of endowment to create a good that is collective yet specific (a particular mosque, or school and so on). Al-Shatibi's ruling was intended to fight the practice, which was widespread at his time in al-Andalus, of using *waqf* revenues for the undifferentiated funding of a general category of collective service (for instance, all mosques in a town) and therefore as a supplement to the sultanic treasure (*bayt al-mal*) (Masud 1995 [1977]: 93). The protection of *maslaha*—al-Shatibi argued—requires an adherence to the particular will of the endower, provided it is finalized to *qurba* (coming closer to God).

An important antecedent to this view of an objective common good as in *maslaha* was present in the theology of the Mu'tazila, mentioned earlier in this chapter. This school considered this type of general good as rationally ascertainable, and therefore as well fitting into a rational concept of divine justice. The limit of this theory consisted in that it could not spell out the actual mechanisms of judgment and legal reasoning for attaining the common good. In other words, this approach was not able to bridge the theoretical gap between means (moral and legal actions) and the end of the common good (ibid.: 131). The Mu'tazila thinkers faced a problem similar to the dilemmas encountered by the Stoics and Cicero (see chapter 3), for they did not yoke the *telos* of action to a solid mechanism of reflective praxis as *phronesis*. On a purely theological level a strong theoretical view of action as the one elaborated by Aquinas remained largely latent in Islamic thought. Far from counting as a "gap," this latency reflected a stronger praxic orientation to the problem of linking *phronesis* to *telos*. This combination between the latency of a one-shot theological solution and the engagement with a theory strictly linked to praxis makes the juridical, yet theoretically informed approach of al-Shatibi particular important as a parallel, yet different solution to the problem, faced by Aquinas, of finding the most rational means to ends apprehended by an intellect tuned into the supreme good.

The solution pursued by al-Shatibi highlights the relation between *phronesis* and *telos* from a practical and legal angle that helps elucidating some of the general nodes encountered in the process of upgrading practical reasoning into public reasoning. It shows a conception that makes quite transparent how reflective *phronesis* is linked to command, while it cannot be defined by authority alone. God's command—according to most theologians, including al-Ghazali—has to coincide with the *maslaha* of man, but "in order to decide that something is *maslaha*, even to say that God's commands are based on *maslaha*, some criterion outside of these commands has inevitably to be accepted" (ibid.: 145). *Istislah* represents therefore nothing less than the specific phronetic criterion to ascertain and seek the *maslaha* on which God's commands are based.

Parallel to this discovery by al-Shatibi, Ibn Taymiya derived from the view that all of God's commands are based on *maslaha* an argument for attacking the weakness of the assumption by the Muʿtazila that there is a coincidence, almost by default, between what is morally obligatory for man and the moral command by God. Ibn Taymiya's view of *maslaha* helped fill the gap between the two levels, through stressing the moral responsibility of man in seeking *maslaha*. While he denied that there can be a *maslaha* that is not revealed in scripture, he conceded that there might be *masalih* (specific goods rooted in given situations) not found by the *faqih* in a source text. This is what makes necessary an active seeking for these goods in the context of a given interaction, situation, or legal case.

While Ibn Taymiya did not endorse *istislah*, he and his pupil Ibn al-Qayyim (1292–1350) defined a less phronetic but more political obligation of actively searching for *maslaha*, an obligation incumbent on every Muslim. They called it *al-siyasa al-sharʿiyya*. A literal translation of this formula (whereby *siyasa* means "politics") cannot render its meaning, which on the one hand comes close to *maslaha*, but on the other lays stress on the collective, legitimate, and finally political character of the activity of seeking the common good (Masud 1995 [1977]: 148–49). It is remarkable, however, that the most radical view of *maslaha* was issued by another Hanbali scholar contemporary of Ibn Taymiya, Najm al-Din al-Tufi (d. 1316). He unambiguously declared *maslaha* to be the overriding principle of *shari'a*, and as such superior even to scripture and consensus. In view of the fact that both the textual sources and the opinions on which the consensus rested were fragmented and inconsistent, the pursuit of *maslaha* as common good was according to al-Tufi the only possible criterion allowing for a coherent method of deliberation (ibid.: 149–50). While radically innovative on the theoretical level for subverting the traditional hierarchy of legal principles, this position was not of great practical help and methodological significance from the viewpoint of the theory of action, since it did not problematize the phronetic criteria necessary for seeking *maslaha*.

It is possible then to see al-Shatibi's concern for *maslaha* as the culmination of a strong tradition of reflection on the phronetic character of human action that climaxed during the Axial Renaissance. Yet it is also symptomatic that al-Shatibi's work occurred at the sunset of that renaissance. His theoretical elaborations were stirred up by the serious socioeconomic changes that Andalusi society was experiencing in the fourteenth century. These upheavals made a reliance on analogy and precedent in jurisprudence insufficient to solve legal cases and raised the necessity to reconstruct broader principles of Islamic law from which to derive rulings (ibid.: 55). Al-Shatibi inherited from the earlier discussions, which spanned the period from the eleventh century to his own epoch, the view that the objectives (*maqasid*) of God's will, and therefore of the *shari'a*, are simply the *maslaha* (the good, the interest) of the people. He was particularly straightforward in seeing the finality of the *shari'a* as coinciding with *maslaha*. We find here a view of *maslaha* that is at the same time strongly objectified and quite concrete, similarly to the pristine Roman view of *res publica* (see chapter 5). The main difference is that as a theoretical notion denoting good or interest, *maslaha* was also immediately applicable to the modalities of legal reasoning. It should be remarked that in his work on the philosophy of law, al-Shatibi manifested his outright distaste for any purely intellectual or theological discussion of *shari'a*. Wherever unrelated to questions immediately relevant for action and judgment, such an abstract discussion was, in his view, hostile to the scope of *shari'a* itself. It was precisely on the basis of such a radically anti-intellectualistic platform that al-Shatibi delivered the most compelling theoretical formulation of Islamic notions of "common good" and "public weal."

Thus al-Shatibi was induced to stress in a straightforward manner that in legal reasoning one must give priority to the results of action in order to check whether it serves the purpose of the law (ibid.: 123). Far from being an expedient method of legal reasoning, the principle of *maslaha* in al-Shatibi's approach is a basic concept upholding human livelihood in all its dimensions: material, emotional, and intellectual (ibid.: 114, 151). The differentiated and plural human *masalih* (those essential to forge and maintain the link between man and God: the human self, procreation, property, and reason) are brought together into a system including in a hierarchical order a series of other goods that are either needed by man, or commendable to pursue. The result is a comprehensive yet flexible notion of *maslaha* coinciding with the objectives of the law, even if plural and concrete *masalih* are the actual object of the inductive phronetic reasoning of the jurist applied to discrete cases (ibid.: 151–52).

Al-Shatibi also introduced a welcome element of complexification—and, at the same time, of distinction—at the intersection between the discursive tradition and the world of practice and "common sense." He insisted on distinguishing between the *masalih* as defined in the discourse (*khitab*) of the lawgiver, and as found in the world of human life and relations. The latter are no pure *masalih*, but are mingled with hardship and discomfort. It is habit and practice (*'ada*) that customarily define certain things as *masalih* and other as *mafasid* (nuisances, discomforts). This specification indicates that practical, common sense is not purely receptive toward needs, but has also a definitional and, as it were, discursive capacity (ibid.: 155).

Social practice therefore reveals a first layer of interpretative *phronesis* in actors' seeking of *maslaha*. This is not a specialized enterprise led by expert knowledge, but is in the hands of the commoner, so it is—we could say—common sense-driven. On the other hand, the discourse of *shari'a* does define the *masalih* in an absolute way. Coherently with the function of prophetic discourse, this definitional task is functional to the goal to inculcate a telic sense of right and wrong in human agency and practical rationality via learning in action, without which action would degenerate into a pure utilitarian hunt for fully predefined, discrete and separate goods.[7]

It is in such a field of enduring tension between the complexity of the social world where goods and ills are not found in a pure form, yet can be defined as such by agents, on the one hand, and the moral command of *shari'a* to do good and prohibit evil, on the other, that agential *phronesis* develops. It takes form on the bedrock of the connotation of man as a free agent (*mukhtar*) who is responsible for his acts, not only morally, but also legally. In those cases where neither habit or custom, nor the *shari'a* provide a clear definition of what is right or wrong, *ijtihad*, intended as the methodical endeavor to find creative solutions through reasoning, has to be exercised. Admitting the importance and legitimacy of *ijtihad* is for al-Shatibi essential to deliberation. After weighing all hypothetical solutions to a case for which no clear answer to whether a certain action is right or wrong (like for instance eating carrion when indispensable to survival, in case no food is available) can be found, the decision of the *mujtahid* has to be considered legally binding (Masud 1995 [1977]: 156–57).

While the complexity of the social worlds and the intricacies of the process of defining and adjudicating *maslaha* are incontestable, this awareness does not justify a relativistic conception of *maslaha*. Al-Shatibi firmly distinguishes *maslaha*, which carries the connotation of "interest" in the sense of "public weal" (even without the specification of being *'amma*, that is, common, general, public, as in the frequent expression *al-maslaha al-'amma*) from the pursuit of particularistic interests, personal preferences, and passionate desires. The Andalusi jurist clearly reaffirmed that *maslaha*, while responding to the objectives of the *shari'a*, is finalized to emancipate human actors from the dictates of passion and make them the faithful servants of God (ibid.: 158). He relentlessly clarifies that *maslaha* is the engine itself of God's law in that it serves human welfare and the removal of hardship in general. It is therefore present as a genus in all rules, to be retrieved by the phronetic approach of jurisprudence aided by the application of the method of *istislah*. In contrast with the hierarchic-dualistic model of the subject prevalent in Christian Europe, and which liberal modernity will not dissolve but normatively consolidate (see Santoro 2003 [1999]; see chapter 5), in the Islamic case the superior interest is not the target of a pure volition of a virtuous subject, but emerges through interaction: it is intrinsically intersubjective. *Istislah*, as the phronetic and jurisprudential method to ascertain and adjudicate goods in a given situation, is, therefore, a genuine intersubjective approach.

It is revealing that one synonymous of *istislah* used by al-Shatibi is *istidlal*, which does not mean "finding a good" in a given situation but "finding the right sign" (Masud 1995 [1977]: 161–62). At a closer scrutiny one discovers that al-Shatibi's theory of law by necessity reposes on a theory of language that compares the *shari'a* issued from prophetic discourse to an "ordinary language" in the Wittgensteinian sense, a language game with intrinsic limits of formalizations, which however shows communicative strength in facilitating intersubjective understanding and connectivity.

Al-Shatibi's philosophy of law configures therefore a distinctive solution to the theoretical problem underlying the phronetic nature of action (see chapter 2). The Andalusi scholar maintained quite straightforwardly that "the judgment (*hukm*) is not derived on the basis of what meanings are posited (*wad'*) for the words but on some other basis, that is the aspect of following actions (*iqtida' bi-l af'al*)" (ibid.: 175). Al-Shatibi explains the enigmas of the regulating impetus of the "logic of practice" (see chapter 2) by invoking the *ummi* ("common" or "ordinary") character of prophetic discourse, its being addressed to the commoner. One cannot understand *shari'a* and its objectives without referring to the common sense of the addressees of the Qur'an. Clearly—and this sets the prophet Muhammad apart from his predecessors—the *ummi* disposition of the receptor of the Qur'anic message matches the character of the speech of *al-nabi al-ummi*, as Muhammad is designated in the Qur'an, that is, "the common prophet," or "the prophet of the commoners."

The ordinary character of prophetic speech might seem to clash with the notion of the miraculous features of Qur'anic discourse. However, the latter was understood as rooted in the immediacy or unmediated power of the word. Indeed, Muhammad was considered illiterate, and the written recording of the Qur'an is a later process determined by the practical needs of tradition-making, on whose necessity, significantly, the prophet was completely silent. Clearly the Qur'an, which means recitation or precisely speech, was intended to supersede the previous scripture, allegedly contaminated by impious and unscrupulous people who had manipulated God's word for mundane interests. This time God speaks to Muhammad through Jibril (Gabriel), and the prophet in turn transmits the revealed word to his followers who retain it by heart. This is why the Qur'an is held to have been recited and transmitted in "pure Arabic."

Al-Shatibi clarifies that the first level of intelligibility of *shari'a* rests on its being cast in ordinary Arabic, and is therefore context-bound. The ideal speech situation configured by the Qur'an and the circumstances of its initial transmission build, nonetheless, a second level of intelligibility that is universal since translatable in all existing languages. This level operates via a mechanism of retrieval activated by the type of reasoning promoted by al-Shatibi, consisting in inductively extracting collectively valid meaning from the text on the basis of the presumption of *maslaha* that helps instituting universal intelligibility. In other words, it is through the method of *istislah* supported by the objectives of *shari'a* that the ordinary language of prophetic discourse is translated into a universal language upholding and regulating social practice. Its phronetic dimension is brought to a level of sophistication that helps transcending the closed boundaries of a given primordial community, and therefore constitutes a high point in the pursuit of universality by discursive traditions issued of the axial breakthrough. The analogical method of *qiyas*, in its double constraint of being text-bound and based on a binary, scarcely reflective, and trivialized Aristotelian logic, is considered insufficient for responding to the axial promise of universality (Masud 1995 [1977]: 178–79).

Al-Shatibi goes one step further when he clarifies that the attribute *ummi* as used by the Arabs for designating themselves and their language was also intended to differentiate them from the Greeks and all civilizations of antiquity that rested on literacy and on the massive use of the written world, while the Arabs preferred oral transmission and tradition. Clearly—and al-Shatibi was aware of that—this inclination toward the spoken word changed quite rapidly in the first two centuries of Islam, mainly as an effect of Islam's rise and rapid spread. This process also encompassed the recording first of the Qur'an and then of *hadith* collections and encouraged the flourishing of the written sciences of the law, theology, philosophy, not to speak of medicine and other sciences in which the Arabs attained excellence. In spite of the consolidation of these cultural legacies, al-Shatibi's insistence on the *ummi* character of the Islamic *shari'a* as well as of the prophetic discourse from which it originated signifies a relativization of the importance of those axial traditions of the written world which culminated in philosophy, but lacked prophetic voices, like in the Greek case.

Al-Shatibi's theory puts in evidence how in the ingredients of what he—and indeed many Muslim reformers inspired by him up to our times—saw as the superior axial universality of Islam, the civilization of the written world played the role of a sufficient condition for the spread and consolidation of the civilization, while prophetic discourse in its pure *ummi*, ordinary form was the necessary one. This observation can be linked to what some scholars have evidenced as a likely concurrent meaning of *ummi* as referred to Muhammad, his language, and the Arabs in general. It is a meaning derived from Hebrew, which indicates "the people of the world in general," therefore with a meaning close to "gentile." Muhammad as the "gentile prophet" would then highlight an additional dimension of axial maturity of his message, that is its capacity to transcend its first level of being *ummi* or native and confined to a given community of ordinary language seeing itself as the chosen people. This second meaning of *ummi* could then be linked to the asserted character of Muhammad's prophecy as completing and sealing the whole chain of Semitic prophecy, by projecting the prophetic tradition toward embracing the people of the world in general, that is "man" (ibid.: 179), as the "common man." In this sense, more than a late manifestation of the axial breakthrough, the rise of Islam can be interpreted as an early manifestation of the Axial Renaissance.

Even if the reference to Ibn Sina (Avicenna) is not explicit, it is apparent how al-Shatibi's argument depends, consciously or not, on the theoretical approach to prophetic discourse developed by Islamic philosophers, in spite of al-Shatibi's ostentatious disregard for philosophical discourse, and in particular for Aristotelian methods. It is known that he was also trained in philosophy. The Andalusi scholar, who not unlike Ibn Sina considered not only Muhammad but all his prophetic predecessors and their laws (*shara'i'*, plural of *shari'a*) as admonishing and exhorting their people to the right path through a discourse formulated in ordinary language, has the merit of putting on its head the elitist approach of Ibn Sina. Instead of assuming a high truth made understandable and palatable to the commoner who cannot command the sophisticated rational discourse of the philosopher, al-Shatibi takes entirely the perspective of the common social and legal actor and asserts that a legal obligation can only be legitimate if the corresponding rule can be understood by its addressees. Thus there is no responsibility of the legal actor without a comprehension of the law.

This is also the part of al-Shatibi's argument where it appears most clearly that, on a social-theoretical level, one cannot rely on a self-enclosed view of ordinary language matching a Bourdieuian "logic of practice" (see chapter 2). Any self-sustaining practice requires efficient communication, and it is the understanding and active seeking of *maslaha* that makes communication among human actors possible via agreements on shared goods and methods to attain them (ibid.: 179). Here it also appears that the interpretive task of the jurist is only feasible as an extension and upgrading of the phronetic activity residing in the practice of ordinary people. This basic layer of practice, however, incorporates a knowledge of *maslaha* through *shari'a* and its intelligibility. In this sense, *maslaha* has not to be taught and inculcated *ex nihilo* by a class of *'ulama'*, neither does it ground obligations for the elite of knowledge alone. Obligation in the *shari'a* is rational and *therefore* universally comprehensible. The task of the jurists is to keep open and functioning the circles of communication, by seeking in *maslaha* the methodological guidance that is necessary for helping solve those problems that the commoners cannot solve on their own. The condition for performing this job is to cast into a *ummi*, comprehensible, ordinary language the solutions sought under the umbrella of the universalistic method of induction provided by *istislah* (ibid.: 181).

Faced with the problem of how to deal with what by his time was a well established spiritual elite, the Sufis, who had recruited wide masses of commoners and had penetrated many civic institutions, al-Shatibi drew a distinction between the ordinary people who act on the basis of self-interest (and therefore need the guidance of *maslaha*), and the Sufis, whose approach to *shari'a* obligations he considered extraordinary and therefore not setting the standard rule for the commoner. He called the Sufis "the people who disregard their self-interest," and saw them as consciously at odds with the common sense of right and wrong of the ordinary people. Though it is known that al-Shatibi did not sympathize with the Sufis, he justified their approach as indirectly beneficial to how *maslaha* orients the legal actors toward the balanced middle between the opposite extremes of too much hardship and too much laxity in performing obligations, thus echoing a well-known Aristotelian motive concerning the virtues (ibid.: 192–93). He saw that the vigorous emphasis on piety and asceticism of the Sufis was useful to counter the looming risk of a fall into laxity by the commoners. Sufism worked as a permanent correction to this danger, in spite of the purported lack of regulative strength of this correcting device in strictly legal terms.

It remains that al-Shatibi's view of the legal actor, of his obligations and of the notion of *maslaha* underlying both action and obligation, was based on a view of the actor not as a "subject" of virtuous or vicious conduct, or simply of rights and duties, but as a genuinely relational agent, who discharges duties incumbent on him/her, whose origin and justification are firmly inscribed in the axial triangular relationship between *ego, alter*, and God (see chapter 1). Whereas Sufism represents the closest approach in Islam to constructing a subjectivity of virtue and excellence through an ethic of renunciation—the closest therefore to the monastic path, whose legitimacy was explicitly denied in a famous *hadith* by the prophet Muhammad—al-Shatibi considered the Sufi path as subsidiary and not central to the Islamic view and practices of the common good.

In spite of the evident differences with the synthesis achieved in Christian Europe by Aquinas, al-Shatibi's challenge of Sufi asceticism's claim that only the negation of selfish interest can be a basis for true obedience to God echoes Aquinas's response to the challenge of the new monastic orders. The common answer was that self-interest is not denied by the notion of obedience to God, since conformity with the will of the Lawgiver (based on *maslaha*) is what constitutes obedience to the law of nature (ibid.: 196). By framing the pursuit of self-interest so as to fit into *maslaha*, this pursuit appears not only as legitimate, but as necessary for common welfare. This apparently simple answer pushed al-Shatibi—similarly to Aquinas—toward clarifying and complexifying the view of the legal agent and the category of intention in a way that, while it added sophistication to his theory, also put in evidence its points of vulnerability.

Trying to deepen the problematization of "interest," for al-Shatibi the legitimacy of *huzuz* (what we can translate as "self-interests") is to be affirmed to the extent they gravitate toward *maslaha* and not toward the servitude of passions (*hawa*). The problem is that the socioanthropological foundation of *huzuz* is in a notion of social practice and habits (or *'ada*, a category of Islamic legal thinking close to "custom") which is too self-explanatory in al-Shatibi's system. In his view, practice, custom, and the pursuit of legitimate self-interest therein feed into a sort of natural law whose relationship with *shari'a* had been scarcely problematized in Islamic legal philosophy. Aquinas offered a more convincing and systematic approach to the relationship between *lex naturalis* (natural law) and *lex aeterna* (divine law) as reflected in the evangelical new law or *lex nova* (see chapter 3). Al-Shatibi's distaste for Aristotelian approaches and in general for the speculative theology that had largely relied on Aristotle was doubtless a limiting factor for his theorizing. It was certainly an obstacle to using an explicit notion of natural law.

Yet his avoidance of a concept of natural law strengthened his emphasis on the factuality of common sense, habits, and customs and on their power to define social relationships and orient contentions about the goods. In this sense, al-Shatibi anticipates Vico's approach to the problem of how to define the nexus between human interaction and the common good (see chapter 5). While Vico had to cope with the natural law discourse (and with its metamorphosis through modern legal thinkers), al-Shatibi could do without it. The terrain on which al-Shatibi's theory sought to vindicate its coherence and comprehensiveness was delimited by the nexus between action and intention. His strategy differed from the Christian Thomistic theory of will (*voluntas*), which was still dependent on the Augustinian construction of the sinful subject.

Al-Shatibi maintained that intention (*niyya*) is necessary for an action to be considered as such. The social actor as a *mukhtar*, that is as an agent of choice endowed with freedom of the will, manifests, through acting, his intention to obey to the commands of the Lawgiver (reflecting the underlying search for *maslaha*) or to disobey. Seeking *maslaha* is therefore a requirement for a correctly directed intention, which is in turn indispensable to act (Masud 1995 [1977]: 206–7). This definition of intention is invoked to eliminate the residual ambiguities of al-Shatibi's dealing with passions, self-interests, and the common good. Ultimately the commitment to *maslaha* and the orientation of the agent's self-interest to it become a matter of the phronetic reason inherent in directing intention, more and before than being ascribable to a principled "subjective or personal responsibility" of the free agent. Al-Shatibi admits that in his phronetic seeking to do good, *ego* may happen to do harm to *alter*. The agent therefore should concur to the definition of *maslaha* in every specific case by supporting his pious intention with a reflection upon the consequences of action.

This operation requires going beyond the appearance or the simple assumption of good and bad. It needs an analysis of the complex ways in which benefit and discomfort are intermingled in social life (ibid.: 209). Therefore, the agent's intentionality has to include a layer of reflexivity. Reflecting about the consequences of one's action is the highest form of *phronesis*, in spite of the fact that it is no antidote against macrosociologically defined, unintended consequences of action, which can be only ascertained after the fact, and therefore cannot be covered by the higher, collective dimension of *maslaha*. This proactive form of *phronesis* is applied through *ijtihad*, as expounded earlier, which in al-Shatibi's approach is defined as "a process in which one exhausts one's efforts to one's full capacity in order to acquire exact or probable knowledge to reach judgment in a given case" (ibid.: 230).

Modern social theory, and Habermas within it, is also concerned with the social technologies that are deputed to "anticipate" and neutralize such unintended consequences. The analysis of the work of al-Shatibi as part of the genealogy of the public sphere thus provides a useful background for evidencing by contrast those shortcomings in the contemporary social-theoretical reconstruction of the public sphere that are built on a misconstruction—probably an inevitable one, from a modernist viewpoint—of tradition's repertoires for conceptualizing and regulating interaction and its communicative dimension (see chapter 6 and conclusion).

It is possible to say that the radically axial character of Sunni Islam lies in the fact that the sense of right and wrong based on knowledge postulated by its discursive tradition was never considered—ever since the time of Muhammad, and less than ever in the pristine Muslim community of Mecca, before its migration to Medina—a special competence of any distinct, specialized, or even consecrated social stratum or intellectual group. This claim is also supported by the fact that the parts of the Qur'anic revelation that have been located in the Meccan period of

Muhammad's preaching mostly concern general principles and narratives, a situation that encouraged and even made necessary the *ijtihad* of the commoner. The situation gradually changed with the establishment of a strong Muslim community in Medina and the subsequent expansion back into Mecca, in the whole of Arabia and elsewhere. Whatever the historical truth, for the narrative of the tradition as elaborated upon by al-Shatibi, the building of a specialized legal field was an inevitable consequence of the complexification of social relations in the growing Muslim community. Yet the only measure for assessing the legitimacy and effectiveness of the jurists' work could only be their capacity to respond to the needs and questions raised by the commoners.

For al-Shatibi, with regard to elementary legal questions that only require the application of general principles the exercise of *ijtihad* is open not only to all Muslims but also to those who do not believe in God and prophethood and are not committed to *shari'a*. Only the answering of more complex questions requires juridical skills and a profound understanding of the objectives of *shari'a*. The *muftis*, that is those jurists in charge of delivering legal opinions (*fatwas*), are qualified to exercise this higher forms of *ijtihad*, which turns them into the truly successors of prophetic discourse (Masud 1995 [1977]: 233). A *mufti* capable to act as a *mujtahid*, as a practitioner of *ijtihad*, is a sort of practical philosopher and community leader. According to al-Shatibi, in order to underpin his authority in delivering *fatwas* — the legal responses to ad hoc questions posed by commoners — he has to ensure that his own words and deeds adhere to the content of his *fatwas*. We see here that the foundation of law's authority with regard to its transmitters and interpreters is not based on personal charisma, but is not diluted in an impersonal institutional role either. Authority maintains its "transpersonal" character that is at the core of the reconstruction of the social bond performed by axial civilizations and their discursive traditions (see chapter 1). Trust and communication as essential to action and judgment can only be rooted in this transpersonal dimension.

Finally, al-Shatibi considered the efforts at performing *ijtihad* as manifestations of a truly independent type of reasoning reflecting the unity of intent of *shari'a* and geared to issuing clear rules on particularly controversial cases: therefore as one major antidote to potential disagreement. *Ijtihad* stands out as the highest reasoning tool for securing understandings on the most delicate issues where *maslaha* is sought and legal solutions provided. Whatever residual disagreement among various practitioners of *ijtihad* is left, it is due to the obvious human limitations in seeking *maslaha* that can never fully reflect the unitary and uncontradictory character of *shari'a*'s objectives. *Mujtahids* (practitioners of *ijtihad*) and *mufti*s are humanly imperfect carriers and transmitters of God's perfect function as Lawgiver. Residual disagreements are differences within *fiqh*, that is jurisprudence, and not a breach of *shari'a*. Al-Shatibi could invoke the authority of previous towering scholars who endorsed different and even clashing systems of thought, like the theologian al-Ghazali and the philosopher Ibn Rushd (Averroes), for affirming that the prudent avoidance of destructive disagreement is what piety in the final analysis is about (ibid.: 241). On a pair with the issue of disagreement is the notion of social and legal change. While the objectives of *shari'a* are based on unchanging principles, the *'awa'id* (habits, practice, customs) are not. Therefore, since these *'awa'id* are also governed by the *shari'a*, the implementation of the *shari'a* should respond to the changes in habits and practice.

To conclude, al-Shatibi's legal philosophy contributed to the definition of *maslaha* as a general principle of common good to be applied to each discrete case where specific goods are sought and not just wherever scriptural sources are silent or the consensus of the jurists mute. Since in al-Shatibi's view the overall power of *maslaha*, though residing in the objectives of the *shari'a*, can only be retrieved and put to work through an inductive work of generalization, the result is the view of an ongoing process of agential *and* relational responsibility for authoring and authorizing the kind of social practice that defines the common good. This is the point where al-Shatibi's philosophy of law is blurred into an overall social theory of high significance for meaningfully linking social action, social interaction, and social order, and for securing the micro-macro link that will be crucial to modern theories of the public sphere (see introduction and conclusion). It is a momentous contribution to the definition of repertoires of intersubjective understanding and connectivity linking authority, trust, and communication.

Both Aquinas and al-Shatibi, as leading representatives of the Axial Renaissance in Latin Christendom and Arabic Islamdom, clearly transcended the axial dichotomist polarization between *civitas terrena* and *civitas Dei* best epitomized by Augustine in Late Antiquity, toward the end of what we might call the primary axial cycle. It is fair to say that the South-Italian theologian and the Andalusi jurist represent the culmination of a process that reconstructed axial formulas in an almost proto-sociological fashion by focusing on the agential capacities of the "commoner." Yet it is also possible to observe that as a representative of the Islamic philosophy of law and of a strong view of *maslaha*—though not an uncontested one both during the Axial Renaissance and in the

modern era (cf. Hallaq 2001; Zaman 2004; Opwis 2005; Masud 2005)—
and more generally as an Islamic theorist of the social bond, the common
good and the public weal, al-Shatibi has the merit of overcoming the
unsociological oversubjectivation of agency that has affected Christian
Europe's genealogy of the subject (see chapter 3).

His theory deserves attention for its coherent adherence to a
relational view of the agent as *ego* involved with *alter* on all nodal
issues attending the construction and maintenance of the social bond: in
a double sense, as participant in, and as observer and judge of social
interaction. In his theory, the agent's responsibility is upheld without
falling into the trap of oversubjectifying its volition. Probably less cogent
in purely theoretical and theological terms if compared to the masterful
architecture of its Thomistic counterpart, al-Shatibi's approach holds a
stronger potential for a socioanthropological reconstruction of social
agency under modern constraints.

# Chapter 5

# The Implosion of Traditions and the Redefinition of Common Sense

## Reconstructing *Res Publica*: An Axial Enlightenment?

As mentioned in the introduction and at the beginning of chapter 3, it is not my goal to engage in a macrocivilizational comparison. My aim so far has consisted in evaluating the cross-civilizational and genealogical potential within the larger Western heritage for reconstructing a theory of practice-*cum*-communication generated from within axial traditions. In this genealogy, the work of al-Shatibi examined in the previous chapter provides a theoretically strong linkage between the synthesis elaborated by Islamic thinkers, on the one hand, and the reconstruction of public reason in European modern thought, on the other. Among them, two prominent characters are Benedict (Baruch) de Spinoza, a heir sui generis to Andalusi high culture and Islamic philosophy, and Giambattista Vico, who reworked the Augustinian and Thomistic heritage to answer some of the new questions raised by the pioneers of modern thought such as Machiavelli, Hobbes, Grotius, and Descartes. Vico also laid the seeds for turning key axial theological and juridical ideas into a genealogical approach nurtured by a socioanthropological theory of the origins and evolution of the social bond, and of the concomitant emergence of ideas and practices of connective justice, the common good, and the public weal (see introduction). Vico so provided key insights into the tensions determined by the metamorphosis of "axiality" into "modernity."

We have seen in chapter 3 how the ideals of the *respublica christiana* resisted strong institutionalization. The same socioreligious movements that had simultaneously revitalized the Church institution and civic life bred seeds of innovation and transformation that undermined the already unstable medieval equilibrium of practices and institutions. The thirteenth-century climax of innovative thought that culminated in the work of Aquinas began, soon after his death, to wind down, lose institutional coherence, and break up into its ideational components, both civic and religious (Hollweck and Sandoz 1997: 32). Fourteenth-century scholasticism is itself a symptom of the demise of the Axial Renaissance within Latin Christendom. Against a commonly held opinion, this scholasticism was hardly a development of the Thomistic synthesis, which was put to the margins of thought and teaching during the era of transition to modernity (MacIntyre 1990: 149–69).

In chapter 3 we have also seen that since the eleventh century the monastic and civic revivals had exerted pressure on the categories inherited from Latin Christian Late Antiquity. These concepts proved only partly able to absorb and regulate the new demands. Virtually all new movements and discourses aimed to fit their own priorities into the Christian order, but at the same time they operated, even if unconsciously, so as to disrupt the same order. This can be said even of the achievements of Aquinas, combining synthesis and innovation. The revival of Aristotelian concepts was ambiguously related to those aspects of the emerging sociopolitical realities which were utterly at odds with the scarcely differentiated model of the Hellenic *polis* (Voegelin 1997b: 110).

An overreaction to the neo-Aristotelian approach to the fragmentation and complexity of late-medieval social worlds came, not surprisingly, from within Franciscan scholarly milieus. Its immediate result was a deconstruction of Aquinas's work, which, far from simply updating the Aristotelian system, had rejected the most static and ethnocentric dimensions of the same system. While Thomas had focused on linking Christian faith to Aristotelian *phronesis*, the Franciscan William of Ockham laid the conceptual fundaments that severed their linkage. He made faith, once the hub of the axial triadic construction of the social bond, a stand-alone feature of a new type of subjectivity. This was the prelude to the erosion, and later disruption, of the triadic link (see chapter 6).

This intellectual movement, particularly powerful among the Oxford Franciscans, inaugurated a pietistic reinterpretation of practical rationality, whose socioeconomic importance was on the rise in the expanding urban worlds. Classic *phronesis* was retrieved and adapted in the vague fashion of people's "common sense." However, subjectified faith did not fit automatically into this diluted view of practical rationality. The main consequence was that faith was increasingly divorced from the civilizational process of tradition-building that had been revitalized during the Axial Renaissance. This process could hardly incorporate the critical approach that Thomas had instituted as essential to the revivification of the Christian tradition through the establishment of an organic link between a revitalized axial faith and the deepening needs of practical rationality (Hollweck and Sandoz 1997: 39). Aquinas himself was not completely innocent of this development, for he had been the champion of a quite radical shift that, while not suppressing the role of the Church, put the essence of Christianity mainly if not entirely in faith.

Facing challenges of a new magnitude and invigorated by the incorporation in the orthodoxy of the new movements and their rapid success, the popes themselves contributed to absolutize faith, along with other key categories of the tradition. The word *fidelitas* carried through the Middle Ages the double meaning of feudal submission and loyalty in the faith that is *fides*. Intentionally or not, this ambivalence was exploited by the papal authority in folding the Christian *fides* into the feudal *fidelitas*, so as to capitalize on its use value as a vector of political obligation. Facing the challenge of rising imperial ambitions especially at the time of the emperor Frederick II, the popes of the epoch worked not only to accommodate a so redefined *fidelitas* to the new reality of emerging autonomous kingdoms (Voegelin 1997b: 90). They also used *infidelitas* as a tool to combat the rising secular enemy by stressing his tyrannical lust for power (*dominii cupido*) (ibid.: 93). In these efforts to contain secular powers, the center of the Church happened to transform the discursive tradition of the *respublica christiana* into an arsenal of rhetoric expediency finalized to power politics.

This development deserves closer attention, since it provides the first segment of a longer trajectory ushering into the genesis of European modernity. The process was less an outright collapse, than a slow implosion and subsequent cannibalization of the discursive tradition of Latin Christendom. Up to a certain point of rupture—represented by the political theories of Machiavelli and Hobbes and by the political developments which nurtured their theories—this process consisted of attempts to revitalize, not to destroy tradition. The paradox was that most such attempts eroded the internal resources of tradition and its capacity to glue its various components. For the earlier mentioned papal attempt to contain the rise of an anti-axial logic of power and governance built on the autonomous sovereignty of the temporal domain, the idea of the *sacrum imperium* needed to be preserved as the antithesis of imperial tyranny and as the glue of a commonwealth of independent national principalities. Yet this approach required a *fidelitas* toward papal authority as the institutional wager of the collective freedom from tyranny, in the unity of the ideational and mystical body of the *respublica christiana*.

It was in this sociopolitical context of attempted revitalization of the governance idea of the *sacrum imperium* that its key actors gained an acute consciousness of the limitations and potentials of its peculiar structure, residing in nothing less than the claim to represent the realm of God on earth. The paradox was that this potential proved unfeasible for the papal approach while it provided the ideational key to the legitimization of the absolute sovereignty of the rising nation-states.

Through the long period of erosion of the propulsive impetus of the Axial Renaissance it became much clearer, in a way that was perceived as partly painful and partly liberating by various key social and institutional actors, that the realm of *imperium* had to be rooted in the *saeculum* (the "world") for all its duration, so that the *saeculum* became the autonomous token of the primacy of immanence against transcendence (Voegelin 1997b: 91). Evidently both the supporters and the rivals of the postulates of papal supremacy shared the same overriding concern for the *saeculum*.

Another key contender in the intellectual battles of the age, the anonymous author of the *York Tracts*, in a spirit close to the innovations of the most radical wings of the new monastic movements, identified the "world" with the "Christian people," that is with a noninstitutional Church traveling across the *saeculum* (ibid.: 99). His advocacy of an independent interpretation of scriptures unbound by tradition and by the guidance of the Roman Church clearly anticipates key arguments of the Protestant Reformation (ibid.: 101). The mundane concerns and the egalitarianism of the anonymous of York are just a further twist to Aquinas's assertion that the *lex nova* (the "new law" of Christianity) is written by grace into the hearts of the faithful, before being a written law. We do not have here a party (hostile to the pope) that anticipates modernity and another party (supporting the pope) that resists it (as claimed by most analysts, see also Santoro 2003 [1999]: 71–88). There are partly conflicting and partly overlapping reinterpretations of tradition which will bear differently on the emerging new forces of modernity.

At the political level, which saw the formation and consolidation of nation-states, one can certainly speak of a collapse of the order of the *respublica christiana*. Yet at the level of the capillary structures of the social order of Latin European Christianity—those structures affecting the construction and maintenance of the social bond—it was more the case of an implosion of the order. To put it succinctly in classic Weberian terms, one could say that salvation turned increasingly "innerworldly," with a focus on the value of human endeavor per se in fulfilling the kingdom of God on earth (Szakolczai 2001b: 356–60). However, some qualifications and revisions of this Weberian scheme are required.

Parallel to developments in the cities and in the rising nation-states, the clerics began to assume the characteristics of what we term "intellectuals." These were no longer an organic sprout of the *respublica christiana*, but found their identity and operated on an increasingly "liminal" terrain. MacIntyre has convincingly shown that through its ambivalent fate Aquinas's work and legacy, far from representing the citadel of an ossified tradition, became a major platform of such intellectual liminality (MacIntyre 1990: 149–69). Yet a fortiori this is true of the rivals of Aquinas and of the enemies of the papal primacy, among whom William of Ockham ranked prominent on both a theoretical and a political level.

The deep transformations of the sociopolitical order that stretched the period conventionally identified as "early modernity," from the sixteenth to the middle of the eighteenth century, brought about a host of national, and often absolutist, monarchies that launched new programs for mobilizing large-scale resources and for forging new collective identities. These transformations were facilitated by imaginative, discursive, and reflective endeavors culminating in the postulation of a "state of nature" of man as left on himself, fearing all others, and dominated by an overwhelming instinct of self-preservation. This radical theoretical option allowed for a new reconstruction of the triadic scheme that had sustained the maintenance of the social bond and of the sociopolitical order well into the Axial Renaissance.

This time around, however, the reconstruction work was done in the absence of prophetic voices. It was, till the middle of the eighteenth century, more a job of piecing together afresh the stones of the broken edifice, than the evocation of a new order via a compact, though "metastatic," discourse (see chapter 1). When a new principle of order was proclaimed, as in the case of Machiavelli and Hobbes, it often consisted in a negation of the axial principle that had thus far limited the arbitrary creativity of sovereign power. This reconstruction work was mainly performed by those thinkers whom Eric Voegelin has labeled the "political realists" of the epoch. Their realism did not diminish, but rather exalted their liminal position. Their basic operation of finding the base of sociality in the individual (an axial construction), his powers (which axial traditions had recognized but tamed through the triadic link), and fears (well known to axial discourse but sedated through the promise of rewards for doing good) made them hardly popular among the popular masses of their societies, ever more shaken by pious passions.

The advocates of a strict separation of the *civitas Dei* and the *civitas terrena*—among them political realists like Niccolò Machiavelli (1469–1527), Thomas Hobbes (1588–1679), and Benedict (Baruch) de Spinoza (1632–1677)—did not attempt to generate a new balance between the two spheres as in the Gelasian scheme of the Low Middle Ages, but took for granted a permanent instability of their relations. This was due to the fact that the increasingly neat distinction between "religion" and "politics"—which Aquinas himself had contributed to draw—did not to match the motivational machine through which new social movements, most of which took the form of socioreligious aggregations, were generated. These movements launched political challenges to institutional authorities on the basis of the reasons of the "spirit." As shown by Voegelin, far from subsiding, this type of challenge intensified in the modern age (Voegelin 1998a: 131–214; Szakolczai 2001b).

In the process of solidification of such reasons of the spirit in a world that increasingly recognized the autonomous sovereignty of politics as incarnate in the modern state, the premises for what we call today "fundamentalism" were laid down. Clearly, this tendency emerged as an essential component of the antinomies of the modern order. On the other hand, the gradual "discovery of society," whose seeds we also found in Aquinas's theory, created a new awareness of the material mechanisms of constitution of the social bond. However new the formulas for justifying this bond, the underlying evocations of order had to follow, morphologically though not in content, inherited axial formulas. "Individuality," and "sociality" were conceptually radicalized at the same moment when their relations became more complex and required new forms of power to be governed.

In this chapter I attempt to show that an important and early dimension of the European Enlightenment was also and by necessity "axial." More specifically, I put in evidence how the sophistications of the Thomistic system, the theoretical epitome of the Axial Renaissance of Latin Christianity, were not dismissed at once, not even among the movements and thinkers issued from the Protestant Reformation. Thomistic influences were still present in Presbyterian-Calvinist university teaching in Scotland well into the eighteenth century (MacIntyre 1988: 209–40). I also suggest that in the work of the political realists and especially of Hobbes, the *tabula rasa* that they did of the axial bond of connectivity consisted less in a zeroing of the merely conceptual legacies of prior axial transformations, than in an implosion of the public world itself within which clerics had performed their task. As acutely observed by Voegelin, by reference to Hobbes as well as to all great realist thinkers of the era,

when a civilization disintegrates and men scurry to shelter under its fragments . . . the erection of fragments of reality into cosmic absolutes has for the realistic thinker the consequence that his larger world becomes a *private* world. The question of what is *public* is always determined by the socially dominant evocation of the time. The realistic thinker becomes a private person because he has no public before which he can display what he observes in his larger world without incurring fierce resentment that may lead to disgrace, persecution, and possibly death, as in the case of Socrates. (Voegelin 1998b: 59–60)

In other words, axial categories were still influential and were indeed radicalized by the new liminal thinkers and movements, while the value of key concepts inherent in traditional ideas of public reasoning had to recoil into a newly defined, autonomous realm of value, the "private sphere." In parallel, the religious reformers of the sixteenth century, led by Luther and Calvin, opted for a drastically new foundation of the order of the fading Church institutions. According to Voegelin, this attempt failed grossly at the institutional and intellectual levels, brought about further fragmentation, and allowed for the spiritual movements to be hijacked by the newly emerging forms of power, monitoring, and control promoted by the autonomous political spheres hegemonized by the states (Voegelin 1998a: 217–68). This process unleashed waves of religious and political fundamentalism (most prominently merged in Oliver Cromwell and his "Puritan revolution," the first of the "great revolutions" of the modern era) or what Voegelin called "political religions": the kind of movements and formations that around two millennia of axial hegemony had quite effectively prevented or tamed.

The secular realists defied this process through which a newly defined religion compromised with the new political formations. Machiavelli, Hobbes, and Spinoza attempted to recreate a principle of social cohesion in a world of new power particularisms. It is not by chance that all of them were isolated in their own time and were accused of atheism and immorality, for they attempted to diagnose and reconstruct the social bond from a traditionless viewpoint and were thus particularly stubborn in rejecting any confuse reformist accommodation of religion. Hobbes's diagnosis was uncompromising in that while Christianity had affirmed that the triangular relationship of *ego*, *alter*, and God guarantees the cohesion of all mankind, his moral atomism postulated no less than the illusory character of the charitable fundaments of the social order. He faced the task of reconstructing a principle of order without *caritas*, one situated outside of the cohesive benefits of the axial triangle of *ego-alter-Alter*/God. In his approach, human beings were apprehended as isolated monads constituting disintegrated multitudes, only connected by random antagonism and mutual dread (Voegelin 1999: 47–72). Hobbes's state of nature best exemplifies the type of society that only acknowledges external goods of effectiveness (see chapter 1) and whose members are caught in an acute and permanent competition for the acquisition of those goods (MacIntyre 1984 [1981]: 196).

The merit of this appalling vision was its clarity. In contrast to the contractarian shortcut preferred by thinkers contemporary to Hobbes or others after his time, who provided an ideological cover to the new techniques and relationships of power incorporated in the modern state, Hobbes, like the other sensible realists of the epoch, inflicted a deadly blow to public reason and its *telos*. As observed by Voegelin,

> Hobbes was crystal clear in saying that man is condemned to find no repose in this life, for the simple reason that there is no such a thing like a telos or *summum bonum*. The terrible consequence of the loss of the *fruitio Dei* is that man in his creaturely loneliness and weakness must create the image of his own omnipotence. (Voegelin 1999: 63)

The bedrock of this new creation is the fear of death. An adamant realist like Hobbes had to admit that reason *as such* is powerless, nothing more, as also admitted by Grotius, than the capacity of "reckoning." The main calculation that reason can deliver concerns the confrontation with the outer world and reflects the ongoing risk of *ego* incurring a violent death at the hand of *alter*. Lacking a *summum bonum* ("supreme good") man finds in death a *summum malum* ("supreme evil") that works as an anti-*telos*. The ensuing apology of the absolute power of the Leviathan over the children of pride is not simply for Hobbes a possible—or recommended—political option from among a whole typology of forms of government, but the only reasonable conclusion of a reckoning with the destructive human forces that have to be subdued in order to ensure social life and civil peace (ibid.: 71).

While the obstinate but rigorous diagnosis of Hobbes leaves no place for discussion and is divorced from the language of axial discourse, Spinoza offers a more open approach with clearer links to tradition, since he was heir to a more composite philosophical heritage. As suggested by Voegelin, with Spinoza, the son of a Sephardic Jewish family that had resettled in Amsterdam due to the Catholic persecutions in al-Andalus, "the Mediterranean irrupts again into Western thought" (ibid.: 126). He pieced together diverse elements, some of which echo the most daring visions of Islamic philosophy and rationalist speculative theology—those most strenuously combated by the Muslim legists (see chapter 4)—and delivered a highly original reinterpretation of the relation between individuality and sociality. For Spinoza, God is the all-encompassing substance, is identified with nature, and deprived of any anthropomorphic attributes. Man can only realize his own nature and pursue the good in company of other men. For him, political society should be constructed in such a way that the pursuit of good is possible for the largest number (ibid.: 128).

Spinoza recombined key elements drawn from Jewish, Christian, and Islamic traditions in order to achieve a revolutionary synthesis. Interestingly—and at odds not only with traditional theologies but also with modern liberal anthropologies (see chapter 6)—neither man nor God are conceived by him as a personality. *Acquiescentia* is the key word of his recipe of good life. The human personality is extinguished in the experience of being an undulation in the flux of natural necessity and divine order. Spinoza's *acquiescentia* cannot be properly translated in any modern European language. As noticed by Voegelin, it simply means *islam*, that is trustful surrender to God (ibid.: 129), though this is closer to the Islam of the philosophers than to the Islam of the *'ulama'* (see chapter 4). Quite clearly, this vision unsettles axial *telos*, but strives toward an arduous, piecemeal, and therefore potentially revolutionary reconstruction of another type of *telos*. Human beings are multitudes, as recognized by Aquinas, but not ineluctably disintegrated, as asserted by Hobbes.

As all other natural beings, human beings, in their multitude, exist by the power of God, so that the extent and nature of their power to act is coextensive with the sparks of power they receive from God. From this perspective, the modern legal discourse of "rights" is an exoteric device, an almost superstitious symbolization inadequate to capture the human capacity to act and communicate. While men are by nature multitudes individually empowered by God, the problem of commanding right and prohibiting wrong cannot be answered by looking at preordained catalogues of injunctions, but is only raised at the moment individuals pool their powers into a common power. Thus they create rules concerning the relation between *ego* and *alter*, to be extended to the collective life of wider multitudes. A life of man as an isolated Hobbesian power monad is not only theoretically inconceivable—since it is human beings who pool their powers —but contradicts a life of reason, security, and comfort. Spinoza radically innovates in delivering a view of the common good as the product of a conscious option for power sharing, while radically renewing, yet not rejecting, the idea of a shared higher good. This idea cannot be erased if the new human *telos* is a good life of reason and *acquiescentia*. Correspondingly, the body politic is a variable entirely dependent from the fluency of the existence of human multitudes and from the ability of human powers to create the proper and creative balance among themselves, among their powers and capacities to act and communicate (ibid.: 132).

Spinoza clearly saw that the ruptures in the medieval Christian civilization, far from realizing a new freedom, had unleashed sectarian passions in the form of unredeemed wills to power. His "Jewish-Islamic" mysticism of reason and restraint (largely unrecognized by commentators, with few exceptions: e.g., Strauss 1965; Albiac 1987), which he proposed as the only key to a balance of powers leading to collective enjoyment, was a radical antithesis to the sectarian furor unleashed by the Protestant Reformation (Voegelin 1999: 131). For all the merits of his daring and intriguing vision, his view remained confined to elitist circles. In Spinoza's vision God as the supreme good risked being privatized by an individualist ethics (ibid.: 136), unless a new public sphere be reconstructed through the pooling of human powers. This last proposal remained however undeveloped. The new perspective was not able to absorb the pious passions of early modernity that, though manipulated by subsequent waves of self-appointed reformers, had real roots in the sensibilities of urban strata in continual upheaval and was strictly related to a process of socioeconomic modernization which perpetually recreated those marginal and liminal spaces that nurtured the movement.

On the level of deconstruction of traditional narratives, Spinoza coherently argued that the image of God as legislating from his throne is an anthropomorphism produced by biblical parabolic discourse and prophetic speech, and is the equivalent of the axial claim that the moral universe is moved by a transcendent will. Consequently, if evaluating the primal structure of "law" as regulating human society and nourishing civic institutions, Spinoza—as Vico, even more strongly, after him—was eager to appreciate it as the creation of the human imagination, intentionality, and power, while admitting that these factors are variably related to tradition and revelation (Preus 1989: 90). Religion is nothing more and nothing less than the prophetic discourse aiding human powers to create rules and sociopolitical orders.

This approach reflects Spinoza's rejection of what was to become one main weapon in the conceptual arsenal of some influential currents within later Enlightenment thought, the idea of a "natural religion." From the Spinozian viewpoint this idea is an absurdity, because religion is instituted by human power and creativity. It is not inscribed by God in the human mind as part of a repertoire of "common notions." Vico's position on this key issue will be more nuanced and will clarify the extent to which a reinterpretation of axial value, based on transcendence, was necessary to ground the common within modern society. Nonetheless it would be difficult to understand Vico's Axial Enlightenment without the critical reassessment of religion as prophetic discourse performed by Spinoza.

For Spinoza, in order to judge the truth of religions, one should evaluate their capacity to institute justice and *caritas*, which clearly do not exist—here he agrees with Hobbes—in the state of nature (Preus 1989: 90–91). The truth of religion is in its social effects. Religion is constituted pragmatically for its appeal to the imagination of the commoner and for instilling in him/her the dispositions that cement the social bond. Spinoza's acknowledgement of revelation is in the form of prophetic imagination and parabolic discourse, which have the merit of grounding, simultaneously, religion and society, neither of which could have seen the light by a purely reflective reason alone. For Spinoza, religion is historically based on prophetic discourse trying to bring justice in harmony with the practical needs of the common people and therefore instituting the very notion of the common good.

This is a genuinely secular approach, in that the exhortative discourse of faith is conceived as a conversation between human agents and does not need to be located, theologically, in God, who matters indeed, but as the impersonal initiator of human power. This vision also implies that the authority used in this conversation is legitimate if it adheres to the function of religious discourse and does not degenerate into the manipulative activity of stirring up wrong beliefs, which Spinoza calls superstition and considers the source of fanaticism. Spinoza's rejection of priesthood in all religions is due to his conviction that this form of institutional consecration of authority inherently fosters superstition. Prophecy, on the other hand, is to be taken seriously in that it "really includes ordinary knowledge" (Spinoza 1951 [1670]: 13).

Anticipating Vico, Spinoza identifies the common origin of religious and social institutions. Both thinkers begin with the consideration of social utilities and necessities as the condition of human endeavor and creative power. This approach is also in continuity with al-Shatibi's plural notion of *maslaha/masalih*, which, as we saw in the previous chapter, has a more articulate meaning than "common good." The two modern thinkers still cope with a phronetic type of human power, which has to be nonetheless entirely redefined, since its nexus with a traditionally conceived *telos* has now been severed. In Spinoza, this operation is still based on shaky ground (cf. Tosel 1985). While it is clear to him that rule by fear cannot secure enduring human cooperation for the common good, he postulates the necessity for the human agent to develop an inner awareness of the shared

184 &ZeroWidthSpace; *The Public Sphere*

utilities and necessities and therefore of sociable conduct. This awareness originates in a moral self-restraint (*conatus*) channeled to the pursuit of a higher good, provided by religion to the masses (Preus 1989: 91). Here we find a clear echo of the approach of the Islamic philosophers (see chapter 4).

Spinoza's work still suffered from a high degree of sociological indeterminacy concerning the relations between human power and the necessary, ongoing creativity of social action and communication. Giambattista Vico (1668–1744) shifted the focus of his analysis toward a level still underrepresented in the writings of the Dutch thinker. He looked at how the necessities and utilities of social life could be grasped by some form of common sense, existing prior to reflection, reason, and even to language, and antecedent to any purportedly human capacity to enter into contractual arrangements and define the corresponding "rights." In search for a new fundament of the social bond, Vico—unlike the radical "laic saint" Spinoza—has been portrayed as a pious Catholic by some, and as an astute radical thinker in a conformist garb by other commentators. He made a new step toward the secularization of *telos* by capitalizing on his likely knowledge of the strengths and weaknesses of the work of his Dutch predecessor (Morrison 1980; Stone 1997: 302–5).

In Vico's opinion, the founders of human civilization were neither the philosophers, nor the axial champions of prophetic speech, whose job was to match the imagination of the people they addressed. Discourse had to rest on some prior and more solid form of knowledge. The founders of human society and of religion, Vico infers, could only be "poets." What defines them is not the production of a specific form of art but nothing less than the articulation of notions of common good via their keenly imaginative grasp of the necessities and utilities of social life (Preus 1989: 92). In other words, necessities and utilities have to be first captured creatively and imaginatively before they can be pursued via understanding among humans, supported by the moral discourse of the prophets or the rational discourse of the philosophers.

In this chapter I deepen the analysis of Vico's theory of common sense as the essential bedrock upon which he reconstructed a post-axial type of public reason. His approach is "enlightened" for he clearly saw the artificial character of the social bond, while also acknowledging the role of pre-axial and axial discourse in its production. However, while he benefited from the liberating effect—also on a methodological level—of the *tabula rasa* brought about by the modern political realists, he drew his theoretical and argumentative resources from axial traditions and turned them into a *New Science* (the title of his main work) of the social bond, of society, and of the role of religion therein. He can be thus considered one of the main founders of modern social sciences and humanities in general and even of sociology in particular (Hösle 2001: 89), especially of a "comparative historical civilizational sociology" (Nelson 1976). The importance of his contribution to the history of modern European thought has been acknowledged, though in various forms, by contemporary social thinkers like Horkheimer, Habermas, and in particular Apel (1978 [1963]). He had the rare capacity of being a cultural critic and a civilizational theorist at the same time.

Though deeply familiar with such authors as Augustine and Aquinas, Vico took advantage of his profound knowledge of the Greek and especially of the Latin classic humanities (Naples, the place where he was born and spent his entire life, was the biggest city in modern Europe combining a Greek origin and a Roman legacy), more than, like Spinoza, of the scriptural heritage of biblical prophecy. Building on this combination of a sufficient acquaintance with the axial heritage and a discrete but committed participation in the disputes that animated the Republic of Letters linking European eighteenth-century scholars in a particularly homogeneous intellectual public sphere, Vico was the architect of a cleverly though cautiously subversive, proto-genealogical approach to modernity. Vico's genealogy attempted to unveil latent continuities—looking backwards—between the essentially secular character of political modernity, the axial heritage and the role of prophetic religion therein, and the pre-axial, pagan institutions of divination and sacrifice. His thought was as much analytic as diagnostic. He thus warned against what he saw as the looming danger of a new barbarism of abstract communication and self-centered reflection which he identified with Cartesian modernity (Miner 2002).

Though he often antagonized his contemporary Neapolitan Spinozists, in whom he saw a capricious radicalization of Cartesian approaches, he inherited from Spinoza two crucial elements of social and philosophical thought: the view of the close relationship between religious and civic institutions, and an engagement with the continuities and discontinuities between imagination and rational discourse. Vico's approach frequently highlighted the inevitability of ruptures and the necessity of new methods of analysis informed by socioanthropological insight and a historical perspective. His main work, the *Scienza Nuova*, declares this ambition in its very title. Apart from the necessity of the new, it is the meaning of "science" that we need to explain. For Vico, this is not just the theory, but the practice itself of a new mode of understanding human and social life (Mazzotta 1999: 60). He was the first European thinker to stress the importance to situate the practices of particular social groups in historical perspective and to spell out the heuristic value of continuities and discontinuities in the evolution of human society.

At the outset, his program was not only a countermanifesto to the approach of political realists like Machiavelli, Hobbes, and Spinoza, but also an alternative to the visionary prophets of modernity like Giordano Bruno and Francis Bacon. He wanted to show the deficits of sociological plausibility of a theory of the social world understood as dominated by absolute power volitions, simulations, and dissimulations. Yet he also wanted to refute those visions of the new where claims to freedom were given a purely metaphysical foundation, as in the work of his Campanian fellowman Giordano Bruno, a witness and martyr of a secular faith in the absolute power of the human subject. Vico's main strategy in the *New Science* highlighted the necessity of a new discourse matching the axial idea of *phronesis* with the modern idea of freedom (ibid.: 7).

## From Poetic Imagination through Jurisprudential Practice to Public Discourse

To start with, Vico refused, unlike most of the other thinkers of his age, and in particular of the political realists, to proceed on the basis of an immediate and unambiguous delimitation of the "political." This option was part and parcel of his genealogical approach, in itself hostile to pre-fabricated definitions, which suppress the complex and perpetually shifting character of the order of human society and of its conceptualization. Yet he was deeply interested in the conceptual dictionary underlying symbolic evocations, beliefs, intellectual styles, and institutions. He was also aware that any approach to the object of his exploration, the genesis of the social bond, had to cope with an entity that had been taking possession of the realm of politics for some centuries. This novelty in European and human history was the modern state and in particular its claim to absolute sovereignty (Mazzotta 1999: 12).

One of Vico's main lines of argumentation was that from the viewpoint of the Roman law tradition the origins of institutions are far more complex than apparent in what he considered the naïve fairy tales of the modern theorists of natural law—first of all of the Dutch law theorist Hugo Grotius—who propagated a one-dimensional and anthropologically emasculated notion of "man" and his "nature" as a kind of inverted paradise. At the root of this difference there are wide diverging approaches, between Vico and the contractarians, to the relationship between law and power (Voegelin 1999: 91; see also Fassò 1971). It is Vico's notion of the relationship between phronetic reason and institutional practice that sets him apart from most of the modern theorists of law, politics, and legitimate order. The modern state is for him a singular power machinery neither to be left to itself, nor to be resisted, or for a human subject to be uncritically co-opted into. For Vico such a state cannot be the source for a theory of law and justice. His attack on Grotius is based on methodological considerations affecting the positioning of the phenomenon of law vis-à-vis the state and on the necessity to take this ambivalent positioning under scrutiny genealogically and not apologetically. It is unsurprising that the apex of Vico's *New Science* is jurisprudence, which he intends as simultaneously a philosophy of law, a theory of justice, and a systematic reflection about how to cope with the state, more than as a static and uncritical theory of state law in the style of the political realists or the contractarians. Vico was adamant in denouncing the methodological and ideological fallacy of his rivals by invoking the typically genealogical awareness of the arbitrary character of beginnings:

> In expounding [their] doctrine, its three great proponents—Grotius, Selden, and Pufendorf—should have begun with the beginning of the nations, since this is when their subject begins . . . But all three of them made the same mistake of beginning in the middle, that is, with the recent ages of civilized nations, in which people are enlightened by fully developed reason . . . I begin my discussion of law from the most ancient point in history, the moment when the idea of Jupiter was born in the minds of the nation founders. The Latin word for law is *ius*, which is a contraction of the ancient *Jous*, Jove or Jupiter. (Vico 1999 [1744]: 154–56)

From his earlier treatises to the successive editions of the *New Science*, Vico's work highlights how by evolving from communities based on custom to societies ruled by law, human beings acquire an increasingly adequate concept of the core idea of justice, the conception of the *aequum bonum* ("equitable good"), which is a good very close, if not equivalent, to al-Shatibi's *maslaha* (see chapter 4). From there Vico's genealogy unfolds, tracing the trajectory of development of the social bond and its forms. It is therefore a genealogy of tradition, not a genealogy of wills to power that are merely parasitic on the narratives of tradition. The option for beginning "from the most ancient point in history" is tantamount to diffidence for every arbitrary vision of a state of nature subordinated to the ruling imperatives of the modern state. It opens up the search for a source of the social bond that is furthest away from the wills of power that lurk behind the "conceit of the scholars." This source "can be traced to the first societies, in which goods were distributed not in a purely arbitrary fashion, but always in accord with some apprehension of the good" (Miner 2002: 44).Vico's genealogy is a "pious" one: not substituting the wills to power of his contenders with an absolute diffidence toward every beginning, but zeroing into the phronetic dimension of the social bond factually and not normatively: into the "fact" of the understanding between *ego* and *alter*, a fact to be explained by a focus on intersubjectivity and not to be explained away by an obsession with "power" as a purely subjective volition and determination through which *ego* shapes him/herself and subdues *alter* to his/her will to power.

It is from the fabric of Roman law and jurisprudence that the method and content of this science of the social bond is to be retrieved. This science needs to incorporate symbolic representation and language as the condition for any formulation and institution of order, since language preserves, buried underneath the weight of history, layers of knowledge and wisdom. Vico's answer to the political realists is a clear move from the centrality of the sovereignty of the state to the priority of language, which he treated in an extraordinarily concrete way and with a "materialistic" sensibility (Mazzotta 1999: 33–34).

> All the primary figures of speech are corollaries of poetic logic. The most luminous figure, and hence the most basic and common, is metaphor . . . all metaphors based on analogies between physical objects and the products of abstract thought must date from an age in which philosophies were just beginning to take shape. (Vico 1999 [1744]: 159)

Vico's diffidence toward the self-enclosed theories of philosophers, including the contemporary philosophers of law, opens the way to a much deeper exploration of the communicative dimension of the social bond. Vico hypothesizes that the first lexicon that grounded Latin and Greek as languages was provided by the several thousands naturalistic deities instituted in ancient Latium and Greece (ibid.: 177). Before being objects of worships, deities incorporated modes of social action and relation. They were the intermediary imaginative symbols between things and facts, on the one hand, and utterances, on the other.

Vico was well aware—against the "fairy tales" of the contractarians—of the huge gap in social complexity between his own times and those remote origins of authority and law that impacted the simultaneous foundation of religious and civic institutions. It is the consciousness of this gap which helped him develop his genealogical approach. Unlike later, full-fledged and conscious genealogists for whom public reason is merely the cover of wills to power, he kept firmly to the goal of reconstructing the genesis and evolution of public reason within tradition. For pursuing this goal, the power machinery of the modern state could not be taken for granted but had to be reckoned with, along with the complication of public speech through games of simulation, which inspired so much of the baroque sensibilities of the epoch. Pure power is no longer a heresy but something to be explored carefully in its multiple aspects, many of which are related to the ambivalence and lack of innocence of language (Mazzotta 1999: 63).

Vico postulates neither an essentially good—like axial authors—nor bad—like many modern realists—nature of man, but focuses on the genealogy of civic institutions and the law as potential providers of justice. A revised Thomistic understanding, folded into baroque sensibilities, looms behind this approach: *phronesis* is a virtue of the practical intellect that however depends on *poiesis*, signifying the creative power of imagination, which inevitably needs an externality, either in material form, or as *alter* to *ego* (ibid.: 225). The I-Thou relationship is then made more concrete, and its dialogic dimension (see chapter 1) is more realistically absorbed in a more generally agonic field of relations. For Vico poetry is a simultaneously imaginative and practical approach to the world which first makes possible the social bond and thus produces religious and civic institutions. The social bond is intrinsically creative and communicative: agents act upon things, need a material basis, and deploy various amounts of violence. This understanding makes obsolete any putative antagonism—which Aquinas also carefully avoided but that Islamic philosophy inherited from Plato and transmitted to modern European thought via Spinoza—between the truth of the poets and prophets (intended as a particular type of poets), on the one hand, and the truth of the philosophers, on the other. In other words, Vico accepts that the philosophers know reality better only if they acknowledge the crude beginnings and the violent origins of both religion and society, and do not depict either of them as either God-given or produced by man's reason.

Vico attributes a crucial role to poetry as *poiesis* because of its capacity to articulate heterogeneous voices of experience. This is the first condition for transcending particularistic interest (ibid.: 57). Communication and understanding would not be possible without *poiesis*. By this train of argument, Vico crosses the way of Plato, a crucial hero of axiality who dismissed poetry outright in favor of philosophy. For Vico, Plato's mistake was to locate the origin of justice in the speculations of the philosophers, instead of looking at the *sapienza volgare* ("vulgar wisdom") of the wild founders of gentile humanity (ibid.: 135). The *New Science* endorses Plato's quintessential view of justice as the supreme good, but works at bringing down his abstractions (whether educational, legal, or political) to the particularities of the heterogeneous and fragmented social world (ibid.: 98). Human beings know the world of civil society because it has been forged by them, but this form of knowledge was, at the beginning, poetic knowledge. This is a critique not only of Plato but also of Bacon, whose visionary philosophy of pure power relied on unadulterated forms of knowledge situated outside of the realm of poetry (ibid.: 100).

The theoretical core of Vico's *New Science*, which simultaneously defies the king of ancient philosophy and the prince of the modern worshipping of science's omnipotence, is that the popular leaders of ancient gentile peoples spoke in poetic language and through signs. Spinoza had already asserted that "those whom the Gentiles called augurs and soothsayers were true prophets" (Spinoza 1951 [1670]: 52). Vico goes a full step forward in explaining who these poets/prophets were:

> By virtue of this imaginative creation, they were called poets, which in Greek means creators. Great poetry has three tasks: (1) *to invent sublime myths* which are suited to the popular understanding; (2) *to excite to ecstasy* so that poetry attains its purpose; and this purpose is (3) *to teach the masses to act virtuously*, just as the poets have taught themselves. The natural origin of this human institution gave rise to that invariable property, nobly expressed by Tacitus, that frightened people vainly 'imagine a thing and at once believe it,' *fingunt simul credunque*. (Vico 1999 [1744]: 145)

Far from being a purely expressive function, the powerful deployment of imagination was the engine of all basic religious and civic institutions. Poetry was sustained by memory—not by chance considered the mother of the Muses—that is the condition for any tradition of discourse and cumulative path to knowledge (Mazzotta 1999: 143–48). Long before Axial Age theory was formulated, Vico counters the preemptive erasure, performed by this theory, of any capacity of value-creation in preprophetic and prephilosophic (i.e., pre-axial) forms of knowledge. Vico proposes that the root of all later conceptualizations of transcendence—like in the subsequent waves of both Abrahamic religion and philosophical metaphysics—lies in the fear of thunder that grounds the highest deity Jupiter and with it the very idea of authoritative fatherhood that is, therefore, inherently imbued with a transcendent force. Apart from the image of Jupiter's thunder, what anticipates later modern genealogies and critiques is that Vico sees the constitution itself of social power as a necessarily intersubjective and communicative mechanism that is one with the alienation of power and relies on the "moral effort" or *conatus*. Power is alienated to the "God-Father" at the very moment an intersubjective and primordially communicative relation is constituted among humans. Transcendence is an inevitable, metaphysical and cognitive by-product of an unavoidably anthropological, more than theological, alienation.

> We must begin with some notion of God that is found in even the most wild, savage, and monstrous people . . . When people fall into despairing of any natural assistance, they desire something higher to save them. But only God is higher than nature, and this is the light which God has shed on all people . . . So we must begin with the popular metaphysics . . . which proves to be the theology of the poets. From this, we must seek that terrifying thought of a deity which imposed form and measure on the bestial passions of these lost men and made them human passions. Such a thought must have given rise to the *moral effort, or conatus*, which is proper to the human will and which restrains the impulses that the body urges on the mind. By means of this effort, such impulses can be completely suppressed by the sage, and can be directed to better ends by the good citizen. (Vico 1999 [1744]: 125)

Vico explains that the proto-patriarchs, whom he calls the "giants," acquired a basic, rough capacity and will of self-restraint in the very moment they were able to experience fear, which coincided with the acquisition of a capacity to cast this fear into a character with a shape, a name, and above all a power: Jupiter, whose wrath targets the lewd (Miner 2002: 91). Moreover, he showed that this moral technique, or *conatus*, can only be produced as an intersubjective, communicative, though primordial "common sense," entailing a modicum of violence of *ego* on *alter*. Violence is neither the cause nor the consequence of dread but is rather part of a larger collective process: the fear of thunder is not a fear induced by a specific other, but by several *ego*s on themselves through the collective construction of the Other: "while they can escape from the thunder into their caves and hideaways, they cannot escape from their fear of it that easily, for it is a sound that in some way points beyond itself" (Shotter 1996: 6).

Here lies exactly the root of a transcending *poiesis* grounding the first imaginative universals, and from there of language at large. This is also the origin of all religious and civic institutions and forms of authority sustained by *phronesis*, whose remotest origin in Vico's account precedes the crystallization of vernacular languages. Law itself, the pivotal institution of human commonwealths, is a direct offshoot of this capacity to act and react in common via symbolization. It is therefore not the convention imposed by Leviathan on subjects imbued with fear of concrete others. For Vico the beginning of human agency is in a simultaneous genesis of fear and language, a fear that points to a transcendent Other and therefore founds the human capacity to transcend any discrete, situated fear via creative imagination and the resulting "common sense."

His modern perspective helps Vico to view this pre-axial *poiesis* as a key sociological factor in the constitution of the intersubjective social-communicative bond. This approach inoculates against the risk of a sociological duplication of axial discourse (see chapter 1). The alien element of externality and potential transcendence is as original to the first constitution of religion as the commonality of the first sensory topic—the symbolization of Jupiter as a prototypical "heaven" deity, and the concomitant weary look upwards or pointing out with a finger up there—unleashed as a response to thunder. Therefore, more than simply the beginnings of "religion," this is the origin of the directive, instructive, and exhortative dimensions inherent in language games. Vico's theory helps explain the remote origin of axiality itself—what axial theory has difficulty to do—and shows its processual character more than its being an abrupt rupture or the original creation of prophets and philosophers.

Vico pays all due attention to the role of human creativity in shaping social practices and institutions and tries to give a name to this combination of *poiesis* and *phronesis*. He calls it *senso comune*, "common sense." Vico considers reason as an ordering principle of human relations, but only as part of a continuum of human creativity steeped in mythical imagination.[1] The *senso comune* of gentile history precedes the irruption of revelation into history and provides the first symbolic substratum to rational penetration. The *senso comune* places myth squarely at the fundaments of the *civitas* and therefore invalidates all transhistorical speculations on the origins of civil society (Mazzotta 1999: 145–47) which would climax in the second part of the eighteenth century in the Anglo-Scottish, and later Anglo-American liberal tradition (see chapter 6).

In the final analysis, Vico considers *senso comune* not only the matrix of religious discourse, but also the point of origin of any civilizational course. Common sense animates the primordial religious, civic, and legal institutions, and in particular the unreflected ideas without which these institutions, which take nourishment from reflexivity in routine times, would not have come into existence. This approach relativizes the axial overemphasis on reflexivity as the main source of institution-building. Rational reflexivity would have no role without this original and "factual" stock of sense. Reflexivity brings a civilizational course (the Vichian *corso*) to its zenith, but a balance can only be kept if rationality does not erase the stock of common sense and related practices on which the institutions repose.

As observed by Voegelin, "the meaning of the *corso* is the refinement of an initial, dense, unreflected substance to a maximum of rational differentiation" (Voegelin 1998b: 133–34). An excess of reflexivity and differentiation destroys the balance and leads to what Vico defines as a barbarism of reflection and calculation, the abyss toward which untamed modernity might push us, especially when articulated through a politics of pure power (Miner 2002: 73). This danger becomes abysmal when language games degenerate into pure power games, like in a purely Machiavellian or Hobbesian world of social relations:

> This barbarism of calculation turns such people into beasts even more savage than did the primitive barbarism of the senses . . . decadent peoples practice an ignoble savagery, and use flattery and embraces to plot against the life and fortunes of their intimates and friends. (Vico 1999 [1744]: 488)

Vico's theory helps us discern the contours of the crystallization of religious discourse within a wider, compact, civilizational course leading up to the public use of reason. On a second move, we can also extract from his theory additional elements for a systematic understanding of the traditionalization of religious discourse as part of the wider process of reconstruction of practical rationality and public reason, in the framework of a theoretical enrichment of Axial Age theory.

A first principle is firmly and even iconically formulated by Vico: the necessity to understand the original nexus between religious and civic institutions. Vico shows us the centrality of the altar in the drawing that he locates at the beginning of the *New Science*, by which he conveys the key notion that the civic world was brought into existence by the practices of divination, which along with sacred burials and sanctified marriages represents the first manifestation of common sense. These increasingly institutionalized practices not only build the symbolic structures of the social worlds, but are also their communicative infrastructures and their source of intelligibility (Mazzotta 1999: 240–41). He reiterates the point that the origin of civilization is in religion intended as compressor of pride through terror:

> And piety originated in religion, which properly consists in the *fear of divinity*. The heroic origin of the world "religion" was preserved among the Romans, according to the scholars who derive it from *religare*, to bind. For this verb refers to the chains which bound Tytus and Prometheus to mountain cliffs, where their heart and organs were devoured by an eagle, the symbol of the frightful religion of Jupiter's auspices . . . Chained under the mountains by their frightful religion of thunderbolts, the giants checked their bestial habit of wandering wild through the earth's great forest. Completely reversing their customs, they now settled down, hidden away in their lands (*fondi*), so that they later became the founders (*fondatori*) of the nations and lords of the first commonwealths. (Vico 1999 [1744]: 208)

Here we see a possible clue to a much stronger continuity between poetic and prophetic religion than maintained by Axial Age theory and cognates. Vico's notion of religion as the original human institution is a creative adaptation from the thought of Spinoza, in particular of the latter's analysis of biblical prophecy as imaginatively shaped discourse (Spinoza 1951 [1670]: 27–42). This train of argument leads as far as to view the institution of the social bond and its underlying promise of connective justice between *ego* and *alter* as being also, simultaneously, the origin of religion (Preus 1989: 72–73). Vico brings this point even further and, anticipating Durkheim (see chapter 1), sees primordial social institutions not just contractually constructed and subsequently sanctioned by deities, but deities themselves from the foundation moment (ibid.: 92). Interestingly, this further move is deeply unsettling for the notion of the social contract itself. Both Spinoza and Vico revealed the inherent power of symbols and narrations, without constructing an alternative source of social order out of them, as did the contractarians. The theory of the social contract did not dispel, but indeed reintroduced in a new guise what Vico called the "conceit of the nations," that is the credulity of ethnic or religious groups in that their own foundational myths—concerning the origins of their laws and sacred texts—were literally true (ibid.: 77). In this way, such modern interpreters—so Vico's criticism—failed to distinguish between meaning and truth.

This critique of the contractarians' early collusion with what will later become ethnic nationalism was anticipated by Spinoza, though in a less radical formulation (see Balibar 1997 [1985]). More in general Spinoza had laid the basis for dispelling the simplifications of the theory of the social contract with his doctrine of the imagination and of its relation to reason. In his *Tractatus Theologico-Politicus* (1951 [1670]: 1–282) the Dutch thinker had attempted to show—echoing the Islamic Mu'tazila thinkers and philosophers like Ibn Sina (see chapter 4)—that scriptures (*pace* all theologians) are not about any speculative knowledge of God or his attributes. Prophetic discourse, nourished by imagination, was not speculative but parabolic and enigmatic, dense of bodily language and finalized to admonishing and exhorting the commoners to right behavior and the observance of divine law. So the prophets communicated the imperatives of piety, *caritas*, and justice to the masses. This approach neatly corresponds to what Vico saw as the assignment of the poet: to communicate *inter rudes*, that is, to make words intelligible to the unrefined people (Preus 1989: 80). Based on creatively random and nonrational association of images, the imaginative universals of poetic and prophetic speech constituted for him "common sense" (ibid.: 83–84). So they were also the effective tool for creating understanding and, a step further, they were the source of meaning allowing for founding institutions among humans.

While prophetic discourse framed a type of moral exhortation nourishing common sense, including the basic sense of moral self-restraint described by Vico as *conatus*—a sense inherent in language-in-use—the common notions of reason were for Vico just one stage further in the developmental trajectory of human knowledge. His clarification of Spinoza's approach and his overcoming of the latter's residual Cartesianism resided nonetheless in the affirmation that the origin of the universal is already located at the primordial imaginative stage and is not the product of the subsequent rational reflection (ibid.: 85). Yet Vico did not set aside the issue of the relation between poetic and prophetic discourse by fully conflating them. He first made obsolete the assumption of a rigid separation between the poetic fiction of the Gentiles and the true salvational path inaugurated by the Jews. On a second step, he acknowledged to the latter a higher form—thanks to God's revelation—of protection from error: he saw value-creation in the Bible as an enduring antidote against the looming idolatries of the emerging secular worlds. However, Vico rejected the reading of biblical discourse as fixed in a text and therefore self-enclosed. Poetic imagination and related common sense are for him the permanent basis of reproduction of the biblical *logos*, which can only speak to the people as poetic discourse (Mazzotta 1999: 244).

This is the juncture where Vico radically departs from Spinoza. The Bible, according to the Dutch thinker, is no longer a holy book for the

Jews or the Christians, but a text from which to derive a rationalist ethics, which in turn can help, if interpreted without superstition, to spread religious tolerance. From Vico's viewpoint this step of reducing religion to moral philosophy is the premise to its transformation into a political instrument. Not by chance does Spinoza endorse the formula of *cuius regio eius religio*, so that for the sake of civil peace rulers are legitimized to authenticate the sense of the Bible. Vico in the *New Science* rejects Spinoza's view of a rational religion and the related conception of the republic as based on a balance between different sects securing tolerance. Vico objects that religion cannot be reduced to an arena for seeking expedient calculus and geometric accommodations only to tame the fury of a sectarianism unleashed by self-appointed defenders of true religion.

More importantly, Vico endorses the rejection of any reification of divinity, which he sees as one of the leitmotivs of the Bible. He questions the method of the interpretation of the Bible as a self-enclosed text uncontaminated by sediments of common sense and common piety. Last but not least, he rejects the principle of the separation of religious/sacred and political/profane spheres itself, so dear to all modern political realists, who here mirror the discourse and interests of the absolutist state that claims unrestrained sovereignty and control over society. For Vico the Bible is not simply a text, it is a living tradition. The religious imagination that is part of tradition is not separated from the social worlds but liminal to them. And it is the permanent source of renewal of religious traditions (Mazzotta 1999: 251).

As tied to religious imagination, common sense is strictly related to, albeit not identical with, piety. This is the point where Vico's approach becomes more normatively axial. According to him, both common sense and piety have to be combined in the task of reconstructing the common good the basis of the complex civilizational sediments inherited by European modernity. Once we are faced with "religion" and "politics" as spheres that are kept distinct by the exigencies of the modern European absolutist states, we have to remember the complex ways through which they are interrelated in shaping phronetic action. They cannot merely represent separate fields of social activities, but have to function as converging imperatives of a public conversation. Religion should be given due attention in political theory and praxis as a force that can become tragically divisive if subordinated to modern power politics, as it happened in the aftermath of the Reformation and especially with the Wars of Religion (ibid.: 254).

For Vico (not unlike Spinoza, but also similarly to al-Shatibi: see chapter 4) piety, from a scholarly viewpoint, consists in reconstructing a unity of converging goods relentlessly and realistically, by recognizing differences in interest. Differences in the social worlds are not irreducibly, atomistically heterogeneous, but are shifting and overlapping modes of dialogue and conflict. Therefore, public discourse is called to serve as the engine of a reconstructed political order in which Christians are liminally and strategically situated inside and outside of society, inside and outside of history. This liminality is the sole positioning that allows for a distancing from pure power politics and permits recognition of difference (Mazzotta 1999: 255).

The incessant reconstruction of public discourse is linked by Vico to a new idea of discursive tradition within religion. For the Dominican Finetti, Vico's contemporary and rival in a dispute over the authority of scripture, tradition reposes on the written, revealed word (*verbum scriptum*). Yet Vico found inspiration in another Dominican scholar, the seventeenth-century Spanish theologian Francisco Suarez, whose similarities of approach with his Muslim Andalusi predecessor al-Shatibi we have previously noted (see introduction). Suarez had shown how a tradition rests on a *regula animata*, on a "living rule." The Council of Trent (1545–1563), which promoted the so-called Catholic Counterreformation, went beyond scripture and revelation in its definition of tradition and included in it the entire spectrum of conciliar decrees and the whole ecclesiastic *magisterium*. Vico went much further and in another direction, thus secularizing the approach to tradition, while perfecting its sociological import. He considered that the poetic "vulgar traditions" are also "providential," though they are completely autonomous from scripture and revelation. They facilitate access to an understanding of the Bible via common sense and are indispensable to grasp the historical workings of what Vico still calls "providence" for reasons that are integral to his approach in the *New Science* and are not theological in any narrow sense (ibid.: 247).

Vico worked to conceptualize the mythical, creative, and "ethopoietic" kernel of Catholic tradition, without having to buy into any specific version of its dogma. Vico's commentators diverge in their interpretation of his frequent reference to "divine providence." For some, like Mazzotta (ibid.: 251–52), it indicates Vico's commitment to a renewed understanding of the Catholic tradition, in direct contrast to Machiavelli's *fortuna*, finalized to make sense of human history and human society. For others, like Israel (2001: 664–71), it is no more than a cautious key word for indicating the due course of human history, without risking exposure to the Inquisition. After all, so the argument, even the "atheist" Spinoza often referred to divine providence.

This interpretative contention among specialized exegetes of the work of Vico is not quite relevant from the viewpoint of the present work. I understand Vico's references to providence as signaling the fact that any viable civic and social institution has to be supported by a strong axis between common sense and a telic orientation of human action. Providence is basically a token of just this *telos*, as the pole toward which *phronesis* is oriented. He probably adds a meaning that in sociological jargon we would call the "unintended consequences" of human action which do not disrupt, but feed into a civilizational course. This is best exemplified by his theory of the emergence of public reason through a violent class conflict, which I explain later (cf. Jacobitti 1996). Over and again, Vico's stress on the role of divine providence is directed against the view that viable civic institutions might be built on a reconciliation of conflicting interests per se, or on a view of "natural law" that covers just such diverse and conflicting interests. The telic dimension represents the mechanism of social coordination warranted by an orientation to the common good that he sees best enshrined in the Roman law notion of *ius* ("law; right"). Quite untheologically, he frequently refers the notion of providence to the genesis and evolution of Roman law much more than to any specifically religious tradition.

The telic orientation of human action also provides the basic platform for Vico's dealing with the relation between public reason and practical rationality, via a theory of justice and law. Reason is for Vico not the same as Cartesian rationality. *Ratio* is in Vico's vocabulary a quite exact translation of "law," in that it incorporates the layers and sediments of "vulgar wisdom," social practice, and common sense. This understanding of *ratio* does not empower the rational thinker to lay a claim to govern the city, nor does it justify the contention that the city and the world should attain salvation and prosperity by reason as such (Mazzotta 1999: 68). There is simply no "reason as such." *Ratio* can only be—as in its original Latin meaning—simultaneously rule and phronetic reasonableness. It therefore relies on the thick and hybrid sediments of the facts-shaping force of human creativity, which incorporates bodies and acts upon them. Reason thus conceived is the only tool for preempting the permanent risk of sociopolitical disintegration of modernity, caused by a self-interest left to itself and legitimated as such by so many apologists of modernity (ibid.: 93, 152, 164).

This approach embraces an issue that has embarrassed many modern thinkers intent to formulate rules of reasons: the question of authority and its relation to power. Vico is extraordinarily outspoken and "materialistic" in asserting that authority is primarily conferred by ownership.

Only on a second step does authority become consecrated and objectified in earnest and binding formulas, which are the prototypical form of the law, before it is finally metamorphosed into the authority of jurists.[2] These are the scholars who are versed in the *phronesis*/prudence of law, that is jurisprudence, and who under normal conditions can only deploy their moral and legal authority if a ruler, mostly a monarch, is capable to secure political order. Ownership, that grounds authority, is strictly linked to the institutions of marriage and patronage and, much at the confluence of both, family. These are the fields that Roman law characterizes as private (ibid.: 165).

> Fathers in the family state must have exercised monarchical power which was subject to God alone. This power extended over the persons and property of their children, and to a greater extent over those of the family servants, *famuli*, who had sought refuge on their lands. This made them the first monarchs of the world. (We must interpret the Bible as referring to such men when it calls them patriarchs, which means "ruling fathers.") (Vico 1999 [1744]: 101)

Thus, it is not surprising that the source of authority is in the private sphere delimited by Roman law. However, in the framework of this legal tradition, the private origins of authority and the public deployment of a discourse on the common good are reconciled by the rationality of the law. The private-public nexus is here quite different from its later modern reinterpretations, starting with those provided by the Scottish Enlightenment, in the context of its elaboration on the notion of "civil society" (see chapter 6). The nexus in Roman law lies in the distinctive force of *ius* to turn private assertions of authority into the public authority of a law that regulates how particular and collective goods are constituted and transacted upon and what their relationships are.

Vico is well aware that interpretative conflicts in the field of law at large are no pure dynamics of scholarly agreement and disagreement, but reflect permanently shifting configurations of power. For Vico these conflicts are due as much to class struggles as to other types of social strife. After all, law is no pure reading of reality but is tied to coercive orders. However, he is also convinced that law, in spite of having its root in the appropriation of authority as property, in the power relations between master and servant, father and son, husband and wife, patricians and plebeians, and in spite of the reality of ongoing power struggles, works as an antidote against the fragmentation of reason into an anarchical matching of particularistic interests. The condition is that, however conflicted and dialectical its emergence, law is formulated in such a way to be an ordinance of reason for the common good and not an expedient matching of strong interests (Mazzotta 1999: 167). Here Vico is very much in the tradition of Aquinas, de Vitoria, and Suarez.

Yet also in close analogy with al-Shatibi's approach to legal philosophy (see chapter 4), the authority of the law, though rooted in an obscurity of judgment on heterogeneous and particular matters, is upgraded by Vico into universal *ratio* via induction mediated by the phronetic search for equity and justice. But this upgraded meaning of law's authority cannot be apprehended in purely speculative terms, by deduction from a divine will or *logos*. It should be grasped through a consistent socioanthropological analysis of institutional transformations. Practices of reprisal and revenge were symbolically transformed into the technique of feigning force via denunciation and suing. Thus in the genesis of law, the brutal but also solemn and "heroic" impetus of the application of sheer force was preserved. Without preserving this bodily language, there would be no such form of reason like law. The switching back and forth between lawfulness and symbolic acts is at the root of the practice itself of public discourse. The original, poetic metaphors of truth, which were taken literally in archaic times, have been subjected to permanent erosion and distortion over time, as shown by philologists. Law appears under the guise of a sublimation of poetry, as a new form of *poiesis*, since its formulas are believed and performed by social and legal agents, and so create reality (ibid.: 169). In this way, Vico redirects Spinoza's principled, philosophical dichotomization between truth and superstition into a social analysis of their factual interrelatedness in the genesis and evolution of all religious and civic institutions.

It is known that *persona* is simultaneously a theatrical and a legal term. Hobbes used this concept in order to reconstruct a distinctively modern notion of the public. For him, a person is "he, whose words or actions are considered as representing the words or actions of another" (Hobbes 1996 [1651]: 106 [80]). The person is then identical to the actor on stage and in common conversation, so that to act or to impersonate (oneself or somebody else) belong to the same category. This notion of the person allowed several modern authors to separate the visibility of utterances and actions from the alleged hidden domain of the soul, or "inner forum" (Voegelin 1998b: 67). Now, once again, Vico shows that the genealogy of the person and its impact on the public sphere are much more complex than maintained by even the most acute of the modern political realists. While Hobbes's view was immediately plugged into the dimension of "playing a game" (indeed a game of power and interest), Vico warns us that the *persona* or mask as found in archaic theatrical scripts is first of all an imaginatively corporeal form.

If it is a representation—and in a sense it is—the *persona* is inseparably imaginary and concrete; it is representation precisely because it comes from a mind incapable of radical abstractions of a philosophical type. Moreover, its relationship to power is not as flat as maintained by Hobbes, and is necessarily mediated by authority. In its mimetic form, archaic theatrical impersonation is a subtle game of revealing and concealing the power of a patrician family or of its hero and "family father" (*pater famil-ias*), since it is originally staged in the marketplace. Far from being "on stage" in a purely theatrical—and therefore safe—sense, this imperson-ation does expose the actor to violence as much as the impersonated hero is exposed to it when he publicly displays the power inherent in his position of authority. There is, in other words, no Leviathan behind the level of staging, who protects the actors against violence. The modalities of violence related to acting and enacting power can be symbolically metamorphosed through the process of evolution of the law from these archaic and theatrical origins, but cannot be definitively erased by Leviathan.

It is impossible to understand the genesis of Roman jurisprudence and of its basic notions of *personae*, *res*, and *actiones*, according to Vico, without paying due attention to this distinctive mechanism of employ-ing corporeal forms in order to communicate abstract concepts. This is exactly why Vico asserts that ancient jurisprudence *was* poetry, represented in the Roman forum like in the Athenian *agorà*. The marketplace, as the public arena hosting the exchanges of all possible goods, brings to the fore separate worlds with their colliding or overlapping catalogues and notions of goods. There would be no marketplace and no public forum, however, without discourse. Not by chance the god supervising exchange in the marketplace is Hermes/Mercury, who is also the hidden god of communication.[3]

What Vico helps us see is that while the solemn formulas of the law cover a higher notion of *res publica* or the common good (corresponding, in Islamic terms, to *maslaha*), they concretely operate at the bottom of the social bond by helping establish a dialogic relation between strangers, in spite of the structural imbalances of power among actors on the marketplace and in society at large. Before it becomes a formula for the pursuit of the common good and public weal, law is thus inevitably and simultaneously a reflection of power relations and an ambivalent acknowledgement of otherness. Law entails the promise of a harmo-nious conversation, but also the tragic potential of violence looming behind every encounter (Mazzotta 1999: 170–71). Vico invokes nothing less than Socrates's authority for arguing that laws (in the plural) precede philosophy in helping forming universals by induction through pulling together similar particulars and then constituting a uniform genus on the basis of the principle of utility common to all. Plato completed the move, according to Vico, in observing that only through debates in public assemblies one overcomes particular utilitarian interests and makes the *ratio* of justice prevail. Socrates suggested a novel, singular method for seeking goods out of scattered cases, while Plato devised the public procedure for securing the application of the method (ibid.: 172).

Yet this definition of justice is the achievement of a highly sophisticated, Hellenic type of axiality. Before this level is reached (see chapter 1), a crude concreteness prevails in the pursuit of the common good, which cannot derive from making sense rationally out of a complex social reality, but has to be built upon the most ambivalent dimensions of the *ego-alter* relationship and the attending power imbalances. Only coping with otherness can finally vindicate public reasoning. The image obsessively evoked in the "Poetic Economy" section of the *New Science* is the refugee or guest. Vico concentrates on this character for tackling the crucial issue of the origin of cities. He finds this origin in patrician families, colonies, and asylums, which were the first hospices, and where the strangers received were considered guests (ibid.: 174).

> Cadmus founded Thebes, the oldest city in Greece, on a refuge. Theseus founded Athens on the Altar of the Unfortunate . . . Romulus founded Rome by opening a refuge in a clearing. As the archetype of a city founder, Romulus and his companions established Rome according to the plan of the refuges that gave rise to the ancient cities of Latium . . . refuges were the origins of cities, whose invariable property is to protect their residents from violence. In this manner, from the multitude of impious nomads who found refuge and safety in the lands of the pious heroes, there derived Jupiter's graceful title, the Hospitable. For such refuges were the world's first hospices, and the first people received there were the first guests or strangers, *hospites* in Latin, of the cities. (Vico 1999 [1744]: 241)

This encounter between the guest/stranger and the host/autochthonous was the type of *ego-alter* relationship that received the strongest sacralization. Zeus/Jupiter is not only the god of thunder who insinuates fear, but also the host-god who protects all strangers and punishes any wrong committed against them. Pagan and biblical myth are joined by how Jupiter shares one crucial attribute with the "Yahweh of Hosts." The arrival itself of the stranger—something for which the host/citizen should be permanently prepared, since it is utterly and inherently unpredictable, and this is why asylums were instituted—testifies the existence and importance of the other, not only as a single other, but as social worlds other than one's own, yet to be made—under the threat of godly sanctions—accessible to one other. The place of the encounter among the hero and father, on the one hand, and the refugee and would-be-servant or client of the hero, on the other, is an altar also because it is the place where, in those crude beginnings of human civilization, the docile fugitive was adopted but the violent stranger was slain and sacrificed (ibid.: 11–12).

The relationship between host and guest is inherently reciprocal, yet unbalanced. The notion itself of reciprocity is always imperfectly incorporated in all proto-institutions of patronage and marriage, entailing essential power imbalances. Yet the asylum also represents a litmus testing ground of an exchange that configures a sort of proto-friendship, an inviolable gift that binds forever *ego* and *alter* in spite of all disparities. It thus provides the grounding stone of the social bond, of the related chain of intimations of connective justice, of civility. As an institution, the asylum is prior to—and the condition for—any injunction of commanding good. However, Vico is well aware that the constructed relation in the refuge cannot erase strangeness, which lingers on. This is the point of entry of prophetic discourse and of what Voegelin called a "leap of faith." This step fixes the triangular relationship between *ego*, *alter*, and God and the concomitant partnership in faith between *ego* and *alter* which the "pre-axial" piety of the asylum was not yet able to contain.

Before that leap occurs, *hostis* means both guest and enemy. Vico embarks on an archaeology of civic unrest, grounded on the fact that the heroes and the refugees, the fathers and the servants, the citizens and the guests turned into the conflicting classes of the patricians and plebeians in Rome:

> Commonwealths . . . were born of a crisis provoked by the family servants against the heroic fathers. For when the servants rebelled, the fathers united themselves into orders to offer resistance; and then as a united order, the fathers sought to placate the servants and restore them to obedience by granting them a kind of rustic fief. At the same time, the fathers found that their own family powers—which can be understood only as a sort of noble fiefs—were now subjected to the sovereign civil power of the new ruling orders. And the leaders of these orders were called kings, for as the most courageous they had led the fathers during the servant rebellion . . . in no other manner can we

understand how civil power grew out of family powers, how the public patrimony emerged out of private patrimonies, or how the foundations of commonwealths were laid by a social order which is made up of the few who command and the multitude of plebeians who obey. (Vico 1999 [1744]: 102–3)

The use of a paradigm drawn from Roman history and Roman law helps Vico draw a theoretically richer picture than any compulsive reference to the axial drama of the Athenian *polis* (which he, however, also takes into account as a secondary source of historical examples). From Vico's perspective, it is clear that Aristotle's political theorizing is not enough. The Greek philosopher's approach is too static to appreciate the importance but also the ambivalence of the command of piety that prefigures the right of asylum (Mazzotta 1999: 175). From the first, unbalanced yet "providential"—in Vico's sense—encounter between the patriarch and the fugitive, a tight dynamics of conflict unfolds. Its providential aspect for Vico resides in the process of turning the cycle of conflict, violence, and suffering into a higher form of the social bond, the institution of the *res publica*:

> The contentions between urban social orders seeking equal rights are the most effective means of making commonwealths great . . . This is the second principle of Roman heroism. Such heroism was attended by three public virtues: the plebeians' highmindedness in seeking to gain civil rights by means of the patricians' laws; the patricians' fortitude in keeping the rights within their order; and the wisdom of the jurists in interpreting the laws and extending their benefits as new cases came to trial. These are the three intrinsic reasons by which Roman jurisprudence distinguished itself in the world. (Vico 1999 [1744]: 106)

A major sociological node consists in how the public spirit of the law emerged out of a monarchical power that was a direct emanation of the private patrician power of the *patres familias* (Voegelin 1998b: 139). The public good originates from a conflicted *ego-alter* relationship transposed from the microlevel of the original encounter in the asylum to a macrolevel of class struggle in the city. The rebellion of the subaltern is essential to bring about the transformation of archaic law—which was secret and literally owned by the patricians—into a transparent and equitable rule instituting rights, first the property rights and the right of marriage for the plebeians. Yet this transformation of the law would be moot without the jurists' prudence in interpreting and applying it. However, it should not be neglected that Vico is realist enough to appreciate the capacity of the dominant class to preserve the sociopolitical order from chaos, without destroying the fundaments of the commonwealth, which are then turned from "heroic" into "civic." Vico is well aware that this preservation is made possible by the fact that the patricians continue to command a considerable amount of violence, not unlike the moment when the asylums were grounded. A further implication—though not one explicitly highlighted by Vico—is that the order-function of the dominant class, which is a metamorphosed form of authority perpetuated within the civic commonwealth, poses intrinsic limits to the public reason incarnated by jurisprudence, which is then called not only to keep and restore equity to the microorder of interactions but also to preserve the public order.

This is a dynamic but realistic view of the rise of public reason. The example provided by the history of Roman society evidences the immanent combination of conflict and recreation of the social bond. This process established the necessity of new laws both in content and in form, or better with regard to the degree of their accessibility and understanding for the commoners. It also included the shift of the Roman state from monarchy to republic, with ever new transformations resulting into the grounding of new cities and the influx of new guests/refugees.

In Vico's reconstruction the emergence of the *res publica* out of the "heroic contentions" between the estates or classes was not the mere result of a pure sociopolitical process, but was made possible by the way in which the plebeians styled their own communicative approach by creating distinctive mythical evocations that subverted the one-sided, class-based, formulaic sacredness of archaic law. The process of turning public the law, both in the sense of making it accessible and understandable (no longer a monopoly of the patrician *pontifex*), and in the sense of making it fit into the idea of a popular commonwealth of equal citizens, was a complex development. Being aware of this complexity as elucidated by Vico should inoculate us from any temptation to postulate the emergence of public reason as a simple evolutionary process (Voegelin 1998b: 139). The process required nothing less than the formation and crystallization of an alternative symbolization and of a counterdiscourse by the rebelling clients. It is through this contention that a new form of speech, based on vernacular language, was created. The key moment in the process is an act of incredulity by the plebeians, and therefore the collapse of the heroes' pretension to be of divine origin. The immediate consequence of this act was the emergence of a postulate of, first of all, existential equality:

> in their heroic contentions with the nobility, the plebeians at Rome protested that the fathers chosen for the senate by Romulus "had not

descended from heaven," *non esse coelo demissos.* In other words, the founders of the patriciate did not have the divine origin of which the patricians boosted. Instead, Jupiter was equal for all. (Vico 1999 [1744]: 165)

While the family fathers unite into a bond reflecting an emerging class consciousness, the plebeians start to understand themselves not only as united by a common, antagonistic class interest, but also as representing *the* common good through their request of new, equitable, and transparent laws. In other words, at the very moment they, the subaltern, develop a class consciousness, they also create the very idea of a good that transcends all classes. They author the crucial passage from the particularistic and authoritarian *res patria* (the secretly managed interest of the fathers) to the equitable and potentially universal *res publica* (the transparently adjudicated common interest).

This transformation can only be accomplished by changing the terms of the symbolic understanding of the two classes: "Power is maintained by a disproportionate allocation of resources . . . but the resources are more cultural than material in character. They are primarily linguistic" (Miner 2002: 118). The importance of Vico's almost proto-Gramscian approach to power and class (cf. Jacobitti 1983) cannot be overestimated, since it reflects a sociological sophistication unknown to later theories of "civil society" (see chapter 6). This approach also spells out the inherent ambivalence of the family of notions related to publicness, which simultaneously reflects a class consciousness and the claim to represent the general interest. Moreover, against Machiavellian accounts, Vico denies that the foundation of the republic could be the result of the application of an ingenious will to power based on calculation, and supported by force or fraud. Social actors are not individual leaders but collective actors. Most importantly, the formation of a subaltern class releases a new language and the beginning of what we call discourse: "just as heroic or poetic language was created by the heroes, vernacular or popular language was created by the populace, who were the plebeians of the heroic nations" (Vico 1999 [1744]: 181).

Indeed, the subjection of the plebeians, also called *vernae* (from which "vernacular," as plebeian language), had been allowed not only by the sheer force of the patrician fathers but by their heroic language, dense with metaphor, metonymy, and synecdoche. Against this type of language, Vico suggests that the rebelling clients discovered an altogether different trope of speech, namely irony, that was developed in the narratives (called "fables," like those of Aesop in Greek and Phaedrus in

Latin) that the plebeians used to unveil the lack of justice in a system that legitimated the "lion's share," the privileges of the patricians. Vico saw the necessity of such a new language for transitioning the human activity of claims-making from imaginative genres to a discursive kind of communication, thus diluting, though not erasing, authority, by transposing it into the authority of the laws.

This kind of speech is articulate and inherently public, while suitable for the promulgation of equitable laws. The method of public speech rooted in the authority of the common good needed not only the means to articulate concepts through words and letters, but also a more sophisticated arguing capacity. This capacity was provided by Socrates through perfecting the induction of universals from particular maxims and commands via abstraction and dialectic reasoning. Yet the full-blown Greek-axial philosophy of Plato and Aristotle has by necessity its fundament in the complex and conflicted origin of social custom, rooted in common sense and common speech but also mediated by dramatic and bloody class struggles (ibid.: 122–23).

Vico equates the foundation of the republic and the concomitant public rank of the law with the beginning of the "third age," that is the human age or the age of reflection (very close indeed to the Axial Age), following the age of the gods, when thunder and terror laid the basis for human *poiesis*, and the heroic age, when private estates and hospices were grounded. We see here why the asylum builds a critical and vital, though fragile nexus between the private estate and the public commonwealth, the *res publica*. It incorporates the embryonic tensions and contradictions that will lead to the plebeian revolt and to the constitution of the *res publica*. Concomitantly with the rise of a republican arena, the power of mythical *poiesis* declines and reflective philosophy starts its ascent. However, the *mente eroica* (the "heroic mind") lives on in the contentions of public assemblies. Good laws cannot see the light and be fully appreciated without a "heroic" substratum that survives in the symbolic constitution itself of any legal litigation. This means that each and every public contention, from the legal adjudication of particularistic interests to constitutional battles, keeps the imprint of a fierce heroic challenge (Mazzotta 1999: 139–43). Outside of philosophy, in the public arena, there is no such a thing as a "pure" speech.

Vico's main argument cannot be fully appreciated without considering the "discovery of the true Homer" that is at the core of the *New Science*'s thesis according to which the origins of common good and public speech are to be sought in the fundaments of the social bond laid down in the divine and heroic ages. Within these ages, Homer represents the last, crucial phase, immediately preceding the irruption of the age of men, and vividly witnessing the full maturation of imaginative universals before their transformation into conceptual ones. This part of Vico's investigation is decisive for understanding the character and merit of his genealogical approach, which preempts any Nietzschean temptation to typologize—indeed, quite ungenealogically—a heroic moral as opposed to a moral of pious concern for the common good.

Through his attention to Homer's construction of the undifferentiated, heroic proto-virtue (conflating strength, magnanimity, a cunning judgment, and an embryonic piety periodically tempering excesses of wrath), Vico also intends to differentiate his approach from Plato's strategy that refurbished the Homeric encyclopedia to the benefit of his own philosophical mythopoiesis, as an axial straight path that leads up to the contemplation of justice. Vico rejects this shortcut and appreciates Homeric poetry on its own merit, for representing the encounter of plural worlds and therefore for protecting heterogeneity from the risk of a (political or philosophical) authoritarian manipulation and centralistic homogenization.

The statue of Homer is depicted on the cover page of the *New Science* as towering among the fragments of history. Homer, the "blind," shows his back to the source of light in a patent reversal of the sage in Plato's cave. Homer does not speak from the vintage point of a transcendent look upon human history. Therefore, he represents the proto-commoner, still involved in heroic contentions, and who stands prior to any philosophic or prophetic discourse, caught within his own world view that is in fact a form of blindness—much like the poet, in his creative *poiesis*, is blind to the causes and effects of his own activity. But the emblem of the *New Science* stands above Homer. It is God's eye refracted on the breast of a woman who represents Lady Philosophy, from where the light is further refracted on Homer's back representing the commoner's capacity to act. This capacity is based on a phronetic reason whose origin is not, as in Aristotle and Aquinas, in the articulation of virtues and passions internal to soul, but in bodily *poiesis*. This is the immediate creative force that underlies subsequent stages of linguistic articulation and vernacularization, and the concomitant waves of "publicization" (Apel 1978 [1963]: 360) of discourses of equity and justice through popular movements (ibid.: 358–64).

This substantial Vichian dissonance from axial postulates, which according to Karl Apel is also essential to understanding Kant's later notions of practical and public reason (ibid.), redesigns the relationship between the concept of a worldly immanence of reason and the human capacity to transcend any given situation into intersubjective value. The viewpoint of God's eye in the frontispiece is what Vico calls providence and is simultaneously transcendent and immanent to human history, rescuing it from the randomness of the tragic plots masterly depicted by Machiavelli (Mazzotta 1999: 160–61). Vico's strategy for countering the subterranean world of power arcanes does not consist in upholding a naïve ideology of the transparency of public discourse supported by an uncontaminated vision of Platonic justice. Vico rather dramatizes the human actor's incapacity of avoiding chaos without resorting to a patient and laborious *phronesis* oriented to a provident *telos*. In the era of men, the main weapon against the simulations of both existing and would-be tyrants, well-learned (unlike the naive heroes) in the modern technique of domination, is a prudential discourse (ibid.: 89).

Vico considers rhetoric the art of public discourse combining memory, invention, and judgment, whereby the persuasiveness it seeks is intended not to manipulate, but to thicken the scope of the audience's imagination and receptivity (ibid.: 70). In the modern era, public speech becomes an increasingly sophisticated arsenal of prudence and eloquence, even more so due to its facing ever more powerful techniques of power. In other words, Vico is skeptical that the sheer power unleashed by modernity can be tamed and channeled without renewing the tradition of a compassionate and prudential attendance to the common good.

## Across the Modern Breakthrough: The Spiral *Ricorso* of Tradition

From Machiavelli to Hobbes, the early modern genealogy of values had affirmed the primacy of force over discourse. For Hobbes, in particular, it was the competition for power that engendered the divisive dynamics of warfare, which in turn determined the spectrum of social values. Without denying this materialistic genealogy of values per se, but rather making it much more complex, Vico's answer is that the world of speech is also, intrinsically, a world of *agòn* (competition) and action. Its genealogy is more realistic and crude than the one proposed by the political realists and consists in the process of turning physical into symbolic violence, suppression into challenge. This is a "pious genealogy" representing a realistic alternative to the unbounded practice of the war, both between classes and among nations.

The displacement of litigation and of its resolution from the battlefield to the courts and parliaments is not an irreversible conquest, but reflects the trajectory of any civilizational course. Any such course might be subject to collapse and subsequent relaunch, and this is the meaning of Vico's *ricorso*. This is an intentionally ambivalent word that means not just a new course, but also something like a second appeal in court, the pursuit of a second chance. This is where a managed shift back to Plato's *Republic* becomes necessary. Whereas Machiavelli and Hobbes warn of a principled anarchy of human society if untamed by coercive power, Plato showed that a city can only become a city through recognizing that nobody is self-sufficient (ibid.: 75). Vico's hero, whom he opposes to the antiheroic characters of the erudite libertines of his time—with their practices of dissimulation and their exaltation of uncontaminated wills to power—is the *homo honestatis*. *Honestas*, which would be reductive to translate as "honesty," consists in recognizing the boundaries and limits of the self, in merging the religious virtue of *pietas* and the civic virtue of *aequitas*. It is a capacity to act in pursuit of the good via acknowledging *alter* and his legitimate interest to pursue good in a likewise way (ibid.: 50).

In his work *Respublica christiana*, Grotius had argued—in spite of the intent declared in the title—in favor of the dismantling of this idea as shaped by the Axial Renaissance. Grotius preferred to search for the common by looking into some generic character of mankind. Symptomatically, this pursuit did not prevent, but encouraged a postulation of the civilized nature of man as found in the most affluent, powerful, and Christian-reformed nations of northwestern Europe in opposition to the other, uncivilized or less civilized nations of the world. White man (better if Protestant) became the standard of mankind at the moment he was preparing for an unbroken series of colonial and imperial undertakings, thus exhausting out any universal idea of law: including the law of the nations or the international law so dear to Grotius and to the modern contractarians and natural law theorists. This is particularly evident in Grotius's *The Freedom of the Seas, or The Right which Belongs to the Dutch to Take Part in the East Indian Trade*, an unequivocal title for a book in which he theorized about the right of the Western sea powers to arrange and lead the mercantile exploitation of the world. He was quite straightforward in stating that denying this kind of law was tantamount to erasing the fundaments of human fellowship, mutual service, and of nature itself (ibid.: 55–56). Putting the will to power at the basis of law could not have been more explicit.

Vico's *Diritto universale* is an implacable indictment of this theory of law. Attacking Grotius, along with Selden and Pufendorf, he dismantled their theories by deploying a philologically and historically sophisticated argument to show how far apart the origins of Roman law and Roman political institutions—whose heritage the Dutch theorists of law claimed for themselves—were from the imagination of the new natural law theorists. Their basic fault was of a genuine ethnocentric nature, consisting in the assumption that if a law is given, legitimate, and well functioning in a specific social and institutional context where it guarantees order and prosperity, it must be equally legitimate in any other social constellation. A fatal error of this theory resided in the idea that society is based on a type of contract whose presuppositions are enshrined in the practices and interests of the rising bourgeoisie (Cooper 1998: 16). Not unlike the patricians' claim of having a divine origin, this was a class-based presupposition, which in turn derived from a gross anthropological distortion and simplification.

The new philosophers of natural law considered human nature as already civilized by religion and law and bracketed out the processes that simultaneously produce and reproduce religious, civic, and legal traditions. In other words, these modern European thinkers lost sight of their positioning *within* a civilizational discourse and tradition, so that the only option left was between being a liberal and a libertine: either to erect one's civilizational values into an absolute system (therefore effecting an implosion of the civilizing tradition and its complexity), or to reject those values in toto (what amounted to a collapse of the tradition). The only way out of this dilemma that threatened the loss of the civilizational heritage was for Vico in the pursuit of a genealogical method for understanding man's own historicity, by bringing the mythical evocations of the civilizational formulas within intellectual and analytic grasp, and finally by situating oneself critically and liminally toward the original and permanent engine of the civilizing process, that is, the *senso comune* rooted in creative *poiesis*.

The first, analytical effort was directed by Vico to the examination of the *corso* of a civilization, whereas the second, diagnostic and genealogical undertaking was to enucleate what the *ricorso* is about. Voegelin and other commentators have pointed out that for Vico the *corso* is epitomized by the gentile myths of Roman history, while Christianity represents the *ricorso* (Voegelin 1998b: 136). It is true that the rise and unfolding of the Christian tradition represents the matrix of an axial *ricorso* for the genealogist steeped in this tradition, and having to cope with the implosion of the myth of the *respublica christiana* of the Axial Renaissance (ibid.: 118). However, the *ricorso* can also be any such genealogical reconstruction, from whatever contingent positioning of the genealogist within a civilizational course. In this, more general sense, the *ricorso* is not Christianity, but the post-axial reconstruction of any axial tradition from within modernity.

Only the predicament of modernity makes possible a genealogical approach to the civilizational link between *corso* and *ricorso*.

To give the *ricorso* a plastic vigor, Vico shows us in the frontispiece of the *New Science* its spiral shape, which depicts the simultaneous closure and openness of a circle that introduces a difference at each turn, and is always eccentric to the other circles in the spiral. Clearly, a *ricorso* is not just a figuration of epochs, but a method of seeing, thinking, writing, and reading. As stated by Mazzotta, it is "history's second chance or appeal." Modernity's curl sharply sticks out of the spiral of universal history. In this momentous achievement that is the theory of *corsi e ricorsi storici*, Vico's personality and style of writing, which has puzzled many commentators, reveals a singular combination of humble archaeology of the common sense and prophetic evocation of the common good (Mazzotta 1999: 231).

Drawing further conclusions from Vico's method for the analysis of sociohistorical transformations, we learn that it is especially in the formative periods of rupture and new foundation that rational reflection and practical knowledge are summoned to solve problems of reconstruction of the sociopolitical order. If this does not occur, extant civilizing traditions either implode or collapse. A kind of accelerated *phronesis* functioning as *ethopoiesis* is required in these fractures (see chapter 1). *Phronesis* demands here an extraordinarily strong interpenetration with the idea of justice, and this, unfortunately, cannot be left to *senso comune* alone. But it cannot be delegated to the speculations of ancient and modern philosophers either.

Looking through the abysmal breakthrough, Vico could not trust the self-taming and self-healing powers of modernity, as the failure of law and the outbreak of new and ever more destructive wars since after the last Wars of Religion of the sixteenth and seventeenth centuries testified. The *New Science* foregrounds Vico's sense of modernity as the *possible* advent of a new public discourse that differs from that of the past, a discourse, however, that cannot stem from a cult of power and of the self, least loosing its integrity as a civilizing discourse. The power of discourse can be easily erased by any discourse of pure power, which would deprive discourse of its potential openness reflecting the ambivalence of the axial constitution of the social bond, and would fragment it into the wills to truth-*cum*-power that it, ideologically, covers. Vico's *New Science* does not dramatize his role as either a classic philosophical prophet of the caliber of a Plato, or a modern prophet of power and control like Bacon. He appears as a genealogist attempting to redeem the soul of modernity as a special *ricorso* of tradition and not as a self-propelling project based on a self-sufficient, abstract reason nourished by a narcissistic removal of the past.

Vico insistently decried the "conceit of the nations," the self-illusion of cultural uniqueness and unity entertained by various peoples since the antiquity, as one of the main threats to the integrity of phronetic reason in the modern era. With the new techniques of power, monitoring, and control nourished by technological achievements and by the strengthening of the machinery of the modern state, the danger highlighted by Vico became even more acute. By the time of Vico, the eighteenth century, the various national communities were starting to deploy ever more comprehensive ideologies of the nation which turned symbolic assets of a shared mystical body (a complex Christian idea) into full-fledged political projects. In the process, the *telos* of the original symbolic power of the Christ was perverted and reconverted and the civic, legal, and religions institutions were subjected to totalizing visions of power (Hollweck and Sandoz 1998: 26; Cooper 1998: 9).

There is no ready-made alternative like a city of God on earth, a lesson easily drawn from the failure of the more radical versions of the Protestant Reformation. The residual Christian character of the *res publica* within the European *ricorso* lies in not surrendering to the self-taming promise of modernity's power. As we will see in the following chapter, Vico's approach to civility will be largely shared by the modern theorists of civil society, but in ways that will flatten out the complexity and historicity of axial traditions and lead to its reductionist essentialization at the service of modern commercial society and the modern state.

# CHAPTER 6

# THE MODERN PUBLIC SPHERE: TRANSFORMING PRACTICAL REASON INTO PRUDENTIAL COMMUNICATION

## The Private and the Public Spheres

We have seen in the previous chapter how the implosion of axial traditions generated the modern quest for a new definition of human agency, autonomy, and creativity, and how this demand brought about new kinds of tensions, paradoxes, and attempted solutions. In this chapter I turn the attention to an attempt to redefine the axial triadic relationship between *ego*, *alter*, and *Alter*/God governed by faith and practical reason into a basically dyadic *ego-alter* relationship administered by trust and prudential communication. This approach, which will yield the modern public sphere in an accomplished, Habermasian sense—as the "third sphere of society" (see introduction)—was not only an attempt to modernize tradition in socially constructive ways—largely through a specification of the basic tenets held by the contractarians—but also a reaction and a critique to the positions of the modern political realists (see chapter 5).

The process metamorphosed the notion of public reasoning by making faith and religion invisible in public life and by turning them into forms of regulation of the social bond, in the guise of "trust" and "morality." These were considered publicly acceptable engines of social cohesion, since more in tune with the new demand for individual agency and autonomy and at a safer distance from axial notions of divine command—though still susceptible of a religious coloring and still benefiting from a religious vocabulary motivating the individual to virtuous action. Yet virtue lies now increasingly in the capacity to accumulate goods of effectiveness (see chapter 1).

This attempted solution to the problem of reconstructing the social bond took form and gained currency within important intellectual circles variously linked to momentous socioeconomic transformations in some parts of northwestern Europe, but finally became paradigmatic for the liberal tradition as a whole. In some important instances these developments are linked to the remaking and relaunching of the classic notion of *societas civilis*, in the guise of a "civil society," consisting of multiple dyadic ties of trust nurtured by a "moral sense" of affection among individuals. To this extent, the contractarian approach was complemented by an insistence on a quite ahistorical version of a sense of communion among human beings, a moralized notion of "common sense" no longer imbued with Vichian tension and creativity (see chapter 5).

Efforts at reforming and remolding faith into an increasingly secular trust proved to be crucial to the modernization of the public sphere. The emergence of a self-sufficient notion of trust incorporated the type of intersubjective agency best fitting the demands of the emerging social classes and actors of the new era. It laid the fundaments for the crystallization of a new sense of publicness, functionally delimited from privateness, underlying the new public sphere. Concomitantly, the mutation of the agent's social and communicative rationality was effected by a transformation of *phronesis/prudentia* into a calculative and reflective, conveniently communicative type of prudence. I attempt to show that this major change is probably the kernel of the "semantic coup" perpetrated from within the Anglo-American liberal tradition against traditional and early modern notions of common sense and the common good (cf. Münkler and Bluhm 2001; Münkler and Fischer 2002). To this end, I explore the metamorphosis of notions of practical rationality and public reason implied by the recasting of the agent's rationality, for which I mainly draw from the analysis of Alasdair MacIntyre. I also elaborate upon Adam Seligman's analysis of the genesis of modern trust as the product of dramatic transformations in specific parts of Europe.

Seligman's main argument is that modern notions of the social bond, like in the elaboration of the concept of "civil society" by eighteenth-century Scottish moralists (also known as the Scottish Enlightenment), entailed a primacy of a redefined private sphere, and thus influenced the restructuring of the public sphere as an important, yet derivative field of social action and communication. This development marked a departure both from the notion of the private realm as developed in the tradition of Roman law and from the dialectical genesis of the public domain out of the dynamics of social encounters and conflicts as diagnosed within the modern, continental, humanist tradition that culminated in the work of Vico (see chapter 5).

It comes as no surprise that as a result of the transformation the new private and public spheres were made to fit the capitalistic formations of the new era. However, the new approach obscured the diagnosis of modernity as intrinsically dynamic and conflict laden and produced transhistorical views of the public sphere and of its relations to the private sphere. The new private sphere no longer reflects a sociological combination of authority and practical reason as in the Vichian account. The emergence of a new type of public sphere did not erase patriarchal authority but rather disguised and mystified it. It also became a largely ideological reflection of the emerging economic discourse and of the role assigned to the nuclear family as a unity of reproduction of workforce and of preservation and transmission of accumulated capital.

The essentialized private sphere acquires a new centrality in constituting and explaining the social bond and the morality of social life in general. The reconstructed public sphere retains and rearticulates an important function of *res publica*, since the last test of effectiveness of any social bond is seen in the morality deployed through public encounters. However, a public sphere so defined and its force of moral cohesion are considered structurally and not dialectically — through dynamics of class and cultural conflicts — derivative of the private sphere.

This structural dependence of the public sphere on the functions of reproduction of the private sphere is complemented by its functional relation to modern state regulation. The public sphere is reconceived as a static, moderately communicative, conflict free relay between the relationships in the private sphere based on interest (contract) and affection (friendship, love), and their combination (marriage, the family patrimony), on the one hand, and the normative force of the modern state that puts to work its monopoly of force to guarantee the emerging public order and mechanisms of generalized exchange, on the other.

In the final Habermasian version of this strand of theory the public sphere will assume the function of facilitating a rational deliberation on the common good among private citizens. Before reaching this stage, and at a more fundamental level of provision of glue to social relationships, in the approach of the Scottish moralists the public sphere was designed to make visible, disseminate, and legitimize notions of generalized exchange, without which contractual transactions among private individuals would have lacked the necessary stability. "Generalized exchange" characterizes here an unconditional, taken for granted, self-reinforcing, and therefore eminently normative code of behavior governing the social interaction, the modalities of communication, and the contractual transactions among social actors warranted by ties of confidence (Seligman 1997: 79–81).

Generalized exchange denotes a "systemic" type of order. While Seligman and others indicate in Mauss's theory of the gift a prototypical, anthropological—indeed pre-axial (see chapter 1)—example of generalized exchange, it cannot be overlooked that the idea of generalized exchange itself, and its application to all forms of the social bond, crystallized in those sociohistorical environments where the transformations of the private and public spheres took place. This happened in the context of emergence of paradigmatic forms of self-sustaining commercial and industrial capitalism, supported by the growth of contract law and supervised by a modern state apparatus.

The deliberative dimension of the public sphere can be here interpreted as a communicative extension of its function as the terrain of generalized exchange. This level of public exchange allows individuals to relate to each other and transact in a regulated, nonpristine way that makes obsolete the face-to-face dimension of encounters and transactions. The public sphere becomes "shared standards of anticipation" among social actors who do not share the same social and communicative spaces (Eickelman and Salvatore 2002: 105–10). Shared anticipation is on the one hand a functional facilitation of individual agency oriented to the pursuit of goods of effectiveness. On the other hand, it allows for a regulated coordination and monitoring of individual actions through public authorities. In this sense, it is hard to see how this communicative-deliberative dimension could become an autonomous source of order for a "third sphere" of society seen as distinct from the economic sphere and from the system of bureaucratic steering of populations (see introduction).

In light of this approach the emerging modern public sphere appears like the dowry brought in by private citizens for a marriage of convenience with the state. This public sphere is still dependent on the Hobbesian covenant that grounds and legitimizes the Leviathan forever, while it also expedites the transition from absolutist to representative forms of government, first liberal, then liberal-democratic. In the very moment when the public sphere is entrusted to an increasingly democratic Leviathan, the regulating mechanisms of the state appropriate its communicative dimension that is first oriented to facilitate exchange, via the standardization of contract law that defines, channels, and regulates the most productive types of transaction among actors. These actors are then considered endowed with a capacity to communicate efficiently and prudently their own interests in order to match them contractually with the interests of others.

What private citizens are allowed to do is to transform the Leviathan first into a liberal and then into a democratic power machinery, but the nature of the covenant, along with the makeup of the public sphere, is not affected by the transformation. As Habermas will show, the mass democracy of welfare states does threaten to diminish the deliberative potential of the public sphere and even to fold it back into the private sphere, so that "public spiritedness" is reabsorbed into the dominance of private concerns, while the citizen becomes a client. However, an essential dependence of the public from the private sphere was probably grafted into its birth as a modern "third sphere." But let us take stock and explore the genealogy of this type of public sphere that social science literature characterizes as distinctively modern, and therefore as the quintessential, or even the only possible public sphere at all.

The theory of civil society by the Scottish moralists departed from an Aristotelian and even Thomistic notion of the common good or *res publica*, pivoted on the natural affection among human beings that facilitates the constitution of the social bond and is mainly nurtured by prudence (*phronesis*), justice, and *caritas* (see chapter 3). These theorists, however, transformed this axial concept into a different tool for looking at social relationships and at society at large (MacIntyre 1988: 209–59). The first among the leading thinkers of the Scottish Enlightenment, Francis Hutcheson (1694–1746)—whom I single out, following MacIntyre, precisely because the earlier sketched conceptual metamorphosis is most visible in his argument—wrestled with the tension between justice (a notion central to all axial political, legal and religious traditions: see chapters 1 to 5), on the one hand, and interests (not an entirely modern concept either: see in particular chapter 4), on the other, while he still affirmed the primacy of the former. His deductive method of reasoning—contrasting with the Roman law tradition of induction that had been elaborated upon by Hutcheson's predecessors within the Scottish moral philosophy tradition well into the eighteenth century—transformed justice from a *telos* inherent in legal interaction into a conceptual cover of rights of individuals making claims on each other within particular social relationships and circumstances.

In order to pinpoint this new idea of justice, Hutcheson (2002 [1728]) had to admit that reasonable action cannot be grounded on practical reason (*phronesis*), but has to rely on the structure of individual motivations, which are affected by interests. Interest itself has to be considered as based on a particular passion, self-love. This was still the classic, Augustinian concept of *amor sui*, which, however, in the process, through Hutcheson's as well as Hume's and Adam Smith's elaboration, was redefined as "vanity," an essential motor of motivation of human action operating through other's perception of one's actions.

The breakthrough here is in that self-love is no longer a negative and diabolic force, but a factor essential to the emergence of the social bond and of civil society. Reason is no longer sufficient to ground morality and sociality, since it now depends on motivations, which in turn rely on affections that are never in themselves good or bad. An action becomes bad only if it is based on an excessive passion vis-à-vis the other and if it is not monitored by the actor's self-love that, through a desire for recognition through the other, normally works as a disciplining engine (MacIntyre 1988: 267). The injury of traditional notions of common good and public reason was consumed through diminishing the autonomy and authority of reason. The *ego-alter* connection is still the focus of this kind of theory. It is rather the notion of the self that reabsorbs some of the functions of mediation and communication that were formerly located in the interaction itself, in the intersubjective mechanism of the triangle *ego-alter-Alter*/God.

The place of reason, which earlier traditions saw as a phronetic form of rationality culminating in a capacity of public reasoning geared to the common good or *res publica*, is replaced by a practical "moral sense." This term was first used by the Third Earl of Shaftesbury (1671–1713), but it was John Locke (1632–1704) who explained the underlying idea. The moral sense is an inner, basically passive capacity of discerning good and bad based on a mildly reflective kind of sentiment (Jensen 1971: 35–43), naturally possessed and developed by the human self. This capacity allows man to know what is good, and to orient and order one's actions toward the good on the basis of the impulses determined by rightly guided passions and sound interests. In Hutcheson's words, this moral sense becomes "a social feeling of partnership with mankind" (MacIntyre 1988: 268).

This conception, which originated from anti-Hobbesian trends of reflection on the human nature, marked a revolution in the definition of the common good. Yet in Hutcheson, who had been trained in scholastic philosophy and belonged to a family of Presbyterian ministers, it was still largely expressed in Aristotelian terms and through a religious vocabulary. While an author like Vico was wrestling to piece together in a dynamic fashion the subjective and objective dimensions of a prerational and premoral, but symbolically dense common sense and of a rationally apprehended common good geared toward justice (see chapter 5), the Scottish moralists were on their way to theoretically pinpoint a simplified, naively realistic, and transhistorical notion of a shared sense for the good as moral and rational almost (if not entirely) by default (Jensen 1971).

Axial *phronesis* develops through the tension and trial of the *ego-alter-Alter* relationship, while the moral sense erases the material and communicative tension and moralizes the terms of the relationship. Clearly, *Alter*/God as the tamer of tension becomes less relevant, while still playing—as it will become evident with Adam Smith—a role in the mechanisms of recognition between *ego* and *alter*. The premises are laid for turning the sharp triadic engagement into a mild dyadic game where *Alter* is given a somewhat honorary, basically functionless (yet often symbolically overloaded—like with the logo *In God We Trust* on the dollar bills—and potentially ideological) position.

This transformation occurred in parallel with dramatic economic and political upheavals that made desirable a tight coordination between the emerging subject/citizen/economic actor and the modalities of governance of the surging liberal state (Santoro 2003 [1999]). As evidenced by MacIntyre, this step required a rejection of the moral theories that were still dominant in seventeenth-century Scottish universities, whether Calvinist or Aristotelian, and was accompanied by a reinterpretation of religious practices. In the era of the Scottish Enlightenment "both preaching and devotional literature were . . . presented in styles well calculated to arouse, stimulate, and guide passions, affections, and sentiments" based on "introspective self-examination" (MacIntyre 1988: 268–69). We can describe this epistemological break as the emergence of a "first person" approach to sociality. The exhortative dimension injected by axial discursive traditions into public speech was not erased, but rather condensed in the moralizing skills of the speaker. This happened at the cost of severing its phronetic link (which Vico had striven to preserve and reformulate) with an idea of *res publica*.

In spite of this radical rupture, some theoretical arguments employed by Hutcheson can be seen as a continuation of axial views (see also Gobetti 1997). He stressed that humans have to use the powers of reason and speech in order to implement their life obligations and so contribute to the common good. He still agreed on seeing government as deputed to remedy injuries to rights which are the consequences of breaches of natural law, a law that would be self-sufficient if human beings did not violate others' rights and behaved more wisely and impartially (MacIntyre 1988: 262–65). However, unlike Vico's view of the social conflict, which resulted in an original synthesis of the theories of axial philosophers and modern political realists, the Scottish thinker, when confronted with the reality of moral disagreement, which was visibly on the rise within the commercial society of his time, saw that what appeared to be public conflict was not really so. For him disagreements can be only caused by diverging rational assessments of the public effects of action, while the moral sense secures uniformity of judgment (MacIntyre 1988: 278).

Clearly, the main preoccupation of this type of theory was with establishing a principle of social cohesion, so that we can see, after Vico, another significant entry point into the key questions of modern sociology. The uniform character of the moral sense applied to dyadic relationships was intended to provide this glue. It is also interesting that this theory had difficulties in demonstrating the moral primacy of the public over the private without creating a tension with the newly established economic but also affective centrality of the private sphere as the locus of a new type of social bond, namely "trust":

> Should any one ask even concerning these two *ultimate Ends, private Good* and *publick [sic!]*, is not the latter more *reasonable* than the former? . . . If the meaning of the Question be this, "does not every *Spectator approve* the Pursuit of publick Good more than Private?" The Answer is obvious that he does: but not for any *Reason* or *Truth*, but from a *moral Sense*. (Hutcheson 2002 [1728]: 144]

Subsequent authors will make the approach to discourse and reasoning as deployed from within modern public spheres more sophisticated, but the basic thrust of Hutcheson's argument will remain central to this strand of theory, up to Habermas himself. While the primary judgments are those immediately provided by the moral sense, correct reasoning about the cause and effects of action is the alleyway to a secondary type of moral judgment conducive to agreement about the public good. Here are the seeds—in opposition to Vico—for a vision of the public sphere as the arena of deliberation that is formed through an ordered adjudication of diverging interests and opinions. Correctness of reasoning guarantees consensus and excludes ongoing conflicts based on a diversity of class locations and cultural identities of the actors.

This was a quite fragile and transitional solution to the redefinition of public reason, yet it aroused the attention of a vast audience that encompassed merchants and lawyers. The "moral sense" theorized by Hutcheson captured the code of generalized exchange as understood in the epoch, and matched what people were increasingly perceiving as an enduring and indeed "natural" source of sociability. The conceptual sacrifice that was necessary for bringing about this change was double: reason was considered inert in motivating social action and human nature was declared unchanging through all ages and cultural domains.

The main theoretical restructuring of social agency resulted in postulating a common morality as the engine of the motivational prism of the agent. This transformation recompacted the agent and his/her relation to the normative structures of society and to its codes of generalized exchange, but at the cost of diminishing the sociological insight into the tense genesis of the social bond and into the delicate functioning of repertoires of intersubjective engagement and understanding initiated by the axial breakthrough.

Hutcheson's contemporary and colleague David Hume gave coherence to the rupture by radically disassociating moral philosophy from the notion of the public inscribed in Roman law.[1] Hume matched Hutcheson's notion of reason as practically inert and the view of human nature as invariant with a more coherent centering of the social bond on the first person, on *ego*. However, in order to explain the existence of social relationships, he had to embed this principled egotism in a third-person viewpoint—this time however not constituted, as in the axial triangular relationship (see chapter 1), by a symbolic-communicative bond between *ego* and *alter*. The third person is now a pure viewpoint and takes the form of an observer. Key to forging the link are what Hume calls the "indirect passions," those mediated by an idea, first pride and humility, and which are formed as a response to the actions of *alter:* more precisely as a response to *alter* who is in turn responding to *ego*, who firmly keeps the center stage.

It is therefore in the game of mutuality engendered by passions, whether harmonious or antagonistic, that the self forms the view of being loosely integrated in what we might term, lacking a better expression, "a community of selves," whose identities are determined by a tight network of ascriptions where the "community of others" plays a mirroring function (MacIntyre 1988: 290–92). Since everybody is both *ego* and *alter*, the axial tension of their engagement is eroded and gives way to a mechanism of coordination based on a system of shared anticipations configuring a collective function of monitoring individual actions. The emerging code of generalized exchange moderates the risk of a too *ego*-centered expression of passionate attachments and assists human beings in adopting impersonal standpoints in their judgments, so producing an ordered reciprocity of their actions.

The weakness of this argument is that a socially ordered world—the emerging commercial and civil society of Scotland and England—is very much presupposed and not explained by the theory. The basis for such an order is the inviolability of private property and the satisfaction of consumers. Far from being universal, this social order—and the mechanisms through which pride, love, hatred, and humility become social-communicative media for the negotiation of interests and standpoints—reflects too closely the world views of the eighteenth-century landowning class and their clients (ibid.: 295–97). This approach makes Hume's theory representative of a wider anthropological mutation effected by modern liberal theory, but also helps understand why successive, even rival approaches to social action and social order had to include ever more refined views of "civil society." These new approaches will be generated from within the same liberal strand, through a different combination and dosage of first- and third-person perspectives.

There are two main ways for summarizing this momentous transformation in more stringent sociological terms. The first one is essentially related to the link between the social agent and his motivational prism, and therefore concerns the nature of social action. The second one consists in the relational dimension of the interaction between social agents, thus affecting the definition of cooperation and collective action and of its symbolic-mediating structures. The mutation at the level of social action was generated by a transformation of *phronesis/prudentia* into calculative prudence in determining the rationality of the agent. In what follows, however, I focus more directly on the level of social interaction, through examining the transformation of "faith" into "trust" as a motor of human cooperation and the limits inherent to this metamorphosis.

## Faith into Trust?

In his analysis of the new nature of the social bond and of the related conception of civil society as theorized by the Scottish Enlightenment, Adam Seligman shows that according to this approach cooperation cannot be afforded on the basis of sole interest, but needs an element of unconditional recognition by *ego* of *alter*'s dignity and capacity to act (Seligman 1997: 44–62). This is, in his opinion, the meaning of the vague "moral sense" postulated by the Scottish moralists: a form of pristine trust, the most secure glue of a dyadic *ego-alter* relationship. Yet it is also at the root of the derivative, public trust of generalized exchange and "shared standards of anticipation" that prevent, according to Hutcheson, the formation of serious and enduring disagreements in society. The key to the formation of civil society, both in its private and public components, is the pristine trust among private individuals. Trust so defined is the only possible means allowing for cooperation among people situated outside of clearly defined, "traditionally sanctified" roles—to use Seligman's vocabulary, which is well in tune with the lexicon of the sociology of modernity.

Seligman evidences the drastic rupture that allowed for the emergence of trust as the glue of civil society. It is in the passage from a model of social relationship between *ego* and *alter* that is mediated by the common faith in God (the Axial triad *ego-alter*-God), to a dyad linking *ego* and *alter* without any symbolic-communicative mediation by such a third instance. According to Seligman, the transformation corresponds to a passage from faith to trust as the main cement of society and therefore— through making faith obsolete socially and increasingly a matter of private choice—by turning human communities into a civil society. Unlike faith, trust—Seligman observes—does not include the certainty of remuneration. While within faith-based relationships it is the transcendent otherhood that helps the human self to know him/herself and to connect to his/her terrestrial otherhood through a common fellowship in God, the situation with trust is different. It spells out a reciprocal recognition of the other's dignity and capacity to act, irrespective of the outcome of the interaction, or at least without providing any guarantee about possible outcomes. These can no longer be sanctioned by a chain of traditionally sanctified role expectations. Unlike the "call" of faith-based discursive traditions, trust can be offered and accepted, but not demanded (ibid.: 74).

Not by chance, the character of this ideal-typical form of trust—and its deeply "unconditional" character, or its being rooted in an assertion of the agential and communicative capacities of the self to reach out to other—is best exemplified by the modern notion of friendship (cf. Silver 1989). This type of relationship is clearly private according to liberal theory, thus providing the flip side to interested contractual ties, for being by definition a noninterested kind of relationship: a "different sort of commerce" (Silver 1997). Axial notions of friendship, most notably the Aristotelian one, were genuinely public, geared to the pursuit of the highest goods, via the co-practice of public virtue among friends sharing the same *telos* of action (cf. Hutter 1978; Carnevali 2001). The kind of trust that provides consistency to modern forms of friendship is essentially private, as when two people share whatever futile interest or passion, even a hobby. It is essentially the fact that ties of trust can be established irrespectively of the seriousness or futility of what is shared, outside of any ascriptive social roles or statuses—including those of being virtuous citizens—that singles out this model of friendship as distinctively modern and quintessentially liberal.

Trust consists here in the possible recognition of a stranger as a friend for whatever reason. We understand from this example that it is not a certain pattern of relationship or role ascription that grounds trust, but an unconditional element of recognition of *alter*'s capacity to act, as one with his "human dignity." Any pre-given role-based and value-oriented identity of *ego* and *alter* cannot be a condition for placing and nurturing trust. The shared identity that is the outcome of the trusting relationship is therefore the outcome of reciprocated trust. Indeed, trust can also be based on trivial grounds of commonality that one "discovers" in the other. The shared identity is the product of, and not the springboard for the establishment of trust.

In Seligman's reconstruction, it becomes crucial, though problematic, to determine the extent to which this model differs from the calls to faith and conversion within Abrahamic traditions which are directed to people who belong to different communities, not sharing the same language and values, that is, to "strangers." If we recall the model of recognition of the stranger as a guest by Vico (see chapter 5), which is even pre-axial in nature, one wonders if modern friendship is essentially built on completing the transfer of sacredness from the place of the recognition (the hospice) to the person (the stranger as guest). More important, one wonders whether this shift occurs at the cost of erasing the obligatory character of the recognition for the maintenance of the social bond, since there is no longer a specific physical or institutional place (the refuge, the *agorà*, the forum) sanctifying this acceptance of the other. In other words, recognition of *alter* is subject to the moral discretion of *ego*.

There probably is a principled misunderstanding of "tradition" that goes with such an explanation of the origin of trust, overstating the modern character of the recognition and its relevance in providing a new type of social relationship. What is certainly new within modernity is the frequency and intensity of encounters among strangers, which can hardly be regulated by role games anchored to specific, sanctified places or arenas. Yet even assuming an ideal-typical trajectory of faith metamorphosing into trust by erasing the mediation of transcendence and transforming the social bond from triadic to dyadic as suggested by Seligman, it is difficult to accept an accomplished transition of faith into trust within any type of modernity. This is problematic even for those areas of Europe considered as the cradles of modern industrial society and modern liberal thought.

These doubts are afforded not only because unlike the Scottish moralists, John Locke, the father of modern political liberal theory— whom some authors consider a "transitional" figure for his reliance on

Calvinist theology (Dunn 1969)—viewed trust without faith as not sufficient to warrant the social bond (and indeed much of the constitutional and political history of the United States shows the high degree of discursive reversibility of the trust model back into faith).[2] It is more because faith can always be used to draw a preliminary boundary between the category of people among which one might find individuals to trust and those who are excluded as untrustworthy since they either do not entertain the same values or are bound to obey some authority unconditionally. Locke's use of "faith" in the argument is spurious if compared to traditionally axial functions of faith as providing the glue to the triadic partnership between *ego*, *alter*, and God. Locke excluded the Catholics from trust by denouncing that their faith is untransparent and authoritarian. It seems that Locke's invocation of faith and his definition of faith's link to trust reflect to a large extent the legitimization of sectarian mistrust brought about by the Protestant Reformation. His position is quite representative of liberal invocations of faith as a condition for trusting other and of God as the ultimate enforcer of contractual obligations, since an authoritarian Leviathan—one that is institutionally called to manipulate faith—cannot be always trusted.

This problem is recognized by Seligman, but finally played down for being basically a question of transition to modernity, made obsolete wherever and whenever political cultures acknowledge the importance of subjective autonomy. Clearly, the argument is circular, and he is compelled to demonstrate his point by referring, by contrast, to the scarce differentiation of notions of faith and trust in what he calls "non-Western" social worlds, traditions, and languages, like in Hebrew (and, we might add, in Arabic), where the terms for trust and faith belong to the same triliteral root (*alef/alif, mem/mim, nun*). He neglects, however, that a similar problem occurs in European languages as well, like in Italian, which was also the language of Machiavelli, who first theorized about the secular character of the social bond.

There is in contemporary Italian a differentiation between the interpersonal link or attitude of *fiducia* (close to "trust") and *fede* ("faith"), though both derive from the Latin *fides*, a "pre-axial" notion denoting the type of social bond well exemplified by the primordial encounter that grounded the asylum and the master-servant bond, theorized by Vico (see chapter 5). Unlike *fiducia*, *fede* denotes the act of bowing to God's will and providence, of making oneself a devote servant of a master of justice and mercy. However, to assume an accomplished differentiation between *fiducia* and *fede* in language and practice would be incorrect. It seems to me that even today there is an overdetermination of the secular *and* economic-transactional character of the notion of *fiducia* that obscures a more complex genealogy and a residual overlapping with the meaning today entrenched in *fede*.

Even in the act of placing trust (*fiducia*) within purely interpersonal, *ego-alter* relations there is a connotation of surrender to some "higher" power or at least to some socially and humanly unattainable determination that transcends both the assessment of *alter*'s trustfulness and more generally the dynamics of the *ego-alter* relationship. To see in this type of trust an investment exclusively into *alter*'s capacity to act, an unconditional recognition of his agency, would be an ideological exaggeration. Not only Machiavelli, who was never a champion of faith, but also later Italian Enlightenment thinkers still used *fede* with a meaning closer to today's *fiducia* (Pagden 1988). In other words, the differentiation of meaning between *fiducia* and *fede* is never—also due to sheer semantic contiguity—as complete and sharp as between "trust" and "faith" in Seligman's reconstruction. This assessment reinforces the impression that the theory that Seligman tries to reconstruct is mainly an Anglo-American liberal idiom.

On the other hand, if we stay at the level of linguistic-semantic analysis suggested by Seligman, the Arabic of the Qur'an, that is the medium of a powerful manifestation of axial transformations (see chapter 4), possesses a family of words for faith and trust stemming from the earlier mentioned, Semitic, triliteral root (*alif/alef, mem/mim, nun*), and another set originating from another root (*wa, kaf, lam*), with a more mundane meaning, but equally applying (like the other root) both to man-God and to man-man relationships. The difference of meaning is here determined by the degree of mundane versus transcendent character of a certain act or relationship. Therefore, while Seligman is wrong in assuming that non-Western languages often lack a differentiated set of words expressing mundane trust, the Arab idiom of faith and trust confirms that any hypothesis of a complete differentiation of meaning between "faith" and "trust" can hardly be generalized as an evolutionary rule. Seligman's point is then only valid as a correct observation of the emergence of an Anglo-American tradition, whose decisive breakthrough he plausibly locates in authors of the eighteenth-century Scottish Enlightenment.

At a deeper conceptual level, one could object to Seligman that asserting that faith entails the certainty of remuneration, while trust requires a bet on the future, is a gross misunderstanding of faith that, as he himself notes, can be seen as stemming from the momentous and traumatic I-Thou relationship of man to God: like with Moses in the thornbush episode or when Abraham was called to sacrifice his son (cf. Seligman 1997: 22). This was also a completely gratuitous kind of act, implying dread and the deepest disorientation. As Seligman admits, the "transcendent otherhood, precisely in our ignorance of it, stands as the root of all knowledge of self and . . . as a referent to all attempts to *know*, in fact to place confidence in, the more terrestrial others of our life" (ibid.: 46).

More recently, Seligman has accepted that this axial moment is "modernity's wager" (Seligman 2000). He thus suggests that the moment of pristine trust among *ego* and *alter* is not only fragile, but in the final analysis does not rest on an autonomous basis. This sounds, however, as a retroactive normalization of his analysis of the genesis of the Anglo-American tradition, within which God's presence is frequently and conveniently invoked, often as a witness to the metamorphosis of axial tradition and of the model of modernity (not seldom nourished by religious vocabulary) enacted through it. Indeed, this tradition stands out for its sui generis pretension of overcoming all traditions, yet for being caught in the same kind of dynamics and ambivalence of all other traditions. It is a tradition characterized by the erosion of *telos* and the emasculation of *phronesis*. The consequence is that a retroactive vindication of "modernity's wager" is a purely individual act of faith, or, better, "belief," which cannot affect the assessment of the social and political working of that tradition. It confirms in an extreme way the primacy of the private sphere of personal belief and individual choice within the Anglo-American tradition.

Trying, again, to generalize, one can suggest that a possible difference between faith and trust is more in the fact that faith, in order to be effective and self-sustaining, finally commands obedience and a corresponding terminality toward the highest good, while trust entails a commitment to an open-ended relationship. This committed directionality, however, permanently faces strictures and closures, demands of terminality that cannot be absorbed by the ongoing investment or bet in *alter*'s agency and morality. Viewed in this way, it is not difficult to detect a notion of trust at work in axial traditions which is related to *telos* and is articulated through *phronesis*. For example, the Qur'an and more generally the Islamic tradition—especially in its Sufi manifestations—encourage and regulate subjective investments into relationships with the other. Yet they define the limits of such investments that, if reached, threaten to make those relationships twisting toward worshipping *alter*: this would result in the ultimate sin of *shirk*, consisting in associating a human creature to the creator. This approach reflects a consciousness of the fact that a really open-ended human relationship, albeit possible, would end up in tragedy and self-destruction.

The sin of *shirk* reflects a heightened phronetic consciousness of the complex workings of human relationships. In particular it reflects the idea that by absolutizing human attachments one runs the danger of exposing oneself to human caprice and lust of power, so missing the benefits of trusting in God's mercy. The Sufi tradition, at the zenith of its development during the Axial Renaissance (see chapters 3 and 4), went one step forward by recommending to relativize all human friendships, in order to become a friend, a *wali*, of God, a notion that condenses the Islamic idea of saintliness (Chittick 1992: 56).

The anthropological and sociological logic of this principle is that in order to be a trusting member of human society one has to keep a phronetic balance that puts appropriate value in differentiated types of relationships, while maintaining a telic coherence and determination through a systematic avoidance of an overinvestment in any specific relationship. This type of thought is also at the basis of the ideals of love as *agape* and of a patient and practical investing into *alter* as *caritas*, adopted and developed by Christianity. The basic engine here is the axial domestication of the prototypical, pre-axial master-servant relationship depicted by Vico. Real access to *alter* is given by being his servant, which is in turn only possible by serving the only legitimate, ultimate, master, *Alter*/God. The pope's title of *servus servorum Dei* ("servant of God's servants") crystallized during the Axial Renaissance. Islamic tradition insistently elaborates on the Abrahamic idea that in order to be master on earth, man has to be God's faithful servant.

Here, the anthropological and sociological insight is that by erasing all authority—like in the idea of "pristine trust" among human beings—what is left is bare power. Then the capacity to shape and govern relationships, communities, and societies is seriously eroded. Therefore, even if we stick to the specific paradigms of Anglo-American historical experience and social theory, one can hypothesize that faith and trust are much more overlapping than neatly distinguished signposts of social action and interaction. Trust emerges as a sort of backup of faith when faith is no longer institutionally autonomous and authoritative. More than an alternative modality of social relationship, trust denotes the weakening of the terminality of action guaranteed by specific authorities and the strengthening of another kind of terminality that takes the form of an "unconditionality."

According to Seligman, and in spite of the often romanticized valuing of friendship within the Anglo-American tradition, the unconditionality of trust is best epitomized by contract law, which could only be institutionalized via the Leviathan's guarantee of its application. The open-ended character of the relationship implied by trust, if realistic at all, can only work on the "disinterested" side of the *ego-alter* relationship as friendship, while on the interested side of a contractual relationship a notion of calculative reason and a corresponding model of the actor have to be matched by a state that successfully monopolizes the exercise of force in order to enforce the respect of contracts. This type of governance is essential to the "maintenance" of the subject, for keeping it functional and feasible as a "social actor." The type of trust to which Seligman refers to can only be conceived where a state has been configured as a machine of power shaping bare life: where it is called to de-differentiate a society that is perpetually fragmented through the multiplicity of differentiating roles and social subsystems (cf. Agamben 1998 [1995]).

Seligman's pristine trust aspires to play the role of the rare and precious salt in the modern social system but makes little sense if abstracted from the distinctive functioning of this type of system. It is therefore its "liminal" status that has to be questioned. Seligman defines trust as liminal, in the sense elucidated by Victor Turner, as "betwixt and between," "beyond the categories (or roles) of any systematic division of labor" (Seligman 1997: 45). The difference with Turner's main example of liminality, that is, the ritual constitution of *communitas*, is that with trust

> the liminal moment of unconditioned belief is predicated not on the sameness or identity of the participants but on their very difference or otherness. What one trusts is some unknown, unverifiable aspect of *alter*'s behavior (or response) which, while existing beyond system classification (as does ritualized communitas), makes no claim to the essential identity of the participants in the interaction. It is in the very otherness of the *alter* that one puts one's "faith" [*sic!*] and not in any communality of traits shared. (ibid.)

Yet far from appearing as liminally precious in warranting a new type of social relationship, trust looks like a weak, only partly metamorphosed or rather imploded form of faith (ibid.: 50; Prandini 1997). This blind alley is only avoided by making explicit the relationship of trust to the public sphere, by elucidating the passage form private trust to public "confidence," as the code of generalized exchange illustrated earlier. However, if we posited a clear and permanent mechanism of transformation of the pristine trust of the private sphere into a principle of generalized exchange, then we would have as a result a type of publicness close to Durkheim's principle of organic solidarity, which Seligman considers as a diluted, highly functionalized, and nonpristine variant of trust.

The Scottish Enlightenment represents a major watershed in that its core arguments helped crossing the threshold from moral philosophy to what we call today social theory or social thought. It radically recast the symbolic-communicative fundaments of the social bond and so laid the rails on which the basic sociological conceptualization of action and order for the two centuries to come will roll. This eighteenth-century innovation reached its zenith, in terms of coherence and systematization, with the contribution of another anglicized Scot, Adam Smith (1723–1790), a pupil of Hutcheson and his successor to the chair of moral philosophy at the University of Glasgow. He was determinant in transplanting the new theoretical approach into the genetic asset of the emerging Anglo-American tradition. MacIntyre suggests that the crack within the earlier tradition of Scottish moral philosophy that relied on Calvinist but also on Aristotelian concepts and arguments and the follow-up English appropriation of the main motives of the Scottish Enlightenment went hand in hand with England's quasi-colonial encroachment upon Scotland that unfolded in the course of that century.

The work of Adam Seligman has been helpful in reassessing the new type of complexity and fragility of the theoretical approach of those authors who laid the founding stones of the Anglo-American tradition of social theory and of its capacity to frame and explain social action and cooperation and collective deliberation.[3] What was required by this type of theory analyzed by Seligman was a more subtle short-circuiting of private trust and public confidence, which evokes what Adam Smith called an impartial observer. This "great inmate of our breast" surrogates God in the triadic model of social relationship and functions through *ego*'s thirst for recognition through *alter* vectored by "vanity" or "approbation." This drive is at the root of the successful socioeconomic activity performed by a type of self whose sociability is "constituted by the refraction of our actions in the eyes of the other" (Seligman 1997: 111). Trust refracts systemic constraints on the psychological makeup and the ensuing public competences of the actor; it is a far cry from Turner's liminality.

> When I endeavour to examine my own conduct . . . and either to approve or condemn it, it is evident that, in all such cases, I divide myself, as it were, in two persons . . . The first is the spectator, whose sentiments with regard to my own conduct I endeavour to enter into, by placing

myself in his situation . . . The second is the agent, the person whom I properly call myself . . . The first is the judge; the second the person judged of. But that the judge should, in every respect, be the same with the person judged of, is as impossible as that the cause should, in very respect, be the same with the effect. (Smith 1853 [1759]: 164–65)

This is a sociological clarification of Hume's mechanism of responsiveness of *ego* to *alter*, whose anthropological basis is the typical notion of "moral sense" or "sympathy" of the Scottish Enlightenment: in other words, responsiveness to *alter* is carried by recognition of *alter*'s agency, via pristine trust. However, pristine trust plays here the mere function of an anthropological stimulator of publicness, but cannot provide the sociological and political engine for a modern public sphere to function. An increasingly internalized instance of control over all acts to which one has to respond publicly cannot exist without the intrusive or discrete role of Leviathan, which not only monopolizes the use of violence and threatens to punish the indocile subjects, but also holds the monopoly over the definitional power of law. Only so can law become positive convention and govern the myriad of dyadic *ego-alter* relationships of which society consists (Santoro 2003 [1999]; cf. also Haakonssen 1981; 1996).

Here the unconditionality of trust ends up showing a dependency on historically given, powerful, and increasingly institutionalized definitions of the nature and hierarchy of social goods, culminating in public goods. While this nexus between the private dimension and the public projection of trust provides a general norm to the definition of public goods and to the legitimization of mechanisms for the distribution of private goods (Eisenstadt and Roniger 1984), in the emerging Anglo-American model the attainment and fruition of all goods—even those most clearly public—depend on the unassailable unconditionality of the contractual freedom of the individual; far from liminal, this is the kernel of the "system."

Seligman admits that "it was in the Anglo-Saxon countries" that this form of trust built such unconditionality upon which system confidence and generalized exchange also rely (Seligman 1997: 85). "Contractual freedom," however, can never be justified on purely "natural" terms, since it has to be based on contract law, which, as a law instituted and guaranteed by Leviathan, poses limits to the agent's freedom. This distinctive type of law, a genuine product of the legal dimension of the Anglo-Saxon, later Anglo-American tradition, "stresses the free choice of the contracting parties and the responsibility each has to attend to their own interests. It is a principle whose emergence dates, not surprisingly, to the early seventeenth century" (ibid.: 87).

The unconditionality of the ties of trust grounding the social bond became an "externality" in the economic process: a good sui generis that cannot be traded; a prerogative of Leviathan. Traditional notions of social goods and the common good were replaced by the view that economic action regulated by the rules of the market and contract law (adhering to and confirmed by the rule of law) is by default "morally" oriented to the common good and apt to institute a convenient and flexible set of public goods that the market cannot produce (cf. Dumont 1977). The basic nature of this social unconditionality taking the function of an economic externality does not change but is rather strengthened at the passage from liberal to welfarist capitalist economies, with such provisions limiting contract freedom like minimum wage and unions' negotiations of collective contracts.

In the process through which this type of theory emerged, the traditional notions of the social bond were eroded not by a decay of "faith" as such (there have been several revivals and awakenings of faith in the Anglo-American world well into the twentieth century, with variable relations to institutional politics), but by the weakening of its institutional underpinnings in the wake of the rise of commercial and industrial society and of the consolidation of the modern state. By the time Adam Smith wrote successive editions of his *Theory of Moral Sentiments* (Smith 1853 [1759]) in the second half of the eighteenth century—the last in 1790 (cf. Raphael and Macfie 1976)—he ever more clearly saw generalized exchange as rooted in the market. This view was also a consequence of his diagnosis of an increasing social differentiation and in particular of the differentiation of an economic sphere. Therefore, one gains the impression that it is the Smithian notion of the market that is shaped according to the emerging logic of publicness as based on generalized exchange, that is, on the provision of public goods—first of all Leviathan's enforcement of contract law—delimiting exchange among units of interest and therefore creating new rules, including those that economic theory likes to see as "immanent" to the market.

In other words, it is not the public sphere, as often decried, that risks succumbing to a "market logic" in modern societies, but quite the other way round: it is the liberal definition of the market that, detached from traditional definitions of the marketplace, was made to fit a convenient definition of publicness as the site of generalized exchange. Market was abstractly redefined as a set of self-sustaining rules shaping the identity of socioeconomic actors and their rationality. As social differentiation progresses, an imploded publicness, delimiting the social and communicative infrastructure of generalized exchange, takes shape. This type of publicness is impoverished of underlying notions—and even more of practices—of public reasoning and of the common good, if they do not result directly from conventional, lawful, and morally acceptable types of social interaction and communication. Such publicness is also in a permanent tension with the pristine trust of the private sphere, since the empathetic, mutual recognition among agents in private is turned into a mechanical and functional responsiveness in public. Publicness is ever more exchange and ever less reasoning. However, it is exchange supported by a (moral) "sense." "For the new regulating factor is not a (procedural or substantive) rationality given *a priori* but is both a consequence of social interaction and an original passion. It is a feeling that, being universal, creates shared value" (Santoro 2003 [1999]: 163).

What is most striking, however, is that the Smithian principle of the impartial observer makes the public sphere simultaneously functional and dependent both on the private sphere and on the state. As evidenced by Santoro,

> the engine of Smith's moral psychology is "seeing" . . . This "power" of others' gaze cannot but recall Bentham's *Panopticon* . . . Smith's depicted society is a huge Panopticon where all of us, becoming impartial spectators, occupy the watchtower. (Santoro 2003 [1999]: 164–65)

The Panopticon, however, was not only too expensive. It was also made obsolete by a commercial society supported by an increasingly discrete Leviathan, a process that helps make every comrade an attentive, meticulous—and democratic—observer. The result is that "in social interaction the individual replaces God as the regulator of her and others' behaviour" (ibid.: 165; cf. also the interpretation of civil society in Foucault 1979; 1991; Burchell 1991).

## The "Habermas Effect"

This turning point in the crystallization of the Anglo-American, liberal tradition represented a challenge for continental and rationalist forms of Enlightenment thought. How to keep and develop that democratic potential, while restoring or possibly upgrading the primacy of public reason? After all, the continental Leviathan was not so fast in adopting restraint in its techniques of governance as it happened in the Anglo-American world. This predicament made the refoundation of public reason on an autonomous basis ever more urgent.

A mainly continental tradition of "civic virtue" emerged in competition with the Anglo-Scottish civil society. While adhering to the dyadic character of the *ego-alter* relationship and to the agential and autonomous character of the social actor, the "republican" tradition of civic virtue found a shortcut to a definition of publicness that incorporated the classic ideal of *res publica* and grounded collective deliberation on the power of the "We." Seligman convincingly argues that the civic virtue invoked by the republican tradition, whose roots go as far back as to Machiavelli and which has been mainly associated with Jean-Jacques Rousseau (1712–1778), is theoretically weaker than the "civil society" approach. It is almost a variant of the same approach, yet adapted to a different, more complex institutional context. "Civic virtue" was also appropriated by a dissident stream within Anglo-American liberal theory best incarnated in the ideals of the American revolution (Pocock 1975). Yet the republican tradition remained an attempt to revise the liberal tradition through selectively incorporating concepts or symbols drawn from older traditions of the common good. It represented a radical version of the liberal tradition more than a real alternative, while it diluted the innovations of the idea of civil society as reconstructed by Seligman.

The German philosopher Immanuel Kant (1724–1804) took up these challenges at a more profound theoretical level and aimed to reintegrate an updated notion of the common good into the train of the Anglo-Scottish reflections of the eighteenth century. We saw that the root of a traditional conception of the common good was still present in the main arguments of the Scottish Enlightenment, via Aristotelian elements and residues of Roman law. The branch of the Enlightenment represented by Kant attempted to square the circle via a simultaneous underpinning of the primacy of the *ego*, that is, the first person perspective, highlighted by Smith, and by devising a permanent converter of the *ego*s' volitions into third persons' ethical concerns. This was a revision of the Smithian mechanism of the sheer "eyes" of *alter ego*, which tuned publicness into the inwardness of "conscience." The idea of *Publizität* in Kant condenses in a sociologically vivid way his idea—grounded in sophisticated philosophical speculations that do not need to be summarized here—that the responsible, private individuals who obey in principle to the absolute ruler (in his society, the Prussian king) would be able, on the ground of the reason, morality, and responsibility that they possess as individual private persons, to develop a competence to form groups for discussing issues of common concern.

No doubt this Kantian claim was not purely normative, but also based on observing social and communicative developments in European bourgeois society. We have on the one hand a reference to responsible persons as privatized individuals. On the other hand, these individuals are defined by Kant as moral beings endowed with something more specific than the vague "moral sense" of the Scottish Enlightenment, which was the root of pristine trust. For Kant individuals are not means to each other, but they are each other's ends. Addressing and pursuing the common good first through discussion and deliberation (complemented by the subjects' compliance with its implementation through the benign Leviathan represented by the Prussian state) is part of their identity as individual moral beings (cf. Kant 1963 [1784], 1983 [1795]).

However, Kant's *Publizität*, still largely relying on a legalistic notion of publicness as public law, is excessively formalized and abstract, if compared with the conception of trust developed by the representatives of the Anglo-American liberal tradition. Kant's solution to the problem is usually perceived by them as circumventing the horizontal and interactional dimension of trust and providing at best a more sophisticated but scarcely practical account of the roots of moral obligation (Hollis 1998). From the viewpoint of the Anglo-American tradition, the Kantian option can even appear as trapped in a conceptual circularity, in that it makes trust a self-legitimizing token of rationality, rather than the bond of society emerging out of the dynamics of social relationships. It thus raises more complex issues of "governmentality" (those concerning the internalization of self-limitation and self-control, or self-discipline and self-policing) than the main representatives of the Anglo-American tradition are willing or able to recognize.

Seligman (1992: 15) even surmises that Kant's approach kills the idea of civil society, without which, according to this tradition, a public sphere cannot exist. The Anglo-American, liberal tradition is at odds with the idea of governmentality or it turns governmentality (like in the earlier mentioned combination of a Smithian and a Benthamian perspective) into a pure device for pushing the subject to transcend his particular passions and interests and assume a position of impartiality. This step is considered essential to building the kind of judgment that takes into account the public gaze and public interest, and so grounds publicness.

In his book *The Structural Transformation of the Public Sphere* Habermas (1989 [1962]) attempted to give historical and sociological plausibility to a basically Kantian idea of publicness. Referring to historical cases from the seventeenth and eighteenth centuries in England, France, and Germany, he first reconstructed the simultaneous emergence of notions, practices, and functions of a bourgeois type of publicness. Habermas put in evidence that the reasons why people from bourgeois milieus got together and what they talked about were in most cases related to quite mundane and self-interested issues rooted in private concerns: like discussing stock exchange trends or prices of colonial commodities, in such places like English coffee houses. But the practice of discussing these issues rooted in self-interest and contract-oriented cooperation triggered a self-propelling dynamics through which people started to debate problems of a different nature, like ways to protect their legitimate private interests from potential abuses of the ruler.

Clearly, in the process, a public sphere emerges well beyond Kantian formalistic presuppositions, through the carving out of an autonomous communicative space: although still tied to private interests, a public sphere thus shaped is no longer functionally squeezed between a benevolent Leviathan guaranteeing rights and a remote realm of private trust providing the existential bedrock and the moral fundament of those same rights. Thus, public discussions were the source for methods and forms of organization apt to represent an emerging common interest consisting in proactively protecting private interests from government's arbitrary intrusions.

Clubs and associations were grounded, whose goals could be scaled up to the formation of political parties. This is exactly what marks the passage from a bourgeois civil society (*bürgerliche Gesellschaft*) to citizenship, and what grounds the modern public sphere in the final analysis, according to Habermas. The common good is here defined not by reference to a shared view of a hierarchy of goods, but through developing via open discussion the citizens' capacity to pursue cooperation and define their common interest. Such cooperation is consciously willed and, as far as it works, unhindered by arbitrary power games and various forms of raison d'état or power abuses. It seems therefore that Habermas's view of the public sphere merged the prior idea of civil society of Hutcheson and the Scottish Enlightenment—mildly filtered through Hegel's dialectics of historical progress—and Kant's moral view of publicness.

Habermas quite clearly subscribed to the notion of a civil society grounded in the private sphere, that is, in the world of self-interested individualism, contractual relationships, and competition. But on a second level he saw the public sphere as emerging by a sort of communicative upgrading, more than a metamorphosis, of the dynamics of civility. He summarized the process that yielded what he called the "social structure" of the public sphere in sentences like the following one that has puzzled many readers: "The bourgeois public sphere may be considered above all as the sphere of private people come together as a public" (Habermas 1989 [1962]: 27).

At first the public sphere depends on the private sphere (coherently with the view of the Scottish Enlightenment), but then, as it gradually takes root in the emerging institutions of participatory citizenship, it becomes an autonomous arena where at issue is not just the avoidance of disagreement through a correct recognition of the public good, but the process itself of its definition through deliberation. However, according to Habermas the further rooting of the public sphere in the procedures of twentieth-century welfare mass democracies divested it of its original cohesive power, which had the potential to represent an alternative both to the sheer market forces and to the purely coercive and administrative steering of the population through the state (ibid.: 181–250). The implosion of publicness is thus complete, and the "Habermas effect"—consisting in upgrading civility into communicatively based mechanisms for a collective definition of social goods and deliberation about political goals—is severely eroded.

For Habermas, however, the prototypical formation of the public sphere in eighteenth-century northwestern Europe remains the historical paradigm for the reconstruction of the same form of social cohesion epitomized by a trust-based civil society and a solidarity-oriented platform of public deliberation, under shifting social conditions and historical circumstances. What facilitates building the public sphere, in the original like in other situations, is the coming together of citizens for discussing and deliberating on issues affecting the common good, through which this common good is defined in a consensual, procedurally ordered, not traditionally transmitted—or imposed—way. Habermas reinjected the intersubjective agency of Hutcheson's moral sense into the publicness constituted by Smith as a discipline of interaction, mutual judgment, and strategic speech.

The result of the operation is that the common good cannot be discerned separately from the process through which citizens come together and engage with each other's judgments. Citizens go public not in spite of, but by virtue of their own private interests and passions and only then, by meeting fellow citizens and interacting with them in a procedurally transparent way, they are trained into public spiritedness. In his later theory of communicative action, Habermas specified that both the private and the public spheres belong to the lifeworld (see chapter 2), as opposed to the systems of capitalist production and of administrative steering (Habermas 1987 [1981]: 113–97). It almost seems that the upgrading of private interest into power-free public discourse for the determination of the common good redeems the former from being an immediate or a subordinate reflection of capitalist interest—and an expression of the political culture of specific parts of the West. Yet if we move from the theoretical concept of "communicative action" to the historical paradigm of the "third sphere," it is difficult to overlook issues of political culture and of "Western primacy."

Either way, do we have the passage from the first to the third person (seeing the self through the other, and so establishing the common good) in ways that differ from the Smithian paradigm of coordination of *ego*-centered private interests based on impersonal rules and procedures anchored in the moral dispositions entailed by being a citizen? While the passage from the first to the third person remains problematic outside of the Smithian scheme, we find in Habermas a shift—or rather a shortcut—from the "I" to the "We," and so the grounding of collective deliberation on the "collective identity" of a body of self-conscious citizens—an idea inherited from the "civic virtue" oriented, republican tradition. A synthesis between the theory of the public sphere, the theory of communicative action, and the grounding of collective identity leading to constitutional democracy is achieved in the later *Facts and Norm* (Habermas 1996 [1992]), where the only secure way to vindicate public reason is identified with a democratic constitutional process. Apart from the high degree of theoretical sophistication maintained by Habermas throughout, what is evident is a gradual narrowing of his approach on the main paradigms of the Anglo-American liberal tradition and its republican ramifications.

Even after the Habermasian detour, one is left with the impression that the work on the notion of the public sphere has not redeemed the paradox, well illustrated by Seligman, of its ultimate resting on a genuinely private trust. The circle has not been squared, and we have reached an impasse in the middle of a Vichian *ricorso*, which is nothing less than the coming to maturation of European modernity. The famous cry that Benjamin Nelson, one of the pioneers of the analysis of the cultural origins of modernity, uttered forty years ago—and that has deserved the approving attention of Seligman (1997: 99)—is ever more valid: can moderns be brothers only by becoming others? (Nelson 1969 [1949]: 136). This painful question strikes at the core of the modern, Habermasian notion of the public sphere, which does not solve the riddle of the constitution of the social bond, the *ego-alter* relationship, and its communicative dimension. Is the modern public sphere built on the implosion of a traditionally consecrated, axial type of public reason? Is it based on a surrogate of brotherhood among what were formerly *ego* and *alter* and are now a multitude of others? Does it sanction a simultaneous implosion of faith into trust and of the principle of common/public good—sanctioned by both Roman law and Islamic law—into a publicness reduced to a phronetically weak but functionally (and sometimes discursively) strong public projection of private trust?

# CONCLUSION:
# AFTER GENEALOGY—
# TOWARD A PLURALIST THEORY
# OF THE PUBLIC SPHERE

## Axial Traditions and the
## Anglo-American Tradition

This work has argued that the long-term genealogy of the public sphere spirals around continuities and discontinuities in the constitution, management, and transformation of the character of human action, of the social bond, and of related patterns of communication. I have attempted to show that this process depends on the construction of inter-subjective repertoires of engagement, understanding, and connectivity, via the shaping of the symbolic-communicative nexus among agents (chapter 2). To this end, I have reconstructed a notion of axial traditions as dynamic ensembles of arguments and practices—not as rigid charts of prescriptions and norms, but as modalities of constructing relationships and facilitating communication among human agents.

Such traditions emerged from the Vichian, pre-axial "heroic age" and were shaped in the Axial Age (chapter 1) to provide creativity to the laborious work of shaping human connectivity and of providing stability to the management of the social bond. I have then focused on the key transitional epoch of the Axial Renaissance both within Latin Christendom and Arab Islamdom (chapters 3 and 4). The focal drama of the emergence of the modern public sphere out of the discursive tradition of Latin Christendom took place during the eighteenth century at the passage from the Axial Enlightenment exemplified by Vico—who elaborated on developments from the Axial Renaissance which took place not only within Latin Christianity but also within Sunni Islam—to the trajectory of the later Enlightenment (chapter 5). The zenith of this trajectory of transformation was reached through the work of thinkers of the Scottish and German Enlightenment and, even more clearly, through its late twentieth-century social-theoretical systematization by Habermas (chapter 6).

The mainstream modern approach to the public sphere as the space of production of the modern social bond and in particular of its communicative dimension bracketed out some of the key critical questions raised by the Axial Enlightenment. I have analyzed these modern approaches in their ambivalent relation both to their own standards of evaluation (rationality, openness, universality) and to the wider antinomies of modernity, that is, to the combination of constructive and destructive forces, like the tension between movement and institution, which cannot be easily framed by those standards (see introduction). The view of the public sphere as a comprehensive "third sphere" is the result of the dilution of these antinomies (see introduction).

By way of conclusion, I would like to invest the results of my analysis into a diagnosis of the Enlightenment solutions condensed into the mature, modern, Habermasian idea of the public sphere. This evaluation might facilitate approaching other, non-Western and/or nonmainstream modern elaborations of public reasoning which have not crystallized into a comparably stable and self-enclosed notion like "public sphere/third sphere." These alternative patterns are relevant not only as parts of the genealogy, but also as sociological configurations with growing and manifold interconnections with the mainstream model of the public sphere. I refer here in particular to an Islamic and to a "Vichian-European" alternative notion of the public sphere, whose seeds have been explored in chapters 4 and 5. This conclusion is also a call for a theoretical pluralization of the analysis of the public sphere which is coherent with Habermas's stated intention not to confine the range of application of public sphere theory to the triumphant liberal tradition of modernity and in particular to "Jefferson's fortunate heirs," that is, to the Anglo-American tradition (Habermas 1996 [1992]: 62–63).

Yet without an analysis of the premodern trajectory of the idea of *res publica*, imperfectly translated as "common good," Habermas's model appears as a mere token of universality devoid of sensitivity for the conflicted implications of the transcultural genealogy of the public sphere. It ignores how this idea became partly autonomous from specific political regimes during the Roman and medieval empires, indicating a *telos* of interaction and communication at both a micro and a macrolevel. The trajectory of this idea—in analogy with the Islamic *maslaha* or *maslaha 'amma*—incorporated a juridical and a religious dimension that are absent or weak both in the ethno-political connotation of "common good" like in nationalist discourse, and in their successor notions laying an emphasis on *demos* or the "people" as the depositary of sovereignty—both dimensions being prefigured and conflated in the elaborations on the Greek *polis* as a model.

The emergence of the public sphere in its distinctively modern shape within the triumphant Anglo-American tradition and their continental variations was made possible through dissolving the symbolic-communicative mediation (via religious commitments and juridical arguments) that secured a practical nexus between *phronesis* and *telos*. This step was performed through the autonomization of the subject as a "social actor" and through the proceduralization of "communication" as a realm of mutual understanding between *ego* and *alter* ideally unencumbered by authority, power, and the attending symbolism. Whatever the dynamics of transformation, the situation today is one where modern understandings and practices of the public sphere exist alongside traditions of argument and action that authorize public reasoning on the basis of a practical rationality more directly related to the axial triadic model between *ego*, *alter*, and *Alter*/God. These traditions do not fit neatly into the proceduralist (as to "communication") and reductionist (as to the nature of the "social actor") straitjacket of the public sphere.

It is necessary therefore to overcome the limit we found in social theory, which consists in confining tradition to the familiarity patterns of inherited customs and habits. Especially when considered within their axial dimension, traditions imply and sometimes necessitate, for their emergence and maintenance, drastic ruptures of familiarity which destroy or erode family and kinship ties and subordinate them to the triangular partnership in faith between *ego*, *alter*, and *Alter*/God. This call for rupturing familiarity and custom is evident in the life and message of leading prophetic voices like Jesus and Muhammad. In many ways, this is the essence of their prophetic speech. However, the dynamics of rupture, reconstruction, and renewal is matched by epochal efforts at comprehensive resystematizations of axial legacies, such as during the Axial Renaissance of the late Middle Ages. In other words, a nonreductionist conceptualization of tradition is necessary in order to recognize alternative trajectories to the formation of public spheres.

A critique of the modern concept of trust as a weak backup of traditional faith (see chapter 6) assumes a paradigmatic value in the attempt to reopen the genealogy of the public sphere to the possibility of coexisting—partly interlocking, partly conflicting—approaches. Revisiting for a moment the argument of Adam Seligman on trust is particularly important in this context. On the one hand, he considers trust "as no more than an artifice of society," produced within the major transformations that led to the emergence of a commercial and industrial type of society (Seligman 1997: 22): "Trust ... enters into social relations ... when ... systematically defined role expectations are no longer viable" (ibid.: 24–25). Here trust appears as an exclusively modern phenomenon characterizing societies held together by forms of solidarity based on contractual relations (ibid.: 37). It is the exponential increase in the indeterminacy and negotiability of non-ascriptive roles within modern societies that seems to allow for the emergence of trust so defined (ibid.: 39).

On the other hand, Seligman admits that the basic paradigm of rupture in the configuration of the social bond which allowed for the emergence of trust at the social system's limits is best exemplified by the idea of an axial breakthrough. This applies particularly well to the last product of long-term axial transformations, namely Islam (ibid.: 27; cf. also Salvatore 1997; see chapter 4 of the present work), a discursive tradition that supplied legal, theological, and political arguments to the work of upgrading tribal solidarities into a potentially universal brotherhood in the common faith. Seligman refers to Eric Voegelin's own redefinition of the axial breakthrough as a dramatic reshaping of the social bond through a leap of faith mediated by the discourse and symbolism of the prophets (Seligman 1997: 27–28). Yet after admitting the importance of axial faith Seligman locates it in a world of basically static traditions, in contrast to modern trust. He thus reverts to the most conventional, negative and static definitions of tradition within sociology and social theory.

Seligman's reductionism toward "tradition" seems necessary for his deployment of a theory of trust. He basically sees tradition as revolving around honor and primordial identities, while the post-Jasperian, sociological approach to axial civilizations (see chapter 1), which Seligman also takes into consideration, shows the opposite: it is these civilizations that have allowed human society to transcend honor-based, primordial ("tribal") identities as vehicles and regulators of social relations and social cohesion. This can be roughly exemplified by the transitions from the heroic values of the Homeric world to Greek philosophy, or from archaic Judaism to the systematic interpretation of Torah, and even more strikingly from the *jahiliyya* (the pre-Islamic "pagan" world of "ignorance" and "anarchy") to Islam. Even after their first eruption, axial traditions encompassed not only the canonization and preservation of values and truths, but also entailed continual reforms and ruptures, in a spiraling challenge between orthodoxies and heterodoxies.

The latest ruptures occurred at the dawn of modernity through the Reformation and in particular Calvinism. The subsequent transformations of the Calvinist stock of ideas about man and God into the concept of pristine, agential trust by Locke, the Scottish Enlightenment, and Adam Smith, have to be situated within a longer chain of relocations of the axial stock of phronetic ideas providing cement to the social bond. The modern breakthrough, concomitantly with the emergence of the modern state and modern commercial society, relocated the burden of the maintenance of the social bond along with its symbolic-communicative patterns from a flexible, triadic management of the relationship centered on God or rather His representatives (the speech and laws of the prophets and their successors, the axial scholars and clerics) into a new field of tension, linking the autonomous agent directly to a state monopolizing not only force but also the power to determine conventions. The idealized recasting of this scheme into the Habermasian view of autonomous subjects engaging in a discourse finalized to mutual understanding and so constituting a public opinion restricting the power of the state and legitimizing the popular will facilitated the subsequent transition from liberal to liberal-democratic society.

Seligman reminds us of Benjamin Nelson's emphasis on the individual's responsibility to God "for the welfare of his soul and the well-being of his brother" as the main marker of the axial breakthrough (Nelson 1981, quoted in Seligman 1997: 47). I have avoided an anachronistic focus on a hermeneutics of the self as the genesis of traditions and have directed attention to the transformations in the mechanisms of mediation of the *ego-alter* relationship as the most distinctive axial motive (see chapter 1). My genealogical analysis did not pursue the unveiling of hidden power motives in the building of the axial triadic relationship between *ego*, *alter*, and God, but concentrated on exploring the displacements of the patterns of mediation, which necessarily implicate relations of power.

While retracing trajectories of development of public reasoning based on specific notions of the *ego-alter* relationship and on their symbolic-communicative mediation, I have critically elaborated on the work of Alasdair MacIntyre (see introduction, chapter 1, and chapter 2). He has convincingly stressed the contingence not only of the emergence of traditions but also of their unfolding in history, of their ruptures and transformations. His argument on traditions is informed by a view of dynamic transformations of axial visions (MacIntyre 1988: 360). This dynamic approach requires a stress on historical contingence which encourages looking at the reconstruction of social relations performed by and within traditions sharing a common kernel in spite of all differences. MacIntyre's soft historicism, unlike Hegelianism, immunizes the social theorist against the claims to absolute knowledge which we saw emerging with modern thinkers and were later aggravated by Hegelian dialectics.

MacIntyre's approach is neither relativist nor perspectivist (that is, genealogical in a Nietzschean sense). Against any temptation to turn genealogy into a purely deconstructivist game, he stresses a contingent, ongoing, yet progressing mechanism of validation and invalidation of the "moral scheme" (the management of *ego-alter* relations) within and among traditions. This process often attains a point where the reflection and revision of the narratives of a tradition by their practitioners produce retroactive patterns of correction and revision and also overarching theories of the fundaments of the same tradition (cf. MacIntyre 1984 [1981]: 270).

In the case of Latin Christian and Sunni Islamic traditions, we could observe processes of reform and sharpening of the tradition, also affecting the level of definition of the type of action required from the practitioners, and the ingraining of this type of action into structures of civic life and social governance. This kind of development can be made sense via MacIntyre's view that a tradition has the character of a movement. If successful, this movement makes practitioners and leaders increasingly aware of its direction and alerts them to the necessity to perfect the influence of the movement on the practitioners and on the institutions, through the stimulation of ongoing inquiries and debates on how to best organize the pursuit of the goals of the tradition, that is, good life, the common good, and salvation. (MacIntyre 1988: 326). At some stage of maturity, a tradition might produce a kind of theoretical work consisting in conceptualizing its main activities (ibid.: 359): it can move from narrative to metanarrative. A good example of this step is the Islamic discipline of the foundations of phronetic knowledge, known as *usul-al-fiqh*, whose most astute representatives help us understand the range of applicability of the notions of *phronesis* and public reasoning in terms that transcend the specific challenges faced by Islamic traditions (see chapter 4).

MacIntyre is also outspoken in suggesting that a key maturity test for a tradition occurs when its adherents confront new, different, and even incompatible discourses that present problems of incommensurability. It might be the encounter with another, rival tradition, but also, and more powerfully, the facing of an entirely new constellation of power, like in the rise of modern states in Latin Christian, Western Europe, or later, in a colonial setting, in the Middle East. This is the moment when one can observe how a variety of crucial resources of a tradition, of its leaders and practitioners, is put to trial:

> An ability to recognize when one's conceptual resources are inadequate
> in such an encounter, or when one is unable to frame satisfactorily what

others have to say to one in criticism and rebuttal, and a sensitivity to the distortions which may arise in trying to capture within one's own framework theses originally at home in another are all essential to the growth of a tradition whose conflicts are of any complexity or whose mutations involve transitions from one kind of social and cultural order to another and from one language to another. (MacIntyre 1988: 327)

One major limit of any tradition in passing this kind of test, according to MacIntyre, is when it faces one key claim of liberal modernity, namely the assumption that the texts and discourses of all traditions should be susceptible of translation into the liberal idiom of modernity. Yet this intimation of commensurability often bounces back on the liberal modernity's claims to universality. The latent or explicit intellectual "imperialism" of such claims is thus exposed in ways that differ from how several other traditions, like the Catholic and Islamic ones, have defended and justified their own imperialistic drives. During the last quarter of the second millennium CE this expectation of universal commensurability has turned the liberal tradition into a new, awe-inspiringly tradition, in tune with the forces of a modern capitalist economy, state bureaucracy, and modern warfare: in other words, with what Habermas calls the "system." The liberal tradition thus appears as a tradition sui generis. Yet it is increasingly unable to defend its monopoly over the "original" model of modernity. The extent to which the modernity issued of the liberal tradition aspires to retain its primacy as the original type of modernity and so to dictate the standards of modernization also outside of the West can therefore only be measured by the extent to which it is the "winning" type of modernity on a global scale.

Yet the weakness of the liberal tradition lies, paradoxically, in its original strength, and particularly in its claim to represent the natural structure and evolutionary trajectory of entire societies and increasingly of the whole world society. However, observers and theorists—including Habermas—do not cease to stress that society is ultimately based on multiple and often fragmented life forms. In particular, if "society is the historical condition in which speakers act and are acted upon, speak, hear, and overhear" (Asad 2003: 187), then we should admit, with MacIntyre, that "there is no way to give us an understanding of any society, including our own, except through the stock of stories which constitute its initial dramatic resources" (MacIntyre 1984 [1981]: 216). The inherent pluralism and agonism of the public sphere of modern societies, intended as a coexistence of different traditions and approaches to public reasoning, is difficult to deny. The crystallization of a dominant metanarrative of the public sphere by reference to a given tradition is a possibility but not a necessity. In a modern pluralist setting the normative claims inherent in how a public sphere functions can only be validated by a broad, transcultural dynamics of debating and defining the common good and the more discrete public goods in which it is articulated.

MacIntyre's approach facilitates viewing not only a coexistence of traditions but also their possible conversation in the formation of culturally diversified public spheres. The condition for a successful conversation is not to disguise differences and obfuscate conflicts behind the bars of rigid proceduralist cages. MacIntyre's view contrasts both with the relativist denial of the possibility of rational debate among rival traditions and with the radically perspectivist assertion of the impossibility of making truth-claims from within any tradition, based on the postulate that truth is just will to truth and that will to truth is nothing else than will to power (MacIntyre 1988: 352; see also MacIntyre 1990; Milbank 1997; Miner 2002). From the viewpoint of the invitation to a conversation among traditions, postmodern relativism appears as the "inverted image" of the scarcely critical self-understanding of the dominant streams within the Enlightenment and also of the limits of any "immanent critique" of modernity. What the perspectivist-relativist and the Enlightenment strands have in common is the inability to recognize the rationality of traditions and their capacity to ground and sustain public reasoning. *Pace* Burke, who appealed to traditions to buttress his antirationalist political-ideological conservatism, traditions are both historically and in the contemporary world the necessary springboards for rational argument and reflection (MacIntyre 1988: 353). The answers to relativism and perspectivism are not to be found in any theory of rationality that originates from one specific tradition, but in "a theory embodied and presupposed by [traditions'] practices of enquiry" (ibid.: 354). After a genealogy of traditions, theory is still what one needs to work on.

The success of the Anglo-American liberal tradition from the eighteenth to the twentieth century and its capacity to set the new normative parameters of the public sphere should be carefully assessed through a look at how it gain benefits from the internal weaknesses of the rival and predecessor traditions: in particular from their limited capacity to update inherited views of *phronesis* on the basis of the major economic and political revolutions that upset the *respublica christiana* from the thirteenth century onward. On the other hand, it is a dangerous simplification to see in the Vichian approach a radical—and preemptive—contestation of the liberal modernity of the Anglo-American tradition (see e.g., Lilla 1993). The complexity of Vico's reception by the Anglo-American tradition is now being explored in quite explicit terms (see Danesi 1995).

## The Complex Genealogy of the Public Sphere

Combining MacIntyre's approach to traditions with some key insights of Vico and Voegelin into an examination of the relationship between social practice, religion, and sociopolitical order, I have attempted to apply a revised genealogical method to the study of the emergence of the public sphere. I conceived of this method as different from a Nietzschean-Foucauldian, perspectivist and poststructuralist approach (cf. also Salvatore and LeVine 2005). My goal has been not to operate a deconstruction but to improve understanding of the ideational limits of a social theory exposed to the liberal bias of the Anglo-American tradition. One main result has been to suggest a way to demystify the necessity of a strong integration between the concept of the public sphere and the notion of civil society, a link that is—as also confirmed by debates in the 1990s—the trademark of the Anglo-American social thought tradition and of their continental ramifications. This conclusion seems in line with Eisenstadt's consideration that

> civil society entails a public sphere, but not every public sphere entails a civil society, whether of the economic or political variety, as defined in the contemporary discourse, or as it has developed in early modern Europe through direct participation in the political process of corporate bodies or a more or less restricted body of citizens in which private interests play a very important role. We do indeed expect that in every civilization of some complexity and literacy a public sphere will emerge, though not necessarily of the civil society type. (Eisenstadt 2002: 141)

The axial notion of human partnership in God and the ensuing patterns of collective action and public reasoning for the common good are rooted in more ancient thought than theories of civil society with their cognates and derivatives. I have attempted to demonstrate that a first layer of crystallization of public reasoning was provided by sophisticated specifications of this axial approach, namely by those political visions that we associate with the conflicted, "communitarian" experience of the Greek *polis* (especially Athens) elaborated by classic philosophy, especially through the triad of Socrates, Plato, and Aristotle. Yet a second layer of historical experience and reflection was tied to the not less conflicted emergence of the Roman republic grounded on the idea of *res publica* and the notion itself of the "public," as a category of collective "good" developed from within Roman law.

This specification of the "common" as the "public" good was determinant for all subsequent developments of any notion of publicness. Against all ungenealogical presumptions of a sharp divergence between the idea of the "common" (as mainly traditional) and the notion of the "public" (as eminently modern), or between authority based and procedure oriented pursuits of common and public goods, I showed that at the moment of its definition—as epitomized by the Vichian contention between patricians and plebeians, and in particular by the outcome of this challenge—the "public" was by necessity based on the "common," though it also departed from it in specific ways, without however suppressing it. The public domain as the sphere of pursuit of public goods resulted from an articulation and convenient reduction of the axial idea of a common or supreme good of all humanity (ranging from good life in this world to salvation in the thereafter) mediated by jurisprudential discourse. This notion of public as qualifying a specific type of good or goods was the result of a simultaneously practical, political, and jurisprudential process of setting limits to the private domain of property and patronage (and to the private power of the *pater familias*), thus instituting the very public goods that are accessible to citizens deprived of a propertied status, devoid of private estates (chapter 5).

Clearly this notion of publicness was not limited to define the moral and legal boundaries of a bargaining among propertied private citizens, though this was one key type of interaction occurring in the public domain. Traditional views of publicness were not bent toward a sheer formal distinction between the private and the public sphere, but were part of a more organic view of the socio-legal-political order, including a combination and hierarchy of goods. The *res publica* is therefore a good sui generis because it is nonnegotiable. It becomes for many authors belonging to different epochs and civilizations (starting with Plato and Aristotle) the condition for the pursuit of all other social and human goods in any post-axial society.

Alongside and partly before the Greco-Roman crystallization of the idea of publicness, the idea of the hierarchy of goods was powerfully enshrined in all Abrahamic traditions, which intensely interacted—and at times conflicted—with the values and standards of the Greek and Roman social worlds. Within these powerful manifestations of axial transformations, the notion of the individual as responsible for his conduct toward God and simultaneously toward his brothers (and, increasingly, sisters) was tied to the notion of a common good and of social goods derived from it, to be pursued by following divine injunctions. Here an idea of self or the person emerged in a triangular relationship, whereby interactions and transactions between *ego* and *alter* were mediated by the common faith in God. Common faith is here the engine to the common good. The biblical commandment to love *alter* as oneself and the Qur'anic injunction of commanding good and prohibiting evil are basic instances of this kind of imperatives. The Decalogue explained the intimate link between commandments related to what is due to God and what is enjoined in order to be fair to the brothers.

The "Habermas effect" consisting in turning private concerns into public deliberation on the common good via the virtue of communicative action to build a collective We-identity is too sharp a passage to account for the complexity and variety of such long term, interlocking trajectories of notions of publicness and of their influence in social life—not to speak of the variety of their institutionalization, constituting a specifically political macrosphere of interaction which this work could only deal with tangentially. Habermas did recognize, at a later stage of his work, the intervention and mediation of appropriate "cultural traditions," that is, the "something else" that should be postulated as the condition for producing "overlapping consensus" and so justice and common good. Yet his demand on tradition (mostly reduced to "familiarity" and "culture") to pass a test proving its suitability as the ultimate source of "communicative action" can only be a test of suitability as a medium for the internalization of procedures of consensus through its practitioners (see chapter 1).

Thus in order to explain the switch from practical rationality to public reason, the forms and limits of "communicative action" have been encapsulated in an ideal-typical communicative form called "discourse ethics" (cf. Apel 1988; Apel and Niquet 2002), consisting in "the exchange of arguments and counterarguments as the most suitable procedure for resolving moral-practical questions" (Habermas 1996 [1992]: 447). While I recognize that the value of the idea of "communicative action" resides in the irreducibility of human action to any technique (cf. Joas 1991 [1986]: 99), the variety of forms of argument and reasoning, including those that have been hegemonic in specific legal, political, and religious traditions, should be acknowledged and analyzed as something different from mere lifewordly inputs into a singular machinery of communicative action of basically uniform modern societies. They should be recognized and valued in their diversity and complexity, which include a capacity to institute consensual forms of procedural reason both through a work internal to traditions and via interaction and dialogue among various traditions.

My analysis has not been finalized to assigning these various forms of reasoning to specific "types" of public reasoning. The goal was rather to offer a crosscutting, transcultural trajectory of the shaping and transformation of patterns of public reasoning, which typified views of modern publicness are not able—even not for the sake of a social theory that aspires to universality—to take over, fix, and turn into a singular norm. Habermas himself was ready to concede on the cultural variability of moral contents of public reasoning, but he has insisted on a uniform formula of "procedural rationality" that does not pay enough attention to hegemonic configurations and shifts of authority in the making of cultural traditions (cf. Salvatore and Amir-Moazami 2002; Salvatore and LeVine 2005).

"Communicative action" and the underlying forms of procedural reason risk therefore to appear as elegant hieroglyphs of a much more complex and conflicted rationalization of the *ego-alter* engagement, as hyperformalized communicative abstractions that hardly tackle the inherently intersubjective issue of the "leap of trust," the crux of the modern establishment of civility-*cum*-publicness as diagnosed by Seligman. He honestly admitted that we need a convincing notion of interactional trust in order to pinpoint the procedural rationality of communication, while, however, the increase in social complexity worldwide makes trust a normative standard detached from the reality of practical understandings among social actors. The conceptual stricture and the inherent normative fragility of trust retroact negatively on public confidence, since private, pristine trust, and public, systemic confidence, though distinct, can only develop in parallel from the viewpoint of the model—which I have criticized—of the simultaneous rise of civil society and the public sphere.

At the present state of development of this model, publicness risks becoming increasingly sterile either as an etiquette of "political correctness," consisting in minimizing incidents among individuals or groups, or in the guise of an approach to overstrategize public communication, or even through a hyperjuridification of social interaction. The wave of interest and debate on civil society and the public sphere of the 1990s was largely the result of the wish to compensate for these mounting deficits. However, the ongoing transformations in the economic and political spheres, which have produced the modern idea of civility, make it impossible to overcome a problem (Seligman 1997: 154–57) inherent in the compact anthropology of the Anglo-American liberal tradition. Seligman, though committed to that tradition, admits: "The idea of the individual as unconditionality . . . was too demanding a principle, one that carried too much baggage" (ibid.: 172). Once the dyadic and agential dimension of the *ego-alter* relationship had been overloaded with expectations, it was difficult to redress its balance through a communitarian reassertion without jeopardizing the model.

In this work, I have outlined a genealogy of the public sphere without proposing a countertheory situated at the same level of analysis. The task that has guided my exploration has been to genealogically situate "public reasoning" as a sociologically plausible specification of the scope of the exercise of reason and therefore as a method for collective deliberative action not caged in a given "sphere." My work hypothesis has been that conceptualizing a noncaged public would free it from a polar yet asymmetric relationship to the private. We could so recognize in publicness the ethical and sometimes political apex of an experiential and institutional continuum (Weintraub 1997: 37), or at least of a spectrum with fractures and leaps—like between the *oikos* ("household") and the *agorà* ("public square")—which does not result in a sharp polarization of "spheres." At the other end of the spectrum we do not find a private sphere where interest and affection are exclusively formed, but everyday practice shaped through learning processes within a series of familiar social settings (not only the transformed "household" of the modern bourgeois nuclear family) leading to the formation of dispositions orienting deliberation at a collective level.

Within such a spectrum, the development of deliberation assumes a crucial importance especially in the form of the disposition of *phronesis* (a Greek notion) or *prudentia* (its Latin version), which is the discerning faculty to find out and apply the most appropriate means to attain determinate goods. The ordering of goods, on the other hand, depends on a parallel, deeply intersubjective or connective capacity, that is, the definition of justice, which derives from the exercise of judgment, first in less-than-public, "lifewordly" (though not necessarily private) settings, and, second, within public arenas of debate and contention. Phronetic judgment and the interactive apprehension of justice are the twin pillars of an experiential and agential spectrum that is common to several traditional articulations of publicness, and not only to those relying on monotheistic religions (MacIntyre 1988: 183–208). It is the yoking of practical rationality to the interactive exercise of judgment that continually reproduces what I have called "connective justice" or simply "connectivity."

One could object that what one leaves out with this approach focusing on connective justice is the level of state governance particularly dear to modern political realists like Machiavelli and Hobbes and further studied by thinkers of the caliber of Hegel, Marx, Gramsci, Weber, Foucault, and the like. Here governance affects the redefinition of "citizenship," no longer containable within an obsolete "Greco-Roman" republican vocabulary—not to speak of the limits of prophetic speech—also because of its tight interference with the novelties and transformations of capitalist, profit-oriented entrepreneurship. In other words, with the earlier proposition of looking at trajectories that are situated before or outside the emergence and crystallization of the Anglo-American liberal tradition and its significant continental peripheries, one could be criticized for being able to just sketch the expansion of the rationality of the *oikos*. One could be accused of missing the essential novelties of the "public sphere," intended as reposing on the modern, Protestant and post-Protestant dialectics of "inwardness" and "publicness" unfolding in the shadow of an increasingly democratic Leviathan.

## Reconstructing Alternative Approaches to the Public Sphere

Yet we can also see it differently, on a double level. First, the alternative trajectories with deeper historical rooting and more complex genealogies than those culminating into the Anglo-American tradition result from a series of leaps, variably defined as "leap of being" or "leap of faith" by Voegelin, preceding and being the condition for what Seligman called, analogically but problematically, the "leap of trust" that grounded modern notions of the private and public spheres. Second, far from being by necessity oppositional and revolutionary in a modern world mainly shaped by liberal values, the nexus between *phronesis* and justice is a structuring element on which the modern state and the capitalist economy themselves are largely parasitic (cf. Sandel 1984: 91), even when this nexus is not very visible since nested in microstructures of power and social relations not subject to visible institutionalization. Probably modern, rational bureaucracies (whether efficient or less efficient according to Weberian criteria) would not be viable in implementing their blueprints of management of the population, if a sufficient number of their officials did not practice, on a daily basis, phronetic deliberation: despite the fact that this kind of judgment is basically extraneous to the bureaucratic logic of formal rationalization and to the related ideology of surveillance (cf. Jonsen and Toulmin 1988).

Admittedly, this argument has been from the beginning one of the main weapons in the arsenal of the so-called communitarians (cf. Sandel 1984). However, Alasdair MacIntyre, who has fiercely rejected this label for his own work, has criticized communitarians for not going beyond a weakly diagnostic approach to some shortcomings of liberalism (especially the stigmatization of its alleged "individualistic excesses"), while in reality sharing its basic assumptions: in particular the key to liberal civil society that they found in the postulation of a "moral sense" (MacIntyre 1998 [1997]): 244). He has convincingly argued that "the values of communitarianism are also to be found in the state's ragbag of values and they were there long before the name 'communitarianism' was given to them" (ibid.: 245). In this sense, communitarianism is the last defensive ditch of the Anglo-American tradition, not its challenger.

MacIntyre shows that in the final analysis there is a large gap between the extent to which state institutions are able to be parasitic on notions and practices of the common good for their survival, on the one hand, and the goals of social movements, to the extent they are articulations of local needs, on the other. These are movements that challenge the arrangements of bureaucratic power ever and again, since the latter do not possess—unlike the movements—a systematic capacity of mapping needs through phronetically and permanently updated, participatory inquiry, open argumentative challenges, and collective learning (cf. LeVine and Salvatore 2005). This consideration also helps situating the legitimacy of public authority vis-à-vis the potential of participatory action from below:

> That some people rather than others should exercise power through political office is not necessarily a mark of oppression. What is always oppressive is any form of social relationship that denies to those who participate in it the possibility of the kind of learning from each other about the nature of their common good that can issue in socially transformative action. (MacIntyre 1998 [1997]: 250)

We do not have here a "lifeworld" facing the "system" like in Habermas's account, but I doubt that we have two different causalities either, one functional, and one immediately practical, or even two forms of will and notions of freedom, like in Ferdinand Tönnies's paradigm of *Gemeinschaft* versus *Gesellschaft* (Tönnies 2001 [1887]). Any dichotomist typology obscures a much more dynamic tension that not only affects all traditions but is also internal to the logic of action and interaction within modern societies. Conscious of these deficits inherent in social theory, one should nonetheless acknowledge that Habermas tried—also through a selective use of the pragmatist heritage—to sketch a deeper layer of publicness through the analysis of the "rational potential inherent in everyday communicative practices," in order to dissolve "the tension of the abstract opposition between norm and reality" (Habermas 1996 [1992]: 442). However, the resulting theory of communicative action places too high a demand on the rationalizing and consensual virtues of communication and neglects even more drastically than his theory of publicness (that had the merit of including a historical analysis of concept formation, though bent to prototypical idealization) any alternative trajectory of public reasoning. An unsolved issue seems then to be concealed by the excessive centrality of the notion of "communication." This concept appears at first sight sociologically neutral, but is in tension with the notion of practice that is—as evidenced especially by MacIntyre—central to the alternative traditions of public reason (see chapter 2).

The public sphere cannot be the form of a singular, albeit universalizing, tradition. The notion of the public sphere can regain theoretical coherence and conceptual plausibility—also for framing empirical analysis—only if carefully reconstructed by drawing on the conceptual resources of a plurality of partly overlapping and partly conflicting discursive traditions. But it is also legitimate to raise doubts as to whether a sustained, theoretical, transcultural rereading of the public sphere would leave this concept intact. Probably the notion of the public sphere—even in the form restyled by Habermas after his theory of *Öffentlichkeit* was filtered through the more general theory of communicative action—is in itself sociologically overdemanding not only for the non-Western world, but also for large parts of it. It cannot capture the actions for reclaiming the common good performed by several social (including socioreligious) movements.

The premises and promises of communicative and deliberative action are not automatically geared toward this kind of "sphere." And it is not enough to allow for the possibility of "plebeian," alternative or counterpublics that, according to Habermas, are "the periodically recurring violent revolt of a counterproject to the hierarchical world of domination with its official celebrations and everyday disciplines" (Habermas 1996 [1992]: 427). In the very moment when the reclamation of the common good crystallizes into Habermas's publicness, it induces a movement of implosion of the pluralism inherent in public reasoning, of its mechanisms and forms of argument sustained by shifting configurations of authority and modalities of its contestation. Since they are built on a variety of potentially consensual yet conflicted procedures, models and styles of arguing cannot be caged into a singular form of procedural rationality. No doubt the dense symbol of the "sphere," the idea of the public sphere as the "third sphere" of society, and the essentializing character of the private-public dichotomy that far exceeds its originally flexible and dynamic function in the Roman law tradition, would need to be critically tackled by any alternative theory of publicness.

Admittedly, a certain implosion of the variety and complexity of public reasoning into a highly functionalized view of the public sphere, characterized by a high degree of formalization of the mechanisms of argument and response, is sociologically unavoidable in the context of modern societies that need to match functional differentiation with efficient communication. This is also discounted in Habermas's picture of the "publicness lost" of enlightened bourgeois individuals, which originally consisted of "self-regulated, horizontally crosslinked, inclusive, and more or less discourse-resembling communicative processes supported by weak institutions," a configuration, therefore, inherently unstable and unsuitable for mass welfare democracies (ibid.: 437).

However, it is not just the overinstitutionalization and bureaucratization of publicness in a welfare state context, decried by Habermas, that severs its link with practical rationality. The problem resides mainly in turning publicness into a normative ideal, based on the morality of the enlightened modern subject per se, whereby the "inwardness" as a source of morality builds the necessary flip side of "publicness." This subject-centered model obscures the relational delicacy of the social bond, which I located at the theoretical center of the genealogy proposed in this work. The concurring view of the legislating force of the "inner forum" of the subject is at the root of the "irrelation to politics" that Koselleck denounced, shortly before the appearance of Habermas's book on the public sphere, as the latent impairing factor that contemporary modern societies have inherited from the Enlightenment drama of the application of absolute reason to absolute power (Koselleck 1988 [1959]).

To conclude, this genealogy of the public sphere departing from axial traditions does not deny the possibility of a theory, or a metanarrative, of the public sphere. It shows that the dominant theory is in need of deep revision, but also that competing approaches based on historical experiences other than those originating from the—thus far—winning models of northwestern, European modernity might legitimately aspire to reconstruct such a metanarrative and compete with a revised

Habermasian one. Indeed, even within the West at large, an alternative European and an Islamic theory (also based on the challenge represented by the participation of populations of Muslim background in European public life) might be in the making. They both possess the potential to develop a universal theoretical range, not limited to a particular region or "civilization" but extended to the West and the rest (cf. Salvatore 2006). Far from representing an antitheoretical stance, the present work's genealogy delineates the possibility and maybe necessity of several competing, dialoguing, and overlapping theories of the public sphere.

# NOTES

## Introduction: The Genealogy of the Public Sphere

1. Yet the inclusion of a compact post-Protestant view of religion as an inward source of morality in Habermas's model would not damage, but rather strengthen it. It would put into sharper relief the dialectics between inwardness and publicness that underlies the model. Habermas himself has been frequently invoking religion in recent works (1997), not to speak of his dialogue with Joseph Ratzinger (Habermas and Ratzinger 2004). Religion was one major focus of the speech that he delivered upon receiving the peace prize of the *Börsenverein des deutschen Buchhandels* in October 2001. True, this occurred right after 9/11, but the attention of sociologists of religion and even theologians to his theory goes back to debates on the theory of communicative action (see Arens 1989; 1998; Browning and Schlüsser Fiorenza 1992; Mendieta 2000). It is important to examine how the notion of religion was transformed from within the Anglo-American tradition and other strands of Enlightenment thought into an instrument for articulating the inwardness-publicness dialectics in the context of profound socioeconomic and political transformations (see in particular chapters 1 and 6).

2. One can hypothesize that the 1968 sociopolitical movement contributed to cooling Habermas's interest in Vico and to strengthening the reasons for his attack on Gadamer's hermeneutics as the last bastion of defense of the authority of tradition. Yet it is also remarkable that Habermas worked on Vico during the most markedly neo-Marxian phase of his work.

## 1 Religion, Civilization, and the Redefinition of Tradition

1. This is not the place to engage in a punctual genealogy of this type of vision, which goes beyond U.S. social theorists and embraces German social philosophers of the nineteenth and twentieth century (including Hegel and Cassirer). This is an additional reason why it is probably wrong to identify this family of approaches to tradition with "communitarianism" in toto. The case of Robert N. Bellah is particularly important not only because of his centrality in U.S. sociology's endeavors to cope with modernization theory, but also for his earlier reliance (in parallel and probably in a dialogue with Eisenstadt), on

Jaspers's concept of the Axial Age (Bellah 1964; for an assessment of Bellah's impact as a sociologist of religion who was also a public intellectual see Alexander and Sherwood 2002).

2. A caveat and a disclaimer on the use of *telos* and *phronesis* in this work are appropriate. The relationship of contemporary social theory to these two classic concepts is highly ambivalent. While the general ambition of the grand social theory is to minimize their use or make them obsolete (Habermas's theory of communicative action is a good example), they often resurface, if not as concepts, as icons of the need to reconstruct social theory on a new basis. For example, they were the names adopted by a self-declared progressive social science journal (*Telos*) and a comparably oriented book series (*Phronesis*). Since my aim in the first part of the work (chapters 1 and 2) is more limited and consists in reconstructing a viable sociological notion of tradition, referring to *telos* and *phronesis* becomes useful for they are an essential part (indeed the engine) of the notion itself of tradition as historically constructed and instituted in the Euro-Mediterranean civilizational area. There is no need here to either minimize or to iconize these two notions. Since the final goal of the present work is a genealogy of the public sphere (chapters 5 and 6) based on an analysis of traditions as platforms of public reasoning (chapters 3 and 4), the task of following the metamorphosis of *telos* and *phronesis* into modern concepts of agency and communicative action is key to this genealogy.

3. Ideally, the metatheoretical elaboration on the notion of tradition as a tool for the genealogy of the public sphere, and the application of the genealogical approach to the analysis of specific traditions should be conducted simultaneously. For obvious reasons of exposition I alternate between both, by giving—as I did so far—a certain priority to the former axis of inquiry, namely to tradition.

4. In contrast with this view, Bourdieu applied his basic notions of field, interest, and capital to the "religious field" (Bourdieu 1971), while treating all types of interest, though historically contextualized and particularized, as morphologically uniform in their basic orientation to the to acquisition of wealth and even more of power (Calhoun 1993: 71).

## 2   Bridging Imagination, Practice, and Discourse

1. What is intended by "poetic" will be further elucidated in chapter 5, in the discussion of Vico's theory.

2. MacIntyre's idea of social practice was partly inspired by Wittgenstein (Knight 1998: 10). The closeness of MacIntyre's concept of tradition to the notion of life form is explicitly acknowledged by him (MacIntyre 1988: 391) and elaborated upon by other authors in a similar fashion (cf. Shotter 1996).

3. This passage is also quoted by Joas (1991 [1986]: 114).

4. Here MacIntyre's argument shows a substantial convergence with Habermas's approach, especially with some among his more recent works (cf. Habermas 1996 [1992]).

5. "A great deal of human action happens only insofar as the agent understands and constitutes him or herself as an integral part of a 'we' "(Taylor 1999: 36).

6. There seems to have been no mutual dialogue, or even referencing, between Habermas and Elias in spite of the fact that they dealt, in crucial parts of their work, with the same phenomenon, namely the differentiation of a bourgeois culture in eighteenth-century France and Germany.

## 3  The Public Reason of the Commoner

1. Coherently with the genealogical approach of this work, I analyze the Axial Renaissance and the thought of its leading representatives (in particular Aquinas within Latin Christendom and al-Shatibi within Sunni Islam: see chapter 4) through the lenses of the interpretation provided by twentieth-century critical representatives of the same traditions: Alasdair MacIntyre and Eric Voegelin for the Catholic tradition, and Fazlur Rahman and M. Khalid Masud for the Islamic tradition (see chapter 4). Differently from the modern thinkers analyzed in chapters 5 and 6, I renounce to refer directly to the work of Aquinas and al-Shatibi and focus on a critical reexamination of how their work is reinterpreted and reappropriated by contemporary scholars.

2. The importance of this late-medieval epoch and in particular of the transformations of the thirteenth century variously associated with the new religious movements and mendicant orders and their impact on modern European paths of development has been emphasized by a diverse array of social theorists (see e.g., Chirot 1985; Mann 1986; Santoro 2003 [1999]). The late-medieval crystallizations of the Axial Renaissance were part of a hemispheric-wide movement consisting in a combination of challenges, which in several cases were determined by the confrontation with "non-axial" nomadic populations (cf. Pollock 1998; Wittrock 2001; Rahimi 2006). The analysis of these transformations touches upon and alters the Weberian interpretation of the emergence of a specific European path to modernity as a blend of the so-called feudal, papal, and urban revolutions, and especially of the emergence of European universities (cf. Nelson 1981; Arjomand 1999). Weber's failure to provide a comprehensive analysis of both medieval Catholicism and Islam as discursive traditions with complex institutional ramifications (see Walker Bynum 1987; Friedrich Silber 1995; Salvatore 1996; Schluchter 1987) has resulted in a sociological overemphasis on the Protestant Reformation as a key moment of post-axial transformations, immediately impacting the rise of modernity.

3. However, the potential tensions cannot be denied. As pointed out by MacIntyre, Aquinas's formulas are particularly compatible with the reflections on forms of socioeconomic life that are alternative to the

conceptions of commercial and civil society due to emerge in a mature phase of a capitalism (see chapter 6), and have therefore a structural affinity with a potential "road not taken" by Marx in his *Theses on Feuerbach* (MacIntyre 1994; see chapter 1).

4. Alasdair MacIntyre, speaking from within an original approach to the Catholic tradition, has convincingly argued that the most innovative legacy of Aquinas cannot be found in the work of Thomistic and neo-Thomistic theologians (MacIntyre 1990). A recognition that the Dominican monk implanted unique seeds for a modern yet alternative view of the public sphere belongs therefore to a wider research program within critical social theory (cf. Finnis 1998; Milbank and Pickstock 2001). Far from having significance for the self-enclosed theoretical current known as neo-Thomism, this dimension of Aquinas's work could be considered determinant in laying the basis for an approach that is alternative both to communitarian-collectivistic and to liberal-individualistic conceptions of the social bond and public reason. Neither should Aquinas's work be considered, at any time, the exclusive legacy of the Catholic Church. It was probably influential on some currents of seventeenth-century Scottish Calvinism, prior to the so-called Scottish Enlightenment (cf. MacIntyre 1988; see chapter 6).

5. This key-point of Aquinas's theory will be developed by Vico in stronger socioanthropological terms that dispense of strictly theological references and make more transparent its potential for an alternative, yet European theory of the public sphere (see chapter 5 and conclusion).

6. For the sake of the genealogy of the public sphere, Aquinas's use of the notion of "multitude" would deserve more attention, also because this concept has been recently reevaluated within approaches seeking to recuperate a viable public sphere out of a situation, determined by the long-term liberal hegemony within modernity, where we face a "publicness without the public sphere," a systemic function deprived of its basis in solidarity-oriented communicative action (see Virno 2002 [2001]: 29–32). This issue is examined in chapter 6 and in the conclusion. Suffice here to remember that while several works often exalt Spinoza (see chapter 5) as the modern theoretician of the multitude, they tend to neglect the seminal contribution of Aquinas in the same field (an exception is Agamben 1993 [1990]).

# 4 The Collective Pursuit of Public Weal

1. In this chapter I pay particular attention to the work of Fazlur Rahman and M. Khalid Masud as modern interpreters of a discursive tradition, here Sunni Islam, on a par with their counterparts Eric Voegelin and Alasdair MacIntyre to whom I referred in chapter 3, with regard to Latin Christianity. Their approach should then be not taken at face value, but reflected upon as part of the genealogy of the tradition from within which they write.

2. "Orthodox" is here a very imperfect translation of *sunni* (Sunni), the adjective of *sunna*, which is, as exemplified so far, a notion comparable to *doxa* but not identical with it, in that it denotes a more complex and fragile, yet also more consensualist process of crystallization of doctrine.

3. This occurred in particular through the work of Spinoza, a thinker of Jewish-Sephardi origin, heir to the rich theoretical heritage of al-Andalus, from where his family fled due to the Christian persecutions (see chapter 5).

4. The Hanbali school was also the only one among the four canonical schools to retain—well beyond the era of the Axial Renaissance—a mobilizing function as a source for solidarity-based socioreligious movements, on a par with Sufi orders, while all other legal schools lost their cohesiveness as movements by the twelfth century (Levtzion 2002: 109). It is therefore far from surprising that the leading Hanbali reformer Ibn Taymiya, mentioned earlier, who decisively contributed to shape and stabilize the notion of *shari'a*, was also a Sufi, although he was particularly vocal in censuring Sufi practices and doctrines that were incompatible with the Qur'anic roots of piety and were enmeshed in what he considered un-Islamic popular cultures (Makdisi 1974).

5. These were rulers whose authority (*sulta*) did not enjoy a direct religious legitimacy, unlike the caliph who was in principle the successor of Muhammad as the leader of the political body of the Muslim community.

6. It would be important, yet outside of the scope of the present work, to attempt a Weberian comparison of paths of institutionalization of urban structures of self-governance or lack thereof (see Arjomand 1998; 1999).

7. This will be indeed the simplifying "discovery" of several authors within European modernity, one fiercely contested by Vico (see chapter 5).

## 5 The Implosion of Traditions and the Redefinition of Common Sense

1. For a contrast to Habermas's reductive view of myth's role in shaping communication, cf. Bertland 2000.

2. "I take the word authority in its primary sense of property, in which sense it is always used in the Law of the Twelve Tables. Thus, in Roman civil law, people who grant rights of ownership were called *auctores*" (Vico 1999 [1744]: 150).

3. This authority is often incarnated by a specific institutional figure monitoring exchange and countering the lingering chaos, like the Greek *agoranomos* or the Islamic *muhtasib* (Crone 1987: 108). Not by chance, the latter's function, the *hisba*, has been often equated with the fundamental Islamic injunction to "commanding good and prohibiting evil," a fundamental command of *shari'a* not limited to the marketplace.

## 6    The Modern Public Sphere: Transforming Practical Reason into Prudential Communication

1. It might appear surprising that Hutcheson still made numerous references to Justinian's *Institutiones*, the main authority in the Roman law tradition inherited through the Middle Ages (MacIntyre 1988: 282–83).
2. Locke's point was the following: How can you trust a contract partner if he is an atheist and does not fear the only ultimate sanction to broken promises, the wrath of God? But also, how can you trust a Catholic if he will only obey the pope?
3. The work of Seligman also facilitates understanding how the legacy of this theoretical school weighs on mainstream social theory up to the recent, largely frustrated rediscovery of civil society and of the public sphere of the 1990s (Seligman 1992; 1997; 2000).

# REFERENCES

Abaza, Mona, and Georg Stauth. 1988. "Occidental Reason, Orientalism, Islamic Fundamentalism: A Critique." *International Sociology* 3, 4: 343–64.

Agamben, Giorgio. 1993 [1990]. *The Coming Community*, trans. Michael Hard, Minneapolis: University of Minnesota Press.

———. 1998 [1995]. *Homo Sacer: Sovereign Power and Bare Life*, trans. Daniel Heller-Roazen, Stanford, CA: Stanford University Press.

———. 2000. *Il tempo che resta: Un commento alla Lettera ai Romani*, Torino: Bollati Boringhieri.

Albiac, Gabriel. 1987. *La sinagoga vacia. Un estudo de las fuentes marranas del espinosismo*, Madrid: Hiperion.

Alexander, Jeffrey C., and Steven J. Sherwood. 2002. "Mythic Gestures: Robert N. Bellah and Cultural Sociology." In *Meaning and Modernity. Religion, Polity, and Self*, ed. Richard Madsen, William M. Sullivan, Ann Swidler, and Steven Tipton, Berkeley: University of California Press.

Apel, Karl-Otto. 1978 [1963]. *Die Idee der Sprache in der Tradition des Humanismus von Dante bis Vico*, Bonn: Bouvier.

———. 1972. "Communication and the Foundations of the Humanities." *Acta Sociologica* 15, 1: 7–26.

———. 1988. *Diskurs und Verantwortung. Das Problem des Übergangs zur postkonventionellen Moral*, Frankfurt: Suhrkamp.

Apel, Karl-Otto, and Marcel Niquet. 2002. *Diskursethik und Diskursanthropologie*, München: Karl Alber Freiburg.

Aquinas, Thomas. 1981 [1265–1273]. *Summa Theologiae*, 22 vols., Westminster, MD: Christian Classics.

———. 1975 [1259–1265]. *Summa Contra Gentiles*, 5 vols., Notre Dame, IN: University of Notre Dame Press.

Arens, Edmund, ed. 1989. *Habermas und die Theologie: Beiträge zur theologischen Rezeption, Diskussion und Kritik der Theorie kommunikativen Handelns*, Düsseldorf: Patmos.

———. 1998. "Das religiöse Verständnis der Theorie des kommunikativen Handelns." In *Religion als Kommunikation*, ed. Hermann Tyrell, Volkhard Krech, and Hubert Knoblauch, Würzburg: Ergon, 241–72.

Ariès, Philippe. 1962 [1960]. *Centuries of Childhood: A Social History of Family Life*, trans. Robert Baldick, New York: Vintage Books.

Arjomand, Said Amir. 1998. "Philanthropy, the Law, and Public Policy in the Islamic World before the Modern Era." In *Philanthropy in the World's Traditions*, ed. Warren F. Ilchman, Stanley N. Katz, and Edward L. Queen II, Bloomington and Indianapolis: Indiana University Press, 109–32.

Arjomand, Said Amir. 1999. "The Law, Agency and Policy in Medieval Islamic Society: Development of the Institutions of Learning from the Tenth to the Fifteenth Century." *Comparative Studies in Society and History* 41, 2: 263–93.

Arnason, Johann P. 2001. "Civilizational Patterns and Civilizing Processes." *International Sociology* 16, 3: 387–405.

———. 2003a. "East and West: From Invidious Dichotomy to Incomplete Deconstruction." In *Handbook of Historical Sociology*, ed. Gerard Delanty, Engin Isin, and Margaret Somers, London: Sage, 220–234.

———. 2003b. *Civilizations in Dispute. Historical Questions and Theoretical Traditions*, Leiden and Boston: Brill.

———. 2005. "The Axial Age and Its Interpreters: Reopening a Debate." In *Axial Civilizations and World History*, ed. Johann P. Arnason, Shmuel N. Eisenstadt, and Björn Wittrock, Leiden and Boston: Brill, 19–49.

———. 2006a. "Marshall Hodgson's Civilizational Analysis of Islam: Theoretical and Comparative Perspectives." In *Islam in Process: Historical and Civilizational Perspectives*, vol. 7, *Yearbook of the Sociology of Islam*, ed. Johann P. Arnason, Armando Salvatore, and Georg Stauth, Bielefeld: Transcript; New Brunswick, NJ: Transaction, 23–47.

———. 2006b. "The Emergence of Islam as a Case of Cultural Crystallization: Historical and Comparative Reflections." In *Islam in Process: Historical and Civilizational Perspectives*, vol. 7, *Yearbook of the Sociology of Islam*, ed. Johann P. Arnason, Armando Salvatore, and Georg Stauth, Bielefeld: Transcript; New Brunswick, NJ: Transaction, 95–122.

Arnason, Johann P., Armando Salvatore, and Georg Stauth. 2006. *Islam in Process: Historical and Civilizational Perspectives*, vol. 7, *Yearbook of the Sociology of Islam*. Bielefeld: Transcript; New Brunswick, NJ: Transaction.

Asad, Talal. 1986. *The Idea of an Anthropology of Islam*. Washington, DC: Georgetown University (Center for Contemporary Arab Studies).

———. 1993. *Genealogies of Religion: Discipline and Reasons of Power in Christianity and Islam*. Baltimore and London: Johns Hopkins University Press.

———. 1999. "Religion, Nation-State, Secularism." In *Nation and Religion. Perspectives on Europe and Asia*, ed. Peter van der Veer and Hartmut Lehmann, Princeton: Princeton University Press, 188–92.

———. 2003. *Formations of the Secular. Christianity, Islam, Modernity*, Stanford, CA: Stanford University Press.

Assmann, Jan. 2002 [2000]. *Herrschaft und Heil. Politische Theologie in Altägypten, Israel und Europa*, München: Carl Hanser.

———. 2005. "Axial 'Breakthroughs' and Semantic 'Relocations' in Ancient Egypt and Israel." In *Axial Civilizations and World History*, ed. Johann P. Arnason, Shmuel N. Eisenstadt, and Björn Wittrock, Leiden and Boston: Brill, 133–56.

Ayubi, Nazih. 1995. "Rethinking the Public/Private Dichotomy: Radical Islam and Civil Society in the Middle East." *Contention*, 4: 79–106.

Bakhtin, M. M. 1993. *Towards a Philosophy of the Act*, Austin: University of Texas Press.

Balibar, Etienne. 1997 [1985]. "*Jus-Pactum-Lex*: On the Constitution of the Subject in the *Theologico-Political Treatise*." In *The New Spinoza*, ed. Warren Montag and Ted Stolze, Minneapolis and London: University of Minnesota Press.

Barns, Barry. 2001. "Practice as Collective Action." In *The Practice Turn in Contemporary Theory*, ed. Theodore R. Schatzki, Karin Knorr Cetina, and Eike von Savigny, London and New York: Routledge, 17–28.

Bellah, Robert N. 1964. "Religious Evolution." *American Sociological Review* 29: 358–74.

———. 1970. *Beyond Belief. Essays on Religion in a Post-Traditional World*, New York: Harper and Row.

———. 1992 [1975]. *The Broken Covenant: American Civil Religion in Time of Trial*, Chicago: University of Chicago Press.

Bellah, Robert N. and Philip E. Hammond, eds. 1980. *Varieties of Civil Religion*, San Francisco: Harper and Row.

Bellah, Robert N., Richard Madsen, William M. Sullivan, Ann Swidler, and Steven M. Tipton. 1985. *Habits of the Heart. Individualism and Commitment in American Life*, Berkeley and Los Angeles: University of California Press.

Benhabib, Seyla. 1986. *Critique, Norm, and Utopia: A Study of the Foundations of Critical Theory*, New York: Columbia University Press.

———. 1992. *Situating the Self*, New York: Routledge.

Berger, Peter L. 1967. *The Sacred Canopy. Elements of a Sociological Theory of Religion*, Garden City: Doubleday.

Bergmann, Werner. 1985. "Das frühe Mönchtum als soziale Bewegung." *Kölner Zeitschrift für Soziologie und Sozialpsychologie* 37: 30–59.

Bertland, Alexander. 2000. "Habermas and Vico on Mythical Thought." In *Perspectives on Habermas*, ed. Lewis Edwin Hahn, Chicago and La Salle, IL: Open Court, 71–87.

Bourdieu, Pierre. 1971. "Genèse et structure du champ religieux." *Revue française de Sociologie* 12: 295–334.

———. 1977 [1972]. *Outline of a Theory of Practice*, trans. Richard Nice, Stanford, CA: Stanford University Press.

———. 1990 [1980]. *The Logic of Practice*, trans. Richard Nice, Stanford, CA: Stanford University Press.

Bourdieu, Pierre, and Loic J. D. Wacquant. 1992. *An Invitation to Reflexive Sociology*, Chicago: University of Chicago Press.

Bouveresse, Jacques. 1999. "Rules, Dispositions, and the *Habitus*." In *Bourdieu: A Critical Reader*, ed. Richard Shusterman, Oxford: Blackwell, 45–63.

Boyte, Harry C. 1992. "The Pragmatic Ends of Popular Politics." In *Habermas and the Public Sphere*, ed. Craig Calhoun, Cambridge, MA: MIT Press, 340–55.

Brague, Rémi. 2002 [1992]. *Eccentric Culture: A Theory of Western Civilization*, South Bend, IN: Saint Augustine's Press.

Brown, Peter. 1984. "Late Antiquity and Islam: Parallels and Contrasts." In *Moral Conduct and Authority. The Place of Adab in South Asian Islam*, ed. Barbara Metcalf, Berkeley: University of California Press, 23–37.

Browning, Don S., and Francis Schlüsser Fiorenza. 1992. *Habermas, Modernity and Public Theology*, New York: Crossroad.

Buber, Martin. 1983 [1936; 1958]. *Ich und Du*, Heidelberg: Lambert Schneider.

———. 1992. *On Intersubjectivity and Cultural Creativity*, ed. and with an introduction by Shmuel N. Eisenstadt, Chicago: University of Chicago Press.

Burchell, Graham. 1991. "Peculiar Interests: Civil Society and Governing 'the System of Natural Liberty.'" In *The Foucault Effect. Studies in Governmentality*, ed. Graham Burchell, Colin Gordon, and Peter Miller, Chicago: The University of Chicago Press, 119–50.

Burke, Kenneth. 1961. *The Rhetoric of Religion. Studies in Sociology*, Berkeley: University of California Press.

Calhoun, Craig. 1992. "Introduction." In *Habermas and the Public Sphere*, ed. Craig Calhoun, Cambridge, MA: MIT Press, 1–48.

———. 1993. "Habitus, Field and Capital: The Question of Historical Specificity." In *Bourdieu: Critical Perspectives*, ed. Craig Calhoun, Edward LiPuma, and Moishe Postone, Cambridge, UK: Polity Press, 61–88.

Carnevali, Giorgio. 2001. *Dell'amicizia politica. Tra teoria e storia*, Rome and Bari: Laterza.

Casanova, José. 1994. *Public Religions in the Modern World*, Chicago: University of Chicago Press.

———. 2001. "Civil Society and Religion: Retrospective Reflections on Catholicism and Prospective Reflections on Islam." *Social Research* 68, 4: 1041–80.

Chambers, Simone, and Will Kymlicka, eds. 2002. *Alternative Conceptions of Civil Society*. Princeton: Princeton University Press.

Chirot, Daniel. 1985. "The Rise of the West." *American Sociological Review* 56: 181–95.

Chittick, William C. 1992. *Faith and Practice of Islam. Three Thirteenth Century Sufi Texts*. Albany, NY: SUNY Press.

Cohen, Jean L., and Andrew Arato. 1992. *Civil Society and Political Theory*, Cambridge, MA: MIT Press.

Cook, Michael. 2000. *Commanding Good and Forbidding Wrong in Islamic Thought*, Cambridge: Cambridge University Press.

Cooper, Barry. 1998. "Editor's Introduction." *The History of Political Ideas*, vol. 6, *Revolution and the New Science*. In *The Collected Works of Eric Voegelin*, vol. 24, Columbia, MO: University of Missouri Press, 1–22.

Crone, Patricia. 1987. *Roman, Provincial and Islamic Law. The Origins of the Islamic Patronate*, Cambridge: Cambridge University Press.

Crone, Patricia, and Martin Hinds. 1986. *God's Caliph: Religious Authority in the First Centuries of Islam*, Cambridge and New York: Cambridge University Press.

Crossley, Nick, and John Michael Roberts, eds. 2004. *After Habermas: New Perspectives on the Public Sphere*, Oxford: Blackwell.

D'Emilia, Antonio. 1953. "Roman Law and Muslim Law (Comparative Outline)." *East and West* 4, 2.

Danesi, Marcel. 1995. *Giambattista Vico and Anglo-American Science. Philosophy and Writing*, Berlin: Mouton De Gruyter.

Dewey, John. 1927. *The Public and Its Problems*, New York: Henry Holt.

Doody, John. 1991. "MacIntyre and Habermas on Practical Reason." *American Catholic Philosophical Quarterly* 65: 143–58.

Dumont, Louis. 1977. *From Mandeville to Marx: The Genesis and Triumph of Economic Ideology*, Chicago: University of Chicago Press.

Dunn, John. 1969. *The Political Theory of John Locke*, Cambridge, MA: Harvard University Press.

Eickelman, Dale F. 2002. "Foreword: The Religious Public Sphere in Early Muslim Societies." In *The Public Sphere in Muslim Societies*, ed. Miriam Hoexter, Shmuel N. Eisenstadt, and Nehemia Levtzion, Albany, NY: SUNY Press, 1–8.

Eickelman, Dale F., and Armando Salvatore. 2002. "The Public Sphere and Muslim Identities." *European Journal of Sociology* 43, 1: 92–115.

Eisenstadt, Shmuel N. 1982. "The Axial Age: The Emergence of Transcendental Visions and the Rise of Clerics." In *European Journal of Sociology* 23, 2: 294–314.

———. 1985. "Comparative Liminality: Liminality and Dynamics of Civilization." *Religion* 15: 315–38.

———. 1986. "Introduction: The Axial Age Breakthroughs: Their Characteristics and Origins." In *The Origins and the Diversity of Axial Age Civilizations*, ed. Shmuel N. Eisenstadt, Albany, NY: SUNY Press, 1–25.

———. 1992. "Introduction. Intersubjectivity, Dialogue, Discourse, and Cultural Creativity in the Work of Martin Buber." In *On Intersubjectivity and Cultural Creativity*, ed. and with an introduction by Shmuel N. Eisenstadt, Chicago: University of Chicago Press, 1–22.

———. 1998. *Die Antinomien der Moderne. Die jakobinischen Grundzüge der Moderne und des Fundamentalismus. Heterodoxien, Utopismus und Jakobinismus in der Konstitution fundamentalistischer Bewegungen*, Frankfurt: Suhrkamp.

———. 2000a. "Fundamentalist Movements in the Framework of Multiple Modernities." In *Between Europe and Islam: Shaping Modernity in a Transcultural Space*, ed. Almut Höfert and Armando Salvatore, Brussels, Berlin, and Oxford: P.I.E.-Peter Lang, 175–96.

———. 2000b. "Multiple Modernities." In *Daedalus (Multiple Modernities)*, 129, 1: 1–29.

———. 2001. "The Civilizational Dimension of Modernity. Modernity as a Distinct Civilization," *International Sociology* 16, 3: 320–40.

———. 2002. "Concluding Remarks: Public Sphere, Civil Society, and Political Dynamics in Islamic Societies." In *The Public Sphere in Muslim Societies*, ed. Miriam Hoexter, Shmuel N. Eisenstadt, and Nehemia Levtzion, Albany, NY: SUNY Press, 139–61.

———. 2003. *Comparative Civilizations and Multiple Modernities. A Collection of Essays*, Leiden and Boston: Brill.

Eisenstadt, Shmuel N., and Bernhard Giesen. 1995. "The Construction of Collective Identity." *European Journal of Sociology* 36, 1: 72–102.

Eisenstadt, Shmuel N., and S. R. Graubard, eds. 1973. *Intellectuals and Tradition*, New York: Humanities Press.

Eisenstadt, Shmuel N., and Louis Roniger. 1984. *Patrons, Clients, and Friends*, Cambridge: Cambridge University Press.

Eisenstadt, Shmuel N., Wolfgang Schluchter, and Björn Wittrock, eds. 2000. *Public Spheres and Collective Identities*, New Brunswick, NJ: Transaction.

Elias, Norbert. 1976 [1939]. *Über den Prozess der Zivilisation*, Frankfurt: Suhrkamp.

Elkana, Yehuda. 1986. "The Emergence of Second-Order Thinking in Classical Greece." In *The Origins and the Diversity of Axial Age Civilizations*, ed. Shmuel N. Eisenstadt, Albany, NY: SUNY Press, 40–64.

Fassò, Guido. 1971. *Vico e Grozio*, Napoli: Guida.

Finnis, John. 1998. *Aquinas. Moral, Political, and Legal Theory*, Oxford: Oxford University Press.

Flyvbjerg, Bent. 2001. *Making Social Science Matter: Why Social Inquiry Fails and How it Can Succeed Again*. Oxford and New York: Cambridge University Press.

Foucault, Michel. 1979. *"Civil Society" and "Interest."* Lecture, Paris: Collège de France, April 4 (English transcript).

Foucault, Michel. 1991. "Governmentality." In *The Foucault Effect: Studies in Governmentality*, ed. Graham Burchell, Colin Gordon, and Peter Miller, Chicago: University of Chicago Press, 87–104.

Fowden, Garth. 1993. *Empire to Commonwealth: Consequences of Monotheism in Late Antiquity*, Princeton: Princeton University Press.

Fraser, Nancy. 1989. *Unruly Practices: Power, Discourse and Gender in Contemporary Social Theory*, Minneapolis: University of Minnesota Press.

———. 1992. "Rethinking the Public Sphere: A Contribution to the Critique of Actually Existing Democracy." In *Habermas and the Public Sphere*, ed. Craig Calhoun, Cambridge, MA: MIT Press, 69–98.

———. 1997. *Justice Interruptus: Critical Reflections on the "Postsocialist" Condition*. New York: Routledge.

Friedrich Silber, Ilana. 1995. *Virtuosity, Charisma and Social Order. A Comparative Sociological Study of Monasticism in Theravada Buddhism and Medieval Catholicism*. Cambridge: Cambridge University Press.

Gauchet, Marcel. 1997 [1985]. *The Disenchantment of the World. A Political History of Religion*, trans. Oscar Burge, Princeton, NJ: Princeton University Press.

Geertz, Clifford. 1973. *The Interpretation of Cultures. Selected Essays*, New York: Basic Books.

Gellner, Ernest. 1981. *Muslim Society*, Cambridge: Cambridge University Press.

———. 1991. *Plough, Sword, and Book*, London: Palladin.

Gerber, Haim. 1994. *State, Society and Law in Islam. Ottoman Law in Comparative Perspective*. Albany, NY: SUNY Press.

———. 2002. "The Public Sphere and Civil Society in the Ottoman Empire." In *The Public Sphere in Muslim Societies*, ed. Miriam Hoexter, Shmuel N. Eisenstadt, and Nehemia Levtzion, Albany, NY: SUNY Press, 65–82.

Giddens, Anthony. 1994. "Living in a Post-traditional Society." In *Reflexive Modernization. Politics, Tradition and Aestethics in the Modern Social Order*, ed. Ulrich Beck, Anthony Giddens, and Scott Lash, Cambridge, UK: Polity Press, 56–109.

Gobetti, Daniela. 1997. "Humankind as a System: Private and Public Agency at the Origins of Modern Liberalism." In *Public and Private in Thought and Practice: Perspectives on a Grand Dichotomy*, ed. Jeff Weintraub and Krishan Kumar, Chicago: University Press of Chicago, 103–32.

Goldziher, Ignaz. 1961 [1889–1890]. *Muhammedanische Sudien*, 2 vols., Hildesheim: Georg Holms.

Haakonssen, Knud. 1981. *The Science of a Legislator: The Natural Jurisprudence of David Hume and Adam Smith*, Cambridge and New York: Cambridge University Press.

———. 1996. *Natural Law and Moral Philosophy: From Grotius to the Scottish Enlightenment*. New York: Cambridge University Press.

Habermas, Jürgen. 1977 [1970]. "A Review of Gadamer's *Truth and Method*." In *Understanding and Social Inquiry*, ed. F. R. Dallmayr and T. A. McCarthy, Notre Dame, IN: University of Notre Dame Press, 335–63.

———. 1978 [1963]. *Theorie und Praxis. Sozialphilosophische Studien*, Frankfurt: Suhrkamp.

———. 1986 [1970]. "Hermeneutics and the Social Sciences." In *The Hermeneutics Reader: Texts of the German Tradition from the Enlightenment to the Present*, ed. Kurt Mueller-Vollmer, Oxford: Basil Blackwell, 293–319.

——. 1984 [1981]. *The Theory of Communicative Action*, vol. 1, *Reason and the Rationalization of Society*, trans. Thomas McCarthy, Boston: Beacon Press.

——. 1987 [1981]. *The Theory of Communicative Action*, vol. 2, *Lifeworld and System: A Critique of Functionalist Reason*, trans. Thomas McCarthy, Boston: Beacon Press.

——. 1989 [1962]. *The Structural Transformation of the Public Sphere*, trans. Thomas Burger, Cambridge, UK: Polity Press.

——. 1990. "Vorwort zur Neuauflage," *Strukturwandel der Öffentlichkeit*, Frankfurt: Suhrkamp.

——. 1991 [1986]. "A Reply." In *Communicative Action: Essays on Jürgen Habermas's "The Theory of Communicative Action*," ed. Axel Honneth and Hans Joas, Cambridge, UK: Polity Press, 214–94.

——. 1992. "Further Reflections on the Public Sphere." In *Habermas and the Public Sphere*, ed. Craig Calhoun, Cambridge, MA: MIT Press, 421–61.

——. 1996 [1992]. *Between Facts and Norms: Contributions to a Discourse Theory of Law and Democracy*, trans. William Rehg, Cambridge, MA: MIT Press.

Habermas, Jürgen and Joseph Ratzinger. 2004. *Dialektik der Säkularisierung. Über Vernunft und Religion*, ed. and with an introduction of Florian Schuller, Freiburg: Herder.

Hall, John, ed. 1995. *Civil Society: Theory, History, Comparison*, Boston: Polity Press.

Hallaq, Wael B. 1986. "On the Authoritativeness of Sunni Consensus." *International Journal of Middle East Studies*, 18: 427–54.

——. 1989. "The Use and Abuse of Evidence: The Question of Provincial and Roman Influence on Early Islamic Law." *Journal of the American Oriental Society*, 110: 79–91.

——. 2001. *Authority, Continuity, and Change in Islamic Law*, Cambridge: Cambridge University Press.

Heelas, Paul, Scott Lash, and Paul Morris, eds. 1996. *Detraditionalization: Critical Reflections on Authority and Identity at a Time of Uncertainty*, Cambridge, MA: Blackwell.

Hefner, Robert W. 2000. *Civil Islam: Muslims and Democratization in Indonesia*, Princeton: Princeton University Press.

Hennis, Wilhelm. 1987. *Max Webers Fragestellung: Studien Zur Biographie Des Werks*, Tübingen: Hans Mohr.

Henry, Paget. 2000. "Myth, Language, and Habermasian Rationality: Another Africana Contribution." In *Perspectives on Habermas*, ed. Lewis Edwin Hahn, Chicago and La Salle, IL: Open Court, 89–111.

Hobbes, Thomas. 1996 [1651]. *Leviathan*, ed. and with an introduction and notes by J. C. A. Gaskin, Oxford: Oxford University Press.

Hodgson, Marshall G. S. 1974, *The Venture of Islam. Conscience and History in a World Civilization*, vol. 1, *The Classical Age of Islam*, Chicago and London: University of Chicago Press.

Hoexter, Miriam. 2002. "The *Waqf* and the Public Sphere." In *The Public Sphere in Muslim Societies*, ed. Miriam Hoexter, Shmuel N. Eisenstadt, and Nehemia Levtzion, Albany, NY: SUNY Press, 119–38.

Hoexter, Miriam, and Nehemia Levtzion. 2002. "Introduction." In *The Public Sphere in Muslim Societies*, ed. Miriam Hoexter, Shmuel N. Eisenstadt, and Nehemia Levtzion, Albany, NY: SUNY Press, 9–16.

Höfert, Almut, and Armando Salvatore. 2000. "Introduction. Beyond the Clash of Civilisations: The Transcultural Politics between Europe and Islam." In

*Between Europe and Islam: Shaping Modernity in a Transcultural Space*, ed. Almut Höfert and Armando Salvatore, Brussels, Berlin, and Oxford: P.I.E.-Peter Lang, 13–35.

Hollis, Martin. 1998. *Trust Within Reason*, Cambridge, MA: Cambridge University Press.

Hollweck, Thomas A., and Ellis Sandoz. 1997. "General Introduction to the Series." *The History of Political Ideas*, vol. 1, *Hellenism, Rome, and Early Christianity*. In *The Collected Works of Eric Voegelin*, vol. 19, Columbia, MO: University of Missouri Press.

Hösle, Vittorio. 2001. "Moralphilosophische Erfahrungen mit soziologischen Relativismen. Anmerkungen zur Philosophie der Geschichte der Sozialwissenschaften." *Essener Unikate*, 16: 89–99.

Houston, Christopher. 2004. "Islam, Castoriadis and Autonomy." *Thesis Eleven*, no. 76: 49–69.

Humphreys, S. C. 1975. " 'Transcendence' and Intellectual Roles: The Ancient Greek Case." In *Daedalus (Wisdom, Revelation, and Doubt: Perspectives on the First Millennium B.C)* 104, 2: 91–118.

———. 1986. "Dynamics of the Greek Breakthrough: The Dialogue between Philosophy and Religion." In *The Origins and the Diversity of Axial Age Civilizations*, ed. Shmuel N. Eisenstadt, Albany, NY: SUNY Press, 92–110.

Hurvitz, Nimrod. 2002. "The *Mihna* (Inquisition) and the Public Sphere." In *The Public Sphere in Muslim Societies*, ed. Miriam Hoexter, Shmuel N. Eisenstadt, and Nehemia Levtzion, Albany, NY: SUNY Press, 17–29.

Hutcheson, Francis. 2002 [1728]. *An Essay on the Nature and Conduct of the Passions and Affections: With Illustrations on the Moral Sense*, ed. and with an introduction by Aaron Garrett, Indianapolis: Liberty Fund.

Hutter, Horst. 1978. *Politics as Friendship: The Origins of Classical Notions of Politics in the Theory and Practice of Friendship*, Waterloo, ON: Wilfrid Laurier University Press.

Israel, Jonathan I. 2001. *Radical Enlightenment: Philosophy and the Making of Modernity, 1650–1750*, Oxford and New York: Oxford University Press.

Jacobitti, Edmund E. 1983. "From Vico's Common Sense to Gramsci's Hegemony." In *Vico and Marx, Affinities and Contrasts*, ed. Giorgio Tagliacozzo, Atlantic Highlands: Humanities Press, 367–87.

———. 1996. "Community, Prereflective Virtue, and the Cyclopean Power of the Fathers: Vico's Reflections on Unintended Consequences." *Historical Reflections/Réfléxions Historiques* 22, 3: 495–515.

Jaspers, Karl. 1953 [1949]. *The Origin and Goal of History*, New Haven, NJ and London: Yale University Press.

Jensen, Henning. 1971. *Motivation and the Moral Sense in Francis Hutcheson's Ethical Theory*, The Hague: Martinus Nijhoff.

Joas, Hans. 1991 [1986]. "The Unhappy Marriage of Hermeneutics and Functionalism." In *Communicative Action: Essays on Jürgen Habermas's "The Theory of Communicative Action,"* ed. Axel Honneth and Hans Joas, Cambridge, UK: Polity Press, 97–118.

Jonsen, Albert R., and Stephen Toulmin. 1988. *The Abuse of Casuistry: A History of Moral Reasoning*, Berkeley and Los Angeles: University of California Press.

Juynboll, Gautier H. A. 1983. *Muslim Tradition: Studies in Chronology, Provenance and Authorship of Early Hadith*, Cambridge and New York: Cambridge University Press.
———. 1987. "Some Ideas on the Development of Sunna as a Technical Term in Early Islam." *Jerusalem Studies of Arabic and Islam* 10: 97–118.
———. 1996. *Studies on the Origins and Uses of Islamic Hadith*, Brookfield, VT: Variorum.
Kallscheuer, Otto. 1994. *Gottes Wort und Volkes Stimme, Glaube Macht Politik*, Frankfurt: Fischer.
Kant, Immanuel. 1963 [1784]. "What is Enlightenment?" In *On History*, ed. and with an introduction by Lewis White Beck, Indianapolis: Bobbs-Merrill, 3–10.
———. 1983 [1795]. "Zum ewigen Frieden, Anhang II: Von der Einhelligkeit der Politik mit der Moral nach dem transzendentalen Begriffe des öffentlichen Rechts." In *Werke*, vol. 9, Darmstadt: Wissenschaftliche Buchgesellschaft, 244–51.
Kelly, Michael. 1989–1990. "MacIntyre, Habermas, and Philosophical Ethics." *The Philosophical Forum* 21, 1–2: 70–93.
Knight, Kelvin. 1998. "Introduction." In *The MacIntyre Reader*, ed. Kelvin Knight, Notre Dame, IN: University of Notre Dame Press, 1–27.
Kippenberg, Hans G. 1996. "Warum Émile Durkheim den Individualismus der arbeitsteiligen Gesellschaft religionsgeschichtlich einordnete." *Zeitschrift für Religionswissenschaft*, 4: 113–34.
Kirner, Guido O. 2001. "Polis und Gemeinwohl. Zum Gemeinwohlbegriff in Athen vom 6. bis 4. Jahrhundert v. Chr." In *Gemeinwohl und Gemeinsinn*, vol. 1, *Historische Semantiken politischer Leitbegriffe*, ed. Herfried Münkler and Harald Bluhm, Berlin: Akademie Verlag, 31–63.
Koselleck, Reinhart. 1988 [1959]. *Critique and Crisis: Enlightenment and the Pathogenesis of Modern Society*, trans. Maria Santos, Oxford: Berg.
Krippke, Samuel. 1982. *Wittgenstein on Rules and Private Language*, Oxford: Basil Blackwell.
Leites, Edmund, ed. 1988. *Conscience and Casuistry in Early Modern Europe*, Cambridge: Cambridge University Press.
LeVine, Mark, and Armando Salvatore. 2005. "Socio-Religious Movements and the Transformation of 'Common Sense' into a Politics of 'Common Good.'" In *Religion, Social Practice, and Contested Hegemonies: Reconstructing the Public Sphere in Muslim Majority Societies*, ed. Armando Salvatore and Mark LeVine, New York: Palgrave Macmillan, 29–56.
Levtzion, Nehemia. 2002. "The Dynamics of Sufi Brotherhoods." In *The Public Sphere in Muslim Societies*, ed. Miriam Hoexter, Shmuel N. Eisenstadt, and Nehemia Levtzion, Albany, NY: SUNY Press, 109–18.
Lilla, Mark. 1993. *Vico. The Making of an Anti-Modern*, Cambridge, MA and London: Harvard University Press.
Luckmann, Thomas. 1967. *The Invisible Religion. The Problem of Religion in Modern Society*, New York: Macmillan.
Luhmann, Niklas. 1995. "Kausalität im Süden." *Soziale Systeme*, 1: 7–28.
———. 1998. *Die Gesellschaft der Gesellschaft*, Frankfurt: Suhrkamp.
MacIntyre, Alasdair. 1984 [1981]. *After Virtue. A Study in Moral Theory*, Notre Dame, IN: University of Notre Dame Press.

MacIntyre, Alasdair. 1988. *Whose Justice? Which Rationality?* London: Duckworth.

———. 1990. *Three Rival Versions of Moral Enquiry: Encyclopaedia, Genealogy, and Tradition*, London: Duckworth.

———. 1994. "The Theses on Feuerbach: A Road not Taken." In *Artifacts, Representations, and Social Practice: Essays for Marx Wartofsky*, ed. Carol C. Gould and Robert S. Cohen, Dordrecht: Kluwer, 223–34.

———. 1998 [1997]. "Politics, Philosophy and the Common Good." In *The MacIntyre Reader*, ed. Kelvin Knight, Notre Dame, IN: University of Notre Dame Press, 235–52.

Makdisi, George. 1974. "The Hanbali School and Sufism." In *Humaniora Islamica*, vol. 2, ed. Herbert W. Mason, Ronald L. Nettler, Jacques Waardenburg and Merlin L. Swartz, The Hague and Paris: Mouton, 61–72.

———. 1983. "Institutionalized Learning as a Self-Image of Islam." In *Islam's Understanding of Itself*, ed. Richard G. Hovannisian and Speros Vryonis Jr., Malibu, CA: Undena, 73–85.

Mann, Michael. 1986. *The Sources of Social Power*, vol. 1, *A History of Power from the Beginning to A.D. 1760*, Cambridge: Cambridge University Press.

Mardin, Sherif. 1995. "Civil Society and Islam." In *Civil Society: Theory, History, Comparison*, ed. John Hall, Boston: Polity Press, 278–300.

Margolis, Joseph. 1999. "Pierre Bourdieu: *Habitus* and the Logic of Practice." In *Bourdieu: A Critical Reader*, ed. Richard Shusterman, Oxford: Blackwell, 64–83.

Marmura, Michael E. 1983. "The Islamic Philosophers' Conception of Islam." In *Islam's Understanding of Itself*, ed. Richard G. Hovannisian and Speros Vryonis Jr., Malibu, CA: Undena, 87–102.

Masud, M. Khalid. 1995 [1977]. *Shatibi's Philosophy of Islamic Law*, Kuala Lumpur: Islamic Book Trust.

———. 2005. "Communicative Action and the Social Construction of Shari'a in Pakistan." In *Religion, Social Practice, and Contested Hegemonies: Reconstructing the Public Sphere in Muslim Majority Societies*, ed. Armando Salvatore and Mark LeVine, New York: Palgrave Macmillan, 155–79.

Mauss, Marcel. 1985 [1938]. "A Category of the Human Mind: The Notion of Person; The Notion of Self." In *The Category of the Person*, ed. Michael Carrithers, Steven Collins, and Steven Lukes, New York: Cambridge University Press, 1–25.

Mazlish, Bruce. 2001. "Civilization in an Historical and Global Perspective," *International Sociology* 16, 3: 293–300.

Mazzotta, Giuseppe. 1999. *The New Map of the World. The Poetic Philosophy of Giambattista Vico*. Princeton: Princeton University Press.

McGee, Michael Calvin. 1998. "Phronesis in the Habermas vs. Gadamer Debate." In *Judgement Calls: Rhetoric, Politics, and Indeterminacy*, ed. J. M. Sloop and J. P. McDaniel, Boulder, CO: Westview, 13–41.

Mendieta, Eduardo. 2000. "Modernity's Religion: Habermas and the Linguistification of the Sacred." In *Perspectives on Habermas*, ed. Lewis Edwin Hahn, Chicago and La Salle, IL: Open Court, 123–38.

Merlo, Grado Giovanni. 1997. "Storia di frate Francesco e dell'Ordine dei Minori." In *Francesco d'Assisi e il primo secolo di storia francescana*, ed. Maria Pia Alberzoni et al., Torino: Einaudi, 3–32.

Milbank, John. 1990. *Theology and Social Theory. Beyond Secular Reason.* Oxford: Blackwell.

——. 1997. *The World Made Strange.* Oxford: Blackwell.

Milbank, John, and Catherine Pickstock. 2001. *Truth in Aquinas.* London and New York: Routledge.

Miner, Robert C. 2002. *Vico, Genealogist of Modernity.* Notre Dame, IN: University of Notre Dame Press.

Morrison, James C. 1980. "Vico and Spinoza." *Journal of the History of Ideas* 16: 49–68.

Münkler, Herfried, and Harald Bluhm. 2001. "Einleitung: Gemeinwohl und Gemeinsinn als politisch-soziale Leitbegriffe." In *Gemeinwohl und Gemeinsinn*, vol. 1, *Historische Semantiken politischer Leitbegriffe*, ed. Herfried Münkler and Harald Bluhm, Berlin: Akademie Verlag, 9–30.

Münkler, Herfried, and Karsten Fischer. 2002. "Common Good and Civic Spirit in the Welfare State." *Journal of Political Philosophy* 10, 4: 416–38.

Nallino, Carlo Alfonso. 1942. "Sul libro siro-romano e sul presunto diritto siriaco." In *Raccolta di scritti editi e inediti*, vol. 4, *Diritto musulmano. Diritti orientali cristiani*, ed. Maria Nallino, Rome: Istituto per l'Oriente.

Nashi, Mohamed. 2004. "The Articulation of the 'I,' 'We' and the 'Person': Elements for an Anthropological Approach within Western and Islamic Contexts." In *Standing Trial: Law and the Person in the Modern Middle East*, ed. Baudouin Dupret, London and New York: I. B. Tauris.

Negt, Oskar, and Alexander Kluge. 1993 [1972]. *The Public Sphere and Experience*, University of Minnesota Press.

Nelson, Benjamin. 1969 [1949]. *The Idea of Usury. From Tribal Brotherhood to Universal Otherhood*, Chicago and London: The University of Chicago Press.

——. 1976. "Vico and Comparative Historical Civilizational Sociology." *Social Research* 43, 4: 874–81.

——. 1981. *On the Road to Modernity*, Totowa, NJ: Rowman & Littlefield.

Opwis, Felicitas. 2005. "*Maslaha* in Contemporary Islamic Legal Theory." *Islamic Law and Society* 12, 2: 182–223.

Pagden, Anthony. 1988. "The Destruction of Trust and Its Economic Consequences in the Case of Eighteenth-Century Naples." In *Trust. Making and Breaking of Cooperative Relations*, ed. Diego Gambetta, New York and Oxford: Basil Blackwell, 127–41.

Piattoni, Simona. 1998. " 'Virtuous Clientelism': The Southern Question Resolved?" In *Italy's "Southern Question": Orientalism in One Country*, ed. Jane Schneider, New York: Berg, 225–43.

Pocock J. G. A. 1975. *The Machiavellian Moment: Florentine Political Thought and the Atlantic Republican Tradition.* Princeton: Princeton University Press.

Pollock, Sheldon. 1998. "India in the Vernacular Millennium: Literary Culture and Polity, 1000–1500." *Daedalus* 127, 3: 41–74.

Prandini, Riccardo. 1997. "La fiducia come forma di fede. Alcune riflessioni introduttive ad un problema sociologico." *Iride* 20: 105–25.

Preus, J. Samuel. 1989. "Spinoza, Vico, and the Imagination of Religion." *Journal of the History of Ideas* 50: 71–93.

Putnam, Robert D. 1993. *Making Democracy Work: Civic Traditions in Modern Italy*, Princeton: Princeton University Press.

Raaflaub, Kurt A. 2005. "Polis, 'the Political,' and 'Political Thought': New Departures in Ancient Greece, ca. 800–500 BCE." In *Axial Civilizations and World History*, ed. Johann P. Arnason, Shmuel N. Eisenstadt, and Björn Wittrock, Leiden and Boston: Brill, 253–83.

Rahimi, Babak. 2006. "The Middle Period Islamic Axiality in the Age of Afro-Eurasian Transcultural Hybridity." In *Islam in Process: Historical and Civilizational Perspectives*, vol. 7, *Yearbook of the Sociology of Islam*, ed. Johann P. Arnason, Armando Salvatore, and Georg Stauth, Bielefeld: Transcript; New Brunswick, NJ: Transaction, 48–67.

Rahman, Fazlur. 1979 [1966]. *Islam*, Chicago and London: University of Chicago Press.

Raphael, D. D., and A. L. Macfie. 1976. "Introduction." *The Theory of Moral Sentiment*, by Adam Smith, Oxford: Clarendon Press, 1–52.

Rigon, Antonio. 1997. "Frati Minori e società locali." In *Francesco d'Assisi e il primo secolo di storia francescana*, ed. Maria Pia Alberzoni et al., Torino: Einaudi, 259–81.

Robertson, Roland. 1970. *The Sociological Interpretation of Religion*, Oxford; Basil Blackwell.

Rosenthal, Franz. 1965. *Das Fortleben der Antike im Islam*, Zürich and Stuttgart: Artemis.

Rudnick Luft, Sandra. 1994. "The Secularization of Origins in Vico and Nietzsche." *The Personalist Forum* 10, 2: 133–48.

———. 2003. *Vico's Uncanny Humanism: Reading the New Science between Modern and Postmodern*, Ithaca, NY: Cornell University Press.

Sadri, Ahmad. 1992. *Max Weber's Sociology of Intellectuals*, New York and Oxford: Oxford University Press.

Said, Edward. 1975. *Beginnings*, Baltimore: Johns Hopkins University Press.

Salvatore Armando. 1996. "Beyond Orientalism? Max Weber and the Displacements of 'Essentialism' in the Study of Islam." *Arabica. Revue d'Études Arabes/ Journal of Arab Studies* 43, 3: 412–33.

———. 1997. *Islam and the Political Discourse of Modernity*, Reading, UK: Ithaca Press.

———. 2001. "Introduction: The Problem of the Ingraining of Civilizing Traditions into Social Governance." In *Muslim Traditions and Modern Techniques of Power*, vol. 3, *Yearbook of the Sociology of Islam*, ed. Armando Salvatore, Hamburg: LIT; New Brunswick, NJ: Transaction, 9–42.

———. 2006. "Public Religion, Ethics of Participation, and Cultural Dialogue: Islam in Europe." In *Contemporary Islam: Dynamic, not Static*, ed. Abdul Aziz Said, Mohammed Abu-Nimer, and Meena Sharify-Funk, London and New York: Routledge, 83–100.

Salvatore, Armando, and Schirin Amir-Moazami. 2002. "Religiöse Diskurstraditionen. Zur Transformation des Islam in kolonialen, postkolonialen und europäischen Öffentlichkeiten." *Berliner Journal für Soziologie* 13, 3: 309–30.

Salvatore, Armando, and Dale F. Eickelman, eds. 2004. *Public Islam and Common Good*, Leiden and Boston: Brill.

Salvatore, Armando, and Mark LeVine, eds. 2005. *Religion, Social Practice, Contested Hegemonies: Reconstructing the Public Sphere in Muslim Majority Societies*, New York: Palgrave Macmillan.

Sandel, Michael J. 1984. "The Procedural Republic and the Unencumbered Self." *Political Theory* 12, 1: 81–96.

Santoro, Emilio. 2003 [1999]. *Autonomy, Freedom and Rights. A Critique of Liberal Subjectivity*, Dordrecht: Kluwer.

Schacht, Joseph. 1950 [1935]. *The Origins of Muhammadan Jurisprudence*, Oxford: Oxford University Press.

———. 1957. "Droit byzantin et droit musulman." *Atti dei Convegni, Accademia Nazionale dei Lincei, Fondazione Alessandro Volta*, vol. 12, Rome: Accademia Nazionale dei Lincei.

Schatzki, Theodore R. 2001. "Introduction: Practice Theory." In *The Practice Turn in Contemporary Theory*, ed. Theodore R. Schatzki, Karin Knorr Cetina, and Eike von Savigny, 1–14.

Schluchter, Wolfgang. 1987. "Einleitung. Zwischen Welteroberung und Weltanpassung. Überlegungen zu Max Webers Sicht des frühen Islams." In *Max Webers Sicht Des Islams*, ed. Wolfgang Schluchter, Frankfurt: Suhrkamp, 11–24.

Schnädelbach, Herbert. 1986. "Transformation der kritischen Theorie." In *Kommunikatives Handeln. Beiträge zu Jürgen Habermas' "Theorie des kommunikativen Handelns,"* ed. Axel Honneth and Hans Joas, Frankfurt Suhrkamp, 15–34.

Schwartz, Benjamin I. 1975. "The Age of Transcendence." In *Wisdom, Revelation, and Doubt: Perspectives on the First Millennium B.C., Daedalus* 104, 2: 1–7.

Seligman, Adam B. 1992. *The Idea of Civil Society*, New York: Free Press.

———. 1997. *The Problem of Trust*, Princeton University Press. Princeton.

———. 2000. *Modernity's Wager: Authority, the Self, and Transcendence*, Princeton: Princeton University Press.

Sennett, Richard. 1978. *The Fall of Public Man: On the Social Psychology of Capitalism*, New York: Vintage.

Shils, Edward. 1981. *Tradition*, London and Boston: Faber and Faber.

Shotter, John. 1996. *Vico, Wittgenstein, and Bakhtin: "Practical Trust" in Dialogical Communities*, paper presented to the conference "Democracy and Trust," Georgetown University, November 7–9.

Silver, Alan. 1989. "Friendship and Trust as Moral Ideas: Historical Approach." *European Journal of Sociology*, 30: 274–97.

———. 1997. "Two Different Sorts of Commerce—Friendship and Strangership in Civil Society." In *Public and Private in Thought and Practice: Perspectives on a Grand Dichotomy*, ed. Jeff Weintraub and Krishan Kumar, Chicago: University Press of Chicago, 43–74.

Smith, Adam. 1853 [1759]. *The Theory of Moral Sentiments; or an Essay towards an Analysis of the Principles by Which Men Naturally Judge concerning the Conduct and Character, First of Their Neighbours, and afterwards of Themselves*, London: Henry G. Bohn.

Smith, Wilfred Cantwell. 1962. *The Meaning and End of Religion*, New York: Macmillan.

Somers, Margaret. 1995. "What's Political or Cultural about Political Culture and the Public Sphere? Toward an Historical Sociology of Concept Formation." *Sociological Theory* 13, 2: 113–44.

———. 1998. " 'Citizenship' zwischen Staat und Markt. Das Konzept der Zivilgesellschaft und das Problem der 'dritten Sphäre.' " *Berliner Journal für Soziologie* 9, 4: 489–505.

Spinoza, Benedict. 1951 [1670]. *A Theologico-Political Treatise* and *A Political Treatise*, trans. and with an introduction by R. H. M. Elwes, New York: Dover.

Stauth, Georg. 1993. *Islam und Westlicher Rationalismus. Der Beitrag des Orientalismus zur Entstehung der Soziologie*, Frankfurt und New York: Campus.

Stauth, Georg. 1998. "Nachwort: Geschichte, Modernität, Fundamentalismus. Eisenstadts zivilisationstheoretischer Ansatz zum vergleichenden Studium moderner fundamentalisticher Bewegungen." In *Die Antinomien der Moderne. Die jakobinischen Grundzüge der Moderne und des Fundamentalismus. Heterodoxien, Utopismus und Jakobinismus in der Konstitution fundamentalistischer Bewegungen*, ed. Shmuel N. Eisenstadt, Frankfurt: Suhrkamp.

Stone, Harold Samuel. 1997. *Vico's Cultural History. The Production and Transmission of Ideas in Naples, 1685–1750*, Leiden and Boston: Brill.

Strauss, Leo. 1965. *Spinoza's Critique of Religion*. New York: Schocken.

Stroumsa, Guy G. 2005. "Cultural Memory in Early Christianity: Clement of Alexandria and the History of Religions." In *Axial Civilizations and World History*, ed. Johann P. Arnason, Shmuel N. Eisenstadt, and Björn Wittrock, Leiden and Boston: Brill, 295–317.

Szakolczai, Arpad. 1998. *Max Weber and Michel Foucault. Parallel Life-Works*, London: Routledge.

———. 2001a. "Civilization and Its Sources." *International Sociology* 16, 3: 369–86.

———. 2001b. "Eric Voegelin's *History of Political Ideas*." *European Journal of Social Theory* 4, 3: 351–68.

———. 2003. *The Genesis of Modernity*. London and New York: Routledge.

Tagliacozzo, Giorgio, ed. 1983. *Vico and Marx, Affinities and Contrasts*, Atlantic Highlands, NJ: Humanities Press.

Tarot, Camille. 1993. *De Durkheim à Mauss: l'invention du symbolique*, Paris: Découverte.

Taylor, Charles. 1990. "Modes of Civil Society." *Public Culture* 3: 95–118.

———. 1993. "Modernity and the Rise of the Public Sphere." In *The Tanner Lectures on Human Values*, 14, ed. Grethe B. Peterson, Salt Lake City: University of Utah Press, 203–60.

———. 1999 [1993]. "To Follow a Rule . . ." In *Bourdieu: A Critical Reader*, ed. Richard Shusterman, Oxford: Blackwell, 29–44.

Thévenot, Laurent. 2001. "Pragmatic Regimes Governing the Engagement with the World." In *The Practice Turn in Contemporary Theory*, ed. Theodore R. Schatzki, Karin Knorr Cetina, and Eike von Savigny, London and New York: Routledge, 56–73.

Tönnies, Ferdinand. 2001 [1887]. *Community and Civil Society*, ed. Jose Harris, trans. Jose Harris and Margaret Hollis, Cambridge: Cambridge University Press.

Tooker, Deborah E. 1992. "Identity Systems in Highland Burma: Belief, *Akha zan* and a Critique of Interiorized Notions of Ethno-Religious Identity." *Man* 27, 4: 799–820.

Tosel, André, 1985. "La théorie de la pratique et la fonction de l'opinion publique dans la philosophie politique de Spinoza," *Studia Spinozana* 1, 183—208.

Turner, Bryan S. 1991. *Religion and Social Theory*, London: Sage.

———. 1992. "Preface to the Second Edition." In *Professional Ethics and Civic Morals*, by Emile Durkheim, London: Routledge, xiii-xlii.

van der Veer, Peter, and Hartmut Lehmann. 1999. "Introduction." In *Nation and Religion. Perspectives on Europe and Asia*, ed. Peter van der Veer and Hartmut Lehmann, Princeton: Princeton University Press, 3–14.

Vico, Giambattista. 1999 [1744]. *New Science. Principles of the New Science concerning the Common Nature of the Nations*, 3rd ed., trans. David Marsh, London: Penguin.

Virno, Paolo. 2002 [2001]. *Grammatica della moltitudine. Per una analisi delle forme di vita contemporanee*, Roma: DeriveApprodi.

Voegelin, Eric. 1956. *Order and History*, vol. 1, *Israel and Revelation*, Baton Rouge: Louisiana State University Press.

———. 1994. *Das Volk Gottes*, München: Wilhelm Fink.

———. 1997a. *The History of Political Ideas*, vol. 1, *Hellenism, Rome, and Early Christianity*, in *The Collected Works of Eric Voegelin*, vol. 19, ed. and with an introduction by Athanasios Moulakis, Columbia, MO: University of Missouri Press.

———. 1997b. *The History of Political Ideas*, vol. 2, *The Middle Ages to Aquinas*, in *The Collected Works of Eric Voegelin*, vol. 20, ed. and with an introduction by Peter von Sivers, Columbia, MO: University of Missouri Press.

———. 1998a. *The History of Political Ideas*, vol. 4, *Renaissance and Reformation*, in *The Collected Works of Eric Voegelin*, vol. 22, ed. and with an introduction by David L. Morse and William M. Thompson, Columbia, MO: University of Missouri Press.

———. 1998b. *The History of Political Ideas*, vol. 6, *Revolution and the New Science*, in *The Collected Works of Eric Voegelin*, vol. 24, ed. and with an introduction by Barry Cooper, Columbia, MO: University of Missouri Press.

———. 1999. *The History of Political Ideas*, vol. 7, *The New Order and Last Orientation*, in *The Collected Works of Eric Voegelin*, vol. 25, ed. and with an introduction by Jürgen Gebhardt and Thomas A. Hollweck, Columbia, MO: University of Missouri Press.

Waardenburg, Jacques. 1989. "La personne au-deçà et au-delà de l'Islam." *Arabica. Revue d'Études Arabes/Journal of Arab Studies* 36, 2: 143–62.

Walker Bynum, Caroline. 1987. "Mystik und Askese im Leben mittelalterlicher Frauen: Einige Bemerkungen zu den Typologien von Max Weber und Ernst Troeltsch." In *Max Webers Sicht des okzidentalen Christentums: Interpretation und Kritik*, ed. Wolfgang Schluchter, Frankfurt: Suhrkamp, 355–82.

Walzer, Michael. 1968. "Puritanism as a Revolutionary Ideology." In *The Protestant Ethic and Modernization*, ed. Shmuel N. Eisenstadt, New York and London: Basic Books, 109–34.

Warner, Michael. 1992. "The Mass Public and the Mass Subject." In *Habermas and the Public Sphere*, ed. Craig Calhoun, Cambridge, MA: MIT Press.

Warner, Michael. 2002. *Publics and Counterpublics*, New York: Zone Books.

Weintraub, Jeff. 1992. "Democracy and the Market: A Marriage of Inconvenience." In *From Leninism to Freedom: The Challenges of Democratization*, ed. Margaret L. Nugent, Boulder, CO: Westview.

———. 1997. "The Theory and Politics of the Private/Public Distinction." In *Public and Private in Thought and Practice: Perspectives on a Grand Dichotomy*, ed. Jeff Weintraub and Krishan Kumar, Chicago: University Press of Chicago, 1–42.

Winch, Peter. 1958. *The Idea of a Social Science and Its Relation to Philosophy*, London: Routledge and Keagan Paul.

Wittgenstein, Ludwig. 1974 [1953]. *Philosophical Investigations*, Oxford: Blackwell.

Wittrock, Björn. 2001. "Social Theory and Global History. The Periods of Cultural Crystallization." *Thesis Eleven*, no. 65: 27–50.

———. 2005. "The Meaning of the Axial Age." In *Axial Civilizations and World History*, ed. Johann P. Arnason, Shmuel N. Eisenstadt, and Björn Wittrock, Leiden and Boston: Brill, 53–85.

Zaman, Muhammad Qasim. 2004. "The 'Ulama' of Contemporary Islam and Their Conceptions of the Common Good." In *Public Islam and the Common Good*, ed. Armando Salvatore and Dale F. Eickelman, Leiden and Boston: Brill, 129–55.

# INDEX

*Translation is provided for words in Arabic*

Abraham, 134, 229; *see also* traditions,
     Abrahamic
accountability, 58, 101; *see also*
     responsibility
     of rulers to God, 53, 58
     action, 2, 5, 9, 12, 40
     communicative, 2, 5, 9–10, 12, 17,
          19–21, 27–8, 37–8, 40, 43
     consequences of, 11
     contingency of, 29
     creative, 38
     prudential, 78; *see also phronesis*
     telic-phronetic, 39, 78, 93, 98
     types of, 2, 19, 104, 142
     voluntary, 110, 116–20
administrative steering, 4, 44,
     239
Adorno, Theodor, 32
*aequum bonum*, 187
*agòn*, 65, 78, 189, 209, 249
*agorà*, 65, 110, 201, 226, 255
alienation, 35, 45–7, 191
Alighieri, Dante, 114
altar, 193, 202–3
*amor sui*, 116, 219
Apel, Karl Otto, 76, 87, 185, 253
Aquinas, 19, 109, 114–24, 129, 145, 159,
     166–7, 170, 174–8, 181, 185, 189,
     200, 208, 263, 264
Arabic, 16, 134, 150, 163, 227–8
Arendt, Hanna, 42
Aristotle, 66–7, 114, 116–17, 120, 167,
     204, 207–8, 251–2, 282
Arnason, Johann P., 39, 51–2, 60, 102, 111
Asad, Talal, 48, 72, 83, 85, 90, 126
Assmann, Jan, 8, 56–7

associations, 130, 238
     civic, 150
     urban, 149
asylum, 202–7, 227
Athens, 49, 62–6, 110, 202, 282
audience, 31, 121, 126, 209, 222
Augustine, 84–5, 104–5, 110–11, 119,
     124, 170, 185
authoritarianism, 4–5, 109, 118, 129,
     206, 208, 227
authority, 9, 11–12, 17, 19–21, 26–8, 34,
     44, 51–2, 55–7, 61, 70, 79–80, 83,
     85, 87, 95, 106, 113, 117–18, 123–4,
     130, 134, 136, 140, 149–51, 153, 159,
     169–70, 178, 183, 188, 191,
     197–201, 205, 207, 217, 227, 230,
     245, 252, 254, 257, 259, 265, 266
     foundations of, 27
     imperial, 123, 129
     papal, 106–8, 123, 129, 175
     patriarchal, 201–7, 217
     political, 128, 147
     as property, 198–9
     religious, 21, 34, 101–2, 126, 129–30
autonomy, 5, 22, 215, 220
     collective, 3, 44
axial/Axial, 15, 21, 40, 49, 52, 54, 58,
     94, 122
     Age, 60, 70, 243, 262
     Age theory, 15–17, 28, 49, 51–60,
          70–1, 83, 99, 102, 111, 190,
          193–4, 207
     breakthrough, 2, 22, 28, 40–1, 45,
          49, 52–8, 60–2, 64–5, 69–70,
          72, 82, 91, 93–4, 99, 104, 107,
          109–11

axial/Axial—*continued*
  civilizations, 17–18, 33, 52, 58, 62, 66, 94, 99, 101, 133
  Enlightenment, 21, 29
  genealogy, 22
  pre-axial, 54, 56, 58–9, 63, 65, 91, 94, 185, 190, 192, 218, 226, 227, 230, 243
  Renaissance, 18–19, 57, 62, 66, 99, 110, 111–28
  traditions, 12, 49, 83, 110, 119

Bacon, Francis, 186, 190
Baghdad, 145, 147
Bellah, Robert N., 47, 261
Benedict of Norcia, 108, 124
Berger, Peter, 46–8, 72
Bernard of Clairvaux, 124
Bible, 195–9
body, 92, 125, 151, 191
Bonaventura of Bagnoregio, 117, 123–4
Bonifacius VIII, 129
Brown, Peter, 135–7
Bourdieu, Pierre, 39–40, 77, 88–98, 165, 262
bourgeoisie, 211
brotherhoods, 18, 130, 149–54
Buber, Martin, 40, 60

Calhoun, Craig, 2, 57, 88–90, 98
Caliphate, 137, 147, 152, 153, 265
Calvinism, 246, 264
capitalism, 3, 7, 20, 25, 28, 34, 43–4, 217–18, 239–40, 249, 256, 264
  mercantile, 118
  welfarist, 234
*caritas*, 103–4, 109–14, 120–3, 126–7, 130, 154–8, 179, 183, 195, 218–19, 230
charisma, 24, 101, 108, 122, 128, 139, 169
  prophetic, 59, 86, 138–9, 150
Christ, 109, 124, 127, 128
Church, 18, 85, 104–8, 112, 124, 127–9, 141, 150, 152, 173, 175, 176, 179, 264
Cicero, 103–4, 107, 158

cities, 129, 177
  autonomous, 109
  origin of, 202, 205
citizenship, 97, 103, 238, 256
  participatory, 239
civic virtue, 130, 210, 236, 240; *see also* public virtue
civility, 36, 46, 112, 203, 213, 238–9, 254
civil society, 1, 3–4, 7, 41–2, 97, 190, 192, 199, 216, 220, 223–5, 235–9, 251, 254, 264, 266
  bourgeois, 5, 238
  liberal, 4, 257
  as *societas civilis*, 216
  theory, 20, 206, 213, 219
*civitas Dei*, 104, 107–9, 122, 136, 170, 177
*civitas terrena*, 104, 108–9, 122, 170, 177
class, 8, 9, 26, 58, 126, 130, 153, 205–6, 209, 211, 216, 222
  commercial, 130
  landowning, 224
  middle, 112
  popular, 112, 153
  ruling, 52
  scholarly, 57–8, 85, 139, 145, 165
  struggle, 198–9, 203–4, 207, 217
  urban, 127
clerics, 53, 57–8, 69, 85, 99, 102, 177, 178, 247; *see also* class, scholarly
collective identity, 48, 63–4, 92, 95, 97, 177, 240
colonialism, 210, 232, 238, 242
commercial society, 213, 221, 235, 247
commoner, 2, 82, 85, 87, 89, 91, 99–100, 108, 112, 122–3, 127–8, 129, 136, 139, 141, 146, 148–50, 153, 155, 161, 163, 165, 166, 169–70, 183, 195, 205, 208
  as *idiota*, 128, 136
  urban, 109, 128
common good, 2, 9, 15–16, 41, 43, 62, 80, 100, 108–9, 113, 116, 118, 140, 154–60, 166–70, 171, 173, 181, 183–4, 196, 198–202, 206, 209,

212, 216–21, 234–40, 244, 248, 250–1, 253, 257–8
  as power sharing, 181; *see also maslaha* and *res publica*
common sense, 30, 90–92, 95, 161, 163, 166–7, 174, 184, 191–8, 207, 212, 216, 220
communitarianism, 7, 36, 66–7, 94, 115, 117, 251, 255, 257, 261, 264
community, 50–4, 67, 70, 83–6, 91, 101–7, 113–16, 120–8, 136, 164, 223
  as *communitas*, 231
  Islamic, 133–4, 137–40, 143, 148, 154, 168–9, 265; *see also umma*
  primordial, 164
  of salvation, 86
*conatus*, 184, 191, 195
confession, 111, 127, 128
confidence, 217, 229, 231–3, 254
connectivity, 26, 34, 37–40, 44, 48, 54, 58, 60–1, 65–6, 70, 72, 76, 83, 96, 99–104, 109–10, 125, 127, 133, 136, 148, 162, 170, 178, 243, 255
consensus, 43–4, 46, 73, 96, 112, 140–1, 144–6, 148–51, 156, 158, 160, 170, 222, 239, 253–4, 258–9, 265; *see also ijma'*
constructivism, 23–4
contractualism, 180, 186–8, 194, 210, 215–16
conversion, 85, 102, 111, 124, 134–5, 151, 226
Counterreformation, Catholic, 197
Covenant
  biblical, 53–6
  Hobbesian, 218–19
creativity, 24, 39, 53, 61, 70–1, 78, 81, 90, 135, 140–2, 162, 177, 182–4, 189, 192, 195–8, 208, 211, 215–16, 243
critical theory, 4, 32
*cuius regio eius religio*, 196
custom, 43, 96, 112, 161–2, 167, 170, 187, 194, 207, 245

deconstructivism, 14, 23–4, 31–2, 70, 248
deliberation, 3, 43, 63, 117, 120, 131, 160, 162, 217, 222, 237, 239, 253, 255, 256
  collective, 3, 232, 236, 240
democracy, 7, 18, 62, 64, 240
  mass, 219
democratic politics, 1, 3, 25, 218, 235, 240, 256
democratization, 1, 5, 31
*demos*, 244
devil, 126, 135
de Vitoria, Francisco, 16, 200
Dewey, John, 96
dialectics, 32, 45
  Hegelian, 29, 238, 247
  between inwardness and publicness, 6–8, 11, 14–15, 256, 271
  between orthodoxies and heterodoxies, 55, 61
dialogue, 65, 73–5, 78, 91, 95, 127, 189, 197, 201, 254, 260
*din* (in Islamic theology, the relation between man and God, religion), 143–4
disagreement, 65, 83, 122, 140–1, 145, 152, 169–70, 199
  moral, 221, 224, 239
discipline, 24, 55, 61, 127, 136, 144, 148–9, 220, 237, 239, 248, 258
  as monastic *disciplina*, 85, 112, 123, 125–6
divination, 30, 91, 185, 193
Dominicans, 115, 121–4, 127, 129, 197, 264
*doxa*, 55, 93, 265
Durkheim, Emile, 45–51, 75, 77, 84, 194, 232

*ecclesia*, 104, 106, 128
ecumenic
  age, 113
  renaissance, 11

education, 65, 66, 81, 84, 111–12, 117, 124, 125, 136, 151, 153, 190

*ego-alter* relationship, 9, 27, 39–40, 54–5, 60–1, 97, 111, 114, 120, 144, 179, 202, 204, 215, 220–1, 224–5, 228, 231, 233, 236, 240, 247–8, 254–5

Eisenstadt, Shmuel N., 2, 33, 58, 133–4, 251, 261

Elias, Norbert, 7, 33, 96, 263

elites, 39, 50, 52, 55, 117, 123–4, 129, 146, 148, 152–3, 165–6, 182

empire/Empire, 102–3, 108, 134, 244
 Ottoman, 152, 153, 155
 Roman, 102, 105, 107
 Sacred Roman, 105

England, 223, 232, 238

Enlightenment, 2, 5–6, 17–19, 21–4, 26–9, 32, 43, 70, 105, 119, 178, 182, 199, 228, 235–6, 238, 243, 250, 259, 261
 Axial, 21, 29, 183, 243–4
 Radical, 21, 29
 Scottish, 20, 216, 219, 221, 228, 232–3, 236–9, 247

equality, 101, 107, 143, 204–6

equity, 30, 157, 200, 205, 208
 as *aequitas*, 210

ethics, 63, 78, 87, 97, 182, 196
 discourse, 43, 87, 95, 253

exhortation, 53, 55–6, 58, 60, 65, 83–4, 86, 91, 94–5, 100–1, 126, 134–5, 165, 183, 192, 195, 221

Exodus (biblical), 54, 56, 58

faith, 9, 11, 21, 50, 55, 60, 81, 83, 84, 97, 102, 113, 116, 118, 122, 127, 130, 134, 186, 203, 215, 216, 224–31, 234, 241, 245–6, 253, 256
 as *fidelitas*, 175
 as *fides*, 175, 227
 leap of, 105, 203, 247, 256

familiarity, 42, 245, 253, 255

*fatwa* (in Islamic jurisprudence, authoritative legal opinion delivered by a jurisprudent or *mufti*), 158, 169

feudalism, 112–13, 118, 175

*fiqh* (interpretive-prudential judgment, Islamic jurisprudence), 142–3, 148, 152, 170

forgiveness, 113–14

forum, 201, 226
 inner, 6, 9, 200, 259
 public, 201, 226

Foucault, Michel, 23, 28, 30–1, 84, 125, 251, 256

France, 238, 263

Franciscans, 123–4, 127–31, 136, 174

Francis of Assisi, 122, 125, 127

Frederick II, 175

friendship, 116, 123, 203, 217, 225–6, 230–1

functionalism, 3, 20, 44–8, 50, 57, 77

fundamentalism, 178–9

*fuqaha'* (Islamic jurists), 148–9, 152

Gadamer, Hans-Georg, 20, 37–9, 43, 74, 261

Geertz, Clifford, 47–8

Gelasius I, 106

gender, 8, 9, 101

generation, 37, 38, 50, 78, 80, 82, 83, 86, 89, 95, 118, 137, 139

Germany, 4–5, 47, 238, 263

Ghazali, Abu Hamid al-, 144, 146, 150, 159, 170

Giddens, Anthony, 34, 86, 95

gift, 54–5, 79, 110, 203, 218

good life, 66, 74, 76, 80, 81, 87, 181, 248, 252

governance, 51, 70, 83, 136, 148, 175, 176, 221, 231, 235, 248, 256, 265

government, 105, 180, 221, 238
 liberal, 218
 liberal-democratic, 218
 secular, 106

governmentality, 128, 237

grace, 110, 117–18, 123, 126

Gramsci, Antonio, 146, 206, 256

Gregory VII, 106–8, 112

Grotius, Hugo, 114, 173, 180, 186–7, 210
guest, 202–5, 226
guilds, 150, 151

Habermas effect, 235–53
Habermas, Jürgen, 1–32, 37–45, 61,
    72–8, 82–7, 90–8, 168, 185, 215–19,
    222, 234–40, 243–9, 253–65
*habitus*, 83, 87, 88–93, 130
*hadith* (saying or deed of Muhammad),
    137–44, 164, 166
Hanafi (school of Islamic law), 141,
    156–7
Hanbali (school of Islamic law), 141,
    151, 160, 265
*haqiqa* (inner truth), 147–9
Hebrew, 164, 227
Hegel, Georg Wilhelm Friedrich, 29,
    42–3, 71–2, 238, 247, 256, 261
heresy, 85, 112, 115, 127, 146, 189
Hermes, 201
heterodoxy, 4, 55, 59, 61, 101, 106, 123,
    142, 145, 246
Hobbes, Thomas, 173, 175, 177–83, 186,
    193, 200–1, 209–10, 218, 256
Hodgson, Marshall G.S., 39, 111
Homer, 65, 69, 207–8, 246
Horkheimer, Max, 32, 185
host, 202–3
Hume, David, 219, 223–4
Hutcheson, Francis, 220–4, 232, 238, 266

*'ibada* (the service due to God,
    religious obligation), 135
Ibn Hanbal, Ahmad, 145
Ibn Rushd (Averroes), 148, 170
Ibn Sina (Avicenna), 146, 165, 195
I-it relationship, 40, 60, 72
*ijma'* (in Islamic jurisprudence,
    consensus among the *'ulama'*),
    140–1, 144, 156
*ijtihad* (in Islamic jurisprudence,
    reasoning based on the
    foundational texts), 140–1, 144,
    162, 168–70

*'ilm* (knowledge), 139, 142
imagination, 19, 21, 30, 31, 51, 63,
    69–70, 90, 112, 146, 182–3, 185,
    189–90, 192, 195, 209, 211
    poetic, 91, 186, 195
    prophetic, 90
    religious, 196
immanence, 92, 176, 208
*imperium*, 108, 124, 176
    *sacrum*, 109, 118–19, 124, 175–6
industrial society, 25, 226, 234
injustice, 61, 118
Innocent III, 198
intentionality, 2, 116, 146, 155
inwardness, 6–9, 11, 15–16, 49, 136,
    256, 259, 261
*istislah* (in islamic jurisprudence,
    method of finding a shared good
    in a given situation or
    interaction), 156, 159, 162–3, 165;
    *see also maslaha*
I-Thou relationship, 40, 54, 60, 72,
    114, 189, 228

*jahiliyyya* (pre-Islamic word of
    ignorance), 59, 246
Jaspers, Karl, 51–2, 71, 262
Jerusalem, 49
Jesus, 99, 128, 134, 245
Judaism, 2, 12, 133–4, 158, 256
jurisprudence, 16–17, 93, 187–8, 199,
    201, 204–5, 252
    Islamic, 16, 133, 140–1, 143, 146–7,
    149–70; *see also fiqh*
justice, 14–15, 30, 37, 41, 43, 55, 58,
    60, 64–5, 80, 86–7, 97, 103–4,
    107, 109, 112–14, 121, 144–5, 150,
    158, 183, 187, 189–90, 194–5,
    198, 200, 202–3, 207–9, 212,
    219–20, 227, 253, 255–6
    connective, 11, 30, 56, 101, 173, 194,
    203, 255–6

Kant, Immanuel, 5, 25, 29, 79, 208,
    236–8

kinship, 65, 101, 245
Koselleck, Reinhart, 5–6, 259

language, 29, 32, 40, 42, 73–4, 76, 84,
   91–2, 94, 96, 98, 102, 110, 162, 184,
   188, 189, 191, 195, 206–7, 227, 249
   bodily, 195, 200
   game, 72, 74, 81, 86–7, 192–3
   ordinary, 162–5
   poetic, 58, 190, 206
   symbolic, 26
   universal, 163
   vernacular, 150, 192, 205
law, 43, 82, 107, 115–17, 140–3, 147, 149,
   156–7, 161, 164–7, 189, 199–201,
   204–7
   contract, 218, 231, 233–4
   divine, 56, 82, 103–4, 112, 118, 136,
      166, 194; *see also shari'a*
   Islamic, 160, 241; *see also shari'a*
   Islamic philosophy of, 119, 144–5,
      155–71
   as *ius*, 107, 187, 198–9
   as *ius gentium*, 104
   *as lex aeterna*, 167
   as *lex nova*, 118, 167, 176
   natural, 104, 167, 186, 198, 210–11,
      221
   philosophy of, 16, 117
   positive, 118
   as *ratio*, 198, 200, 202
   Roman, 14, 27, 82, 104, 107–8, 119,
      130, 133, 141, 157–8, 186, 188,
      198–9, 204, 210, 216, 218, 223,
      236, 241, 252, 259, 266
Leviathan, 180, 192, 201, 218, 227,
   231–8
   democratic, 218, 256
life conduct, 14, 50–1, 57, 61, 83, 84, 97,
   101, 110, 152
life form, 72, 83, 90, 262
lifeworld, 5, 9, 38, 43–4, 47, 71, 77, 83,
   96–7, 152, 238–9, 257
   and phenomenology, 43, 46, 71
   rationalization of, 74

liminality, 61, 131, 177, 179, 182, 196,
   231, 233
Locke, John, 5, 220, 226–7, 257
*logos*, 30–1, 52–3, 70, 72, 92, 100, 107,
   195
   divine, 31, 200
love, 126, 148, 217, 218, 220, 224, 230
   divine, 114, 116
Luhmann, Niklas, 34, 86

Machiavelli, Niccolò, 31, 173, 175, 177,
   179, 186, 209, 210, 227, 228, 236,
   256
MacIntyre, Alasdair, 13–14, 21, 24,
   31, 36–42, 63, 66, 70–2, 79–82,
   94, 103, 110, 118, 120, 177, 216,
   219, 221, 232, 247–51, 255, 257–8,
   263, 264
Maliki (school of Islamic
   jurisprudence), 141, 157
Ma'mun, al-, 145
*maqasid al-shari'a* (the objectives of
   divine law), 156, 160
market, 3, 4, 65, 234, 239
Marx, Karl, 29, 41–2, 45, 256, 264
*maslaha* or *maslaha 'amma* (common
   good, public interest), 12, 15, 140,
   156–70, 183, 187, 201, 244
Masud, Khalid, 263, 264
memory, 29, 31, 138, 190, 208
mendicant orders, 112, 122, 124, 126,
   152, 263
mercy, 55, 135, 227, 230
modernities
   alternative, 23
   multiple, 28, 33
modernization theory, 33, 35, 39, 261
monarchy, 205
monasticism, 85, 124–5, 149
   monastic rule, 108; *see also* discipline,
      as monastic *disciplina*, and *Regula*
monotheism, 56, 105, 133, 255
   Abrahamic, 61
morality, 6, 9, 14, 15, 113, 215, 217, 220,
   223, 236, 259, 261

as moral sense, 220–4, 233, 237, 239, 257
Moses, 53, 56, 82, 104, 134, 228
mosques, 153, 154, 158
movements, 12, 24, 48, 55, 83, 92, 108, 124, 125, 128, 174–9, 182, 208, 244, 248, 257, 258, 261, 263
  heterodox, 55, 59, 101
  monastic, 18, 136, 149–51, 176
  pietistic, 147–55
  protest, 27
  religious, 1, 12, 22, 56, 85, 92, 106, 122–3, 129, 149, 173, 258, 263, 265
  sociopolitical, 18, 56, 261
*mufti* (in Islamic jurisprudence, issuer of authoritative legal opinions or *fatwa*s), 169–70
Muhammad, 59, 97, 99, 105, 133–4, 136–8, 148, 163–8, 245, 265
*mujtahid* (in Islamic jurisprudence, practitioner of *ijtihad*), 162, 169–70
*mukhtar* (in Islamic jurisprudence, free agent), 161, 167
multitudes, 118, 179, 181, 204, 241, 264
Mu'tazila (theological Islamic school), 144–5, 158–9, 195
myth, 25, 26, 29, 54, 59, 70, 108, 192, 202, 211
  as *mythos*, 26, 52

Nelson, Benjamin, 240
networks, 45, 125–6, 130, 136, 151, 152, 154
New Testament, 110, 113, 115, 127
Nietzsche, Friedrich, 23, 29, 50, 208, 248, 251
*niyya* (intention), 142, 167
*nomos*, 47–8, 107, 265

obedience, 118, 125, 155, 166, 203, 229
Ockham, William of, 124, 174, 177
*oikos*, 255, 256
Old Testament, 57, 115; *see also* Bible

order
  cosmological, 51, 57, 61, 110, 149
  sociopolitical, 53, 57, 58, 59, 114, 137, 147, 170, 176, 177, 179, 182, 197, 199, 204, 205, 212, 224, 251, 252
ordinary life, 2, 89
orthodoxy, 59, 94, 99, 101, 106, 112, 124, 127, 139–41, 145–52, 175, 246, 265
otherness, 11, 201–2, 231

*paideia*, 125, 136
Papacy, 106–9, 123–5, 128–9, 175–6, 230, 266
*parrhesia*, 110–11, 121–2
Parsons, Talcott, 3, 75, 77–8
participation, 23, 84, 108, 117, 251
passions, 31, 167–8, 177, 182, 191, 209, 220–3, 237, 239
*pater familias*, 201, 252
patricians (in Roman histoy), 27, 105, 199, 201–7, 211, 252
patronage, 27, 101, 130, 199, 203, 253
*pauperitas*, 130
penance, 85, 126–7
Pericles, 62–5, 110
*persona*, 200–1
perspectivism, 24–5, 248, 250–1
Pharaoh, 57
*phronesis*, 11–12, 16, 20, 31, 37–8, 49, 74, 76–9, 82, 88, 92–3, 98, 119–21, 159, 161, 168, 174, 186, 189, 191–2, 198–9, 209, 212, 216, 219, 221, 224, 229, 245, 248, 250, 255–6, 262
piety, 57, 69, 136, 144–5, 148–50, 166, 170, 194–6, 202–4, 208, 265
  as *pietas*, 14, 210; *see also taqwa*, 135, 137
Plato, 63–7, 70, 110, 189–90, 202, 207–12, 251–2
plebeians (in Roman history), 27, 199, 203–7, 252, 258
pluralism, 23, 249–50, 258
poets, 66, 69, 184, 189–91
*poiesis*, 77, 189–92, 200, 207–8, 211–12
*polis*, 62, 64–5, 103–5, 110, 113, 115, 118, 120, 174, 204, 245, 251

political realism, 5, 118, 177–8, 184, 186–8, 196, 200, 208, 215, 221, 256
political society, 3, 7, 181
postmodernism, 28, 29, 250
practical reason, 37, 61, 109, 215, 217, 219; *see also phronesis*
prayer, 111, 124
preaching, 100, 111, 124, 127–8, 134, 149, 153, 155, 169, 221
priesthood, 52, 123, 139, 148, 183
private
  citizens, 217, 218, 252
  law, 130
  origins of authority, 199
  sphere, 7, 44, 80, 179, 199, 216–17, 219, 222, 229, 231, 235, 238, 239, 255
privateness, 49, 216
prophets, 53–61, 69–70, 82, 86, 90–92, 97, 99, 101, 105, 110, 121–2, 126, 133–9, 144, 146, 148, 150, 161–6, 169, 177, 182–6, 189–90, 192, 194–5, 203, 208, 212, 245–7, 256
Protestantism, 2, 8, 15, 17, 19, 48–50, 59, 78, 176, 178, 182, 210, 213, 227, 256, 261, 263
providence, 121, 197–8, 209, 227
prudence, 78, 113, 121–2, 199, 204, 209, 216, 219, 224
public
  exchange, 27, 218
  gaze, 237
  good, 11–12, 16, 17, 41, 103, 130, 204, 222, 233–4, 239, 241, 250, 252
  Islam, 10
  law, 237
  opinion, 152, 247
  order, 6, 154, 205, 217
  as *publicus*, 15
  reason, 11–12, 44, 63, 100, 103–5, 109, 120, 122, 173, 180, 184, 189, 193, 198, 205, 208, 216, 220, 222, 235, 240–1, 253, 258, 263, 264
  reasoning, 2, 9, 11–12, 18–19, 22, 26, 28, 29, 41, 51, 63, 66, 70, 100, 103, 108, 115, 121, 133, 139, 140, 145–7, 155, 156, 159, 179, 202, 215, 220, 244, 245, 247, 249–51, 254–5, 258–9, 262
  services, 151–4; *see also waqf*
  space, 17, 30, 63, 65, 152, 153, 155
  speech, 122, 146, 189, 207, 209
  square, 65, 110, 255; *see also agorà* and forum, public
  utility, 109, 130, 157
  virtue, 110, 204, 225
  weal, 118, 140, 153–4, 156–7, 160, 162, 171, 173, 201, 264
publicness, 2, 6–9, 11, 15–16, 41, 109, 206, 216, 232–41, 252–9, 261, 264

*qiyas* (principle of analogical reasoning in Islamic jurisprudence), 140, 156–7, 164
Qur'an, 59, 97, 101, 134–5, 137, 138, 140, 142–4, 148, 150–1, 163–4, 168, 228, 229, 253, 265

Rahman, Fazlur, 139, 149, 263, 264
rationality
  instrumental, 50
  practical, 9, 40–1, 43–4, 61, 66, 88, 100, 107–9, 120–1, 161, 174–5, 193, 198, 216, 245, 253, 255, 259
  procedural, 13, 75, 77, 85, 87, 95, 254, 259
  substantial, 86
rationalization, 12, 21, 31, 35, 43–5, 47, 50, 74, 108, 114, 254, 256, 258
  bureaucratic, 5
  economic, 12
reciprocity, 104, 203, 223, 225–6
recognition, 197, 220–1, 224–6, 228, 232, 233, 235, 239, 264
reflexivity, 2, 52, 55, 59, 60, 65, 74, 78, 83, 96, 99, 103, 168, 193
  rational, 193
reform, 59, 65, 66, 123, 124, 129, 248
  Islamic, 149, 164

Reformation
Protestant, 18, 19, 48, 51, 59, 176, 178,
    182, 196, 197, 213, 227, 246, 263
refugee, 202–3, 205
*Regula* (of Benedict of Norcia), 124–6
reification, 30, 196
religion
    civil, 25, 36, 46
    natural, 182
    political, 179
    rational, 196
    wars of, 196, 212
religiosity, 48
reprisal, 200
republic, 64, 104–5, 108, 109, 196,
    205–7, 210
    Roman, 103, 252
republicanism, 6, 97, 109, 236, 240
*res publica*, 12, 15, 26, 27, 103, 105,
    107–9, 113, 119, 140, 157–8, 160,
    201, 204–7, 213, 217, 219–21, 236,
    244, 252
*respublica christiana*, 12, 104–9, 112, 123,
    124, 129, 158, 173, 175–7, 210–11,
    250
responsibility, 6, 117, 142, 159, 165, 170,
    171, 233, 236, 247
    personal, 149, 168
revolution, 22, 56, 71, 106, 123, 179, 250,
    263
    American, 236
    European revolutions of 1848, 5
rhetoric, 31, 62–4, 66, 91, 122, 175, 209
rights, 17, 21, 181, 184, 204, 219, 221,
    238, 265
    and duties, 154, 166
rituals, 46, 50, 54, 55, 59, 60, 75, 84, 85,
    93, 98, 101, 136, 139, 148, 151, 231
Robertson Smith, William, 46
Rousseau, Jean-Jacques, 236

*sacerdotium*, 124
sacred, 40, 56, 113, 134, 196, 205, 226
sacrifice, 185, 229

*saeculum*, 136, 176
saintliness, 150–1, 230
salvation, 50, 53, 54, 56–61, 84, 86, 101,
    102, 105, 106, 109, 114, 120, 135,
    176, 195, 198, 248, 252
scholasticism, 174, 220
Scotland, 178, 223, 232
scripture (in Abrahamic religions), 57,
    97, 100, 101, 111, 134, 135, 146, 159,
    160, 163, 176, 195, 197; *see also* Old
    Testament, New Testament,
    Qur'an
secrecy, 6, 50, 204, 206
sectarianism, 101, 134, 182, 196, 227
secularization, 1, 184
Sennett, Richard, 7, 34
Shafi'i (school of Islamic
    jurisprudence), 140–1
*shari'a* (in Islamic theology and
    jurisprudence, the divinely
    ordained pattern of human
    conduct), 136, 143–50, 153, 156,
    160–7, 169–70, 265
Shatibi, Abu-Ishaq, al-, 16, 19, 146, 156,
    158–71, 173, 183, 187, 196, 197, 200,
    263
Smith, Adam, 20, 219, 221, 232,
    234, 247
sociability, 7, 222, 232
    public, 7
social
    capital, 35
    integration, 4, 10, 20, 23, 27, 31,
        43–6, 77, 78, 83
    theory, 3, 13–5, 20–32, 34, 39, 40, 42,
        46, 51, 79, 86, 168, 170, 230, 232,
        245–6, 251, 254, 258, 262, 264,
        266
*societas christiana*, 107, 119–20, 122
Socrates, 64–7, 102–3, 179, 202,
    207, 251
solidarity, 23, 37, 127, 130, 239, 246,
    264, 265
    organic, 45–6, 232

Somers, Margaret, 3–4, 6, 14, 22

sovereignty, 5, 175, 203, 244
  God's, 107
  state, 176–8, 180, 188, 196

speech, 43, 65, 73–4, 100, 110, 121, 124,
    126, 127, 138, 163, 188, 205–7, 221,
    247, 261
  prophetic, 91, 121, 144, 163, 182, 184,
      195, 245, 256
  public, 122, 146, 189, 209, 221
  strategic, 239

Spinoza, Benedict (Baruch) de, 21, 29,
    69, 90, 118, 146, 173, 178–86,
    189–90, 194–7, 200, 264, 265

state
  modern, 12, 26–7, 44, 178, 180,
      186–7, 189, 213, 217–18, 234, 247,
      248, 256
  nation-state, 20, 25, 29, 97, 105, 109,
      176, 177

state of nature, 177, 180, 183, 187

Stoicism, 103, 107, 113–14, 118, 121, 144

stranger, 201–3, 226

Suarez, Francisco, 16, 200

subjectivity, 22, 122, 142, 146, 174

Sufism (tasawwuf), 18, 112, 143–54, 166,
    229–30, 265

summun bonum, 116, 180

sunna (living tradition, orthodox
    practice), 137–45, 148, 150, 265

superstition, 101, 181, 183, 196, 200

surveillance, 125, 257

symbolic-communicative link, 3, 9, 11,
    15, 25, 26, 40, 91, 101, 223, 225, 232,
    243, 247

Syria, 137


taqwa (God's fear, piety), 135–6

tariqa ("the way," network of master-
    disciple relations, Sufi
    brotherhood), 151

tawakkul (faithful trust in God), 148

Taylor, Charles, 2, 74, 92, 97–8

telos, 12, 31, 37–8, 41–3, 54–5, 60, 64–7,
    73–9, 86, 94–8, 106, 110, 113, 114,
    118–21, 142, 156, 158–9, 180–4,
    198, 209, 213, 219, 225, 229, 244,
    245, 262

Ten Commandments (Decalogue), 53,
    82, 104, 253

theocracy, 106–8

thereafter (afterlife), 52, 54, 139, 252

third sphere, 3–12, 20–4, 31, 131, 215,
    218–19, 240, 244, 259

Thucydides, 64

Tillich, Paul, 78

Tocqueville, Alexis de, 7

Tönnies, Ferdinand, 257

Torah, 134, 236

totalitarianism, 4, 5, 116

tradition
  Abrahamic, 3, 9, 15, 25, 27, 57, 67, 69,
      83, 86, 139, 226, 253
  Anglo-American, 6–7, 15, 228–33,
      237, 243–5, 251, 256–7, 261
  Axial, 12, 83, 110, 119, 164, 173, 177,
      184, 211, 213, 215, 229, 243, 246,
      259
  Catholic, 18, 100, 197, 263, 264
  cultural (in Habermas), 73, 253–4
  discursive, 13–17, 22, 38, 54, 56–8, 66,
      69, 72, 74, 77, 80, 83–5, 87,
      89–90, 92, 97–8, 100, 109, 111,
      112, 115, 118, 126, 130, 133, 161,
      164, 168–9, 175, 197, 221, 225,
      243, 246, 258, 263, 264
  humanist, 216
  implosion of, 28, 211
  Islamic, 16, 62, 97, 105, 115, 119, 133,
      143, 148, 181, 229, 230, 248, 263
  liberal, 6–7, 12, 117, 192, 216–17, 235,
      240, 244, 249–50, 255–6
  living, 71, 81, 83, 87, 137–9, 141, 144,
      196; see also sunna
  macrotraditions, 80–2
  microtraditions, 81–2
  republican, 236, 240

transcendence, 25, 27, 51–67, 70–1, 73,
    76, 80, 86, 92–4, 97, 101–3, 105,
    107–9

trust, 9, 11, 19, 21, 30, 97, 117, 123, 124, 135, 136, 148, 149, 151, 153, 169, 170, 212, 215–16, 221–41, 245–7, 254, 266
   leap of, 254, 256
   pristine, 224, 229, 230, 231, 233, 235, 237, 254
   social, 151
   unconditionality of, 217, 224–6, 228
Turner, Victor, 231

*'ulama'* (sing. *'alim*), 139, 147, 149, 151–5, 165, 181
*umma* (the Islamic community of believers), 134, 143, 154
universals, 25, 91, 202, 207
   imaginative, 63, 95, 191, 195, 208
   intelligible, 63, 163
university, 80, 81, 112, 113, 121, 123–4, 127–9, 152, 178, 221, 263
   as *universitas*, 124
*usul al-fiqh* (science of the foundations of Islamic jurisprudence), 154, 248
*utilitas publica*, 129, 157–8

Vico, Giambattista, 19–20, 26–32, 40, 42, 75, 82, 90, 91, 146, 167, 173, 182–213, 216, 220–2, 226, 227, 230, 243, 251, 261, 264, 265
violence, 27, 150, 189, 191, 201–5, 209, 233
Voegelin, Eric, 51, 53–5, 61, 99, 115–18, 127–8, 177–81, 193, 203, 211, 251, 256, 263, 264
voluntarism, 23–4, 39
*voluntas*, 117, 119, 142, 167

*waqf* (pious endowment), 17, 141, 151–5, 157–8
Weber, Max, 12, 46–7, 49–51, 61, 83, 176, 256, 263, 265
Weintraub, Jeff, 6–7
welfare, 45, 103, 154, 162, 167
   state, 5, 219
will, 110, 113, 117, 119, 122, 125, 150
   of God, 126, 166
   to power, 187, 188, 210, 212
Wittgenstein, Ludwig, 40, 71–2, 80, 84, 89, 92, 162, 262